Egypt's Diplomacy in War, Peace and Transition

"Prof. Nabil Fahmy is a preeminent career diplomat who has found success in politics and academia. He has a deep comprehension of the Egyptian reality, dynamics in the United States and the United Nations, and, in particular, the Middle East. He writes from broad experience, extensive knowledge, and a profound understanding of critical issues. In this book, Dr. Fahmy's insights illuminate a whole world for the reader."
—Dr. Nasser Alkidwa, Chairman of the Board of Directors,
Yasser Arafat Foundation, Palestine

"This is a timely and original contribution to the scholarship on the Middle East … Although this is not a memoir in the usual sense, the book also tells us much about the author – one of the prominent diplomats of his generation and the proud son of an equally prominent and courageous diplomat. Dr. Nabil FAHMY writes with the understated, nuanced language of his lifelong profession and the skills and foresight of a University Don."
—Lakhdar Brahimi, Former Foreign Minister, Algeria

"Nabil Fahmy is uniquely placed to write about an important part of Egypt's history, including post 2011. This book is must reading for all who want to shed more light about Egypt's role in international affairs in the last fifty years."
—Marwan Muasher, Former Foreign Minister of Jordan and
Vice President for Studies, *Carnegie Endowment for International Peace*

"Nabil Fahmy a distinguished veteran Egyptian diplomat and a former Foreign Minister is in a unique position to offer a learnt analysis on some of the most important transformative events in Middle East diplomacy. With the region in a tumultuous flux, this is invaluable reading for diplomats professionals, academics, historians and the general public."
—Nabil El Araby, Former Secretary General of
the Arab League and Former Foreign Minister of Egypt

"Former Egyptian foreign minister Nabil Fahmy is widely regarded as one of the most thoughtful Arab diplomats of the past several decades. Analytical and independent minded, he brings his perspective to important political events of the past half a century, with new insights and information, derived from being a key player in these events – especially on American mediation in the Middle East conflict, nuclear proliferation, and Arab relations with Iran. Accessible and informative, this book fills a gap in the literature. Highly recommended."
—Shibley Telhami, Anwar Sadat Professor for Peace and Development at the University of Maryland, and Non-Resident Senior Fellow at the Brookings Institution

Nabil Fahmy

Egypt's Diplomacy in War, Peace and Transition

palgrave
macmillan

Nabil Fahmy
Cairo, Egypt

ISBN 978-3-030-26387-4   ISBN 978-3-030-26388-1   (eBook)
https://doi.org/10.1007/978-3-030-26388-1

Cover illustration: © Egyptian Studio / shutterstock.com
Cover design by estudio calamar

This Palgrave Macmillan imprint is published by the registered company Springer Nature
Switzerland AG.
The registered company address is: Gewerbestrasse 11, 6330 Cham, Switzerland

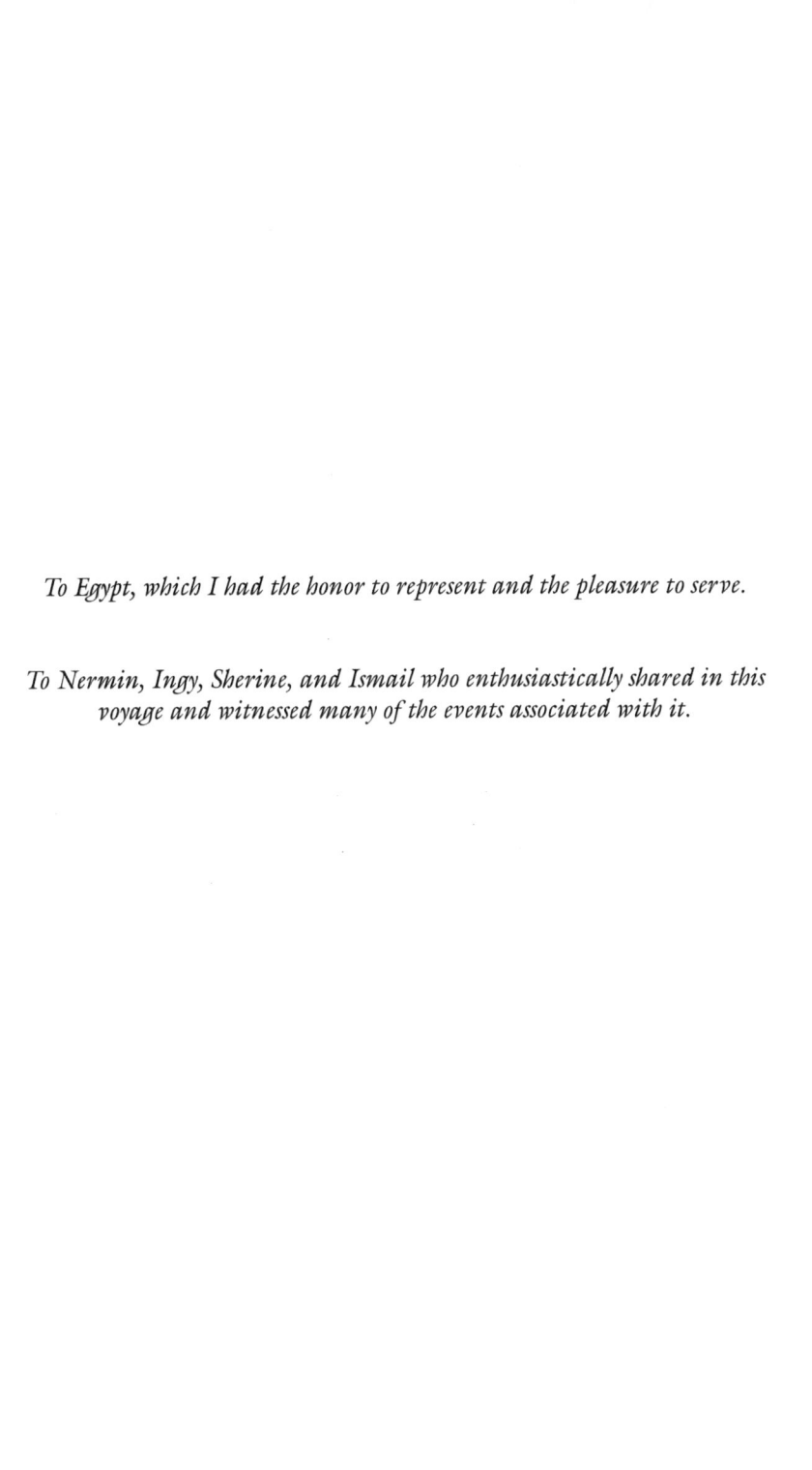

To Egypt, which I had the honor to represent and the pleasure to serve.

To Nermin, Ingy, Sherine, and Ismail who enthusiastically shared in this voyage and witnessed many of the events associated with it.

PREFACE

Reading books written by high-level policy practitioners are entertaining and often insightful, irrespective of the opinions or renditions of events presented. They provide a firsthand account of important events that can be valuable for present and subsequent generations. However, one must read critically because the authors frequently embellish positions to enhance personal legacies or to lay the foundation for future ambitions.

Regrettably, the Arab world does not have a long-standing tradition of government officials and politicians publicly reflecting on what they did and saw during their time in government service, especially in foreign languages. Personally, I have frequently urged retiring Arab officials to share at least part of their experiences, if only for balancing the narratives presented by other interlocutors or adversaries, thus correcting false perceptions abroad. No scholarly work will be perfect; memoirs are even more subjective. Moreover, in the absence of diverse sources and opinions, even the best historians, applying the most rigorous professional analytical tools, will be unable to provide accurate accounts of events or do justice to the different parties who partook in their development and implementation.

Personally, I first began contemplating sharing my reflections on the international events that unfolded during my adult life at the conclusion of my post as the ambassador of Egypt to the United States in 2008. I initially refrained from doing so, concerned that the author, rather than the events, would be the essence of the story. However, after serving as the foreign minister of Egypt in 2013–2014, subsequent to two revolutions, driven by popular demand for good and shared governance, I felt duty-bound to candidly share my experiences, thoughts, and sentiments having lived through historic tests to statecraft and unique diplomatic challenges. The conclusive determinant in my decision to publish was a sense of personal dismay that the past two generations in the Arab world were handing over the Middle East to future leaders in a far worse state than it was when they took charge of it. The least we could do was to share our experiences for others to learn from.

My reflections, which coincidently cover half a century, come essentially in four contiguous periods. First, in the years between 1967 and 1973, as a young adult influenced by the many major developments around me without actually being an influential player. Secondly, in the subsequent five years when my father, Ismail Fahmy, was a government minister in Egypt's inner cabinet, which coincided with the beginning of my own diplomatic career, where I had close access and a bird's eye view of events, information, and decision-making. Thirdly, during the following two decades when I was a senior diplomat in sensitive diplomatic positions, carrying serious responsibilities myself. Finally, being appointed as the foreign minister, provided me with yet another unique prism on and level of responsibility for foreign policy and domestic affairs in a turbulent, changing Middle East.

There were also two other different stops where I was closely associated with ongoing developments in Egypt: from 2008 to 2013 as an academic and between 2014 and 2017 after I left the government cabinet. During both, I was also engaged with an agitated civil society searching for a better future; thus, my commentary is not only on foreign policy but also on the issues of transition and statecraft.

In the concluding chapter of this book, I attempt to offer a general projection of the future of the Arab World despite the fluid and dubious circumstances that continue to prevail.

Noteworthy is that after completing my first draft, close friends and advisers insisted that my internationalist perspective on issues had been tailored over the years by my personal experiences, which therefore needed to be shared to provide a context for the reader to fully understand my reactions and conclusions. Consequently, after considerable hesitation, ultimately at the beginning of this work, I touched upon some personal experiences and anecdotes but only where I felt they would enrich the narrative or provide more texture or clarity.

I hope this material is informative and objective, and provides insight of value to all those concerned with better public order in the Middle East for future generations.

Cairo, Egypt   Nabil Fahmy

SPECIAL ACKNOWLEDGMENTS

Throughout the reflections in this manuscript on international, regional, and domestic experiences, I always had in mind the principles and standards dear to a single unique mentor, my father, Ismail Fahmy. He set the highest standards of integrity and professionalism, yet insisted that I independently made the professional and personal decisions of my time.

ACKNOWLEDGMENTS

International relations always have numerous narratives and involve many stakeholders, without which the story is untold. Thus, I also owe acknowledgments to the distinguished professionals, close friends, and challenging foes who were party to the half-century of events dealt with in this book.

A special word of thanks goes out to my colleagues at the Egyptian Foreign Ministry, seniors, peers, and the younger generation, particularly those whom I worked with directly. Many were part of these events. Some also reminded me of details, as well as helped in fine-tuning the assessments and analyses in this manuscript.

My immediate project team was instrumental in coherently bringing ideas to pen and paper and deserves special recognition. Reem Gehad meticulously and tirelessly did much of the preliminary work in helping me prepare the first draft. Aya Sabry was a meticulous and sharp editor. Leilah Elmokadem and Noman Ahmed Ashraf were worthy research assistants in ensuring that the text was factually correct and consistent. Sherihan El-Sawah patiently and laboriously worked throughout the process in putting all the pieces together over and over again.

I would also like to thank Alina Yurova and her assistant Mary Fata for their valuable expertise and personal efforts in bringing my work to publication with Palgrave Macmillan and, hopefully, in ensuring the widest possible availability to readership.

CONTENTS

Part I Uncharted Destinies   1

1 Personal and Professional Alignments   3

Part II Foreign Policy Challenges and Opportunities   21

2 Geopolitical Upheaval in the Middle East   23

3 No War   47

4 Yet No Peace   85

5 Efforts to Quell Nuclear Weapons Proliferation in the
   Middle East   115

6 New Engagement of Sensitive Neighbors and Long-
   Standing Relations   129

7 An Indispensable but Uncomfortable Relationship   161

Part III   Egypt's Continuous Transitions   201

  8   After Three Decades a Public Awakening Fueling Two
      Revolutions   203

  9   A Nexus of Foreign and Domestic Policy Throughout the
      Interim Period   225

Part IV   Looking Forward   265

10   Towards a Better Middle East   267

Appendices   279

Name Index   369

Subject Index   375

LIST OF FIGURES

Fig. 1.1   Nabil Fahmy, Chairman of the UN General Assembly first
committee meeting   10

Fig. 1.2   Nabil Fahmy, Chairman of UN Secretary General's Advisory
Board on Disarmament Affairs   11

Fig. 3.1   Ismail Fahmy at the White House   50

Fig. 3.2   Nabil Fahmy and Yasser Arafat   66

Fig. 4.1   Joint press conference between Nabil Fahmy and John Kerry   88

Fig. 6.1   Nabil Fahmy and Abdel Fattah El-Sisi   155

Fig. 6.2   Nabil Fahmy, Abdel Fattah El-Sisi, Sergey Lavrov and Sergey
Shoygu   156

Fig. 6.3   Joint press conference between Nabil Fahmy and Sergey Lavrov   157

Fig. 7.1   Nabil Fahmy and George W. Bush   171

Fig. 7.2   Nabil Fahmy and the Obamas at UN General Assembly
reception   194

Fig. 9.1   Nabil Fahmy and President Adly Mansour   239

Fig. 9.2   Nabil Fahmy speaking in a press conference   240

Fig. 9.3   Nabil Fahmy talking in the UN General Assembly   248

Fig. 9.4   Nabil Fahmy and Ban Kee moon   249

Fig. 9.5   Nabil Fahmy in a meeting with the French Foreign Affairs
Minister Laurent Fabius   252

Uncharted Destinies

Personal and Professional Alignments

Born into international affairs, after initial reluctance I made a choice to pursue diplomacy professionally at a time when the world order was being transformed, which defined my life and my career as one of continuous realignment.

I was born in New York City in 1951 to Afaf Mahmoud and Ismail Fahmy, a diplomat at Egypt's Permanent Mission to the United Nations. This coincided with an era of global and national transformation. The cold war was coming to the fore, and a populist movement in Egypt soon sparked a revolution in 1952 that ended the reign of King Farouk and created a republic.

In 1954, Gamal Abdel Nasser, the revolution's heart and soul, succeeded the country's first president and former General Mohamed Naguib. Nasser quickly established an even more progressive and assertive social domestic contract with the Egyptian people, more egalitarian in its approach but regrettably non-inclusive in its application. His foreign policy battles with old and new colonial powers were as challenging, if not even more so, than those on the domestic front. His regional leadership witnessed a meteoric rise and was increasingly perceived as a threat to the interests of old-world powers, particularly the European colonialists. Globally, Nasser's foreign policy gradually tilted toward the Eastern Bloc but in fact only after he and the Free Officers[1] first courted and later rebuffed by the West.

---

[1] Nasser and his revolutionary colleagues were known as the "Free Officers".

© The Author(s) 2020
N. Fahmy, *Egypt's Diplomacy in War, Peace and Transition*,
https://doi.org/10.1007/978-3-030-26388-1_1

My father Ismail Fahmy was known by friend and foe to have absolute professionalism, unwavering integrity, and unfailing commitment to always speak truth to power. This continues to be a strong part of his legacy and widely applauded four decades after he left the office and over two decades after he passed away. As a mid-career diplomat, he had strongly argued against Egypt demanding the withdrawal of the United Nations peacekeeping forces from Sharm El-Sheikh, where they had been stationed since the armistice agreement at the end of the 1956 War, cautioning that Israel would use this as a pretext to initiate military operations against in Egypt. Unfortunately, his warning was unheeded, and the 1967 War was to break out soon after the forces were withdrawn. A few years later, while serving as the Undersecretary of the Foreign Ministry, he again rocked the boat in a seminar hosted by Al-Ahram newspaper in the summer of 1971 by publicly speaking up against what he felt was Egypt's excessively close relationship with the Soviet Union. He argued instead for the pursuit of a more balanced and independent foreign policy with open communications with all major players.

In light of my father's profession, international affairs were part of my day-to-day intellectual harvest. He was a highly distinguished and strong-willed career diplomat who was later to serve as foreign minister (1973–1977). As he rose within the ranks, I had frequent opportunities to meet prominent international and Arab leaders, including United States President Gerald Ford, United Nations Secretary-General Kurt Waldheim, United States Secretary of State Henry Kissinger, Soviet Union Foreign Minister Andrei Gromyko, President Anwar Sadat, and Vice President Mahmoud Fawzy, as well as Arab leaders who were to shape historic events throughout the Middle East.

Accordingly, my upbringing put high-profile international diplomacy and domestic politics in a lifestyle context that deglamorized the idea of meeting high-profile politicians or taking on positions of power. Throughout, it was underscored that public service was a solemn responsibility that required candid, honest appraisals irrespective of the risks or difficulties associated with that.

The diverse intellectually and culturally privileged upbringing of diplomats' children is something to be grateful for, but it does not come without some serious challenges. They often become patently attached to diplomacy, or reject the profession completely, preferring a more stable environment and a direct personal return on their efforts. Personally, I was somewhere between these two extremes, enamored by international affairs, but not initially inclined to pursue a career in diplomacy because of the pressures associated with the constant travel and displacement.

Egypt's strategic geopolitical place mitigated for a traditionally proactive foreign policy. Its diplomatic service, which was established in 1923, played a prominent normative role in establishing the contemporary world order, being one of the founding members of the Arab League, the Organization of African Unity, and the Non-Aligned Movement. In addition, Egypt's diplomatic activities were forward thinking. In San Francisco, while the United Nations Charter was being written, Abdel-Hamide Badawi Pasha, a prominent and distinguished Egyptian jurist, suggested that the United Nations Security Council membership and its rules of procedure should be reviewed after 25 years. He recognized that the global political model would be much different a quarter century later. Today more than seven decades later, the United Nations and its charter and rules remain essentially unchanged in a context of a much different geopolitical model, which is one of the reasons for its increasing inefficiency.

From World War II, through the subsequent Cold War, the collapse of the Berlin Wall to the end of the bipolar world order, Egypt's permanent mission to the United Nations in New York was always seen as omnipresent in the international affairs scene. I vividly remember in the middle of my diplomatic career, while serving in New York in the late 1980s, a French delegate telling me half-jokingly that Egypt acted as if it was the 16th virtual member of the Security Council, often more informed and influential from outside its chambers of the council than some of the member states. This was flattering testimony to Egypt's foreign policy advocacy and activism. It was not an exaggeration then to say that many considered Egyptian diplomacy as an indicator of emerging developments in the Arab world, the Middle East, and Africa. To be a member of the Egyptian Foreign Service was not only an incredible honor but also a solemn responsibility.

I appreciated all this and was enamored by it, but when I graduated with a degree in physics and mathematics from the American University in Cairo (AUC) in January 1974, my father advised me to follow my own path according to my own preferences, pursuing rational career choices which as much as possible ensured me multiple options. This was music to my ears. Entering the job market at a time that coincided with Sadat's open-door economic policies in 1974, where he encouraged the private sector both domestic and foreign. I did not intend to join the Foreign

Service, being more interested in pursuing a career in private business, either in banking or multinational companies.

My professional interests were on my mind, but I first had to finish my obligatory military service, which was to extend for 20 months. However, even before serving in the army, I temporarily took on employment at the Egyptian President's Office of External Communications in February 1974.

My daily tasks included the ciphering and deciphering of the occasional cables that were exchanged at the presidential level with a few countries, or during overseas presidential trips. The work schedule extended over long hours, but the workload was light and very manageable. Consequently, on a parallel track, I studied for a master's degree in management attempting to prepare myself for the marketplace once I had completed my military service.

In the summer of 1975, I had an unexpected fall-out with Ashraf Marwan, the young head of the office, who was the son-in-law of the late President Nasser. I had had a warm and amicable working relationship with Marwan until innuendo generated by petty office jealousies created a misunderstanding between us. Not being at fault and feeling unappreciated, I immediately resigned, fully prepared to return to active military barracks.

As a young graduate and political novice, I did not realize that as an employee at the Presidency, and even more so as the son of the foreign minister, my resignation would quickly become a big issue. I was called in to meet the then newly appointed Vice President Hosni Mubarak, who had oversight over the management of the presidential offices. I had not even had a chance to inform my father of my resignation. He was amused by my brashness but true to his words, he left me to independently navigate my way through my first career crisis, albeit while keeping a watchful eye from a distance.

This was not the first time I met Mubarak. My father had invited President Sadat to attend my wedding a few months earlier. The day before that important occasion, the president asked that we also invite Mubarak, who was still head of the air force, explaining that he was to be appointed vice president the very morning of my wedding, and therefore it would be a good opportunity for him to appear in his new civilian capacity.

Mubarak first patiently and amicably listened to my comments, even accepting my refusal to dwell on the details of the misunderstanding with Marwan, and my reluctance to join his own newly established office. Ultimately, he indicated that as long as I was in military service, I only had two options. I could either work in his office in military gear or in civilian clothes. I ended up completing the rest of my military service dealing with foreign media from the room across from the vice president's.

While serving in Mubarak's office, I received several jobs offers in the banking sector, which I was tempted to accept, but could only do so after the completion of my military service. In the meantime, a very close friend of mine, Ramzy Ezzeldin Ramzy, challenged me to take the Foreign Ministry's difficult and competitive admission exams. Joining the Foreign Ministry was not my priority, but with youthful abundance, I impetuously succumbed to the challenge.

At first, my father did not expect that I would really sit for the exams. However, once he saw that I was seriously preparing, he reaffirmed his earlier career advice, adding that I would have to pass the difficult entry exams on my own merits without any support from him. To my surprise, he did not raise the obvious point that this would raise issues of perceived nepotism. He was placing the responsibility for success on my shoulders, but not encumbering me with issues that he would have to face.

Ramzy and I both passed the exams with high scores. I was slowly edging toward a career in diplomacy; I did hesitate for a moment yet one last time. On the very same day of our induction as new diplomatic cadets in the Foreign Ministry, I received a very lucrative job offer from Citibank with a salary 21 times what I was about to be paid in government. Nevertheless, in March 1976, I took the plunge into Foreign Service, fully committed and resolute to serving my country, approaching my new career not as merely another profession, but more as a vocation that one takes on with deep conviction and that comes with solemn responsibilities.

My father, who was now about to also become my boss, was very clear with me and his chiefs of cabinet Ambassadors Omar Sirry and Ossama El-Baz, his direct assistant Mohamed El-Baradei, and many other future stars of Egyptian diplomacy working in his office like Nabil El-Araby and Amre Moussa. I should work harder than anyone else without any form of favoritism. At times, I felt this was a bit excessive, but it was an important and valuable experience. To me, he simply said be yourself, get into the depths of issues that you have to work on, make well-thought-out decisions, and never compromise your credibility even at the cost of your career. A diplomat's role, he truly believed, was to help in developing state policies that are in the national interests and then execute them to the best of his/her abilities.

Soon enough about 18 months later, he himself demonstrated how resolutely he lived by these tenets. In November 1977, my father resigned from his position as foreign minister to protest Sadat's unilateral visit to Jerusalem, after years of Egypt working with other international players toward a comprehensive Arab–Israeli peace process. Although he was extremely close to Sadat, he did not hesitate to resign because he firmly believed this unilateral step would create a negotiating imbalance between Arabs and Israelis. Thus, it would derail the efforts to achieve comprehensive Arab–Israeli peace that does justice to all parties involved, including the Palestinians. In this way, Ismail Fahmy demonstrated how a foreign minister's relationship with the president could become one of "assertiveness" as per Christopher Hill's model.[2]

At that moment, the immediate question concerning my presence at the foreign ministry suddenly changed from potential perceptions of nepotism, to whether I would be the target of vindictive acts from government institutions, or officials who took exception to my father's resignation. To the credit of the government institutions in Egypt, especially the Foreign Ministry, I was not subjected to any serious prejudice, with very few exceptions.

I continued doing my work under different foreign ministers, including in the cabinet of Ambassador Muhammed Ibrahim Kamel who directly succeeded my father, but also remember well Kamal Hassan Aly who gave me the opportunity to express myself in intergovernmental meetings even when knowing beforehand that I would argue against the policy position that he wanted to have adopted. I also had numerous engagements with Minister of State for Foreign Affairs Boutros Boutros-Ghali, initially with a rocky start, attributed by some to his opposing approach to that of my father's, especially with regards to the Egyptian–Israeli peace talks.

My first full diplomatic assignment abroad was from 1978 to 1982 at the Permanent Mission of Egypt to the United Nations in Geneva. At first, I was the junior diplomat responsible for disarmament and political affairs, especially those related to the Arab–Israeli conflict, two topics in which Egypt was traditionally active and strong-willed.

---

[2] In his book *Foreign Policy in the Twenty-First Century*, Christopher Hill (2015) talks about the different relationships that could exist between foreign ministers and their presidents, categorizing them as either one of "equality"—such as that between Henry Kissinger and Richard Nixon (US, 1973–1974)—or one of a "subordinate foreign minister".

The diplomatic work in Geneva, which hosted a large number of specialized agencies, was highly technical. Going into meetings unprepared was an invitation to be embarrassed because delegations, especially from the industrial world, tended to be heavily staffed with technical support. The nature of the work there was instrumental in defining my diplomatic rigor afterwards.

At the end of my tenure in Geneva, I chose to work at the International Organizations Department of the Egyptian Foreign Ministry in Cairo from 1982 to 1986. Lengthy stays in Cairo were not something most diplomats normally opted for, preferring foreign diplomatic experiences because of the low pay grade domestically. Nevertheless, having traveled often as a child with my father, I was particularly concerned about providing my family with a sense of stability and enabling my children to learn the fundamentals of Arabic, their mother tongue. Over time, these years in which I was close to the Egyptian center of power helped establish my reputation as a diplomatic resource for Egyptian officials and for foreigners as a serious interlocutor on national security, conflict resolution, and disarmament affairs.

Mubarak, whom I considered a stabilizer president who ruled from 1981 to 2011, first focused on ensuring domestic security and stability in the wake of his predecessor's assassination. In terms of foreign policy, he wisely repositioned Egypt back to the center of the Arab world. Different from and maybe because of his experiences with Sadat, he shied away from grand policy schemes. I found myself working in this domestic context for most of my diplomatic career, and in an international arena, that was in itself slowly bidding adieu to the bipolar order.

In the spring of 1986, Ambassador Abdel-Halim Badawi, the permanent representative of Egypt to the United Nations, asked me to join his team in New York. Highly cultured and low-key, Badawi was an expert in multinational affairs who was known to be strongly supportive of his staff. I was happy to come on board and was immediately assigned the senior disarmament file at the first committee of the United Nations General Assembly.

Three years later, still a mid-career diplomat in 1989, I was elected to be vice president of the first committee. The Venezuelan president-elect of the committee was quickly called back to his capital to become deputy foreign minister. The other vice president was from Iran, thus not perceived by Western countries as a politically appropriate leader of the committee even for just a few meetings. This placed the burden of managing

Fig. 1.1 Nabil Fahmy,
Chairman of the UN
General Assembly first
committee meeting

the committee squarely on my shoulders. At the conclusion of its closing session, several of the older delegates thanked me for my effective chairmanship and warmly mentioned that they had now served at the same committee under the chairmanship of the son, after having done so with his father more than two decades earlier (Figs. 1.1 and 1.2).

A few months after I returned to Cairo in early 1991, President Mubarak appointed Amre Moussa as the Minister of Foreign Affairs to bring in new and young blood to the leadership of the Foreign Ministry. After being sworn in on May 20, 1991, Moussa appointed me as his political advisor.

Among the tasks that were assigned to me at the beginning was to support Boutros Boutros-Ghali in his campaign to be elected Secretary-General of the United Nations. It was Africa's turn to lead the organization. There were strong candidates from sub-Saharan Anglophone Africa. In addition, the Arab world was not expected to give Boutros-Ghali support due to his association with Sadat's visit to Jerusalem and the Egyptian–Israeli Peace Treaty. He would also not easily garner many votes from the Islamic world because he was not of the same faith. My personal relations

To Amb. Nabil Fahmy,

Fig. 1.2 Nabil Fahmy, Chairman of UN Secretary General's Advisory Board on Disarmament Affairs

with Ghali then were still quite cold and impersonal. I told him candidly that his chances for election were not strong and explained that our best bet was to have an extended battle between the African candidates because a quick one would go to a Sub-Saharan candidate. I suggested that we start by quickly contacting China to make sure that it would continue to block any attempt to open the race to non-African candidates even if the election process was protracted. I also recommended that he position himself as the representative of French-speaking African countries rather than North Africa. To his credit, Ghali appreciated my candidness, and our relationship warmed up quickly. He went on to carry out the campaign strategy marvelously and win election as Secretary-General much quicker than anyone expected, including myself.

The following seven years as political advisor to the foreign minister, I was always very busy at the center of high-priority events challenges or opportunities at the ministry, at the forefront of which naturally was the Arab–Israeli conflict. Before I realized, six years had quickly passed. I only recognized this when I was surprised that my young son had become a teenager. I realized immediately that I needed more time for my family. My wife, Nermin, who had been the family custodian and who was the shining rock diamond who held it together for us, agreed with my decision to move away from the highly interesting but overly consuming work that I had been entrusted with after one more year.

In 1997, I was nominated to be Egypt's ambassador to Japan, where I served until 1999. These years were an auspicious opportunity to get a second wind in constructive diplomacy, after taking a break from the endless frustrations related to the failures in the Middle East peace process. They also allowed me to expand my experiences by engaging more professionally in economic and trade relations and were an excellent opportunity to get an important primer on Asia, the emerging global force for the next generation.

Friends told me that the Japanese were initially reluctant about my nomination. I was relatively at a young age, and this was to be my first ambassadorial post. The Japanese Embassy in Cairo explained to headquarters in Tokyo that I had a reputation for being a doer closely associated with the center of power in Egypt.

Two months after my arrival in Japan, I had to handle the shock and agony that was widespread because of the tragic terrorist attack at the Deir El-Bahari Temple in Luxor in 1997, where 10 Japanese tourists were killed among 58 tourists and 4 Egyptians. I stood at Narita airport solemnly receiving the coffins of those killed and then boarded the plane myself to return to Cairo because of my father's death. Shocked by this tragedy, the Japanese were very appreciative of this gesture, and throughout my two years, there were professionally exemplary and highly refined.

Ironically, my posting in Japan was instrumental in determining the future direction of my diplomatic career. Because of my travels abroad until the early 1990s, I had not met President Mubarak much after I left his office as vice president back in 1976. Starting the early 1990s as a political advisor to the foreign minister, I was often at the presidential palace for meetings and visits related to the Arab–Israeli file. However, during the first two years in that position, Mubarak inexplicably never acknowledged my presence. Out of respect for his position, I did not take the initiative to engage him either. It was only in 1993 that things changed.

While at the Blair House in Washington DC, the American presidential guesthouse, during one of Mubarak's annual visits to the United States, the president walked across the hallway where his delegation was assembled. Moussa mischievously offered to introduce me to the president who gamely responded, "I have known Nabil for longer than I have known many of the ministers here." A few minutes later, Mubarak called me into his meeting room to ask about my wife, Nermin, and our family. Thereafter through the years, he was always exceptionally courteous and always inquiring about my growing family.

Hosni Mubarak was to visit Japan in April 1999. I was still ambassador there but had already been nominated to serve next in Geneva as Egypt's permanent representative to the European Office of the United Nations. This was a very successful trip, which was meticulously organized by the Japanese.

Mubarak was in a jovial mood, expansive in the issues he raised with me, which I assumed were just small talk or testimony to the president's generally pleasant character. Months later, I would realize that the questions he kept asking me about how best to deal with America were in fact part of his search for a new Egyptian ambassador to the United States.

Bill Clinton's second term as the United States president had seen a slow but constant deterioration in Egyptian–American relations, particularly as the administration became increasingly uncomfortable with Egypt's independent positions and strong support for Palestinians that did not align with American preferences. In 1996, the Congress reviewed the aid package given to Egypt that was adopted after the 1978 Camp David Accords and the Clinton administration put forth a ten-year plan to gradually cut the economic aid by 70 percent without a corresponding increase in the military aid as they had decided for Israel.

Our ambassador in Washington had reached the retirement age, and Mubarak wanted to properly manage these delicate and increasingly difficult relations. The gist of my responses to the questions that the Egyptian president had asked me while visiting Japan was that America was too big to ignore, because it provided vast opportunities and its mistakes had serious ramifications that affected many countries. Accordingly, I argued that hands-on management and continuous engagement with America was necessary, but it was imperative that this included speaking candidly to the United States even where we disagreed bluntly. For me, these two important high-strung countries needed each other. Misunderstandings were problematic and could be averted, and differences of opinions were inevitable and ultimately manageable.

Just before entering his limousine on departure to the airport at the end of his visit to Japan, Mubarak had turned to me and inquired about my age. A long time had passed since I was the 23-year-old army conscript working in the vice president's office and I rashly responded, "I have gotten older." Mubarak retorted, "We are all older. How old are you?" After I told him that I was 48 years old, Zakaria Azmi, his chief of staff, remarked without elaborating that the president clearly had something in mind. I discounted this as small talk, but Azmi argued back, "Do you really think he cares how old any of us are?"

After the visit, Foreign Minister Moussa kept postponing my move from Tokyo to Geneva, without offering an explanation. Then in August 1999, Moussa hinted that I might not end up in Geneva at all. Shortly afterwards, he called again to congratulate me on my appointment as the ambassador to the United States asking me to pass by Egypt to meet the president before flying to my new post.

I arrived early at the "Ittihadiya", the Egyptian presidential palace, in Cairo on October 11, 1999, to find a slow stream of guests gathering. They had just been nominated as members of the new Egyptian cabinet and were waiting to be sworn in. I spent at least 45 minutes with the president that morning in what was a very flattering but odd meeting. The new cabinet and the presidential staff impatiently waited outside.

The president started by insisting that he was the one who nominated me as ambassador to the United States, a remark that he reiterated repeatedly. I thanked him, concurring that all ambassadorial posts were the president's prerogative, especially in positions as important as Washington was, and promised to do my best. His reaction was to repeat that he personally chose me for the job because of my good understanding of the American mentality and my independent streak, which would not allow interest groups on either side to try to influence my management of the bilateral relations. Mubarak then spent the more substantial part of the meeting talking about reasons behind his cabinet reshuffle, especially the justification for removing Prime Minister Kamal El-Ganzouri. I deliberately chose to refrain from commenting on the matter, confining myself to the issues that consumed my attention during my past two years in Tokyo.

All embassies in Washington are at the center of high-stakes diplomacy given America's political and military weight, and this occurs at an increasingly fast pace in almost complete transparency. In essence, I rigorously respected the process of reporting and asking for instructions in a professional manner, but always had to be ready to take my own decisions according to my best judgment, if time was short or instructions did not arrive. More than in any other embassy abroad, in Washington the ambassador inevitably becomes a direct member of his/her country's high-level decision-making élite. There is simply no room or time for complacency, hesitation, or recurrent bad judgment.

These were not easy years neither for Egyptian–American relations nor for Egyptian foreign policy. Our foreign ministers changed frequently, domestic changes in Egypt became imminent, and the Middle East verged toward a period of instability, particularly after the 9/11 events. For me, however, they were particularly opportune in culminating a diplomatic career characterized by rational dispassionate analysis, candid reporting, and rapid decision-making; those were the kinds of challenges that motivated me.

In late 2008, toward the end of my nine-year tenure in Washington, many rumors were circulating in Egyptian circles about what my next assignment would be. Some speculated that I would be taking on the position of foreign minister. Others argued I would be working as a national security advisor to the president.

This was not the first time I was to find myself linked to the position of foreign minister. I had previously been offered the position by Mubarak himself, once in 2001 indirectly after Amre Moussa left the position to join the Arab League as secretary-general, and once again more directly in 2004 after he decided to change Ahmed Maher Moussa's successor. In both cases, I declined due to my lack of interest in public office even though I loved international relations. The second refusal annoyed Mubarak who must have assumed that there was some Machiavellian reason behind my decision.

As I returned to Cairo after this posting, I was fully satisfied with my career in diplomacy and wanted to look beyond government. I was also increasingly uncomfortable with some domestic political trends in Egypt that reflected more centralization and exclusive control of the greatest political party in Egypt, the National Democratic Party (NDP), and a growing contingency of opportunists and carpetbaggers. On arrival with no set plans in mind, I told the foreign minister that I would be ready to help on any ad-hoc assignments, if he requested, but was no longer interested in a formal position or ranking within the ministry.

At the end of the summer of 2008, David Arnold and Lisa Anderson, the then president and provost of the AUC, respectively, came to visit me. They quickly invited me to join the university and create a new school for public affairs. I was taken by complete surprise, never having previously thought of academia professionally. I told my guests that I knew nothing about academia and had not determined my plans. Fascinating and strong-willed, Anderson assured me that all they wanted was leadership on global affairs with a focus on policy. She offered to personally give her support and suggested that she and Medhat Haroun, the Dean of the School of Sciences and Engineering, would be my informal mentors on academic management if needed. Moreover, contrary to my advice that it was too early to do so, she put an offer on the table.

Our discussions took nine months before we reached an agreement, mostly because I was undecided on career paths. As Founding Dean, I established the School of Global Affairs and Public Policy (GAPP) at the AUC in August 2009. Initially trying to explain the logic behind this school to the Egyptian community was difficult. Many did not differentiate between global affairs and political science. Others closer to the government were not comfortable with its focus on governance. Although I was no longer functioning at the Foreign Ministry, an associate in the Egyptian President's Office informed me that Mubarak was inquiring whether this school was part of the American President George W. Bush's public diplomacy campaign, which had been his main tool in sidestepping governments and reaching out to societies throughout the Middle East. I assured him it was not.

I was not a political activist nor had I held any domestic leadership position prior to the historic events that, in late 2010, started to unfold in the Arab world, including in Egypt. They were nonetheless relevant to the work of the school, which was all about good governance. Domestic policy issues gradually became more in the focus of my own personal attention even beyond academia having personally served Egypt for over three decades, albeit more so on international relations.

Two years later, in 2011 when President Mubarak was removed from office and the Supreme Council of the Armed Forces (SCAF) led the nation, Foreign Minister Nabil El-Araby asked me to join him as minister of state for foreign affairs, which is essentially the second principal on foreign affairs in the cabinet. I was just then witnessing the early fruits of my efforts to create a School of Global Affairs at the University, so I declined the offer.

Three months later, I was asked by SCAF to become Foreign Minister, after El-Araby was nominated as the Secretary-General of the Arab League. I again declined, still disinterested in public office and aware of the fluidity, if not chaos, of domestic politics then. The overlap between institutional responsibilities in a crisis would, in my opinion, make it impossible to properly or professionally function as foreign minister for a country as important as Egypt. I was contacted by the then Prime Minister Kamal El-Ganzouri in December 2011 to again be offered the position of Foreign Minister, which I declined yet again.

My engagement in domestic politics had evolved a bit as I joined the newly established Dostour party led by Mohamed El-Baradei. Party politics were a novel experience for me and required a serious learning curve, one that I did not have the tolerance for. I preferred to express myself on the issues but had no real patience for the legitimate but tedious process of domestic consensus making which involved a macabre balance of important and insignificant issues both personal and professional. The later developments of the year after, with the Muslim Brotherhood coming to power, confirmed the veracity of my decision not to accept the foreign minister's position then. There was no way my foreign policy views would have been compatible with those of President Mohamed Morsi with his Muslim Brotherhood posture, which included a religious index of faith rather than borders in determining national security.

In 2013, Egypt erupted again for the second time in three years, an unsurprising but traumatic experience, even for a country with a long history and deeply rooted state institutions. The three years since Mubarak was removed were filled to the brim with legitimate public aspirations for better government and engagement expectations, but had also witnessed serious threats to the nation's very identity as a centric, cosmopolitan, quasi-secular state. The activists of 2011, still committed to the ideal of better governance, remained unsatisfied that their aspirations had been unmet. Egyptian centrists feared for the country's identity and inclusiveness, which they felt was threatened by an Islamist ideology and the Muslim Brotherhood's non-transparent operations. I was always personally uncomfortable with excessive religiosity in politics and governance because of its potentially arbitrary nature. I was however ready to uphold the rights of all, including Islamists, to have a different approach. However, this has to be done within the limits of the nation's constitution, as was done during Sadat and Mubarak's presidency in order to preserve Egypt's identity.

I had not been a prominent or active member of the opposition during President Morsi's year in office and preferred to express myself independently and act individually. In fact, I followed the events as they unfolded mostly through the media. And, I still had reservations about taking on a ministerial position, even that of Foreign Minister, but felt that the country was coming apart and had lost direction. In those circumstances, I was not able to refuse to serve, when again asked to join the Egyptian government after the removal of President Morsi in 2013. On July 16, 2013, I was sworn in as foreign minister, upon the invitation of Prime Minister Hazem El-Beblawi.

My year in office as foreign minister was very challenging domestically, regionally, and internationally. The societal shocks of the two revolutions after over six decades of domestic stability and a considerable deal of political stagnation and even societal apathy were testimony to the rising popular demand for accountability and shared governance. After 2011, Egyptians were no longer willing to succumb to any given authority, and they wanted their country to be assertive and independent. This required a substantial revision of the country's foreign policy approach and choices with an eye on the future. That was my mission.

A Foreign Policy Rebalancement

The Egyptian revolution was fundamentally a call for change in domestic governance; however, the people's demands were undeniably attached to a need for greater national autonomy on the international stage. This, I felt it was imperative to undertake a careful re-balancing of Egypt's foreign policy, through astute, well-calibrated regional and international diplomacy to make sure that the country always had multiple options to choose from.

After less than a week in office as foreign minister in the summer of 2013, I convened a major press conference and laid out an action plan for Egypt to deal with imminent foreign policy challenges and reset its course. The American New York Times correspondent in Egypt casually dubbed this as "The Fahmy Doctrine".

This comprehensive plan set out to provide Egypt with multiple foreign policy options, avoiding overdependence on any single country given the ramifications of such practices during the past 70 years. It attempted to discuss pressing priorities and future challenges on three fronts: the domestic, the regional, and the international. To begin with, there was the obvious immediate need to explain to the world the June 30, 2013, events. Removing a president before the end of his/her term was, of course, an exceptional measure, and this required highlighting that Egypt was facing exceptional circumstances that its citizens could not condone for three more years until the president's term in office would naturally end. To do this, I planned for the Foreign Ministry to establish a special task force and design a media plan to provide a credible and accurate account of the developments in the country and to monitor Egypt's image abroad.

My goals were however much more ambitious and substantive. I was determined also to recalibrate Egypt's foreign policy toward more sustained and proactive regional cooperation in the Middle East, Africa, and the Mediterranean, and toward a rebalancing of Egypt's international relations, particularly with respect to American and Russian relations but also about Asia. Among other things, the plan of action underlined the commitment of Egypt to actively and creatively engage in a number of international issues, including water security in Africa, the Palestinian cause, the situation in Syria, Islamophobia, combating terrorism, and nuclear proliferation concerns in the Middle East.

In essence, this was a foreign policy of diversification, as well as a determination to keep Egypt's eggs in different baskets. This policy seriously considered the changing global and regional political realities as well as the priorities of Egypt's domestic political transition. Equally important, the action plan also worked toward laying the foundation for a future vision beyond the transitional period and including training and empowering younger generations of Egyptian diplomats and restructuring the foreign ministry itself. This was an ambitious project which, while initially only personally conceived by me, was soon to be embraced by all of the senior leadership in government after I had presented it at the press conference. In addition, it was a plan that the Egyptian foreign ministry under my leadership rigorously pursued even in difficult circumstances.

I ultimately left the government in June 2014 in an Egyptian government cabinet reshuffle. Shortly afterwards, Lisa Anderson who had become the president of the AUC asked me to resume my position as dean of the School of Global Affairs and Public Policy. Creating synergies between strong academic foundations and practitioners' experiences had been an enjoyable and fruitful exercise for me for the four years prior to my assumption of the ministerial post in July 2013. I accepted Anderson's invitation without hesitation, but with a clear understanding that I intended to continue my efforts beyond the University to help create a better foundation of governance in Egypt and a more balanced geopolitical structure in the Middle East.

My work has kept me extremely busy for the last few years, with extensive travels particularly across the Arab world, which remains in a very serious state of flux, and across Asia, whose role is globally expanding. At the same time, I have also been drawn into a number of civil society initiatives with the hope of achieving the goals that the Egyptian people expressed through the recent historical developments.

REFERENCE

Hill, C. (2015). *Foreign Policy in the Twenty-First Century*. London: Palgrave.

Foreign Policy Challenges and Opportunities

CHAPTER 2

Geopolitical Upheaval in the Middle East

*The 1967 war was the death knell of Arab nationalism. The Iraqi
invasion of Kuwait in 1990 brought the end of any semblance of
Arab unity. Falsehoods and failed American policies created
regional imbalances, elevating Iran and Turkey's status.*

The Middle East, with the Arab world at its core, has been turbulent since
the middle of the twentieth century. Nation-states were born in the Arab
Gulf area while others were redefined like Syria, Jordan, Palestine, and
Sudan. Yet, others changed both their political direction and their form of
government, most prominently Egypt, Iran, and Turkey. Former European
colonialists, acting to safeguard their interests, or to settle old scores
among one another, were instrumental in determining the present-day
realities of the region through the infamous Sykes–Picot Agreement of
1916 and the Balfour Declaration.

In the midst of all this turmoil, Egypt was geographically, politically,
and culturally at the heart of the Middle East. It was the intellectual beacon, recognized as the leader of the Arab world. Its policies attracted wide
popular support, and its institutional and intellectual depth was often seen
as a model to be emulated by other states as they fought for independence.
She was a stronger proponent of inter-Arab cooperation, the leading force
behind the Pan-Arab movement, and a cofounder in 1945 of the League
of Arab States in Cairo.

© The Author(s) 2020
N. Fahmy, *Egypt's Diplomacy in War, Peace and Transition*,
https://doi.org/10.1007/978-3-030-26388-1_2

Three main events changed the political paradigm in the Arab world and the Middle East, redefining Arab nationalism, reconstituting Arab leadership, and reshaping Egypt's role in the Middle East were the 1967 War, the 1990 Iraqi invasion of Kuwait, and the 2003 American invasion of Iraq. The repercussions and ramifications of these events shook and shocked the geopolitical theater in the Middle East out of its hinges.

THE 1967 WAR: THE DEATH KNELL OF ARAB NATIONALISM

On the morning of June 5, 1967, Israel attacked Egypt by surprise, justifying it later as a defensive preemptive action. As I navigated my way from my home in Zamalek, west of Cairo, to my high school in Heliopolis, northeast of Cairo, my friends and I felt exhilarated as street radio repeatedly broadcasted news of dozens and dozens of Israeli fighter planes being shot down by our armed forces. The only questions that came to my mind then were how many planes Israel could have, and how long would it take to completely defeat its army. Twenty-five minutes later, on arrival to school, there were already whispers that something was wrong.

Later in the day, from friends and family in the Egyptian armed forces, it became evident that the military tide was in fact strongly in favor of Israel. To our shock and dismay, victory was not to be ours. By the end of that short war, Egypt, Syria, and Jordan had suffered thousands of human casualties and substantial material losses. Israel had captured the Sinai Peninsula, the Gaza Strip, the West Bank, the Old City of Jerusalem, and the Golan Heights. The ramifications of that war, however, did not stop there.

The Egyptian society lost confidence in its leadership, as did the Arab world in general. Nasser was discredited and the country's political stature in the region diminished. Arabs were stigmatized by the world as inept failures. Even two years later, in the summer of 1969, as a high school graduate visiting Speakers' Corner in Hyde Park, London, I sensed that while we were being looked upon with sympathy, Egyptians were considered emotional losers who would never be able to change the Middle East's regional realities on the ground.

The political momentum behind Pan-Arabism was the first casualty of this humiliating defeat. Inter-Arab conflicts existed before the 1967 War: The Civil War in Yemen in the 1960s with Egypt supporting the revolutionary republicans while egged on by the British, Jordan, and Saudi Arabia supported the more conservative elements. However, the devastating Arab defeat in 1967 had systemic ramifications for the Arab regional political paradigm, expediting the end of the ambitious short-lived call for Arab nationalism. Egyptian President Gamal Abdel Nasser announced a televised resignation, albeit it was quickly retracted the following day in the wake of large public demonstrations. Some of these were spontaneous, while others unquestionably supported or initiated by government institutions. Nasser's domestic and regional credibility was however shaken and he had to recalibrate his ambitions focusing on domestic affairs, rebuilding the armed forces, and reconciliation with his followers. This gradually laid the foundation for Egypt's shift toward *realpolitik* under Nasser's successor, Anwar Sadat, after his death from a cardiac arrest.

The debate about regional political developments in this part of the world has always occurred in the shadow of one conspiracy theory or the other. A widespread one in 1967 suggested a Western scheme to counter and undermine Pan-Arabism which defied Israeli interest associated with this theory is the assumption that Egypt was drawn into its unfortunate military intervention in Yemen in the early 1960s in order to distract its army and curtail its ability to stand up to the Israeli aggression. True or not, Egypt's adventurism in Yemen had a devastating effect, not only on Egypt's military capacities but also on the economy. Furthermore, it is true that Nasser's challenge to the status quo rendered him a natural target of old and new powers in the West, of non-Arab states in the Middle East, and even of conservative constituencies in the Arab world as well as domestic ones in Egypt. Nevertheless, as head of state, Nasser was politically responsible for the 1967 Naksa (the military defeat) and for Egypt's miscalculated military engagement in Yemen.

The demise of Pan-Arabism was not solely the work of foreign conspirators collaborating against Arab interests. The 1967 War expedited the process but was not in itself the fundamental reason. The inevitable irrelevance of Arab nationalism was a result of its static non-evolutionary nature and its inability to respond to the evolving needs of the different Arab domestic constituencies, especially those that had recently achieved their independence. By portraying Arab nationalism primarily as a rallying cause against foreign threats and corrupt regional monarchs, rather than a movement to build modern, affluent, and proud nations, it became irrelevant and moribund as a younger generation of Arabs emerged with new interests and priorities.

The Arab leaders of the last half century are those primarily responsible for the end of Pan-Arabism. However, it is not an exaggeration to assert that the 1967 War psychologically broke the Arabs and shook the Middle East's political paradigm to its roots. Personally, I think the Middle East continues to suffer from its consequences up until this day.

The 1990 Iraqi Invasion of Kuwait and the End of Arab Unity

Another moment of tectonic change in the Arab region came with the Iraqi invasion of Kuwait in the summer of 1990. Leading Arab and Islamic capitals had been in heated debate over how to preempt the oncoming catastrophe as the Iraqi President Saddam Hussein prepared to invade Kuwait.

Egypt held intensive consultations within its diplomatic and national security establishments on how to proceed. This included a number of heads of diplomatic missions abroad such as Amre Moussa, who was the permanent representative to the United Nations in New York at the time, where I also worked.

The night before Moussa left to Cairo for consultations prior to the invasion of Kuwait, my counterpart in the Japanese mission to the United Nations insisted on a very urgent meeting. Overwhelmed by the regional crises at hand, I grudgingly made time for the Japanese diplomat who asked me whether Hussein would invade Kuwait soon. At that point, the Iraqi president was still threatening an invasion but had not ordered his troops to move across the border. In the absence of clear instructions from Egypt, I hesitated to answer directly but chose to affirm Egypt's concerns about Hussein's actions and explain our efforts to prevent a looming war. I then asked my Japanese interlocutor what had provoked such a pointed question with a great sense of urgency. His response was eye opening, explaining that Japanese construction companies working in Iraq had seen large numbers of Iraqi troops and heavy military equipment moving in the direction of the border, far beyond what would be necessary to bluff or simply threaten Kuwait.

I hurriedly reported this to Moussa before his flight to Egypt. He was initially skeptical about the information but quickly agreed to send an urgent cable to Cairo reporting on the meeting with the assessment of the mission in New York that Saddam Hussein would, in fact, cross into Kuwait imminently. Regrettably, our projection proved correct.

On August 2, 1990, Iraqi troops invaded on the pretext that Kuwait was illegitimately acquiring Iraqi oil by cross-border slant drilling in a shared oil field. Iraq further justified the invasion by reiterating historical claims to Kuwait as being the 19th Iraqi province. Within two days, Iraq had completely taken over the country with the royal family fleeing to Saudi Arabia. The United Nations Security Council quickly called for an immediate withdrawal of all occupying forces. Iraq refused to comply. In January 1991, a United Nations-authorized coalition led by the United States, which included Egypt, Syria, the Arab Gulf Cooperation Council (GCC) countries, and Morocco, intervened militarily to liberate Kuwait.

The Iraqi invasion entailed drastic and traumatic regional repercussions on the Arab world. It divided the Arab world, but most importantly, it prompted the Arab Gulf States to focus on sub-regional cooperation and become fully dependent on American security. For them, this was not simply a territorial disagreement between neighboring Arab states but a full-fledged existential invasion from within the Arab world itself, which was an anomaly in contemporary political relations in the Arab world.

Saddam's irresponsible actions and the inability of the Arab world to prevent his aggression underlined the failure of the assumed collective Arab defense system against possible threats. The inability of this system to liberate Arab territories occupied by Israeli forces was already discredited, particularly with the 1967 War when even more Arab lands were occupied than was previously the case. While there were already attempts at sub-regional coalitions, such as the Gulf Cooperation Council (GCC) which was formed in 1981 exclusively for the Arab Gulf states, and the short-lived Arab Cooperation Council (ACC) which was founded in 1989 by Iraq, North Yemen, Jordan, and Egypt in response to the GCC, the 1990 Iraqi invasion exacerbated the situation, widening the preferences for sub-regional alliances. Accordingly, although Egypt and Syria were part of the United States-led international coalition for the liberation of Kuwait in 1991, the Arab Gulf would depend even less on collective Arab action and even rejected the offer of Egypt and Syria to provide a military security blanket in the future including military assets to ensure Arab Gulf security as had been agreed in the Damascus Declaration of March 1991. Instead, the Arab Gulf states acted to take further steps to ensure more efficient inter-Arab Gulf collaboration.

The invasion of Kuwait, which was preceded by more aggressive and expanding Iranian policies in the region since the Iranian Revolution in 1978–1979, also drove Arab states to seek increased security measures and a security blanket from the United States in particular. Thus, the ramifications of the war did not only break the traditional Arab matrix but also greatly increased the influence of non-Arab regional and international players in the Levant and the Gulf area. Eventually, the security in these regions became almost entirely dependent on international players, be that the United States or more recently the Russian military and security engagement in Syria since 2016.

Some Middle East experts suggest that after being shocked by the Arab oil embargo in 1973, the United States intentionally encouraged Hussein to invade Kuwait in order to decimate the burgeoning Iraqi military capacity and emerging nuclear program. This is perceived by them as an attempt to preempt the emergence of a strong, more independent Arab regional player with control over substantial oil reserves and the potential to pose a security threat to Israel.

Hussein's aggressive actions are to be condemned. Yet, it is important to note that, as the Iraq crisis heightened, the United States was annoyed with the attempts of many international leaders including the French President François Mitterrand, the then Soviet emissary Yevgeny Primakov, and the United Nations Secretary-General Javier Pérez de Cuéllar to search for compromises with Hussein. In December 1990, the American Permanent Representative to the United Nations Ambassador Thomas Pickering approached me in the United Nations delegates' lounge, interrupting a phone call I was on, to express his concern that Hussein would agree to partially withdraw his forces back to only 10 kilometers inside Kuwait. This, he argued, would make the American-led coalition efforts to liberate Kuwait very difficult to justify. Hussein, however, did not take advantage of that opportunity which could have spared him and the Arab world much turmoil.

The Invasion of Iraq: Falsehoods, Failed Policies, and Regional Imbalances

One of the traceable reverberations of the 1990 Iraqi invasion of Kuwait was the American invasion of Iraq 13 years later. The declared reason for the invasion of Iraq was the alleged acquisition by Iraq of weapons of mass destruction. Another general sentiment is that the invasion of Iraq was a reaction to the terrorist attacks against America in 9/11. I believe that was the excuse rather than the real reason. It was not known that Iraq was associated with these treacherous events. A more plausible theory is that the growing neocon influence in America was the driving force behind the decision as part of a strategic objective of diminishing Arab regional powers in the region. Other theories included that George W. Bush seemed committed on writing or completing the legacy of his father who had liberated Kuwait but refrained from entering Iraq and removing Saddam Hussein. I was serving as Egypt's ambassador to the United States when it invaded Iraq.

Even more than previous events, the 2003 invasion of Iraq fueled and legitimized widespread conspiracy theories in the Arab world that its dissemination was a grand Western scheme driven by Israelis and American neocons. Saddam Hussein was evil and treacherous. The American invasion was, however, on false pretense, contrary to the evidence available and a violation of international law. All of this has led some serious analysts to conclude that there was a premeditated American policy to invade. Even conspiracy theory skeptics like myself cannot discount the many actions and accounts that provide ample reason to conclude that a grand design at the expense of the Arab world did in fact exist. There clearly was a determination to ignore or falsify evidence. For example, the United Nations investigator's reports presented by Rolf Ekéus during (1991–1997) did not substantiate the American allegation of the continued existence of chemical and biological weapons in Iraq. The reports prepared in March of 2003 by Hans Blix[1] and then Mohamed El-Baradei,[2] the successive directors of the International Atomic Energy Agency (IAEA), were of a corresponding conclusion that there was no evidence of an Iraq nuclear weapons program at the time of the attack. Similarly, American investigators of weapons of mass destruction, who were led by David Kay, later confirmed that there was no concrete evidence of Saddam Hussein having nuclear, chemical, or biological weapons before the war started.[3] The Director of the United States Central Intelligence George Tenet also later publicly said that the Central Intelligence Agency (CIA) was mistaken about Iraq's inventory of weapons of mass destruction.

Even more damning was that while addressing the United Nations Security Council in February 2003, the Secretary of State Colin Powell, to

---

[1] United Nations Weapons Inspectors Report to Security Council on Progress in Disarmament of Iraq | Meetings Coverage and Press Releases. (March 7, 2003). Retrieved from https://www.un.org/press/en/2003/sc7682.doc.htm

[2] El Baradei, M. (2011 p. 65). The age of deception: Nuclear diplomacy in treacherous times (1st ed.). New York: Metropolitan Books.

[3] Transcript: David Kay at Senate hearing. (January 29, 2004). Retrieved from http://edition.cnn.com/2004/US/01/28/kay.transcript/

justify the upcoming invasion of Iraq, referred to a letter signed by Niger's foreign minister Allele Habibou dated October 2000, concerning Iraq's purchase of uranium as evidence of its involvement in building a nuclear weapons program. During the same Security Council meeting, however, Mohamed El-Baradei, then the director-general of the IAEA, challenged Powell's assertions by pointing out that Habibou had in fact been out of office years earlier than the date of the document, inferring that it was clearly forged. Years later, at a social event in Washington, after Powell left office, I undiplomatically asked him why he had done so, particularly since he was "un-sackable" given his war record and special status. His tired response was, "I had so many battles to fight every day. I was exhausted and they misled me on this."

There were others in the American administration who were actively agitating for the invasion of Iraq while knowing the allegations were unsubstantiated. Secretary of Defense Rumsfeld and his deputy Paul Wolfowitz were among the strongest proponents, the latter being the conceptual thinker among the neocons in the administration. After the invasion, Paul Wolfowitz openly told me that the premise that Iraq had weapons of mass destruction was the only possible way to get consensus in the administration on the decision to attack Iraq, given that it was impossible to establish a direct link between the Iraqi president and Al-Qaeda or other terrorists. It was obvious that for the neocons, restructuring the Middle East was an essential objective in addressing both the perceived threat from Islamist extremists to America; and ensuring Israel's security from regional adversaries in the Arab world would be best served by dismantling strong Arab armies, even if they were not at that moment targeting Israel. Iraq was an opportune target.

In the late summer of 2002 when the American President George W. Bush announced that the United States of America would raise the Iraqi issue at the United Nations General Assembly,[4] I commended this step to the Under Secretary of Defense for Policy Douglas Feith at the Pentagon. Surprisingly, he openly expressed his disapproval for what Bush had just announced, complaining "it would only complicate things and might tie our hands". This antipathy toward a United Nations role before and after the outbreak of military operations was strongly shared by Rumsfeld, Wolfowitz, and Feith.

---

[4] George Bush's speech to the United Nations General Assembly (September 12, 2002). Retrieved from https://www.theguardian.com/world/2002/sep/12/iraq.usa3

The reactions of Rumsfeld, Wolfowitz, and Feith, I believe, clearly indicate that the Bush administration was predetermined to attack Iraq irrespective of what the Iraqis had or did not have in terms of weapons of mass destruction. It is simply implausible that a superpower like the United States did not realize that the information was false. There were too many horrendous unjustified decisions to assume that they were simply mistakes, especially the de-Beatification, the release of the Iraqi army, and the hesitation to hand over the governance to transitional committees of Iraqi leaders. All of this resulted in chaos after the end of the military operations and a quickly rising tide of anti-Americanism as America was seen as an occupier rather than a liberator. Either there was a conspiracy or the hallowed institutional checks and balances in the American system were in fact fictional. I am inclined to believe the former.

The invasion of Iraq was one of the most contentious differences between Egypt and the United States under the presidency of George W. Bush. Prior to that, in the 1980s, Egypt had partially provided arms to Iraq during its war with Iran (1980–1988) with the agreement of the United States. However, President Mubarak was not a fan of Hussein. Even before the Iraqi invasion of Kuwait, when Iraq initiated the establishment of the ACC as a sub-regional counterbalance to the GCC, Egypt only joined hesitantly. As Hussein became more assertive, asking for cooperation and coordination between intelligence services in the four countries, Mubarak immediately retrenched. He had no intention of being part of anyone else's plans or schemes, especially someone as strong-willed and adventurous as Hussein. However, when Mubarak provided military support in the liberation of Kuwait, it was stipulated that Egypt's support would not include entering Iraq itself. The 41st American president did not enter Iraq, but his son George W. Bush, the 43rd president, had a different perspective on life.

When President Mubarak visited the United States during President George W. Bush's first year in office, the Pentagon showed him a simulation of communications and interoperability security system, hoping to convince an already reluctant Egypt to join. At one point, the American presenter showed a map on the screen of the unnamed land theater where they would be simulating the attack. As soon as we were in the president's car, Mubarak said to me that the theater of operations looked very much like Iraq. This been my immediate impression as well.

The Invasion of Iraq was definitely preplanned on the cards and the books quite early. I remember meeting Vice President Richard Cheney before his first trip to the Middle East in March 2002, and highlighting the importance of the Arab–Israeli conflict and the need to move forward. To my surprise, Cheney's frank and direct response was that his focus would be on Iraq. With the benefit of hindsight, this was clearly an indication of what was to come, confirming that the new administration had a premeditated plan to challenge Saddam Hussein and Iraq.

In early fall of 2002, about eight months before the American invasion of Iraq occurred, I sent a formal cable to Cairo from the embassy in Washington asserting that the United States would invade Iraq before the spring of 2003. I explained that the size and composition of the American military that was present in the vicinity of Iraq provided significant indications that the invasion of Iraq was developing and hot weather considerations would make it imperative to act by spring at the utmost. I also sent a substantial report assessing the American neocons in support of this invasion and their backgrounds and ideology.

The then Egyptian Foreign Minister Ahmed Maher contacted me to say that I was known to be calm under pressure, thus both President Mubarak and he were surprised with my rather agitated assessment. I explained that I was not agitated but simply being straightforward and candid as it should be at this level of diplomacy, especially given the seriousness of the issue. A combative but intelligent man, he slightly backed off, inquiring whether I was sure about my conclusions. I had made these assessments based on my reading of American policy, politics as well as the civilian and security stakeholders. Politically, I could sense that the more aggressive members of the administration such as the United States of America Vice President Cheney, Secretary of Defense Rumsfeld, the Deputy Secretary of Defense Wolfowitz, and the Under Secretary of Defense for Policy Feith had gained more ground, and that Bush was leaning in that direction if not the original instigator of the policy himself.

Equally, if not more, important was that I also understood that the United States' military would be the determining factor on the timing and nature of the operation. The Pentagon was of course led by civilians, but the active officers would have a major effect on how the decision would ultimately go and when. As I looked around and listened carefully throughout Washington, I remember being particularly taken by a comment made to me by former Senator Richard Lugar of Indiana, a good friend and an arms control and national security expert. Lugar had said that once the American troops on the ground in the neighboring areas near Iraq exceeded 100,000, there was no turning back without some form of military engagement.

Egyptian–American high-level contacts, including among the military, continued throughout the following few months after my assessment. Slowly, the Egyptian authorities accepted that invading Iraq might actually occur. Tommy Franks, the Commander of the United States Central Command, later wrote in his autobiography that Mubarak had told him that Saddam Hussein had biological weapons.[5] Mubarak told me that he had never made any explicit statement on the matter. Iraq had used chemical weapons against Iran previously and while I cannot definitively confirm what exactly was said, I would not rule out that Mubarak was cautioning about potential threats and not making a conclusive determination.

As spring got closer, the inevitability and irrationality of an American invasion of Iraq became more self-evident. The drumbeats had increased; the administration was deaf to concerns made by its closest allies including the North Atlantic Treaty Organization (NATO) members Germany and France, who opposed the invasion. The Arab states were also divided on the issue at a summit meeting in Sharm El-Sheikh, Egypt. The majority of the countries, Egypt included, opposed the invasion. For their part, the Arab Gulf states were generally supportive of the planned attack. Nevertheless, the United Arab Emirates presented a last-ditch proposal at the summit suggesting that Hussein would have to step down in exchange for safe and dignified refuge, after which Iraq could pursue a new political path. The initiative was well-intentioned, and hypothetically, it could have prevented the war, but informed politicians at the time did not imagine that Saddam would peacefully relinquish power or that Bush would cancel his war plans. The Emirati initiative never received concrete consideration.

As ambassador in Washington, I was instructed to inform the American administration that Egypt was not supportive of the invasion and to also recite a list of dos and don'ts if the inevitable invasion occurred. Our message, among other things, emphasized the importance of ensuring the stability of state structures including the Iraqi army, even if the top echelon was removed. On several other occasions and meetings with the National Security Advisor Condoleezza Rice and other high officials, I reiterated for the record that Egypt did not support the invasion of Iraq.

As the American invasion of Iraq got closer, President Mubarak sent a delegation to Washington for one last assessment, even though he repeat-

[5] Tommy Frank, (2005). Autobiography: American Soldier book.

edly insisted that my assessment seems to be close to realization. Foreign Minister Maher's health had been deteriorating, and the delegation was composed of the National Security Advisor Ambassador Osama El-Baz, the President's Information Secretary Maged Abdel Fatah, and the president's son Gamal. Just before the visit started, Mubarak told me that El-Baz would come back because he was not in good health, and therefore, he wanted me to lead the delegation. He also instructed that his son should be the last on the list, protocol-wise. I assured him that we would handle his son's participation as he had requested, especially that he had no official capacity. I added, however, that El-Baz was already a senior diplomat when I first joined the Foreign Ministry decades ago. Therefore, I was more comfortable giving him the lead. Mubarak agitatedly responded, "I don't care how you sit but you are responsible as my ambassador. And you report the results to me." That was fine with me.

The Egyptian delegation held several meetings with the Americans, especially with Rice and Wolfowitz repeatedly affirming Egypt's opposition to the invasion while providing a long list of guidelines if the invasion occurred anyway. As a consummate professional, Rice listened patiently before posing a series of questions about post-military operations, seemingly attempting to ascertain facts in support of arguments already ongoing within the American administration.

The meeting with Wolfowitz was more consequential for us and reflective of the different postures and "exceptionalism" attitude of the different members of the administration. Wolfowitz was calm and reserved, carefully listening while saying very little, clearly only hosting us as a political courtesy. He was a strong supporter of invading Iraq and was not about to be swayed. Besides, his attitude toward Egypt had been negative from the start, being one of the strong proponents of regime change in Egypt.

As the meeting progressed, the Secretary of Defense Donald Rumsfeld suddenly walked in. To the astonishment of the Egyptian delegation, I included, after quick pleasantries, he looked at me and said, "Ambassador, can't Egypt take him out?" We understood he meant Saddam Hussein, but it was not clear what he literally meant by "take him out". This incident with Rumsfeld was at the precise time that the American Secretary of State Powell was delivering his report to the United Nations Security Council in New York. Rumsfeld invited the Egyptian delegation to a side room to watch the delivery on television, looking at us as if we should be convinced of the open-and-shut nature of the case against Iraq.

As soon as we walked out of the Pentagon, the Egyptian delegation turned to me in astonishment with the rhetorical question: "Do you still believe they are going to war in the next few weeks with all these kinds of questions still up in the air?" I was still confident that I was correctly reading the situation. I did, however, become really worried then and there that America did not have a good plan for the day after and would thus be driven by arrogance and guided by ignorance. The Middle East, especially the Arab world, was about to pay a heavy price for the upcoming debacle.

On March 20, 2003, America invaded Iraq. There was never any doubt that the American military would defeat Iraqi forces. The question was rather the volume of the inevitable costs to Iraqi civilians as well as to the Middle East as a whole. These proved horrendous.

America's Iraqi policies post-invasion were worse than the invasion itself, both devastating and irresponsible to say the least. All Iraqi state structures were disbanded, rather than reformed, and the Iraqi army dispersed with its weapons. It then established a sectarian, rather than a pluralistic, political system, putting in place an executive authority based on an artificial power-share formula of the ethnic, sectarian, and religious constituencies.

Given the ethnic and sectarian diversity of numerous Arab countries in the Levant and Gulf areas, this American policy exponentially brought into play the whole question of identity politics. This rattled the nation-state system not only of Iraq but also of the Levant and the Gulf area especially that this was occurring simultaneously with Iran's increasingly aggressive foreign policy in the Arab world that projected its own status as the protector of the region's Shiites as a means of exercising hegemony. The overwhelming identity in the Arab world was still Arab identity, but failed inclusive governance has led to recurrent domestic discontent including complaints of inequitable treatment by non-Arab constituents in many Arab countries. This needed to be addressed by better governance while preserving national identities, but the American recipes were caustic and divisive.

The promotion of such sectarian-based sentiments rather than Arab national identity in the region was potentially politically damaging to Egypt. The shared Arab cultural identity had in modern history morphed into a political regional one, with Egypt at it apex. Arab nationalism was a platform for political cooperation but not a license to erase the specificity and sovereign identity of each nation-state, or a call for imposing identical policies and priorities throughout the region. Arab nationalism could survive even if Pan-Arabism, which encroached on the nation-state specificity, slowly lost relevance.

Establishing identity on sectarian rather than national terms would greatly weaken the whole concept of extensive Arab cooperation of nation-states. This was a community of states that Egypt best led by example, not by infringing on their sovereignty.

Ultimately, America's post-invasion restructuring plan was catastrophic, especially the dismantling of the Iraqi army, the de-Beatification, or the procrastination in handing over authority to the Iraqis. It made a mockery of statecraft that planted the seeds for sectarianism, divisions, and the rampant expansion of non-state actors, including the Islamic State of Iraq and the Levant (ISIL). It created regional imbalances in favor of non-Arab countries like Iran, Turkey, and Israel, while spilling cancerous poison on the social fabric of the Arab states in the Levant and Gulf areas. The Middle East continues to pay heavily for this debacle, even more than a decade later.

Not Only an Arab Neighborhood: Iran and Turkey

Two years before the American invasion of Iraq, after the 9/11 attacks, the Middle East had been redefined among foreign affairs analysts. Prior to that, in the United Nations jargon, the "Middle East" was usually used to refer to the Arab world, Israel, and occasionally Iran depending on circumstances and topic. This, I think, was essentially the result of historic Anglo-French interferences and the prominence of the Arab–Israeli conflict. However, Iran and Turkey were now generally considered within this region among practitioners. This new definition of the Middle East evolved with the debate over militant Islamic groups in the wake of the 2001 attacks. Given the overwhelmingly Muslim population of these countries, analysts from the West, in particular, began looking at the region from the prism of Islam. It was even further expanded in nomenclature during the presidency of George W. Bush with the birth of the new term "the greater Middle East" to include two other Muslim states, Pakistan and Afghanistan, but this was short-lived and seemed to die down quickly after the American president left office. Personally, I remember being surprised by the incoherence of this idea that seemed to be driven by the primacy of combating terrorism threatening America, a simplistic and false theory that all the region's problems emanated from religion and particularly Islam.

For Egypt, the Middle East included its immediate neighbors in the region: the Arab world, Iran, Turkey, and Israel rather than Pakistan and Afghanistan.

Egypt and Iran are two old and rich civilizations that in fact have always had respect for one another in the past despite their political differences. The political relations between the two countries over the last 50 years have ebbed and flowed, witnessing admiration and cooperation followed by political tensions and adversarial actions. On occasion, enmity has also come into play.

Egyptian–Iranian relations during the rule of President Nasser and around the 1967 War were generally negative, as Egypt tilted toward the Soviet Union and the Eastern Bloc while the Shah of Iran aligned his country toward the United States and the Western Bloc. This created a clear divergence from the previously stable relations. Iran's Shah Mohammad Reza Pahlavi had married King Farouk's sister, which was both socially appropriate and politically astute as an expression of the political weight of the two nations. It is noteworthy that the marriage of a Sunni bride and a Shiite groom did not provoke a contentious religious furor or in fact any debate. It was designed to promote a close alliance between the two leading regional powers in the earlier half of the twentieth century. After the Egyptian monarchy ended with more progressive leadership in Egypt leaning toward the Eastern Bloc, and Iran positioned clearly in the Western camp, bilateral relations between the two countries soured for years.

Following the 1973 War, President Sadat's openness toward the United States reopened the door for a more positive engagement with Iran under the Shah. A good, personal rapport developed between Sadat and Mohammad Reza with Iran. The Egyptian president was to later offer refuge and burial ground to the Shah and his family in the wake of his ouster from power in 1979 after the United States refused to receive its terminally ill former ally.

The Iranian Revolution of 1978–1979 and the rule of Ayatollah Khomeini, the founder of the Islamic Republic of Iran until his death in 1989, established a complicated paradigm in the regional political map as Iran and America parted ways. Arab politics, both its conservative and progressive trends, was shaken as Khomeini aggressively attempted to export the "Islamic revolution" to Iran's Arab neighbors. This was both ideologically and geopolitical motivated. Consequently, when this failed, Iran pursued its goals under the mantra of the oppressed in the Arab world, particularly with regards to the Shia constituencies in the Arab Gulf and the Levant, be that Arabs under Israeli occupation or Shiite minorities in the Arab World. Iran's real motivation was clearly to expand its geopolitical influence and power. A very clear example of this was Iran's support of Assad's Alawite regime in Syria: The Syrian regime is not only of a different Shia sect than that followed in Iran, but it is also highly secular and not ready to accommodate political or ideological associations with an "Islamic" rule. But the Syrian Bath party was at odds with its Iraqi counterpart competing for Arab prominence in the Levant. Sharing a mutual although different antipathy toward Iraq, Syria and Iran became strategic allies.

The new regime in Tehran was firmly opposed to Sadat's pursuit of peace with Israel. Egypt's already warm relations with America and its hospitality of the expelled Shah was also a source of friction between Cairo and Tehran. After his assassination, Iran chose to name one of the main roads of its capital after Khalid El-Islambouli, the soldier who assassinated Sadat. For decades, every attempt to reconcile appeared to break down in futile discussions about removing Islambouli's name from a Tehran Street and ensuring that the Shah's burial place would not become a gathering venue for Iranian royalists. Irrespective of the mutual respect for the cultural heritage of the two nations, the real issue here was whether the Middle East would be defined as mostly Arab but including others, thus led by Egypt, or multicultured and faith-based thus catering to Iran's projection.

Throughout his 30 years in office, President Mubarak was always extremely suspicious of Iran's intervention in the internal affairs of the countries of the region, strongly convinced of its support for extremist groups in Egypt. The negative sentiment was further consolidated by the refusal of the Iranian security services to cooperate with their counterparts in Egypt.

Ironically, the Iranian diplomatic missions overseas, especially in New York and Geneva, would regularly reach out to their Egyptian counterparts to propose the initiation of formal dialogue. Mubarak was never enthusiastic about these invitations but would nevertheless allow for diplomatic contacts, always assuming that they would quickly break down. He was proven right numerous times because Iranian hardliners would ultimately prevail with unacceptable actions or demands. This was so recurrent that on one occasion, Mubarak openly derided his own Foreign Ministry diplomats for repeatedly requesting approval to engage Iran. He even publicly boasted that he was always confident that the Iranians would once again disappoint and embarrass their Egyptian counterpart. It was not clear whether Iran appeared dysfunctional because of a conflict among the diverse domestic political forces, or was it a premeditated Iranian strategy to try to divide the Arab world by engaging its most prominent leader under false pretense. Noteworthy is that Iranian President Ahmadinejad visited Egypt in 2013 to attend the Organization of Islamic States Summit. Iran is an important player in the Middle East, and diplomats tend to encourage engagement, but Egypt would never sacrifice its Arab relations for openings with other regional states.

The same Iranian inconsistencies continued even after the ouster of Mubarak. Egypt, however, added its own inconsistencies to the pot. This was certainly the case during the one-year rule of the Muslim Brotherhood. On a visit to Tehran to attend the Non-Aligned Movement (NAM) summit in August 2012, President Mohamed Morsi decided to touch on raw nerves and sensitivities between Shiites and Sunnis, which left some Iranians perplexed. However, this did not dampen their interest in engaging Egypt by encouraging Iranian tourists to visit Egypt given its Fatimid history and the many Shiite religious sites in the country. The Salafi movement was no less annoyed, they demonstrated in front of the residence of the Iranian chargé d'affaires in opposition to encouraging Iranian Shia tourist visitors to Egypt.

A few months later, as I assumed my position as Egypt's Foreign Minister shortly after Morsi was ousted, the Iranian Foreign Minister Mohammad Javad Zarif was among the very first to personally phone and congratulate me. I had known Zarif for many years with our initial introduction occurring when we were both young diplomats at the United Nations. But this was not at all a simple gesture of courtesy from one diplomat to the other. It was a political move that was quickly covered in the press given the long list of contentious issues between the two countries that had remained unresolved.

Egypt and Iran are highly significant in the Middle Eastern paradigm. It was not surprising that the political forces in each of the two countries would have diverse views on engaging the other. I am confident that Zarif and others in Iran of similar political orientation wanted to engage Egypt. On several occasions, when we met at the United Nations or at the NAM summit in Algeria in May 2014, he made that point in a very straightforward fashion. However, in spite of the Iranian foreign minister's messages, I also saw indications that Zarif did not have much room to maneuver on this issue within the wider circle of Iranian political decision-making. Regrettably, Iran's representative office in Cairo tended to be stocked with security type officials.

Similarly, different institutions within Egypt were much more skeptical about the dialogue with Iran. The security institutions, in particular, continued to affirm that their counterparts in Iran had shown absolutely no readiness to cooperate on outstanding bilateral issues. And, the Grand Imam of Al-Azhar Ahmed El-Tayyeb openly expressed to me his strong reservations about Iran propagating Shiism in Egypt, urging me not to pursue developing relations with Iran as a priority issue.

The concerns raised by the Egyptian security authorities were legitimate and could not be ignored. No attempt to establish even limited cooperation between security services on terrorist issues gained traction. And, there was always the concern that Iran just wanted open engagement with Egypt to infuriate significant numbers of the Arab Gulf States and divide the Arab world. However, I still continued to believe in the importance of having a direct frank and difficult dialogue with Iran to make sure the efficient management of relations including disagreements. For me, a difficult discussion was better than no discussion at all. It provided clarity even if it didn't offer solutions. I would tread slowly and cautiously but kept all options open.

However, it soon became clear that none of the pending security issues between our two countries were getting resolved during the year that I held the Foreign Ministry portfolio. This included issues of terrorism and extremism affecting Egypt domestically as well as antagonistic identity politics within Iran's Arab neighbors.

Iran was the rotating chair of the NAM summit in May 2014 when I met Zarif at the organization's Council of Foreign Ministers that was held in Algiers. He really laid out all the fanfare, with flags of the two countries and live television broadcasting. After the press left the room, Zarif reiterated his welcome and spoke in warm terms about Egypt concluding with a diplomatic suggestion that we turn the page and move on with our relations. I reciprocated his greetings and talked of the richness of the Iranian culture. I very candidly expressed my support for an Egyptian–Iranian dialogue but resolutely indicated my refusal to let bygones be bygones and turn the page. The only way to clearly show that the two countries were serious about engaging each other was to first discuss and try to resolve as many outstanding issues as possible. And, I strongly cautioned against any discussion that was founded on sectarianism or a Sunni–Shia divide. We needed to deal with each other as nation-states, agreeing, disagreeing, and even competing, but legitimately so.

Zarif and I moved toward the side of the room at the end of the meeting, where I asked him to replace the head of the Iranian diplomatic office in Cairo, who was obviously of a security background. He did not directly respond to my suggestion but nodded and said that we needed to have a rational professional diplomatic dialogue between our two countries. Just before we departed, he leaned over and added that "sectarianism was the cancer that would destroy the Middle East".

In spite of our personal relations, an uncooperative approach characterized Egyptian–Iranian relations throughout 2013 and 2014. Egypt had raised concerns about specific extremists who had found haven in Iran and was also anxious about Iranian funding of militant groups in North Africa. The intensity of both of these issues seemed to decrease a little in the early weeks after Mubarak left office. The security services in the two countries did not, however, ever manage to establish a mutual understanding on resolving these points of difference.

Meanwhile, Iran's regional activities at the cost of Egypt's Arab allies in the Arab Gulf, Iraq, and in the Levant had become increasingly aggressive, even more so now that it had much more room to maneuver after the decapitation of its archenemy, Iraq, after the 2003 events. There were some slight indications of readiness to engage in dialogue but nothing that would have made me conclude that President Mubarak's cautionary attitude toward Iran was without merit, even after brief meeting with the reformist Iranian President Mohammad Khatami in Geneva in 2003, an event that was secured after over eight years of extensive diplomatic negotiations.

My serious but carefully measured attempts to encourage Arab–Iranian dialogue throughout 2013 and 2014 continued. During the United Nations General Assembly meetings in the fall of 2013, I suggested to the late Prince Saud bin Faisal, foreign minister of Saudi Arabia, that it was better to directly engage Iran and have tough discussions with them.

Given my strong network of contacts in the nuclear proliferation domain, it was evident in late 2013 that the ongoing negotiations on Iran's nuclear program were serious. I explained to Prince Saud in no uncertain terms that the permanent five Security Council members plus Germany would reach a deal with Iran without delay, and consequently, it was important for Egypt, but preferably Saudi Arabia who was a direct neighbor with more pressing concerns, to start engaging Iran on Arab interests rather than to hear foreign reports on negotiations once a deal was imminent. I added that the Egyptian authorities were not enthusiastic about this suggestion and that they have a good reason, as did his country, to be skeptical about Iran. Therefore, it would be useful first to ask Iran to take concrete confidence-building measures that reflected the commitment of the more conservative elements in the Iranian regime toward true reconciliation with the Arab world.

Prince Saud's initial response was that Iran should issue a declaration of good neighborly relations, but I cautioned that the more progressive political trends in Iran could easily issue such a statement without it being indicative of a serious commitment by the more conservative Iranians whom had been more problematic and were more influential. Something more concrete should be asked for and which, if presented, would reflect the engagement of the conservative factions as well. Singing to the choir would be worthless, I argued. Prince Saud then mentioned that Iran and Saudi Arabia had a bilateral security protocol, which the Iranians were not respecting. He added that Iranian engagement and cooperation in this protocol, in particular, could be a serious beginning.

The following day, while I was attending meetings at the General Assembly, I sought out Zarif. After jokingly commending him on his performance and that of President Hassan Rouhani in courting the international community at the General Assembly, I reminded him that they would ultimately have to return and find ways to live with their neighbors. Zarif jovially responded, "I have known you for long; I was sure that there was something behind your initial flattery." Zarif then asked me whether I could arrange a meeting for him with Prince Saud.

I wanted to preserve positive mood but nevertheless changed my tone, responding coolly that I do not arrange meetings for anyone. Zarif sensed my displeasure, flippantly commenting, "You have not changed since we were both much younger." He then very professionally asked what I had in mind. I argued that a serious Iranian dialogue with the major Arab states, be that Saudi Arabia or Egypt, should be our goal. For any dialogue to be serious, however, it was important to commence around a subject of concrete significance that would help build confidence among the respective institutions, especially those dealing with security issues, suggesting that discussions about discrepancies or violations of the already existing Saudi Iranian security protocol as a starting point.

Zarif was receptive to this idea. He and Prince Saud later both agreed that their security officials initiate contacts on the issues concerning the security protocol. For the next few months, Prince Saud would regularly inform me of the Saudi Iranian contacts, which were progressing reasonably well with plans set to gradually have higher-level meetings among government principals, including the heads of state before the 2014 General Assembly. Regrettably, in mid-February 2014, this whole process broke down completely as the situation in Yemen heated up, with Iran and Saudi Arabia supporting opposing groups on the ground.

Regrettably, several years later now, there are no indications of a new beginning in Arab–Iranian relations; quite the contrary. Between 2014 and 2017, Iranian relations with its Arab Gulf neighbors have taken a strong nosedive. In addition, Iran aggressively extended its influence in the Levant and was significantly more forceful in emphasizing its role in defending the Shia communities in the Middle East. Its support for the Houthis in Yemen was also of great concern.

I have often talked to different Iranian analysts over these last few years. Almost all of them without exception repeat two fundamental points when explaining Iran's regional posture. The first is that Iran was not broken by ten years of sanctions and should be treated as a major regional power. The second is that given the complexity of Middle East politics and the interference of non-regional states in the Levant and the Gulf area in particular, it was imperative for Iran to gain leverage throughout the region, both politically and militarily, in order to fight its battles away from its borders to safeguard its national security interests that are threatened by global powers. To put it in the words of a senior Iranian diplomat whom I talked to in 2016, my vision of the central role of Arab states in this region was flawed because Arabs do not have that much to bring them together. He added that now that the sanctions on Iran have been removed: "It was Iran's era."

One can discuss and analyze Iranian policies and posture in much more detail, but suffice it to say that these two points alone merit serious concern by Arab states, both in the Levant and the Gulf area, even beyond that for Egypt in North Africa.

In 2013–2014, Egypt had a significant number of issues on its international relations agenda. Egyptian–Iranian relations, while important, were not at the top of the list, given the differences of opinions on both sides and the low probability that the diplomatic efforts will be really ripe to bear fruition. Managing relations with Turkey, yet another important and at that point problematic neighbor in the Middle East, was a higher priority on Egypt's foreign relations agenda.

In the late 1980s and early 1990s, Turkey started its successful economic development program under former Prime Minister Turgot Özal. Slowly but surely this provided momentum for a more effective Turkish foreign policy. Ahmet Davutoğlu, who served as foreign minister from 2009 to 2014 under the Islamist-led government, conceptualized an attractive but short-lived "zero conflict" policy with Turkey's neighbors. This occurred only a few years after Turkey and Syria were about to go to war in 1998 over the issue of the Kurdish Workers Party had it not been for the direct intervention of the Egyptian President Mubarak.

The incremental progress in the Turkish regional policies since the 1980s was possible because Turkey always promoted itself as a bridge between the conflicting parties in the Middle East, maintaining relations with both Arabs and Israel. However, after Israel's peace agreements with Egypt and Jordan respectively made direct contacts between these countries, the normal state of play the virtual Turkish bridge between these conflicting parties lost its utility and attractiveness. Turkey then shifted the focus and projected itself as the bridge between Western modernity and moderate Islamic states, particularly as Islamist policies gained prominence in Turkey and the terrorist attacks of 9/11 raised international anxiety toward the Muslim world. This posture served Turkey well, enhancing its stature internationally and expanding its influence regionally in the Middle East.

Indeed, the Arab awakening and the subsequent rise of the chances of political Islam in Tunisia and Egypt raised Turkish regional ambitions once again. But the ouster of the Muslim Brotherhood in Egypt and its decline in Tunisia as well as the Arab Gulf states quickly and severely diminished the resonance of any potential role for Turkey as a bridge with what they called moderate Islam.

Thus, the Turkish reaction to the Egyptian President Morsi's ouster was particularly vociferous. Be it the initiation of the Arab Israeli peace process or the removal of the Muslim Brotherhood from power, it is not an exaggeration to argue that all of Turkey's bridges seemed to collapse because of policies or events in Egypt. Suddenly, its foreign policy mantra of "zero conflict" was transformed into one of conflicts with almost all of its neighbors as its geopolitical ambitions at the expense of its neighbors became more evident.

Nevertheless, in light of the Arab disarray and focus on domestic problems, Turkey has unabashedly made a number of significant shifts in its attitude becoming more assertive in dealing with the new global and regional realities with a view to asserting its influence. It has even revived old historical territorial claims in Syria and Iraq. In the process, it has positioned itself away from the West and Europe to safeguard its interests regarding the Kurdish issue, it has moved considerably closer to Russia, which also regained considerable influence in the Middle East, particularly in the Levant.

As part of its expansionist and aggressive foreign policy, Turkey has also heavily financed several players in Libya, widened its relations in Somalia and East Africa, and created footholds in the Horn of Africa with the objective of pressuring Egypt and other Arab adversaries with interests in the region. Much of this lays the ground foundation for intense geopolitical engagement in the Middle East.

In short, Turkey, like any other country, has its aspirations in the Middle East. However, the vacuum that emerged in the Arab regional influence and the instability that the region witnessed as a result of the ongoing transitions encouraged it to pursue opportunistic policies and even zealous interference in the internal affairs of several Arab countries. It also prompted the engagement of Turkey in cross-border military activities in Syria and even in Iraq.

Over time, a geopolitical imbalance has occurred in favor of non-Arab countries in the region, especially Turkey, Iran, and Israel. Each of them poses a different unique challenge to the Arab world and Egypt; from influence and insurgency to occupation. And, these three countries will continue to resist any Arab regional reassertiveness if at their expense.

In the midst of all this turmoil, Arab diplomacy has been strangely absent. Some Arab countries have provided military support for different protagonists in different conflicts, notably in Libya, Yemen, and in the war against terrorism in Syria and Iraq. None have been conclusive, and diplomatic efforts being made in every one of these cases are being led by non-Arabs or non-Arab organizations.

Another important and alarming factor to consider is the emergence of dangerous non-state actors, particularly terrorist groups such as the Islamic State in Iraq and Syria (ISIS) and the Al-Nusra Front. These groups are essentially homegrown; terrorism in the Middle East is a direct derivative of the breakdown of the social contract and the absence of effective state institutions. But these non-state actors, in different forms and with different identities, have managed to transcend borders with terrorist operations on different continents.

REFERENCES

Bush, G. W. (2002, September 12). *Speech to the United Nations General Assembly.* Retrieved from https://www.theguardian.com/world/2002/sep/12/iraq.usa3

El Baradei, M. (2011). *The Age of Deception: Nuclear Diplomacy in Treacherous Times* (1st ed., p. 65). New York: Metropolitan Books.

Frank, T. (2005). *Autobiography: American Soldier Book*, with Malcom McConnel. New York: Harper Large Print.

Kay, D. (2004, January 29). *Transcript at Senate Hearing.* Retrieved from http://edition.cnn.com/2004/US/01/28/kay.transcript/

United Nations Weapons Inspectors Report to Security Council on Progress in Disarmament of Iraq. (2003, March 7). *UN Meetings Coverage and Press Releases.* Retrieved from https://www.un.org/press/en/2003/sc7682.doc.htm

CHAPTER 3

No War

The 1973 war fundamentally shifted domestic, regional, and global perspectives on the Middle East, with Arabs regaining confidence and respect. Egypt in particular played yet another pioneering role as it battled to make this the last comprehensive Arab–Israeli war and becoming once again a catalyst in reconfiguring global politics as it shifted to a more balanced posture diminishing Soviet influence in the region.

THE 1973 WAR: MAKING PEACE POSSIBLE

The Arab–Israeli conflict, which has persisted since the establishment of the State of Israel in 1948, is the longest ongoing conflict in modern history. Palestinians have remained under occupation, dispersed in diaspora, denied their right to a state, and with no clear hope for the future. The conflict deepened as Israel occupied other Arab territories in other military conquests. Unprecedented human suffering and material losses continued on both sides beyond reason as opportunities for peace were left at the wayside because of failed regional leadership and cynical global geopolitical competition.

In war and peace, Egypt was at the forefront of the regional dynamics in this regard.

Succeeding Gamal Abdel Nasser, Anwar Sadat aspired to move Egypt forward and relieve it from the draining burden of the Arab–Israeli conflict.

© The Author(s) 2020
N. Fahmy, *Egypt's Diplomacy in War, Peace and Transition*,
https://doi.org/10.1007/978-3-030-26388-1_3

He quickly announced a series of diplomatic initiatives. On February 4, 1971, he publicly offered to open the Suez Canal for maritime navigation if Israel withdrew just 50 kilometers from the canal's eastern banks. Israel completely ignored the proposal. Strongly believing that only the United States could influence Israel into returning the occupied territories, Sadat sent his National Security Advisor Hafez Ismail to secretly meet Henry Kissinger in New York on February 25 and 26, and then in Paris on May 10, 1973, in pursuit of a peaceful resolution to the Arab–Israeli conflict. President Nixon was intrigued by this message; his national security advisor, however, was much less enthusiastic. The United States was busy with detente efforts with the Soviet Union, and engaging Egypt or taking on the Arab–Israeli peace process was not a priority for it. Besides, America still looked at Egypt, stigmatized by the 1967 War as a non-influential player.

Kissinger's response, in essence, was that in order to attract the attention of the United States, Egypt first needed to help itself. Sadat realized that to pursue a diplomatic process, he would first have to redress the perception that Egypt had very few options before it. He reluctantly concluded that he had to change the military reality on the ground and consequently took the courageous and historic decision to go to war on October 6, 1973, which the Egyptian armed forces implemented valiantly, given Israel's military superiority at the time. The original objective of the military operation was only to move eastwards to reach the Mitla and Gidi strategic passes in Sinai in order to shake the political status quo. Sadat's ultimate goal was to regain all of Egypt's territories through negotiations, with the war being a precursor for a larger diplomatic exercise.[1]

This war fought by Egypt and Syria did not restore Arab nationalism in the Nasserite tradition, but it brought the Arab world closer. Arab countries from North Africa and the Levant contributed to the war effort. Others from the Arab Gulf provided material and political support. In fact, Algeria, Libya, and Iraq all provided military resources and soldiers, as did several Arab Gulf countries. Particularly noteworthy was Saudi Arabia's late King Feisal's decision to impose an oil embargo on Western markets to apply economic pressure as a response to their military and political support for Israel during the war.

The Egyptian army did not take control of the Mitla and Gidi passes, but it broke the perceived impenetrable Bar-Lev Line that Israel had built on the Suez Canal's eastern shore. That in itself created a new military-political

---

[1] Field Marshal Mohamed Al Gamasy's book (1993). The October War: Memoirs of Field Marshal El-Gamasy of Egypt.

dynamic, shattering the presumptions of Israeli invincibility and Arab incompetence which had prevailed after the 1967 Israeli victory. No longer could the United States or any other country with interests in the Middle East shrug aside the Arabs, whose self-confidence was greatly restored as a result of the war. Even without a complete military victory, Egypt had succeeded in changing the playing field and reestablishing its regional leadership. Sadat now had the opportunity to negotiate peace in the Middle East and diplomatically harvest the fruits of his military efforts, provided he pursued astute, rigorous, and sustained negotiations.

THE TOUGH ROAD OF NEGOTIATIONS

Peace among conflicting parties is often established either through one party's outright victory, such as after World War II, or through a negotiation process that leaves no clear victor or vanquished party. The second paradigm was now available to Sadat. The United Nations Security Council Resolution 242, adopted on November 22, 1967, after the June 1967 War, was considered to be the contemporary founding document of the peace process in the Middle East. Its fundamental "bargain" called for the ending of Israeli occupation of Arab territories in June 1967 in exchange for the right of all states in the region, including Israel, to live in security—established by the "land for peace" tenet.

As the major military battles subsided, the political process gained prominence. Complementing Resolution 242, on October 22, the United Nations Security Council adopted its Resolution 338, which called for a ceasefire and placed the peace process within a comprehensive regional context. The latter resolution placed renewed emphasis on the importance of an overall Arab Israeli peace which once again brought multilateralism rather than separate agreements into play. Egypt and Israel both accepted the resolution the following day (Fig. 3.1).

On October 31, in the oval office President Nixon received Sadat's envoy Ismail Fahmy, a career diplomat who was the Minister of Tourism and a member in Egypt's war cabinet. After the meeting, the president walked Fahmy to his car, a unique exception from protocol with cameras on the White House lawn framing the visit. Even before the reports on the substance of the meetings were out, the message from America, at the highest level, was that in light of the October War, Egypt was again a player in the Middle East with substantial strategic value, especially now that it was repositioning itself away from the Soviet Union.

Fig. 3.1 Ismail Fahmy at the White House

That very same day, Sadat announced the appointment of Fahmy as foreign minister, with a clear mandate to lead the diplomatic efforts toward peace. Sadat and Fahmy strongly believed that it was imperative to change the direction of Egypt's foreign policy. Both were determined to leverage America's new interest in the Middle East to lay the groundwork of the Arab–Israeli diplomatic process.

Sadat was, however, more pro-West, and particularly more pro-America than his newly appointed foreign minister, who believed in engaging all but preserving a healthy distance from major world powers. Fahmy vehemently opposed precooked American and Soviet understandings, which were a precursor to resolutions on the Middle East, insisting that each directly deal with Egypt. After arduous negotiations, he agreed to terms for the first Geneva Arab Israeli Peace Conference which was convened on December 21. This constituted the first renewed effort toward a negotiated Comprehensive Arab Israeli Peace. Even though Syria refrained from participation in the conference, which was a major mistake on its part representing the first break in the unified Egyptian Syrian efforts. In January 1974, Egypt and Israel signed their first Disengagement Agreement to reduce the potential for the outbreak of military hostilities. This was a precursor for what were to be difficult and long negotiations between them.

I had just graduated from the American University in Cairo in February 1974 when negotiations for the second disengagement agreement were ongoing in Aswan, Egypt, with the objective of setting the terms for further withdrawal and better management of the disengagement lines between Egyptian and Israeli troops in the Sinai. It was a tough negotiation process, with the United States showing a clear bias toward Israel to an extent that agitated public opinion in Egypt. I remember sending a handwritten message to my father in Aswan, emotionally cautioning him against hastily agreeing to American suggestions which would be at the expense of what Egypt had achieved during the war. I was later told by the Egyptian Foreign Ministry staff that during one of the tenser negotiating sessions, my father reached into his briefcase and handed my letter to Kissinger. He did not identify who had written it, explaining simply that it reflected what Egypt's youth felt of his efforts.

Even more importantly, however, and in many ways confirming the concerns that existed about American partiality toward Israel, was that at one point during the Aswan second disengagement negotiations, on return from Israel, Kissinger presented Sadat with a formulation that the stipulated parties would agree to an "end of conflict" in exchange for only another partial withdrawal of the Israeli forces to a line to be determined in the agreement. Impatient to reach an agreement, President Sadat quickly nodded indicating approval of the proposal.

Fahmy was much more attuned to the complexities of negotiations, paying careful attention to detail and context. He was concerned about the implications of making such a major concession before the end of Israeli occupation of all Egyptian territories. On seeing Sadat's approval, he silently collected the papers before him on the table and abruptly left the room settling in the garden just outside, visible to all through the large glass windows of the meeting room.

The startled and concerned Kissinger offered to walk out and talk to his counterpart. Sadat's response was equally surprising. He did not seem embarrassed or annoyed that his foreign minister had walked out of the meeting, rather simply explained to Kissinger that the only way to get Fahmy back in the room was to drop the phrase "end of conflict". That is what happened.

This incident was unprecedented in Egyptian politics, shedding great light not only on the strong professional and personal relationship between Sadat and Fahmy but equally so on the stature and self-confidence of both Egyptians. For them, Egypt's interests were of much more importance than protocol. The negotiating environment, however, had been poisoned by the American bias and that round of negotiations failed.

The second disengagement agreement was eventually concluded on September 4, 1975, and signed in Alexandria in a ceremony with Sadat, Fahmy, and Kissinger all present. Nevertheless, rather than signing it himself, Fahmy designated Ambassador Ahmed Osman, the undersecretary of the Foreign Ministry, as the Egyptian signatory in order to convey to Kissinger his reservations about his negotiating approach. It was also a very subtle message to Sadat that the rushed negotiating pace was not allowing Egypt to truly reap the political benefits of the October War achievements.

Indeed, Sadat's increasing dependence on the United States and his exaggerated expectations of the White House support raised concerns among Egyptian opposition. Thereafter, the prominent poet Ahmed Fouad Negm and the composer-singer Sheikh Imam released the song "Sharraft ya Nixon baba" (Welcome Nixon dad) to criticize Nixon's visit to Egypt, which occurred in the midst of his Watergate scandal.

Fahmy, on the other hand, was still committed to a balanced foreign policy and repeatedly attempted to counter Sadat's pro-Western inclinations by developing relations with the Soviet Union in spite of Sadat's resistance. As the years progressed, it became evident that while Egypt's president and foreign minister were both believers in a comprehensive Arab–Israeli peace and in the importance of global Egyptian activism, they had different visions of how this could be achieved. This did not go unnoticed in diplomatic circles and was frequently inferred in the cables sent to Washington by the American Embassy in Cairo. Nevertheless, the mutual respect and admiration between these two Egyptian officials were what kept their relationship intact for almost four years in spite of their differences. Ultimately, the differences in approach to diplomatic engagement would prove too strong and pull them apart.

Efforts to Reconvene the Geneva Conference

The first Geneva Conference had been held December 21, 1973, under the auspices of the United Nations with the United States and the Soviet Union presiding with Egypt, Jordan, and Israel participating. This was an attempt to start a process of cooling down the military theater and to provide a basis for future negotiations to resolve the Arab–Israeli conflict once and for all. This process did not lead to quick results and the wind was lost from its sails, although the general concept remained alive.

Soon after his inauguration, President Carter's newly appointed Secretary of State sent an oral message to Fahmy dated January 22, 1977, affirming that "President Carter attaches the highest importance to making significant progress that year towards a full and lasting peace in the Middle East" and expressing a desire to visit Egypt on February 17 and 18. This was followed by a letter from Carter to Sadat on February 14 affirming the same sentiments.

On March 7, Secretary Vance sent another letter to Fahmy with his reflections on his Middle East trip affirming that "President Carter intends to continue the active role of the United States in seeking a just and durable peace in the Middle East" and that the administration "would be trying to bring together the parties to the conflict to enable them to work out a stable solution to the problems in the area". Relevant State Department talking points[2] about the trip highlighted the conclusions that Vance had drawn from his meetings, including that:

There was a consensus among all concerned that they started work towards reconvening the Geneva Conference in the first half of 1977.

The principal substantive issues are the nature of peace, the withdrawal/territorial questions and a settlement of the Palestinian problem.

[T]he principal procedural issues that must be resurfaced before the negotiations can begin remains the question of Palestinian participation in the negotiating process.

On the 12th of March, the American Charge D'affaires in Egypt summarized the American conclusions about a visit of the Israeli Prime Minister Rabin to Washington explaining that even though it was early in the process, President Carter had listened to the Israeli positions and offered American alternatives for the parties to consider. It was clear from that encounter that the issue of creating a political entity between Israel and Jordan was still critical to both Palestinian and Israeli sides and that their positions on this were highly divergent.

[2] Talking Points. (March 7, 1977). US National Archives. Document number: 1977STATE050667. Film Number: D770078-0789. https://aad.archives.gov/aad/create pdf?rid=49009&dt=2532&dl=1629

The Carter Administration also closely briefed Egypt on its consultations with Arab leaders. Carter summarized the highlights of his discussions with King Hussein of Jordan in the following points[3]:

> [T]hat the failure at Geneva would have serious consequences and that therefore, it is necessary to prepare the ground with care. King Hussein affirmed that an Arab wide delegation should be sent to negotiations.

> King Hussein indicated his understanding that the nature of peace would have to be an element in the settlement negotiations.

> [T]he King reaffirmed that Israel should withdraw from the occupied West Bank, with the possibility open for the modification of the 1967 lines.

President Carter also shared his reflections on his meeting at Geneva with President Assad of Syria, emphasizing the following[4]:

> President Assad reiterated that Syria's position is that, in return for peace, there must be withdrawal to the 1967 borders and this should apply to the case of Jerusalem.

> Assad affirmed that both Arabs and Israelis should focus on economic development that would eventually bring peace.

> Assad accepts the concept of limited, reciprocal demilitarized zones and international observer forces along the borders. President Carter emphasized on the importance of security arrangements in giving confidence to both sides.

As for refugees, President Assad recognized that "the question on refugees presents a complex set of issues that require further study, but the starting point must be the United Nations resolutions calling for repatriation or compensation".

Assad also stressed that the Palestinians should be part of the peace process and that their views must be heard. Following the Israeli elections,

---

[3] Letter from President Carter to President Sadat. (April 29, 1977). US National Archives. Document Number: 1977STATE095780. Film Number: D770149-0005. https://aad.archives.gov/aad/createpdf?rid=77665&dt=2532&dl=1629

[4] Meeting Between President Carter and Syrian President Assad. (May 11, 1977). US National Archives. Document number: 1977SECTO04023. Film Number: D770165-0932. https://aad.archives.gov/aad/createpdf?rid=106357&dt=2532&dl=1629

Secretary Vance was to make another trip to the Middle East, as encouraged by King Hussein.

Needless to say, the Soviet Union was carefully following the process and the United States could not ignore their interest, especially given that they were part of the original Geneva Conference. Vance and his Soviet counterpart Gromyko issued a communique on May 21, 1977, which stated:

> that elimination of the continuing source of tension in the Middle East constitutes one of the primary tasks in ensuring peace and international security.
>
> USSR and the United States, who are the co-chairman of the Geneva Conference, are of substantial importance for achieving just, durable and stable peace in the Middle East… For these purposes, the United States and USSR will be conducting monthly consultations at the level of Ambassadors in Washington or Moscow.

All of this occurred in a general political environment where separate Arab–Israeli peace agreements were not seen as politically viable, with the United States and the Soviet Union both vested interest in appearing to be consulting if not collaborating with each other, in the delicate posturing and dance while pursuing détente in the cold war.

As movement toward reconvening the Geneva conference progressed, Israel outlined its opinion on the next steps in the process.[5] It explained that Israel accepted to participate in the Geneva Talks based on Resolution 338 of the Security Council along with Egypt, Syria, and Jordan. However, Israel stated that "no participant will present any prior conditions for their taking part in the Conference." Israel wanted three separate commissions discussing the Conference issues with each of the three Arab representatives. The original outline from Israel did not include the Palestine Liberation Organization (PLO) as a participant. In the case that the neighboring countries insisted on the PLO's participation, Israel proposed two alternatives:

> To establish, through the good offices of the United States, the aforementioned three mixed commissions in keeping with the method used during the Rhodes negotiations of 1949.

---

[5] Israeli Outline for Peace: The Framework for the Peace-Making Process Between Israel and its Neighbors. (July 7, 1977). State of Israel Archives. File A 4313/1. Along with a letter that was submitted to the US. http://www.archives.gov.il/archives/#/Archive/0b0717068001c167/File/0b07170684cd6be2/Item/090717068507a13b

Or: In accordance with the principle of the "proximity talks" with a view to conducting in the framework of such mixed commissions the negotiations on the conclusion of the peace treaties.

On July 21, Secretary Vance sent an oral message briefing the Egyptians on the Begin–Carter discussions. He explained that Carter, after consulting with all leaders, sent this message to Sadat to express hope that negotiation will still be possible. The message highlighted the different views between the Israelis and the Egyptians on the matters of territory and the Palestinian question. The United States recognized that these differences may not be resolved, but it was indeed important to get a negotiating process started.

Carter also briefed Sadat on the procedural requests and the alternatives that Israel had proposed but mentioned that the United States had neither welcomed nor approved the procedural suggestions. He mentioned that in a follow-up Vance trip to the Middle East, further details on conference procedures will be discussed.[6]

On August 9, Vance provided the Egyptians a readout of Carter's talks with Saudi Arabia's King Khalid, Crown Prince Fahd, and Foreign Minister Saud al Faisal. Prince Fahd suggested that the United States could invite the PLO to participate, stating the importance of their presence in Geneva. He supported that the parties should submit a detailed contribution containing draft treaty language before the conference was seen as extremely useful. On the issue of Palestinian participation, Carter urged Sadat to positively consider the idea of a unified Arab delegation as a means for dealing with the Palestinian delegation problem.[7]

On September 21, after another visit to Washington and meetings with Carter and Vance, Fahmy highlighted the following in his report to Sadat:

- Sadat and Carter had developed a useful personal rapport and the latter expected Sadat to take courageous positions.

[6] Oral message for President Sadat from Secretary Vance. (July 21, 1977). US National Archives. Document Number: 1977STATE170055. Film Number: P840084-1889. https://aad.archives.gov/aad/createpdf?rid=173538&dt=2532&dl=1629

[7] Telegram from Secretary of State Vance to the Embassies in Jordan and Egypt entitled: "American Talking Points" (August 9th, 1977). US STATE DEPARTMENT OFFICE OF THE HISTORIAN ARCHIVES (0830Z Sector 8102) https://history.state.gov/historical-documents/frus1977-80v08/d77

- America would depend on the Egyptians in the pursuit of peace and consider an Egyptian–Israeli peace agreement as an example to be followed by others.
- America was agreeable to the idea that substantive progress, almost conclusive progress, had to be achieved before the Geneva conference was reconvened in 1977.
- America strongly believed in the inevitably of Arab–Israeli normalization as part of the peace agreement.
- United States and Carter's personal support for a Palestinian homeland does not necessarily mean a full-fledged state, but could be achieved through affiliations with Jordan and Israel.
- Americans were procrastinating and not completely transparent about Palestinian Liberation Organization representation even while they had direct and indirect contacts with them.
- America wanted Egypt and Israel to sign or at least initiate a Peace Agreement at the Geneva conference.

Fahmy also informed Sadat that in a separate meeting, Vance had handed him an Israeli draft of an Israeli–Egyptian peace treaty[8] as delivered by Moshe Dayan. Fahmy commented that the draft was replete with normalization and demilitarization provisions upfront and was regarded by Egypt then as a non-starter. It is noteworthy that it was very similar to the peace treaty ultimately signed between Egypt and Israel the following year after Sadat's visit to Jerusalem.

In presenting the Israeli draft, Vance had commented that Israel had focused on the West Bank and had not at all mentioned Gaza. He also indicated that the United States had offered Israel a mutual defense pact which they welcomed but remained to be negotiated.

Vance also handed Fahmy a draft that the Americans proposed for peace agreements[9] between Egypt and Israel and procedures to convene the second Geneva Conference. Fahmy was furious with the American draft, which he felt had endorsed Israel's position. It referred to the 1949 Armistice boundaries rather than Egypt's internationally recognized bor-

---

[8] Treaty of Peace Between the State of Israel and the Arab Republic of Egypt (September 19, 1977). Attached in telegram 6588 from Tel Aviv on September 2. (National Archives, RG 59, Central Foreign Policy File P840081–2175). (See Appendix I) https://history.state.gov/historicaldocuments/frus1977-80v08/d100

[9] See Appendix II.

der, called for the end of hostilities before Israeli withdrawal began, and accepted explicit normalization between the two countries. He told Sadat that he was so annoyed by the draft that he returned both the original and comments to Vance, who took Fahmy's concerns seriously and handed him a revised American text.[10] This was much more accommodating. Egypt also prepared its own draft peace agreement,[11] crafted around traditional end of conflict and peace treaty parameters.

Noteworthy, however, in the second American proposal was the complete absence of any reference to the PLO. Another was that all references to the Palestinians were deleted with the refugee question becoming one of the Arab and Jewish refugees, to be resolved on the basis of United Nations Resolutions that the United States supported. The second draft of the paper, different from the first, also did not include Syria in the working group for the West Bank and Gaza.

One of the outstanding issues was how to include representatives of the Palestinians, and there was a growing understanding with the Americans that the Palestinians would be from not well-known members of PLO. On October 3, Sadat conveyed an oral message to President Carter that Yasser had agreed that the head of the Palestinian delegation to the Geneva conference would be an American professor of Palestinian origin.[12] Palestinian representation, however, remained a divergent issue. Israel was intransigent against speaking to the PLO. America hesitated to do so without the PLO first accepting Security Council Resolution 242 and recognizing Israel's right to exist. The PLO had just been recognized, at the Arab Summit in Rabat, as the sole legitimate representative of the Palestinians, and consequently was not inclined to forgo this particular status.

The pursuit of the Arab–Israeli Geneva conference continued and even intensified the following weeks. The Americans submitted a draft paper on the modalities of convening the Geneva Conference[13] and then revised it after listening to the parties.

---

[10] See Appendix III.

[11] See Appendix IV.

[12] The two proposed Palestinian-Americans were academicians Edward Said of Columbia University and Ibrahim Abu-Laughed from University of Illinois, with the former suggested as the potential head of delegation.

[13] Working Paper on Suggestions for the Resumption of the Geneva Conference (October 5, 1977). US Department of State Office of the Historian Archives. https://history.state.gov/historicaldocuments/frus1977-80v08/d124#fn:1.5.4.2.256.568.4.4

Egypt had preferred that the Geneva conference be a culminating exercise rather than one of protracted and possibly inconclusive negotiations. In the response to Carter on October 19, Sadat reiterated that he had agreed with the general concept behind the proposal in the first American draft, with two suggestions, explaining that the new working paper was a serious departure amending some of the basic points in the original draft. He attached to his letter a formula[14] which he believed would enhance the chances of convening the Geneva Conference. The first element was that the United States, as an intermediary, convene participatory talks with the parties on a paper that "outlines the essentials of peace" with details of the peace agreements to be negotiated in Geneva. He also suggested that if the issue of the Palestinian representation continued to be problematic with geopolitical groups, Carter could consider the Palestinian representation to be part of the Egyptian delegation, or that they be represented by the Assistant Secretary-General of the Arab League for Military Affairs.

Despite several points of concern, Sadat reiterated his support but with the clear caveat that that was conditional on Carter supporting the creation of a Palestinian State, and provided that the approach was agreed upon by the other Arab parties.

On October 22 and 28, the Americans sent an oral message[15] from Vance and then a letter[16] to Sadat from Carter. They reaffirmed their commitment to work for a "draft agreement peace conference" but also conveyed the view that it was futile to continue consultations with the parties on the procedural aspects of convening the second Geneva Conference. They added that instead, the United States and Russia intended to call for reconvening the conference in the same manner used for the initial conference, but with one unified Arab delegation, except where the working group topics were bilateral.

---

[14] Egyptian Response to 1st US Draft on Convening the Geneva Conference and the suggested Formula. (October 19, 1977). US Department of State Office of the Historian Archives (1339Z 17348). https://history.state.gov/historicaldocuments/frus1977-80v08/d133

[15] Oral Message from Secretary Vance. (October 22, 1977). US National Archives. Document Number: 1977STATE252851. Film Number: P850050-2204. https://aad.archives.gov/aad/createpdf?rid=252121&dt=2532&dl=1629

[16] Letter from Carter to Sadat. (October 28, 1977). US Department of the State Office of the Historian Archives. Ref: Cairo 17817 (1351Z 258388) https://history.state.gov/historicaldocuments/frus1977-80v08/d139

Sadat's Visit to Jerusalem

Even before this last turn of events, Sadat had already gotten increasingly impatient with the multilateral diplomacy of reconvening the Geneva Peace Conference. In September 1977, he had initiated secret contacts with the Israelis in Morocco by sending his Deputy Prime Minister Hassan El-Tohamy to meet Israeli Foreign Minister Moshe Dayan. For a very short period, Sadat did not share this with his foreign minister. Fahmy, however, was aware of the talks from Moroccan sources. The Egyptian Foreign Minister continued to work on convening a Geneva II Arab–Israeli Conference to preserve the comprehensive nature of the peace process.

As Sadat's thinking evolved more toward directly and publicly engaging the Israelis, he broached the idea with his Foreign Minister, and they had several discussions about it including on a trip to Romania in October.

Well aware of Sadat's impatience, Fahmy countered and proposed convening an International Conference meeting in Jerusalem with the participation of the permanent members of the Security Council to establish the basis for Peace. This formula would have placed the whole process within the United Nations context, which from 1948 had called for the establishment of both a Palestinian and a Jewish state and the confirmation of a special international mechanism for Jerusalem. In such a context, visiting Jerusalem, while still dramatic, would not have constituted premature normalization or a unilateral recognition of Israel, thus it accommodated Sadat's inclinations while also bringing the international community solidly behind resolving the conflict without providing any unilateral concessions to Israel.

The Egyptian president was not overwhelmingly convinced by this proposal, but nevertheless, he wrote[17] to Carter, reiterating that in his previous letter, he had shared his intention to propose a bold step to accelerate the Arab–Israeli peace process. He informed him of his intention to call for the convening of an International Conference in Arab East Jerusalem, with larger international participation, including the five permanent members of the Security Council. Attached as well was a draft initiative[18] on the

---

[17] "Personal Letter from President Sadat to President Carter". (November 3, 1977). US Department of State Office of the Historian Archives. Ref: (A) para 5, Cairo 17863, (B) Cairo 18232. (2255Z 18241). https://history.state.gov/historicaldocuments/frus1977-80v08/d141

[18] (See Appendix V). Attached with "Personal Letter from President Sadat to President Carter". US Department of State Office of the Historian Archives. Ref: (A) para 5, Cairo

conference. The objective was for the gathering to agree on the essentials for peace in the Middle East and submit its recommendation to be reconvened Geneva conference before the end of December, to develop Arab–Israeli peace treaties no later than June 30, 1978. Sadat closed with a reference that he would announce the proposal while addressing Egypt's People's Assembly on November 9.

Carter promptly wrote back arguing that the suggestion would further complicate the procedural discussions rather than focus attention on completing the United States' effort to reconvene the Geneva Conference before the end of the year.[19]

As planned on November 9, 1977, while speaking before the Egyptian parliament, Sadat made a dramatic announcement, but it was about his willingness to go to the Israeli Knesset in pursuit of a peaceful end to the Arab–Israeli struggle. To emphasize that this was not a separate Egyptian–Israeli effort, he did this in the presence of the Palestinian leader Yasser Arafat, who had been summoned from a visit to Libya.

A few days later, Sadat visited the Syrian President Hafez al-Assad to convince or reduce his opposition to this step, offering to speak on behalf of Syria but bear full responsibility if the efforts failed. The Syrians rejected his proposals.

Fahmy refused to join Sadat on the trip to Syria and tendered his resignation, which was delivered by messenger to the Vice President Hosni Mubarak in a closed envelope who subsequently handed it over to Sadat at Cairo Airport on his return from Damascus.

Fahmy, who avoided any personal criticism of Sadat afterwards, believed that although presidents had the ultimate authority to decide on policy, there were clear fault lines of political responsibility that if crossed, ministers, who also had to safeguard the interests of the nation, should resign. He felt strongly that unilaterally visiting Jerusalem was a major concession that would imply not only the recognition of Israel, but also its jurisdiction over Jerusalem. He knew that a bilateral Egyptian–Israeli agreement had always been attainable. It would remove the Egyptian–Israeli front from the politico-military equation, thus weakening the Arab negotiating position and delay or even completely destroy any prospects for a comprehen-

---

17863, (B) Cairo 18232. (2255Z 18241). https://history.state.gov/historicaldocuments/frus1977-80v08/d141

[19] Letter from Carter to Sadat. (November 5, 1977). US Department of State Office of the Historian Archives. (0129Z 264771). https://history.state.gov/historicaldocuments/frus1977-80v08/d142

sive Arab–Israeli peace and the fulfillment of the Palestinian national aspirations.

Sadat accepted Fahmy's resignation, and the Minister of State for Foreign Affairs Mohamed Riad was asked to replace him, but he quickly declined. Ambassador Mohamed Ibrahim Kamel, who was a close confidant who had been imprisoned with Sadat during their youth, became the next Egyptian Foreign Minister. The president, however, obviously intended to unilaterally determine policy, regardless of what the relevant governmental institutions recommended.

Sadat not only visited Jerusalem, but he also eventually accepted a separate peace agreement with Israel. In 1978, a trilateral summit was held at Camp David, resulting in Sadat signing two framework agreements with Israel at the White House. The first one was a "Framework for Peace in the Middle East"[20] and the other one a "Framework for the Conclusion of a Peace Treaty between Egypt and Israel".[21] The Second document signed was very similar to the first Israeli Draft Peace Treaty that had been submitted even before the Jerusalem visits on November 19. This in effect is testimony that while the Jerusalem visit created tremendous momentum and support for Sadat globally, it did not alter the Israeli concept for peace, or result in greater compromises on their part. In essence, Israel made no significant compromises because of it.

The other agreement, titled "Framework for Peace in the Middle East", was never to see fruition. It supposedly aimed on establishing the parameters that would expand the Egyptian–Israeli bilateral peace into a comprehensive Arab–Israeli peace, particularly on the Palestinian–Israeli track. But it failed for many different reasons, not the least of which was that the right-leaning Israeli government's ideological commitment to keeping the West Bank of the River Jordan as Eretz Israel—the "Holy Land" of supposedly biblical Israel.

Naturally, Sadat would have preferred a comprehensive Arab–Israeli peace. However, in the absence of that, he was ready to accept a bilateral and separate Egypt–Israel Peace Treaty. After the Jerusalem visit, this was an existential and inevitable choice for Sadat. He would have been severely politically discredited had he returned from Camp David empty-handed.

---

[20] Ariel Center for Policy Research (ACPR) http://www.acpr.org.il/publications/books/42-Zero-camp-david-accords.pdf

[21] Egyptian Ministry of Foreign Affairs (No. 17854). https://www.mfa.gov.eg/Lists/Treaties/Attachments/2279/Framework_en.pdf

The Egypt–Israeli Peace Treaty was signed in Washington on March 26, 1979.[22] Israel would ultimately withdraw from all the Egyptian territories, albeit with some restrictions on Egyptian military activity in the Sinai. And, Sadat was rightfully proud of this. Israel was even more greatly rewarded by the peace treaty. With Egypt out of the Arab military equation, it had gained exponentially militarily, having removed any serious possibility of a full-fledged Arab–Israeli war in the future. For Israel, the Egypt–Israel Peace Treaty, not the Framework for Peace in the Middle East, was the conclusive political fruit of the peace process.

Over a decade later, in the early 1990s, as part of an Egyptian delegation, I listened to the Israeli President Ezer Weizman reflect on the different negotiating styles of Egyptians and Israelis. Previously as Israeli Minister of Defense, he had complained to Sadat that his Egyptian counterpart Mohamed Abd El-Ghani El-Gamasy was insisting on a rapid impractical timeline for the withdrawal of Israeli forces from Sinai with Israel wanting much more time. To his surprise, Sadat offered one month more than what Israel had asked for. Weizman was bewildered by the gesture. He recounted that if he had explained in Israel that Sadat offered more than he had requested, no one would believe him, and some would even assume that some egregious plan was in the making by Sadat. Thus, Weizman asked the Egyptian president why he had made this offer, which was more than what Israel was asking for. Sadat quickly responded, "You and El-Gamasy have been negotiating for longer than the difference in the time frame you had each suggested for Israeli withdrawal." Sadat went on, "I don't care if it is one month more, but Israel must withdraw from every centimeter of Egyptian territory. There will be no compromise on land."

Weizman then added that Egyptians had the habit of collapsing their maximum and minimum positions into one from the very outset of negotiations. Israelis on the other hand always started by asking for much more than what they could actually accept. At first, Israel assumed Egypt wanted it to completely capitulate to its demands, which made the Egyptian–Israeli negotiations extremely difficult.

In essence, while Egypt retrieved its territories, the Egypt–Israel Peace Treaty created a political and military negotiating imbalance between Arabs and Israelis. This diminished the probability of a comprehensive Arab–Israeli peace, a goal that remains unattainable even today. Egyptian

---

[22] Egytpian Ministry of Foreign Affairs (No. No. 17813). https://www.mfa.gov.eg/Lists/Treaties/Attachments/2278/Peace%20Treaty_en.pdf

efforts to engage other Arab countries, particularly the Palestinians, in the process were rebuffed by the Arabs. It was suspended from the Arab League until 1989, with the League's headquarters temporarily moved to Tunisia. Israel made no serious effort to encourage the Arabs to believe in the credibility of the ongoing peace process. It did the exact opposite over the following decade, with a full-fledged invasion of Lebanon, the bombing of an Iraqi nuclear reactor, the annexation of the Golan Heights, and the expansion of settlements in the occupied Palestinian territories and repeated skirmishes with Gaza.

History will testify that the October War was a high positive transformative moment for Arab world, almost as much as 1967 was a devastating debilitating one. Sadat deserves credit for the decision to go to war in 1973: He was the one who took this courageous step, even at a military disadvantage after having expelled Soviet military experts in 1972 from his main weapons supplier. Yet, the difficulties of the peace negotiations during Sadat's presidency, and which continue to this day, highlight the arduous process of keeping multiple Arab stakeholders together, as well as the fact that rigorous, precise evaluations and patient negotiations are imperative to successfully negotiate with the Israelis—who are masters of draining you with tactical maneuvers and drowning you in irrelevant detail.

Reviving Multilateralism: The 1991 Madrid Peace Conference

The 1980s and early 1990s witnessed immense transformations and dramatic events, both regionally and internationally. Arabs increasingly drifted apart after the short-lived inter-Arab cooperation during the October War, with the continuation of the Lebanese Civil War (1975–1990), the Iraq–Iran War (1980–1988), the first Palestinian Intifada (1987–1991), and the 1990 Iraqi invasion of Kuwait. Global dynamics also dramatically shifted, with the end of the Cold War, the tearing down of the Berlin Wall, and the dissolution of the Soviet Union.

With all these changes, the Arab–Israeli conflict remained of paramount importance in Middle East and global affairs, with several initiatives put forth including the Fahd Plan, the adopter in Fez Moroco (FEZ) Plan, and the Reagan Plan. The Palestine Liberation Organization was expelled from Beirut, Lebanon, and Jordan relinquished authority over the West Bank of the River Jordan further consolidating the call for an independent Palestinian State. The repeated Palestinian attempts to engage the United Nations Security Council on Israel's expansionist or settlement policies in the late 1980s were met by an American unwillingness to attend to the

Palestinian–Israeli conflict as its focus shifted toward Saddam Hussein's aggressive attitude. Immediately after the liberation of Kuwait, this all started changing with President George H. W. Bush's talk of a new world order. Both the United States and a new Russian leadership knew that the most prominent Middle East issue for Arabs, until then at least, remained the Arab–Israeli conflict. Thus, in spite of their many other concerns, the United States and Russia decided to cosponsor an historic Middle East peace conference in Madrid in 1991, with Israel, the Arab countries on its borders (Egypt, Syria, and Lebanon), a joint Jordanian–Palestinian delegation, and the European Union.

The Madrid Peace Conference was an attempt to revive the Arab–Israeli peace negotiations by merging bilateralism, regionalism, and multilateralism all under one umbrella. In two different tracks, it brought all the Arab and Israeli parties together with international support. It also attempted to tackle conflict resolution and peace building simultaneously. The basic logic behind this approach was that a three-day conference would become the steppingstone to both bilateral and multilateral negotiations to follow. The bilateral negotiations, which started on November 3, 1991, would be about conflict resolution between Israel and Syria, Jordan, the Palestinians, and ultimately Lebanon respectively, with the cosponsors' support as necessary. The multilateral discussions, on the other hand, were about how to expand regional cooperation with a view to facilitating the bilateral negotiations and illuminating what real peace would look like once the conflicts were resolved (Fig. 3.2).

The Madrid Conference, which began on October 30, 1991, was a truly momentous event in that sense. It was also the first occasion where all these adversarial countries were gathered for face-to-face negotiations. Syria attended the bilateral track of this process after having declined to participate in the first Geneva conference. This was only possible after numerous, arduous trips to the Middle East by the American Secretary of State James Baker, complemented by determined Egyptian efforts by Hosni Mubarak and Amre Moussa that ultimately succeeded in convincing the Syrian President Hafez al-Assad to accept the American letters of assurance and attend the conference.

Any such gathering could not be concluded however without a number of surprises and heated fireworks. There were numerous concerns regarding various important details, as well as some symbolic ones like who would sit beside the Israeli delegation. Egypt, the only Arab country at peace with Israel at the time, stood out not unduly concerned where it would be seated.

Fig. 3.2 Nabil Fahmy and Yasser Arafat

Throughout the conference, tensions continuously surfaced between the Israelis and the Palestinians. The Palestinian–Israeli conflict was finally politically recognized not only at the international level but also grudgingly by Israel itself as the crux of the Arab–Israeli conflict. Israel, however, did not miss on occasion to deemphasize the focus on the independent national stature of the Palestinians. It had insisted that the Palestinian delegation at the Madrid Conference, which was led by Haidar Abdel-Shafi, be seated as part of the Jordanian delegation rather than as an independent one. Then it even refused to allow any direct Palestine Liberation Organization (PLO) members to attend at Madrid, insisting on prominence only for Palestinians not affiliated with PLO in hopes of creating dissension and diminishing the PLO Chairman Yasser Arafat's authority. In response, to spite them, the Palestinian delegate Saeb Erekat went into the opening conference session wearing a traditional Palestinian headdress "Kafeya". Nevertheless, it should be noted that the Palestinians at Madrid whether Abdel-Shafi, Erekat, Faisal Al-Husseini, or Hanan Ashrawi, highly credible among Palestinians, were strong supporters of the Palestinian aspirations of national identity as well as their inalienable right to a sovereign state. They also subsequently led the delegation to the bilateral Washington talks that followed with Israelis.

The content and tone of the opening speeches were of particular concern because they would determine the overall environment for Madrid. The United States urged that different delegations remain constructive and even asking to see the statements in advance. At the time, I was working as Foreign Minister Amre Moussa's political advisor.

When asked for the text of Egypt's opening statement, I assured the Americans that Egypt would strongly support Palestinian and Arab rights while remaining constructive about the need for peace as well as the processes to achieve it. I also affirmed that the speech would be critical about the myriad of Israeli positions, which were inconsistent with the prospects of an Arab–Israeli peace, but without undue rhetorical embellishments. However, after a second American request to see the Egyptian opening statement. I assured American Ambassador Daniel Kurtzer that the statement at the opening session would be constructive, but it would not be provided to anyone beforehand.

Indeed, Moussa's opening statement on Egypt's behalf was powerful but positive in its outlook. It was meticulously prepared in the Foreign Ministry, with the initial draft drawn up by Ambassador Reda Shehata and then reviewed by a large delegation including Egyptian intellectuals, well beyond simply government officials. Thus, the statement truly reflected the wider Egyptian sentiments on the issue of the Middle East process at the time, and Moussa was smart to have chosen to do so. His speech was supportive of an Arab–Israeli Peace, consistent with the United Nations resolutions and understandings reached going into Madrid, which included ending the occupation of Arab lands by Israel and providing for a Palestinian state in the West Bank and Gaza, as well as providing security for all including Israel.

Naturally, the speech kicked off with a clear recount of Egypt's peace efforts, emphasizing the basic bargain behind peace being the end of Israeli occupation of Arab territories in exchange for a comprehensive Arab–Israeli peace. It was explicitly clear that a Palestinian state on the 1967 borders, including a capital in East Jerusalem, was a condition sine qua non for the realization of that objective, condemning Israeli transgressions and violations of international law.

The Egyptian statement was well received in the Arab world. The United States, of course, wished it had been more progressive in arguing for the imperativeness of direct Arab–Israeli negotiations. Although expected, the American measured dissatisfaction with the Egyptian speech indeed confirmed that its tone and balance had correctly conveyed Egypt's position on the issue. Everything went reasonably well at the conference until we moved closer toward its conclusion on November 1, 1991.

As we prepared for our closing statement, Moussa called in Ambassador Shehata and myself to discuss the tone and content of his closing speech. A highly capable diplomat and artful speechwriter, Shehata felt that Egypt should emphasize the same points we had done at the beginning, in the same tone. I, however, felt that after having emphasized rights and obligations, we should now lay out our vision for how to achieve comprehensive peace in the Middle East. Moussa asked each of us to draft a speech from our different perspectives and eventually chose my approach, adding his personal embellishments to the draft I had prepared.

As we sat in the closing session with the more futuristic speech ready to be delivered, tensions suddenly rose. The Syrian foreign minister was waving a newspaper clipping of Israeli Prime Minister Yitzhak Shamir depicted as a terrorist. In response, Shamir countered with heated, insidious language regarding Syria. Seated behind Moussa in the plenary session, my colleagues and I started to frantically consult on how to react, recognizing that neither of the two draft speeches would serve the moment. There was very little time to put together a coherent text, and we had not yet even shared our opinions with Moussa sitting before us in the meeting room. As this occurred, I noticed that Moussa was already scribbling on a notepad before him and asked my colleagues to allow him to concentrate. He was not only an accomplished diplomat but also a particularly good Arabic linguist. Under the pressures of time and at a historic event, he was able to craft a strong rebuttal of Shamir's aggressive and arrogant occupational sentiments, while also highlighting the basic tenets of a comprehensive Arab–Israeli peace, exactly the correct balance for the circumstances.

The Madrid bilateral negotiations were followed by other associated bilateral meetings in Washington as part of the same conference efforts. The United States essentially took charge of these negotiations especially between Israel and Palestinians and Syrians. Jordan and Israel had had long-standing secret contacts. Thus, they handled most aspects of the negotiations themselves, with their bilateral peace agreement later signed in October 1994 under King Hussein bin Talal and Prime Minister Yitzhak Rabin.

All eyes were on the Palestinian–Israeli track. Arafat came to Cairo for consultations before the beginning of the direct Palestinian–Israeli negotiations that emanated from the Madrid Peace Conference. He was accompanied by the most significant Palestinian leaders and all those who were subsequently members of his negotiating teams at Madrid, Washington, or later in Oslo. Arafat, who had lived in Egypt, was confident in its leadership and respected the Egyptian Foreign Ministry's tradition of activism and professionalism.

The Arab–Israeli process, especially in its Palestinian track, always drew special attention from Egypt because of its geopolitical consequences and its national security implications. Defending Palestinian rights was something expected of the Egyptian government not only by Palestinians but by Egyptians as well.[23] Consequently, the Egyptian Foreign Ministry generously offered the Palestinians strategic advice and when asked, reactions and proposals on specific issues while remaining careful not to impose on Palestinian decision-making prerogatives. On many occasions, the Egyptian Foreign Ministry would even politically intervene with different international parties to support the Palestinians, including forcefully responding to Americans and Israelis when we felt their positions were inconsistent with a just and lasting comprehensive Arab–Israeli peace. I personally cautioned Arafat very strongly against the Paris agreement signed on April 29, 1994, which made the Palestinian economy hostage to the rules and services of Israel's economy. It remains problematic today.

Amre Moussa and I met Arafat and the other Palestinian leaders in the conference room of the Foreign Ministry's Tahrir Palace offices. They were honorable and passionate about their rights as well as the importance of peace, but many clearly lacked formal negotiating experience. What personally surprised and worried me initially was that Egypt knew only a few of them with the exception of Arafat and a number of others who had moved with him to Tunis after the Israeli invasion of Lebanon led to their eviction. Egypt, in fact, had almost no relations with those who were based in the occupied territories of the West Bank. This, however, was quickly overcome as our engagement with the Palestinian negotiating team intensified and diversified in an intensive effort to help them prepare for statehood.

---

[23] In a poll conducted by Shibley Telhami at the University of Maryland in the first decade of this century, locals of different Arab countries were asked what they considered to be their most pressing domestic issue. Egyptians responded the Palestinian cause. With the events following the Arab awakening, this may have changed, but it was the case back then.

As the ensuing negotiations progressed with little success, Israel consistently played the Palestinian members of the Washington delegation and the senior members of the PLO against each other. Arafat, however, remained the preeminent unchallenged Palestinian leader throughout the process. Ironically, while he justifiably felt that he was subject to the conspiracy of the Israeli delegations in Madrid and Washington, he himself effectively conspired with other Israelis against the Palestinian and Israeli delegations in Washington shortly thereafter blindsiding them with the Oslo process. I guess these practices are a testimony to the pain, suffering, and conspiracies these two people had been through.

Similarly, the Syrian–Israeli bilateral peace negotiations faced significant challenges, considering Israel's 1967 capture and 1981 annexation of the Syrian Golan Heights, actions that were internationally condemned. In addition, while Syria did not possess Egypt's weight in the region, it considered the Palestinian cause part of security in the Levant and in essence Syria's very legitimacy in the Arab world. Syria would never be the first Arab country to reach a deal with Israel or even negotiate with it due to its determination to be perceived as an Arab power. However, its mercantile negotiating approach would also not allow it to be left out once the Palestinians started negotiating with the Israelis directly. To put it in the words of the Syrian Foreign Minister Farouk El-Sharaa after the Oslo process started, "We won't be the first to negotiate [with Israel] but we will not be left out in the cold."

The Syrians and Israelis held several rounds of talks in Washington after the Madrid Conference, focused on territorial and security-related interests. However, the negotiations barely led to any results. With the election of Rabin in June 1992, things looked as if they could change. Indeed, in August of the following year, Rabin delivered an important message to the Syrian President Hafez Al-Assad through the United States Secretary of State Warren Christopher about Israel's willingness to withdraw from the Golan Heights in exchange for a list of Israeli demands pertaining to security and normalization. This message was read out to the Syrians, but never literally handed over in written form. The Israelis complained nevertheless that Christopher had been too transparent. This language provided tempting incentive in the negotiation process, concerning the Syrian border. With Israeli delays and historic Syrian distrust for Israelis, these sensitivities and suspicions further intensified when the Israelis and the Palestinians signed the Oslo I Accord in Washington in September 1993 and the Israelis slowly diverged away from resolving tensions with Syria. Over the years, Israel and Syria held several other talks and meetings, under different Israeli leadership and with the sponsorship of the United States, but these would always fall apart in what became an on-off cycle of negotiations.

To accommodate Israeli interest in creating normal relations of peace, a multilateral track of the Madrid process commenced in Moscow on January 28, 1992. Its aim was to create confidence for the bilateral and provide the space to discuss the post-peace Middle East. It involved many Arab countries that did not participate in bilateral talks with Israel. In other words, it was to give teeth to the Israeli proposed concept of normalization through regional cooperation. Consequently, the multilateral negotiations were originally conceived to start with three working groups: on environment, economic cooperation, and water. Upon the request of the Palestinians and the Egyptians, two additional working groups on refugees, as well as arms control and regional security were established. Only marginal success occurred here. Syria and Lebanon refused to engage in multilateral talks before there was significant progress on their bilateral tracks. Palestinian and Israeli negotiations also stalled quickly dissipating the momentum and enthusiasm toward the multilateral negotiations.

Although the Madrid Conference did not lead to conclusive results in terms of comprehensive peace, it inaugurated a new reality in the Middle East and was thus nevertheless highly significant. Most importantly, it reemphasized the objective of a comprehensive permanent settlement of the Arab–Israeli conflict on all fronts. In addition, for the Palestinians, it was the beginning of wider political recognition of their independent political identity and inalienable right to a State. For Jordan, it opened the door for the conclusion of the Jordan–Israel peace treaty. The conference increased the number of foreign countries beyond the Middle East that recognized Israel and some from the Arab world began a limited form of diplomatic and economic relations with it. In addition, after the conference, Israel succeeded in getting the United Nations General Assembly to revoke its Resolution 3379 that equated Zionism with racism.

The Oslo Process: Palestine and Israel, Face to Face

Putting aside Israeli efforts to place normalization before conflict resolution, and all the diplomatic balancing acts about who was to talk to whom and when, after the first Palestinian Intifada, both the Israelis and Palestinians realized that real progress could not be achieved if they did not find a way to respond to each other's political and security concerns. "There were only so many bones I could break", Israeli Prime Minister Yitzhak Rabin wisely encapsulated when I met him at the Ittihadiya presidential palace in Cairo and asked why he had agreed to the Oslo process. That was the core reason for the Oslo process' initial success.

With other negotiations and events in the ground in play, the official Palestinian–Israeli track of bilateral negotiations in Madrid and Washington slowly reached a stalemate with both Israel and the Palestine Liberation Organization (PLO) focusing on a backchannel for communications directly engaging each other marking a change in each other's diplomatic efforts particularly in Israel's foreign policy. The Oslo peace process thus began January 1993 in Norway, following the efforts of the Norwegian academics Terje Rød-Larsen, who later became the United Nations Envoy to the Middle East, and his spouse, Mona Juul.

Yossi Beilin, a left-leaning Israeli peace advocate and deputy foreign minister (1992–1995), was a strong proponent of direct negotiations with the PLO, in fact the Israeli godfather of the Oslo process. Mahmoud Abbas, better known as Abu Mazen, was the Palestinian equivalent in this respect, although the first Palestinian negotiators in this process were Ahmed Qurei (Abu Alaa) and Hassan Asfour. Ironically, having objected to an independent Palestinian delegation at the Madrid Peace Conference only a few months earlier, Israel was now negotiating with two Palestinian delegations simultaneously, one publicly in Washington and the other secretly in Oslo. Likewise, while the Palestinians had been adamant about getting public recognition in international fora, they were now negotiating more seriously through the backchannel in Oslo, with their own formal delegation in Washington at least initially unaware of this. Both of the two adversaries understood that a continuing stalemate was untenable. Their respective internal politics however made public formal negotiations inappropriate for difficult compromises. The water had to be tested first.

The Oslo process was probably one of the best-kept secrets in Palestinian–Israeli diplomacy. They both tend to leak information as part of their own respective internal diplomatic bickering and political maneuvering. Initially, only four people in Egypt were aware of these negotiations: President Hosni Mubarak, Foreign Minister Amre Moussa, Osama El-Baz as the political advisor to Mubarak, and myself as the political advisor to the foreign minister. El-Baz, who was well connected in Israel and America given his involvement in the Egyptian–Israeli negotiations in the 1970s, was optimistic from the outset, without ever cogently explaining his reasons. The rest of us were initially skeptical, being particularly concerned about the asymmetry in the composition of the delegations: Israeli non-officials versus Palestinian officials close to Arafat. We believed this gave the Israelis significant room to maneuver even if they were surrogate Israeli agents, initially calling into question the seriousness of the Israeli commitment to the process. Nevertheless, we carefully considered Arafat's briefings and remained open-minded.

In Egypt, we all became more attentive when Uri Savir, the director general of Israel's Foreign Ministry, joined the delegation, and after him, Joel Singer, the legal advisor and confidant to Prime Minister Rabin. This essentially erased all potential deniability and indicated that Israel had become seriously engaged in the process. Another important factor was that the texts, mostly drafted by Israelis, started referring to the Palestinians as a people, in terms similar to those used to refer to the Israelis, language that implied recognition of them as a nation. Years earlier, when asked about the Palestinians Golda Meir, the former Israeli Prime Minister responded by questioning their very existence. Oslo was a major shift from that position. I highlighted these developments to Moussa who agreed that the process looked much more constructive than we had originally assumed.

At that point, Egypt's position and advice shifted from one of great skepticism to one of support for the principles evolving with recognition of the potential opportunities in the still secretive Oslo process, while leaving the details and decisions to the Palestinians and Israelis. Gradually, Arafat himself was becoming more confident in the process, but he still felt it necessary to seek Egypt's advice and blessing on a regular weekly basis. He was meticulous in always providing Egypt precise complete texts before they were formally agreed upon. This was generally done through me as political advisor to the foreign minister. At the very last stage, Arafat even asked for an Egyptian legal advisor to review the texts.

Then after eight months of intense but secret talks, the Palestinian–Israeli Oslo I Accord was signed at the White House on September 13, 1993. It was an historic occasion that I attended with Moussa on Egypt's behalf. I watched on the White House lawn as Israelis and Palestinians simultaneously wept out of joy for what had been achieved. But the ceremony was not without its tense moments. Rabin for one was initially hesitant about publicly embracing Arafat on the stage before ultimately agreeing to shake hands after some serious prodding from President Bill Clinton. Arafat was tense and concerned that American Israeli bias would in some form or the other be reflected in special treatment given to the Israeli representatives on stage. There was even some jockeying around just before the beginning of the ceremony about whether the agreement constituted reciprocal recognition by the PLO and Israel before that was put to rest.

The Oslo Agreement,[24] also referred to as the "Declaration of Principles on Interim Self-Government Arrangements" (DOP), set out to establish the general guidelines for the negotiations to come, as well as lay the foundations for a five-year transitional period of Palestinian Interim Self-Government in the West Bank and Gaza. Included in the agreement were measures for the transfer of authority from Israeli military government and its Civil Administration to authorized Palestinians. Noteworthy was that it left more complicated issues like Jerusalem refugees and border delineation to its later stages on the assumption that the auspicious confidence building would have involved between the Israelis and Palestinians. The general objective of the Oslo Accords was to reach an agreement between the State of Israel and the PLO to, for the last time, put an end to decades of conflict, recognize their mutually legitimate political rights, and strive for a state of coexistence that preserved mutual dignity and security.

Any agreement of this stature concluded after intensive and often confidential negotiations on different fronts was bound to be received with skepticism, some legitimate and substantive, some politically motivated, and some out of personal anger or envy from those who felt left out of the process. A number of serious learned Palestinians, such as Edward Said, felt that the agreement lacked detail and clarity and was with an overly prolonged period, consequently making its success or failure mostly in Israel's hands. With the luxury of hindsight, Said's assessment in this regard had proved true. Some Palestinian negotiators in the Washington bilateral track, which had emanated from the Madrid process, also felt a bit aggrieved, raising some concerns about the agreement, but eventually chose to remain in the Arafat fold. Syria felt politically marginalized and led a campaign against both the agreement and Arafat personally. Nevertheless, the Arab and even international yearning for light at the end of the long dark tunnel, where the Palestinian aspirations for statehood had remained for so long, made this flickering light a bright glimmer in the eyes of the majority.

Although I was not initially supportive of the Oslo process because of the informal nature of the Israeli delegation, which did not reflect political

---

[24] Ariel Center for Policy Research (ACPR). OSLO II Agreement: http://www.acpr.org.il/publications/books/44-Zero-isr-pal-interim-agreement.pdf

commitment, I had come around before it was signed. Before its conclusion, it was clearly a formal negotiating format with no deniability. Furthermore, having the Israelis appear to deal with Palestinians as a nation quasi-equally was an opportunity worth testing despite the obvious risks of obfuscation. It was the right step to take for both sides, although a much more tenuous one for the Palestinians. Nevertheless, the ambiguity in language and the assumption of incremental, protracted change based on the progressive building of confidence between the parties did not favor the Palestinians, particularly since the most complicated issues, such as Jerusalem, the right to return, and settlements, were intentionally excluded from the agreement and left to be negotiated in subsequent, follow-up talks. The Palestinians with an internationally recognized cause were nevertheless literally the weaker of the two parties on the ground. If things went wrong, as they ultimately did, they would pay a heavier price with the shifting political mood in Israel as well as the American political bias in favor of Israel.

The Oslo Agreement was to become a reality until defeated by its contractual parties themselves out of Israeli intransigence and the Palestinian inability to take a stand early on with the first aberrations to the process. The Israelis were never held accountable for not implementing Oslo, particularly after Rabin's assassination. As the revolving Israeli governments were constituted on a more conservative, hardline approach, they moved further and further away from the Oslo commitments, which would have gradually given Palestinians more authority over more lands in the West Bank and Gaza. Rabin and Arafat, strong leaders in their own countries, had measured each other up. As Israel changed prime ministers from Shimon Peres to Benjamin Netanyahu and Ehud Barak, this mutual assessment quickly disappeared: Peres was a known quantity to the Palestinians and he also understood Arafat, but he did not have enough support in Israel to take major decisions. Netanyahu was clearly opposed to Oslo, and Barak, a strong believer in his own instincts and capabilities above all others, shared a mutual reciprocated contempt with Arafat. On top of this, Palestinian compromises, especially with regards to postponing implementation of Israeli withdrawals from occupied lands and accepting limited security capacities, brought fewer and fewer dividends. Thus, the direction of the Palestinian–Israeli peace process and its consistency became more distorted and haphazard.

Regrettably, today, decade's later Israel completely ignores the Oslo. It has expanded its settlement activities in the West Bank and prevented the

Palestinian authority from exercising its control on areas designated for that purpose and known under the agreement as Area C. At the same time, it continues to place the onus on the Palestinian authority to preserve security in the West Bank. Mahmoud Abbas, president of the Palestinian Authority and the original proponent of the Oslo process among the Palestinians, is considering withdrawing from it. In short, while the Oslo approach was substantively novel between Israelis and Palestinians and potentially constructive, its long five-year process with all the inherent ambiguities and moving parts was much to the disadvantage of the Palestinians, especially with Israel still the determining force on the territories.

New Realities Face Old Truths: The Middle East and North Africa Economic Summits

The overwhelming optimism that was percolated about creating a new Middle East in the early 1990s after the beginning of the Madrid Peace Conference, and particularly about resolving the Palestinian–Israeli conflict, quickly dissipated as implementation proved difficult especially with continuous settlement activity, ever more so after Prime Minister Rabin's assassination.

Even before Rabin's death, it became clear that a construction of a new reality was unrealistic before conflicts were resolved because the parties disagreed on goals and even the definitions. Israelis, especially Shimon Peres's team, felt that economic development could precede political conflict resolution and, if not so, help create a better environment for it. Palestinians and most Arabs felt that a new Middle East meant changing geopolitical concepts in the region from power politics to cooperativeness, which includes applying equal standards for all, particularly the right to establish an independent sovereign Palestinian state. Egypt, the first Arab state to sign a peace treaty with Israel, shared the Arab view and also felt that a new Middle East meant equal obligations for all, including in arms limitations especially about nuclear and mass destruction weapons, as well as the potential for post-peace engagements. The Americans, less creative than ever, became fixated on repeatedly and superficially arguing that talking was better than killing disregarding, that while true in practice, this is neither enough nor sustainable with continuing injustices.

Trying to do too much at the same time shifted the attention from fully investing and reaping the benefits of the Palestinian Israeli Oslo breakthrough that should have been instrumental in establishing an Arab Israeli peace since it was dealing with the core issue of conflict.

Ultimately, the different players in the Middle East peace process were caught in a seemingly endless cycle of negotiations, meetings, and conferences without serious attempts to respond to concerns of their adversaries; all in a futile attempt to bring to life a new approach without dealing with the old reality on the ground.

Concerning the Palestinian–Israeli track, it became ever more difficult and was further derailed. A series of follow-up negotiations, talks, and even agreements were attempted after the signing of the Oslo I Accords to discuss further details of mutual concern. Egypt's role between the Israelis and Palestinians, in particular, increased, hosting a number of the interim agreement negotiations and ceremonies.

In the spring of 1944, the Gaza–Jericho Agreement in Cairo (which facilitated the establishment of the Palestinian Authority for interim self-government in Gaza and portions of the West Bank) came into effect after considerable live prime time television drama. Yasser Arafat and Yitzhak Rabin initially refused to complete signing the negotiated document because of a misunderstanding about on the size of territory to be handed to the Palestinians in Jericho. All of this occurred while the event was being broadcast live on Egyptian and international television channels, with the Egyptian President Hosni Mubarak, the Egyptian Foreign Minister Amre Moussa, Israeli Foreign Minister Shimon Peres, and the American Secretary of State Warren Christopher standing on stage with the two Palestinian and Israeli principals.

The crisis was ultimately resolved when Rabin promised to send Arafat a letter confirming his intention to review the map of Jericho. Ironically, such a letter already existed in the large folders before the two leaders during the signing ceremony, folders which under the pressure of time they had not fully reviewed or been briefed on in detail. Amnon Lipkin-Shahak, as the head of the Israeli team and former Israeli chief of staff, and I, as the Egyptian official responsible for the Arab–Israeli peace process in the Egyptian Foreign Ministry, knew this and were to laugh about it later when it was all over.

Simultaneously, there were multilateral conferences focusing on issues of regional significance to the future of the Middle East. The highest profile of these were the Davos style Middle East/North Africa (MENA) Economic summits, which were Shimon Perez's brainchild. The inaugural event was held in November 1994 in Casablanca, Morocco, with the aim of encouraging mutual economic exchange and cooperation within the Middle East, as part of the normalization and peace-building efforts. These summits would soon, however, expose the persisting fault lines between Arabs and Israelis and among Arabs themselves.

Developments in the region during those years reflected that the general sentiment was converging around a more comprehensive Arab–Israeli peace as laid out by Egypt starting with the October War. Ironically as this developed, it also raised concerns in Egyptian circles that its pioneering and exclusive Arab role in the search for peace in the Middle East, and consequently its regional eminence, was gradually eroded by its own success as the peace process gained momentum with more Arab states following in Egypt's footsteps, intensifying their engagement with Israel.

As the talks about a new Middle East intensified and preparations for the Casablanca Middle East/North Africa (MENA) Economic Summit gained momentum with draft texts focusing on the new participants in the process, Egyptian diplomacy felt compelled to reaffirm its prominence and pioneering role in the Arab–Israeli peace process. In preparation for the first summit, the United States convened a half-day preparatory meeting at the Council on Foreign Relations in New York. Saad Al-Farargi, a foreign ministry expert on economic affairs, headed our delegation. Two days before the meeting, Moussa asked me to fly to New York and join the delegation to ensure that Egypt's role was not forgotten.

I walked into the meeting room that day a little bit late, with all delegations, including our own, already seated at the table. As I moved across the room, Daniel Kurtzer, a long-time American expert on Egypt and Arab–Israeli issues, came up to me and asked whether we had any particular problems. I tried to assure him that that was not the case. Kurtzer, however a knowledgeable and insightful diplomat and personal friend, responded that given my intensive workload, I would not have flown all the way from Cairo to New York for a three-hour meeting unless there was something that seriously concerned Egypt, or I had a surprising proposal to make. I was both flattered and concerned by the reputation I had acquired; and explained the need for clear and appropriate reference to our pioneering and continuing role in the Middle East peace process. Kurtzer immediately drafted strong commendable language regarding Egypt's role and promised to include it in the concluding document, provided that I did not instigate a debate. That was fine with me. I sat calmly through the meeting as Al-Farargi engaged constructively and professionally on the different agenda items. I flew off to Cairo later that day having spent less than 24 hours in New York without publicly uttering a word formally at the meeting.

Indeed, Egypt's proactive role in the peace process continued on the ground. During the Casablanca summit, as I was sitting with Amre Moussa in his suite hours before the first meeting Arafat asked to see me. On entering Arafat's suite, I found a disturbed, worried leader, anxiously waiting. He asked the Palestinians in the room to leave us alone and as we sat privately, Arafat said, "*Akhi* [my brother] Nabil, I am worried that our cause is being diluted and that the false dreams of a new Middle East will overshadow the more imminent violation of our inalienable right to have a sovereign state." I spontaneously responded that the Moroccan King Hassan II, with his special religious role and being the head of the Jerusalem Committee of the Organization of the Islamic Conference, would safeguard Palestinian rights. To this, Arafat responded, "It is because of the significance of the King's stature that I am worried about Rabin trying to start that here because it could be erroneously inferred that the Muslim world was normalizing relations with Israel."

I shared Arafat's concerns with Moussa who asked me to meet André Azoulay, the political advisor to the Moroccan king, to whom I highlighted the potential embarrassment it would create if heated rhetorical arguments broke out in the presence of the king. When the opening plenary was convened, the tensions were palpitating, especially when references were made to Jerusalem. The Moroccans, however, were astute diplomats, particularly King Hassan II, and they were able to deftly manage the tense meeting without too much commotion. They had clearly talked to both sides before the meeting.

The second MENA Economic Summit was convened in Amman in October 1995, also with some controversy. Egypt was annoyed that Israel was placing the carriage before the horse in the Middle East by underlining Arab–Israeli normalization even before the core issue of ending Israeli occupation of Arab territories had been resolved.

I arrived a day earlier in Amman to prepare for the summit and saw the final draft of Moussa's speech only on his arrival the next day. As usual, it was substantive, well crafted, and sharp in making several points. My first reaction was to commend the text, but to caution the use of the Arabic word "*harwala*" (which could be translated as overzealousness or hastily) in describing Arab overeagerness to engage with Israel. This would offend King Hussein of Jordan and create unnecessary controversy. Other members of the delegation were supportive of this term, and Moussa, who was always strong-willed but keen on hearing diverse opinions, asked me to further elaborate on my reservations. I reiterated that making these comments would provoke the Jordanians much more than create pressure on the Israelis to be generous in their peace offerings. Moussa attentively listened but asserted his prerogative as Minister, affirming that he intended to use the language as presented.

As soon as Moussa had finished reading his statement in the plenary session, Crown Prince Hassan sent his brother King Hussein, a note highlighting what Moussa had said, urging for a strong rebuttal. Hussein, eloquent as usual, responded forcefully that Jordan would always strive for peace, but that Egypt had been the first to be overzealous that way. Tensions were palpable, resonating across and beyond the conference room and the meeting ground outside.

As we walked toward our cars, I insisted that Moussa not speak to the press or anyone else until we had time to reflect and consult. I cut off the American delegation attempting to address Moussa, listening to their admonitions while working our way toward our cars, until Toni Verstandig, then deputy assistant secretary for Near Eastern Affairs at the State Department, suggested that America's response was to move the next meeting from Cairo to Doha, Qatar. I could not remain passive toward both the arrogance of the American presumption that they could manage the Middle East, command or punish whomever, but more so at the naivety and lack of understanding of the region. Notwithstanding the growing role for which Qatar was aspiring for in the region, hosting the next Summit in Egypt was certainly a lot more significant in the context of Arab politics. Angrily and spontaneously, I withdrew Egypt's invitation to hold the next meeting in Cairo. Moussa silently smiled as we walked quickly toward our car. Dennis Ross, the lead American Middle East emissary, immediately intervened to calm sentiments, affirming that they wanted us to hold the next meeting in Cairo as originally scheduled.

After a very short car ride, Moussa and I entered his hotel suite alone where he contacted President Hosni Mubarak to brief him on what had occurred. He then visited King Hussein to calm sentiments as much as possible. Arab public opinion, however, embraced *"harwala"*, codifying it as the mantra of opposition to premature normalization, and placed Moussa high on a pedestal for his public assertiveness. In the end, both Moussa and I were correct: the term had been a resounding success but had also greatly offended the Jordanians.

Ironically, only a year earlier on July 25, 1994, before signing the Jordan–Israel bilateral peace treaty, the two parties met in Washington to sign the Washington Declaration, a non-belligerency agreement between Jordan and Israel. After the official ceremony, President Bill Clinton publicly asked King Hussein and Israeli Prime Minister Yitzhak Rabin, "Tell me the truth, how long have you known each other?" King Hussein did not answer at first. However, when Rabin said "Twenty-one years", King Hussein corrected him by saying, "Twenty years". The story was picked up by reporters and published in the media. Irrespective of the one-year discrepancy, it constituted the first formal public acknowledgment that Jordan had in fact been in touch with the Israelis way before the Egyptians.

The third MENA Economic Summit was held in Cairo from November 12 to 15, 1996, and like any Middle Eastern gathering, it had its tense moments. Egypt had just arrested an Israeli Durzi, Azzam, and accused him of spying. After arriving in Cairo, the Israeli Foreign Minister David Levy suddenly announced that he would not participate in the designated panel unless Azzam was released. Oded Eran Levy, senior advisor, took me aside at the conference venue, explaining to me how adamant Levy was about his position.

In the midst of all of the ongoing events at the conference, there was really no time for small talk or intricate negotiations, nor was it politically acceptable to compromise after Levy's arrogant public statement. I cut to the chase and bluntly responded that the panel would simply go on without Levy. Egypt, I affirmed, would be happy to use the occasion to focus on further promoting its national economic interests and to attract investments rather than promote regional economic cooperation. Ultimately, Levy did not deliver a speech at the conference but sat in the audience during the panel and his team distributed a communiqué of his statement prepared instead. This attracted very little attention throughout the region.

The following MENA Economic Summit after Cairo was held in Doha from November 16 to 18, 1997. The American and Israeli goal was to "openly" normalize Israeli relations with the Arab Gulf states. The hope was that this summit would attract Arab Gulf stakeholders through economic engagement, irrespective of the reality that the political process was slowly dying down. Needless to say, holding the event in an Arab Gulf state for the first time was particularly attractive to the Israelis and Americans, but the hopes for a major breakthrough in relations in spite of the Arab Israeli conflict were naïve and expectations remained mostly unfulfilled.

Egyptian and Qatari relations were just starting to cool then. President Mubarak and Emir Hamad bin Khalifa Al-Thani did not get along. The latter felt that Mubarak had colluded with his deposed father to return him to power. Mubarak felt no empathy for Hamid. Egyptian government officials declined the invitation to attend the summit but left that option open to the Egyptian private sector.

Over the two decades after the last all-out Arab–Israeli War in 1973, with peace agreements between Israel and Egypt and Jordan as well as the Oslo process, a younger generation of Arabs and Israelis were not attuned to the drumbeats of all-out war. In spite of the occasional violent confrontations in Lebanon and Gaza and the tragic suffering of the Palestinians under occupation, this new generation of Middle Easterners wanted to move forward, and for them, the MENA process was conceptually an auspicious tool and modality that could serve as a catalyst in this respect. The MENA process itself was, however, losing steam, and the rising political difficulties caused by the election of a right-wing government in Israel laid it to rest.

The responsibility for this less than anticipated result falls mostly on Israel, ironically probably the most enthusiastic supporter of this process. Without ending the occupation of Arab territories and the establishment of a Palestinian state, the full potential of normal relations Israel was hoping for would not evolve.

Egyptians were not particularly supportive of this process either. Its government institutions were bitter that the Framework for Peace signed between Anwar Sadat and Menachem Begin at Camp David over a decade earlier had not been underscored enough, with Israel reaping the dividends of peace with Egypt without fulfilling its wider regional obligations. There were lessons drawn from its own experiences of bilateral peace with Israel that it could not ignore—the most important being that any new political paradigm had to first resolve the old conflict. Finally, Egypt also felt that this MENA process, focusing on regional normalization, would diminish its singular prestige and leverage throughout the Middle East.

REFERENCES

Al Gamasy, M. (1993). *The October War: Memoirs of Field Marshal El-Gamasy of Egypt*. Cairo: American University Press.

Attachment to "Personal Letter from President Sadat to President Carter". (1977, November 3). US Department of State Office of the Historian Archives. Ref:

(A) para 5, Cairo 17863, (B) Cairo 18232. 2255Z 18241. https://history. state.gov/historicaldocuments/frus1977-80v08/d141

Camp David Accords. (1978). Ariel Center for Policy Research. http://www.acpr. org.il/publications/books/42-Zero-camp-david-accords.pdf

Egyptian MOFA. (1978). *Framework for the Conclusion of a Peace Treaty Between Egypt and Israel. No. 17854.* https://www.mfa.gov.eg/Lists/Treaties/ Attachments/2279/Framework_en.pdf

Egyptian MOFA. (1979). *Treaty of Peace Between Arab Republic of Egypt and the State of Israel. No. 17813.* https://www.mfa.gov.eg/Lists/Treaties/Attachments/ 2278/Peace%20Treaty_en.pdf

Egyptian Response to 1st US Draft on Convening the Geneva Conference and the Suggested Formula. (1977, October 19). US Department of State Office of the Historian Archives (1339Z 17348). https://history.state.gov/historicaldocu- ments/frus1977-80v08/d133

Israeli Outline for Peace: The Framework for the Peace-Making Process Between Israel and Its Neighbors. (1977, July 7). State of Israel Archives. File A 4313/1. http://www.archives.gov.il/archives/#/Archive/0b0717068001c167/ File/0b07170684cd6be2/Item/090717068507a13b

Letter from Carter to Sadat. (1977a, November 5). US Department of State Office of the Historian Archives. 0129Z 264771. https://history.state.gov/ historicaldocuments/frus1977-80v08/d142

Letter from Carter to Sadat. (1977b, October 28). US Department of the State Office of the Historian Archives. Ref: Cairo 17817 (1351Z 258388). https:// history.state.gov/historicaldocuments/frus1977-80v08/d139

Letter from President Carter to President Sadat. (1977, April 29). US National Archives. Document Number: 1977STATE095780. Film Number: D770149-0005. https://aad.archives.gov/aad/createpdf?rid=77665&dt= 2532&dl=1629

Note on President Carter and Syrian President Assad Meeting. (1977, May 11). US National Archives. Document Number: 1977SECTO04023. Film Number: D770165-0932. https://aad.archives.gov/aad/createpdf?rid=106357&dt= 2532&dl=1629

Oral Message for President Sadat from Secretary Vance. (1977, July 21). US National Archives. Document Number: 1977STATE170055. Film Number: P840084-1889. https://aad.archives.gov/aad/createpdf?rid=173538&dt= 2532&dl=1629

Oral Message from Secretary Vance. (1977, October 22). US National Archives. Document Number: 1977STATE252851. Film Number: P850050-2204. https://aad.archives.gov/aad/createpdf?rid=252121&dt=2532&dl=1629

OSLO II Agreement. (1995). Ariel Center for Policy Research. http://www.acpr. org.il/publications/books/44-Zero-isr-pal-interim-agreement.pdf

Personal Letter from President Sadat to President Carter. (1977, November 3). US Department of State Office of the Historian Archives. Ref: (A) para 5, Cairo 17863, (B) Cairo 18232. (2255Z 18241). https://history.state.gov/historicaldocuments/frus1977-80v08/d141

Talking Points. (1977, March 7). US National Archives. Document number: 1977STATE050667. Film Number: D770078-0789. https://aad.archives.gov/aad/createpdf?rid=49009&dt=2532&dl=1629

Telegram from Secretary of State Vance to the Embassies in Jordan and Egypt Entitled: "American Talking Points". (1977, August 9). US STATE DEPARTMENT OFFICE OF THE HISTORIAN ARCHIVES (0830Z Sector 8102) https://history.state.gov/historicaldocuments/frus1977-80v08/d77

Treaty of Peace Between the State of Israel and the Arab Republic of Egypt. (1977, September 19). Attached in Telegram 6588 from Tel Aviv on September 2 (National Archives, RG 59, Central Foreign Policy File P840081-2175).

Working Paper on Suggestions for the Resumption of the Geneva Conference. (1977, October 5). US Department of State Office of the Historian Archives. https://history.state.gov/historicaldocuments/frus1977-80v08/d124 #fn:1.5.4.2.256.568.4.4

CHAPTER 4

Yet No Peace

*The blood and suffering of the 1973 war brought long-standing
adversaries to negotiations—from Geneva to Jerusalem and Camp
David, from Madrid to Oslo then Camp David again and Beirut.
Israel demanded a regional peace but ignored all regional initiatives
and only negotiated bilaterally. Arabs called for comprehensive peace,
but signed separate peace agreements. The United States and the
international community vacillated between process and personalities.
Many lessons were learnt from the longest regional ongoing conflict.*

A Troubled Middle East: America, Egypt, and the Post-Oslo Peace Efforts

As the Middle East peace process oscillated between flickers of hope and
surges of failures after both Madrid and Oslo, the second half of the 1990s
in particular became characterized by a biased American hegemony over
the Middle East peace process that was intense and miscalculating, particularly its Palestinian–Israeli track.

American President Bill Clinton unlike other newly elected American
presidents witnessed Palestinian–Israeli wins early in his tenure. The Oslo
agreement had quickly whetted his appetite for this topic. He, quickly,
overstocked his Middle East Peace Process team at the State Department
and in the National Security Council with overwhelmingly strong supporters of Israel while completely sidelining the Near East Bureau at the

© The Author(s) 2020
N. Fahmy, *Egypt's Diplomacy in War, Peace and Transition*,
https://doi.org/10.1007/978-3-030-26388-1_4

State Department, which dealt with America's relations with the countries in the Middle East.

This was to create a serious imbalance in America's attitude toward the Middle East. Even more dangerously, it blurred the distinction between American and Israeli interests and priorities, which historically and to this day were not always identical. United States Envoy to the Middle East, Dennis Ross, who was the lead American negotiator in the peace process, inferred in his memoirs about this period that his primary objective was to ensure that Israel's interests were served.[1] Thus, as Palestinian–Israeli negotiations intensified with all the expected ups and downs, the Palestinians leaned heavily on an always-ready Egypt for support to counter balance out the American bias toward Israel. This was not only due to Egypt's active role in the Middle East process, particularly with the Palestinian issue, but also due to Yasser Arafat's strong confidence that we did not have an interventionist national agenda on the Palestinian issue. He understood that our only real interest was safeguarding of the Arab identity in order to consolidate Egypt's leadership in the Arab world. For this, Arafat was always depended on Egypt for support in negotiations with Israel. This served Egypt's interests as well.

The Egyptian Foreign Ministry under Amre Moussa would often aggressively intervene on Palestine's behalf. The Israelis and the Peace Process team in the State Department repeatedly expressed discomfort with the Egyptian Foreign Ministry even spreading innuendo occasionally about me but more frequently and more vehemently about Moussa. On several occasions in Washington and Egypt, the American administration maneuvered to exclude Moussa from high-level meetings they were holding with President Mubarak, where his counterpart Madeleine Albright would be present. This was an outright violation of protocol and a precedent that revealed the growing American dislike for Moussa, a proud Egyptian who was neither anti-American nor anti-Israeli by any count. Israeli Prime Minister Rabin was also personally highly critical of the Egyptian Foreign Ministry's role, and explicitly and vehemently criticized Moussa.

By then, the Americans felt that Palestinian perseverance would ultimately wilt out of fear that they would end up with much less if they procrastinated further especially with the determined Israeli settlement policy

---

[1] Dennis Ross memoir (2005). The Missing Peace: The Inside Story of the Fight for Middle East Peace.

eating up more and more land. The American negotiating team would never admit to failure. This seemed fixating on preserving the process rather than achieving substantive progress to ensure Clinton's legacy. On the other hand, Vice President Al Gore, who was running for president, was gradually becoming more cautious and calculative out of fear of failure affecting his presidential ambitions.

For their part, the Palestinians were torn between the realization that they would not achieve their national goals with Benjamin Netanyahu in power and the imperative engagement with Israeli authorities to fulfill the obligations of governance, once Arafat had returned to the West Bank and established the Palestinian Authority. Arafat was in no mood to relinquish his national aspirations but could not ignore Israel's authority on a day-to-day basis. In essence, he was in no mood to say yes but was in no position to say no.

All of these factors increased the challenges of an already volatile peace process. In the fall of 1996, as Israelis and Palestinians attempted to negotiate what was to become the Khalil (Hebron) Agreement to expand Palestinian authority in the Old city, Clinton asked Mubarak to send Osama El-Baz to convince Arafat to be more cooperative in negotiations. While generally amenable to cooperating with the West, Mubarak was always annoyed by the American tendency to choose which of his advisors they wanted to deal with, so he ignored the request.

A few months later, in late December, Clinton again asked Mubarak to send someone to assist Arafat but this time without naming anybody, in particular. I received a phone call late in the evening from Mubarak's Information Advisor with the message that the president wanted me to join Arafat in Gaza the next morning to advise him on what to do, suggesting that it might be useful to take with me a legal advisor as well. No direction was given for what kind of advice I was expected to give. I phoned Moussa, who was out of Cairo, and asked him for instructions. His response was that I knew the strategic policy direction and that I could use my best judgment, assuring me that we would remain in touch (Fig. 4.1).

Early the next morning, I left for Gaza with Mufeed Shehab, an Egyptian legal expert, on a car ride that took five hours. On arrival, Arafat immediately asked for my opinion on language that was being negotiated between Palestinians and Israelis under the auspices of the United States at the residence of the American Ambassador to Israel Martin Indyk.

Fig. 4.1   Joint press conference between Nabil Fahmy and John Kerry

After reading the text, my first conclusion, which I kept to myself, was that impeccable English of the text was an indication that it was either an American or an Israeli draft. The beginning of the text seemed to be amenable and consistent with Palestinian aspirations. The concluding ones, however, negated everything offered at the outset and more. I looked up at Arafat and frankly told him so. He asked me to draft a solid but negotiable text that could be part of a Palestinian–Israeli agreement. I did this before going to my hotel, Al-Tahouna, a small pleasant hotel that was burnt down a few years later amidst the disturbances in Gaza.

Very early at dawn the next morning, I got an agitated phone call from Indyk inquiring about what role I intended to play with Arafat. He felt that I had made an unhelpful contribution by redrafting a Palestinian text that made it even more difficult to accept. My response to Indyk was, "I came to help Arafat reach whatever decision he wanted." I knew the text I suggested was stronger than the one shown to me but felt it still provided a basis for negotiations. I did, however, notice that the language Indyk read to me differed from what I had drafted and in fact was now incoherent. The Palestinian delegate who had conveyed the text to his colleagues had obviously not done so correctly. I kept this to myself and did not tell Indyk that I had thought Americans or Israelis rather than Palestinians originally drafted the language Arafat had shown me.

Arafat was not an early riser, so I waited until midday before going over to his headquarters in Gaza. On arrival, I asked him why he had not told me that the text was originally a Palestinian one. Arafat listened without reacting and changed the subject. Later, as we walked across the meeting room for lunch, he suddenly stopped and in a loud resounding voice said, "*Akhi* Nabil, do you know why I asked you to come and help? You saw what happened yesterday with the draft language: Each one of my Palestinian brothers here lives in diaspora with relations, obligations, and responsibilities towards their host country, many of which have their own agendas. Egypt is the only country whose national agenda does not impinge on the Palestinian national agenda. That is why I wanted you here." I was surprised by his outburst and felt a bit embarrassed for my Palestinian friends around the room, although he was simply candidly explaining the pressures on the Palestinian diaspora.

I spent the next six days in Gaza, helping Arafat consider the texts and discussions the Palestinians were having with the Israelis. The American delegation was composed of Ross, Aaron Miller, the deputy Middle East special envoy at the State Department, and others. Indyk, as ambassador, was also intensively engaged with both sides. I was surprised to watch how easily the Israelis distracted and consumed the Americans with minor details like the size of vacant parking lots or how wide sidewalks were because of presumed security concerns. The Palestinians had clearly not yet decided whether or not any deal was useful to them and procrastinated endlessly taking advantage too of the American obsession with wanting to announce success even if artificial and marginal. By then, the Americans had become addicted to process rather than substance. Both Israelis and Palestinians clearly understood this.

To the dismay of all the negotiating parties, especially the Americans, President Mubarak was daily publicly expressing vehement concern to the media about many of the points being negotiated and which I had been relaying to Cairo. Personally, I became more uncomfortable with the negotiations. They seemed senseless from the Palestinian perspective, providing minor gains in exchange for cumbersome Israeli restrictions, particularly the Israeli control and Judaization of Al-Khalil. I shared my concerns with Arafat, but respected that it was his prerogative to decide on what was acceptable.

On January 6, 1997, I sensed that an agreement was imminent and informed Arafat that it was time for me to return to Egypt because of a number of personal issues. I arrived home before dawn the next day, after another long car ride across the Sinai. Less than an hour later, I received a phone call from Moussa suggesting that we have breakfast with Arafat. To my complete surprise, he also crossed the Sinai that night as well, very shortly after I left Gaza, and was now at the Andalus Palace in Heliopolis, north-east of Cairo.

Two hours later, as Moussa and I were being received in Heliopolis, a smiling Arafat looked at me with a sense of exasperation, repeating, "Why did you leave? Did you think I was going to sign an agreement with that liar?" My response was simply, "I came to give you Egypt's advice, but your signature on a Khalil agreement or not was completely your prerogative as the leader of the Palestinian people." Later, when he met President Mubarak alone, Arafat reiterated that he did not intend to sign an agreement. Arafat concluded that Mubarak's repeated public expressions of concern and my departure from Gaza were clear indications of where Egypt stood on the text of the agreement being negotiated. Ultimately, the negotiations were aborted only to be resumed months later, on a better but not great text, finally leading to the signature of the Hebron Agreement.

A Short Detour to the Syrian–Israeli Track

After I assumed my post as the Egyptian ambassador to the United States in fall 1999, I quickly sensed that the American administration felt there was an opening for negotiated progress on the Syrian front. They later explained that they had drawn this conclusion from contacts with Israeli Prime Minister Ehud Barak and understandings from Prince Bandar bin Sultan, Saudi Arabia's ambassador to Washington. The former had no empathy toward or respect for Arafat and preferred not to deal with him. Moreover, according to the Americans, the Saudi ambassador had informed them that al-Assad was open to deal.

To Mubarak's surprise and dismay, the United States had scheduled a meeting between Clinton and al-Assad in Geneva two days before Mubarak was scheduled to arrive in Washington for his annual spring visit to the United States of March 2000. An annoyed Mubarak felt this reflected a diminishing focus on Egypt and openly conveyed his feelings to me. I assured Mubarak that Clinton would be back and ready for his meeting as scheduled early the week after. I also suggested that the Geneva meeting would be a failure because the Americans had incorrectly assumed that Al-Assad would agree not to extend Syrian sovereignty to Lake Tiberias.

The Americans had never shared with me the language under negotiation. I nevertheless contacted Miller and told him what I thought was being developed, cautioning that they would be mistaken if they assumed that Al-Assad would agree to relinquish sovereignty over any territory. I asserted that Syria may be flexible on security arrangements, but it would not compromise on territory, particularly after Egypt had regained all of Sinai. Miller was non-committal and refrained from confirming anything. He realized, however, that I was well informed.

Before the weekend was over, the American Syrian summit in Geneva had failed, with each side blaming the other for the misunderstanding about whether or not Al-Assad would insist on full Israeli withdrawal from the Golan and to where exactly. When they could not agree on whom to blame, they inferred that Prince Bandar had caused the misunderstanding. On issues of sovereignty, precision and direct clear understandings are paramount.

The Camp David II Summit: Diplomatic Mismanagement

The failed American Syrian summit in Geneva brought the focus once again back to the Palestinian–Israeli track. The United States team quickly geared up for concrete progress, if not a full agreement, before President Clinton left office at the end of 2001. By early summer of 2000, they had planned for an American Israeli–Palestinian summit at Camp David in July. The Arabs could not understand the rush and were both suspicious and perplexed. On the one hand, Barak and Arafat were not even on speaking terms; the negative sentiments were strong and mutual. On the other, both the Israelis and Palestinians tended to be last-minute compromisers, which did not auger well for agreement six months before Clinton would leave office. What then could have been the real motivation behind the American insistence on holding the summit, we all wondered. The political environment was definitely inauspicious.

Arafat was not enthusiastic about the idea of attending the Camp David II Summit and told us so in Egypt. He was suspicious of both Israeli and American intentions. I told the Americans that we did not support convening a trilateral summit that summer because it was bound to fail and recommended that if they insisted on convening it, they should not announce failure when it ultimately happened, better to simply say that the negotiations would be resumed later.

The Americans, however, were determined to move forward in the summer. In opposition to the approach followed in the Oslo process, of not spelling out details and relying on follow-up meetings, the Americans adopted a comprehensive approach that attempted to reach a conflict-ending agreement to resolve all the core issues in a single summit meeting. This would have been great if the timing was right and the summit was well prepared for. That was not the case, however. Upon Mubarak's instructions, I went to the State Department again a few days before the summit and repeated our position to Ross in Miller's presence. I also added that, should the task fail as we expect, they should not announce that the fundamental disagreement was on the issue of Jerusalem, with all of its religious connotations and sensitivities. Negotiating people's conflicting national aspirations was difficult, but negotiating their beliefs about God-given rights was impossible. I also added that it was also of paramount importance that they should not place the blame on one side. Throughout his two terms in office, Clinton had the tendency to applaud both the Palestinians and Israelis for every success, but only to blame the Palestinians for the failures.

Ross challenged my assessment that the summit would fail but assured me that they will neither focus on one particular issue nor apportion blame if there were problems.

Arafat came to the United States to attend the summit with mixed feelings. Although he was very concerned about the summit's expected outcome, he preferred not to reject Clinton's invitation. Prior to the Summit at a dinner hosted by Hani El-Masry, a Palestinian American, for the Palestinian delegation, Arafat told me that the differences between the Palestinians and Israelis on Jerusalem were too wide to be resolved at the summit. He was also certain the Americans would renege on their promise and ultimately blame him for failure. He was proven correct on both counts.

Arafat's relations with his deputy Abu Mazen had gotten increasingly difficult since the signing of the Oslo agreement. He felt the latter was publicly taking hardline irreconcilable positions with the Israelis, hoping to solidify his position with Palestinian hardliners while at the same time preventing anyone but himself from gaining credit with the rest of the world for achieving progress in bringing an Arab Israeli peace closer. This surprised me given that Abu Mazen was the main patron of the Oslo process. But in response to Arafat's request, I crossed the room to join Abu Mazen, asking for his assessment of the prospects of achieving progress at the upcoming Camp David Summit. His responses confirmed Arafat's impressions that Abou Mazen was taking a tough posture at that point. He said that he was always flexible on tactics but would not compromise at all on final settlement issues like Jerusalem or refugees, the outstanding issues to be discussed at the summit.

The responsibility for the failure of the American Israeli–Palestinian Camp David II Summit falls squarely and clearly on the United States administration. It had neither properly prepared itself nor followed through after its conclusion. Years later, I asked a former American official why they had been so insistent on convening the summit in July 2000 without appropriate preparations. I knew that Barak wanted an early meeting to leverage the peace process in his election campaign and that Al Gore, who was a candidate running for president in the United States elections, did not want the summit to be held too close to the November elections, just in case it failed. James Steinberg, deputy United States national security advisor, replied that the United States was concerned that Arafat was going to unilaterally declare a Palestinian state in September 2000. This was news to me.

Another annoying characteristic of American diplomacy at the time was that it expected its friends and allies in the Arab world to blindly support American peace efforts without being briefed on the efforts at hand. The trilateral Camp David summit was held in a closed venue with very limited access, even to the participating delegations. Personally, as Egypt's ambassador to the United States, I made daily phone calls to Palestinian and Israeli delegations off-site but near Camp David. Their briefings were always extensive, entertaining, passionate, and often in contradiction with each other. I would also place a daily phone call to the American delegation at Camp David but was never put through or received a return call during the summit. My daily cables to Cairo were, therefore, reporting on Palestinian and Israeli visions, complemented with my own assessment and analysis.

Toward the closing phases of the Camp David negotiations, President Mubarak informed me that upon the America president's instructions, the

American Ambassador in Cairo Daniel Kurtzer had asked him to persuade Arafat to support Clinton's proposal on Jerusalem. Strangely enough, the request was made without informing Kurtzer, and thus Mubarak, of the content of the proposal. Angry, the Egyptian president asked me if I knew what the proposal actually was. I reiterated what I had said in my cables, that I was providing information from Palestinian and Israeli sources[2] that needed to be taken with a grain of salt but that the American side was not communicating with anybody outside Camp David. Mubarak briskly asked me to convey to the Americans, when they responded to my calls, that he would not give a blind endorsement.

The administration and a number of well-connected American columnists would place the blame for the failure of the summit on Arafat and the Arabs, especially president Mubarak, while in fact, it was fully a failure of American diplomacy.

After the conclusion of the summit without agreement, both Barak and Arafat catered to their more rejectionist constituencies, claiming not to have compromised with each other or succumbed to American pressure. Nevertheless, both sides agreed to continue the negotiation process in September 2000. The second Palestinian Intifada began out of frustration with the whole process but ironically not to the chagrin of either the Israelis or Palestinians, who were catering to their more agitated constituency since the failure of the summer summit.

THE CLINTON PARAMETERS: A LAST-DITCH EFFORT

Despite their anger and frustration, President Carter and his administration clearly understood that the Arab–Israeli peace process would play an important role in defining their legacy. Consequently, they were determined to continue to make further efforts before the changing of the guard. In a message[3] to President Mubarak at the conclusion of the Camp David Summit II, President Clinton had emphasized that while success was not achieved, progress had been made. He also reaffirmed his intention to continue to exert efforts calling for Egypt's support. As the Clinton

---

[2] The Israeli position is summarized in talking point dated July 19, 2000, which purpose is to address the minimum requirements of both sides without violating red lines (see Appendix VI).

[3] President Clinton's message to President Mubarak, dated August 9, 2000, evaluating the Palestine, Israel, America Summit at Camp David (see Appendix VII).

administration entered its closing few months, it tried to facilitate progress toward an agreement between the Israelis and Palestinians by verbally suggesting in December 2001 a set of guidelines for the permanent settlement called the "Clinton Parameters". They reflected that Clinton envisioned the establishment of a Palestinian State in 94–96 percent of the occupied Palestinian territories in the West Bank and Gaza with territorial exchange and giving the Palestinians 1–3 percent of Israeli territory. The Israelis would retain settlement blocks containing 80 percent of the settler population. Security arrangements would be based on an international force, Israeli warning stations, and a continued presence in the Jordan River Valley. Jerusalem would be partitioned on ethnic grounds, and the Historic Basin would have special arrangements. Palestinian refugees would be repatriated essentially to the Palestinian state.

In spite of having been blamed for the failure of Camp David II, Arafat was invited back to Washington, to see President Clinton. On touch down at the Andrews Air Force Base, he asked to see Prince Bandar and me, to ensure Egyptian and Saudi cover for whatever he decided upon. On arrival at his suite at the St. Regis in Pentagon City, Virginia, he had a number of advisors with him including Saeb Erekat, Mohammed Dahlan, Muhammad Rashid (also known as Khaled Salam), and Yasser Abed Rabbo.

Both Prince Bandar and I encouraged Arafat to attentively listen to President Clinton and see if there was an opportunity to move forward explaining that the next American president would not want to immediately engage in a just failed process. Prince Bandar was emphatic that Bush would not touch the Palestinian–Israeli peace efforts if Clinton failed.

After Arafat's private meeting with Clinton, he asked to see us again. When we returned to his hotel, he went into a long slow monologue about how good the meeting was. Prince Bandar started to congratulate Arafat and quickly moving to another room to call the National Security Council at the White House. Arafat looked particularly pale however, and his body chemistry was not one of victorious or even relaxed negotiator. I could sense that something was wrong, so I asked him about the final conclusions which can be drawn from the meeting.

Arafat's tone changed as he explained that the discussions had been excellent until Ross walked into the room and had Clinton backtrack from his constructive positions especially on Jerusalem. Arafat then went on a long testy diatribe about how conniving Ross was, clearly still bitter about how he had been treated by the Americans after the Camp David II Summit. Before Arafat could even finish, Bandar ended his phone call, and announced that he was leaving for his winter house in Aspen, Colorado. Arafat tried to convince him to stay, but he was adamant about leaving and said that I could speak on behalf of both Egypt and Saudi Arabia.

The attempt to adopt the Clinton Parameters failed. The Palestinians, even Arafat, claimed they never formally rejected the Clinton Parameters. Indeed, when I met with Arafat at the Andrews Air Force Base hours later before his departure, he told me that he had "[a]ccepted the Clinton Parameters, with reservations" and asked me to convey this to the American administration. This was not the role of the Egyptian ambassador in Washington, in spite of our support for the Palestinians. Consequently, on the drive back to Washington after Arafat's departure, I had Hassan Abdel Rahman, the Palestinian representative in Washington, relay Arafat's message to Bruce Riedel, the special assistant to Clinton and senior director for near east affairs on the National Security Council. Immediately after that, I spoke to Reidel myself to reiterate the message. He was not sure, however, whether the phrase "with reservations" was acceptable. I immediately conveyed all this by telephone to the Egyptian Foreign Minister Moussa while he was in meetings with other Arab foreign ministers in Cairo. I emphasized that Arafat had given a qualified approval. Some of the officials sitting with Moussa, especially the Syrians, were not fans of Arafat so only later did I also tell Moussa that it was my strong opinion that Arafat should have announced his approval with reservations of the parameters. This would have made it more difficult for the Israelis or Americans to backtrack later, and it would also establish a baseline for the incoming American administration of George W. Bush as well as preempted a negative media campaign against Arafat in America.

Regrettably, by the time Arafat had reached the Middle East after a stopover in Morocco, the formal Palestinian public narrative was mostly about having rejected the Clinton Parameters, focusing on Arafat's courage and stalwartness in the face of severe American pressure, and projecting him as a hero in the Arab world. This was a big mistake. Arafat should have pocketed these parameters and kept arguing for more through the window of the reservations he had clearly left open, making any final agreement contingent on the fulfillment of Palestinian aspirations.

The remaining few weeks before Clinton was to hand over office to Bush witnessed some frantic, useful, but futile efforts on the Palestinian–Israeli track. President Clinton himself gave a long speech explaining his personal vision on Palestinian–Israeli peace, where he went further than any standing United States president had done at the time, by personally, but not officially, supporting the establishment of a Palestinian state.

In January 2001, Egypt hosted the Israelis and Palestinians in Taba under its own auspices where a number of understandings and compromises were reached and compiled in what were called the Moratinos documents.[4] The negotiating parties never formally adopted these understandings. The Israelis questioned the outgoing Prime Minister authority to make such decisions days before an election. Arafat was not ready to be bound by new compromises that might not be binding on the incoming Israeli government. President Clinton and his administration officials briefed the incoming administration on the subject of Arab–Israeli conflict. I was informed by friends close to the White House that the senior Clinton administrators strongly recommended that the incoming administration not take on the Middle East conflict as a priority, describing Arafat as cunning and unreliable.

The Second Intifada, which extended to 2005, brought about heavy international criticism and was used as unifying factor for the more hawkish and conservative Jewish political groups and organizations. The new administration started a campaign to diminish Arafat's control before jumping into Palestinian–Israeli negotiations. They also insisted that the continuation of the American economic assistance to the Palestinian Authority was contingent on Arafat appointing Mahmoud Abbas (Abu Mazen) as prime minister with executive powers.

THE ARAB PEACE INITIATIVE: ANOTHER MISSED OPPORTUNITY

With the terrorist attacks of September 11, 2001, the image of the Arab and Muslim world was deeply shaken. Arab leaders had this clearly in mind as they prepared to meet in the Arab League summit in Beirut on March 28, 2002. Saudi Arabia was eager to reduce criticism from the West, given that 15 of the 19 hijackers in the attacks were rogue Saudis. It was thus not coincidental that the prominent *New York Times* columnist Thomas Friedman was invited to meet Saudi leaders and then wrote an opinion piece with an imaginary memorandum from the American president to

---

[4] Moratinos Documents (2001): http://www.jewishpeacelobby.org/wp-content/uploads/2015/11/TheMoratinosDocument.pdf (see Appendix VIII)

Arab presidents regarding the upcoming Arab League summit and recommending their endorsement of a resolution of peace with Israel.

Arab leaders, led by Saudi Arabia and Jordan, energetically and successfully lobbied for the adoption of an historic document known as the Arab Peace Initiative. If one considers the 1991 Madrid Peace Conference as the starting point for the regionalization of peace, the Arabs at Beirut took several more steps forward in clearly enunciating their readiness to have normal relations of peace in The Middle East after the end of the 1967 Israeli occupation of Arab territories.

In this proposal, the Arabs reaffirmed that the basis for peace in the Middle East was the United Nations Security Council resolutions 242 and 388. However, for the first time ever, they openly declared that all Arab states, not only those directly neighboring Israel, would commit to having normal relations with Israel once it ended its occupation of Arab territories and a Palestinian State was established with East Jerusalem as its capital. After considerable debate on the initiative of Jordan, the Arabs agreed and offered to consider a negotiated settlement for the Palestinian refugee issue in accordance with the United Nations General Assembly Resolution 194.

The concessions offered by the Arabs in the initiative were highly significant, and the proposal itself was wise. The timing, however, was wrong because no real potential for progress existed at that point. In fact, the Israeli Prime Minister Ariel Sharon was literally holding Arafat hostage at his own headquarters in *Al-Moqata'an* in Ramallah, West Bank, from March 29 to May 2, 2002, refusing to allow him to attend the summit and return to the West Bank. Sources also even reported that the Israeli cabinet had seriously considered terminating Arafat. In addition, in typical Israeli tradition, surprised by Arab compromise and responsiveness, Israel asked the Arabs for more details and demanded the negotiation of the content and language of the text of the initiative. This was yet another example of clear evidence that in spite of all the calls for regional peace and normalization, the real problem was that the Israeli political paradigm did not seriously support a two-state solution or agree to withdraw from occupied Arab territories. Therefore, as expected, the Arab Peace Initiative was pocketed and then ignored by the Israelis, without any reciprocal concessions, even though this initiative provided the opportunity for full regional normalization and the permanent end of the conflict.

Regrettably, the Arab Peace Initiative was quickly orphaned, both regionally and internationally. The Israelis wanted the Arabs to move toward peace but were discomforted when they did so. For their part, the Arabs did very little to promote the initiative, probably because its timing was driven by a desire to deflect attention from the anti-Arab and anti-Muslim sentiments after the 2001 terrorist attacks. The Arab apathy essentially resulted in them getting nothing for the concessions they had just made. The international community commended the initiative but refrained from openly embracing it as the basis for negotiation. This progressive and invaluable proposal was thus another important missed opportunity for peace.

THE ROAD MAP FOR PEACE: AND ITS DISTORTION

As the United States continued to reach out to the Arab and Muslim worlds for partners in dealing with terrorism after 9/11, it increasingly understood that pursuing a negotiated Arab–Israeli peace would enable, or at least facilitate, Arab and Muslim cooperation in the war against terrorism. Tensions between Israel and its Arab neighbors both in the West Bank and Gaza as well as in Lebanon also clearly indicated that the status quo was not sustainable.

On June 24, 2002, President Bush announced, as official United States policy, his vision of two states, Palestine and Israel, living side by side, a first for a sitting American president. While doing so, Bush openly called for Palestinians to supplant its current leadership by a democratically elected one and to reform their institutions with support from the international community while denouncing terrorism. These were his conditions for Palestinian statehood. On the other hand, he called on Israel to support Palestinian economic development, to redeploy its forces to the lines of September 2000 as progress was made, and to freeze settlements expansion during the negotiations. This was to be in exchange for Palestinians ending incitements and cooperating with the Israelis on security measures. Both sides were called upon to refrain from unilateral measures that would affect the ultimate result of the Arab–Israeli peace process.

The United States, Russia, the European Union, and the United Nations, jointly known as the Middle East Quartet, quickly embraced the two-state solution concept but, because of differences on issues like the change of the Palestinian leader, could not formally adopt a performance-based road map for the resumption of negotiations until April 23, 2003.

Consistent with past practice, the Israelis, after some grumbling, announced their support for the road map, laying down 14 different reservations and conditions that essentially negated its basic foundation. Sharon had other plans in mind, primarily a unilateral and uncoordinated withdrawal from Gaza, counterbalanced by a substantial increase in settlement activity, as well as the construction of the separation barrier wall in the West Bank, and the extensive strategic deployment of the Israeli security apparatus all the way to the River Jordan. The Israeli military deployment had already started when Operation Defensive Shield, possibly the largest Israeli military operation in the West Bank since the 1967 War, was launched a few months earlier in March 2002. Sharon's message was crystal clear. Israel would seize large chunks of the West Bank where the settlement blocks were under the guise of "realities on the ground". In parallel and not unwittingly, Sharon partially eliminated the "demographic threat" which Gaza represented with its more than one million inhabitants. He also cut the cost of policing Gaza and guarding a few thousand settlers, with no ideological attachment to the land. Simply put, the tactical withdrawal from Gaza was meant as a prelude for a strategic redeployment in the West Bank. As Dov Weissglass, one of Sharon's closest advisors put it, the objective of Israel's unilateral disengagement plan was to "freeze" the peace process.

Egypt, among other Arab countries, complained to the United States that Israel was violating the basic premise of the road map. In spring 2004, in an attempt to entice the Israeli government not to completely reject negotiations, United States' assurances were offered, acknowledging and accepting the permanency of certain settlement blocks that had transgressed into Palestinian territory as well as the application of limits on the number of refugees to be resettled.

The negotiations on these texts intensified just before Mubarak's planned visit to Bush's ranch in Crawford, Texas, a gesture to try to reestablish some personal chemistry between the two presidents after a very tenuous first Bush presidential term. National Security Advisor Steve Hadley and Special Assistant to the President for Middle East Affairs Elliott Abrams had visited Cairo before the visit to brief Egypt on the said assurances. They also informed me of them in Washington. I immediately registered my very strong reservations, on both the content and timing, to Cairo after having already done so to Hadley spontaneously.

After receiving a preliminary report from Egypt on the discussions with Hadley and Abrams, I again expressed my strong reservations to both my American counterparts and to Cairo. America was the main sponsor of the Arab–Israeli peace process. Providing assurances to only one of the adversaries and accepting limitations on the number of Palestinian refugees as well as the inevitable continuation of the major Israeli settlement blocs in the West Bank was not only inappropriate because it created an imbalance, but it was also illogical because it would prejudice the results of the negotiations. Doing so soon after Mubarak's visit would also be misinterpreted as a sign of Egyptian approval or acquiescence to these conditions. Thus, a few days later, I again contacted Cairo recommending that Mubarak cancel or postpone his visit to the United States. This was met by surprise in Egypt, with officials responding that the American president was hosting his counterpart at his home. Frankly, I was flabbergasted and firmly reiterated that I had arranged for the Crawford venue myself and therefore understood its significance. Nevertheless, I repeated my recommendation to the Egyptian Presidential Chief of Staff Zakaria Azmy to postpone the trip to a later date because it would be politically ill opportune with the assurances to be given to Sharon so soon after the visit.

President Mubarak came to Texas in spite of my recommendation. During his meeting with Bush, he twice personally registered our reservations about the assurances to be given to the Israelis. This, however, fell on deaf ears, particularly with President Bush who did not seem to appreciate the seriousness of these steps. During the meeting, Secretary of State Colin Powell leaned over toward me and whispered that President Mubarak should reiterate his position a third time. I asked Mubarak to do so, but he adamantly refused. He had had enough with Bush and suggested that I myself do the talking thereafter.

I explained to President Bush how wrong it was to give assurances to only one of the negotiating parties, contrary to the practice that was so effective in preparation for the 1991 Madrid Peace Conference where all parties got assurances. I also cautioned that the United States should not take unilateral positions on final settlement issues inconsistent with the agreed international norms for resolving the conflict. I urged him to leave these issues for negotiation among the parties. The American president calmly listened but then simply said, "Why are you taking this so seriously Mr. Ambassador? I haven't even read them yet." We were all shocked. Bush then told Mubarak that it was illogical to oppose an Israeli withdrawal from Palestinian territory, even if it was unilaterally and not in coordination with the Palestinian Authority as per the road map. This was either an intentional misrepresentation of the ramifications of the Israeli and American policies or an amateurish analysis of what was about to happen.

I could tell from the expression on President Mubarak's face that he had been completely turned off. After that, he literally refrained from participating in any further substantial discussions at the ranch. The sound of silence was resounding throughout the lunch that followed the meeting. Bush surprised us all after lunch by personally driving Mubarak around the rough terrain of his ranch, bouncing up and down the crevices and creaks. As I followed in another car with Powell, I could only imagine that Mubarak was truly regretting disregarding my recommendation not to come. Along with the discussions being useless, this bumpy escapade in Bush's Jeep over rugged terrain could not have been anything but agonizingly painful for Mubarak who had arrived in the United States with severe back pains.

As soon as we got into the American helicopter to fly back from the ranch to the airport, in the presence of the United States chief of protocol, Mubarak looked at me and said, "Now what do we do with this mess?"

On the short plane flight back, I drafted a letter to President Bush, reiterating Egypt's concerns and rejection of the assurances. Mubarak quickly approved it but, in spite of my prodding, it was only sent off until after he had traveled to Europe and the Americans had formally decided to go ahead with the assurances to the Israelis.

Needless to say, the American assurances did not encourage the Israelis to take more constructive positions in engaging the Palestinians. Quite the contrary, it emboldened them to adopt even more aggressive measures against the Palestinians and toward Arafat in particular.

CHANGING PALESTINIAN LEADERSHIP
AND THE RISE OF HAMAS

As the years progressed, my concerns and expectations regarding Palestinian power dynamics regrettably proved completely true. Palestinian leadership problems would be taken advantage of by their adversaries, and both Arafat and Abou Mazen needed to keep this in mind. I made this point clear to numerous Palestinian visiting politicians that America was important but would never side by them at the expense of the Israelis. Therefore, they needed to be effective on the ground in the Middle East and especially in the occupied territories. America was a closer that could be indispensable, but an "honest broker", it was not. Its domestic politics would not allow for that unless there was a clear American national security concern that made that imperative.

I also told my American colleagues that they were naïve to believe that changing Palestinian leadership would solve the problem Israel was insisting on sovereignty over the West Bank of the river Jordan, which they called Eretz Israel, which they ideologically believed was theirs. I also told them that unless they were determined to soon successfully conclude the peace process, they would burn Abou Mazen by precipitously projecting him to the forefront thus dooming him to become a failed leader. Arafat had the stature to take difficult historic decisions to survive failure. Abou Mazen could take courageous decisions but was much less resilient in the face of failure. Most importantly, the Palestinian–Israeli peace process gradually went from slow to a complete stop.

There is much speculation as to why Arafat passed away on November 2004, in a French military hospital to which he was airlifted from Ramallah. These remain unanswered questions well over a decade later.

Arafat was not infallible, but he was able to represent Palestinians in tenuous, dangerous circumstances. After his death, Abou Mazen was elected president of the Palestinian Authority. Yet even with the godfather of the Oslo Process who endorsed non-violence leading the Palestinians, the Israelis claimed they could not find a Palestinian peace partner. This is a recurrent false allegation especially by the Israeli right. As frustrations grew, violence among Palestinians and the Israelis increased. As much as Abou Mazen was committed to the peaceful resolution of this conflict, his Israeli and American counterparts were not providing him with political dividends to bolster his position among his people. The Americans mistakenly pushed for early Palestinian elections even while diminishing the credibility of the most moderate Palestinian leader among his people.

In an attempt to stop the breakdown of the peace process completely, Egypt held a summit in Sharm El-Sheikh on February 8, 2005, attended by the Palestinians, the Israelis, the Jordanians, and the Egyptians. This was unsuccessful. The head of Egyptian intelligence Omar Suleiman also cautioned the Americans, to no avail, against pushing for early elections in the Palestinian territories. In light of the increasingly difficult living conditions, support for the Palestinian authority was decreasing and popular support for Hamas was on the rise. On the January 25, 2006, Hamas won a parliamentary majority in the Palestinian legislative elections, and shortly thereafter, it violently evicted the Palestinian Authority from Gaza, politically isolating it from the West Bank. Ironically, this may have been even more than what Sharon was driving for with his decision to unilaterally withdraw from Gaza.

This new development left Egypt in particular with a difficult predicament. We were supporters of the Palestinian Authority, clearly uncomfortable with Hamas because of its ideological Islamist foundation as well as its rigid political positions on Arab–Israeli peace. But Hamas was now on our border and we had to deal with that reality. The day after Hamas took sole control in Gaza, I was invited by *CNN* news anchor Wolf Blitzer to appear on his Sunday morning television show. I had not yet received instructions from Cairo but openly said we would deal directly with Hamas on security and transit issues, but not change our political decisions regarding the peace process. As could be expected, there were frequent problems on the border, but ultimately a tense modus vivendi was established.

America, for its part, was not showing much resolve for Palestinian–Israeli peacemaking. In fact, it appeared increasingly distracted by other events in the Middle East including the 2006 Lebanon War which sapped much of the winds out of their sails. As the year was ending, Secretary of State Condoleezza Rice invited me to a closed one-on-one meeting. In spite of her tight schedule and heavy responsibilities, Rice had always been accessible to me. As a Soviet expert, she had not been particularly keen on the management of the Middle East peace process. However, she realized that it would not serve America's interests in the Middle East if the situation on the ground in the Palestinian territories were to explode. At the meeting, she informed me that the United States was contemplating reengaging on the Arab–Israeli peace process, particularly the Palestinian track. President Bush was however hesitant to agree and needed assurances that his Arab partners would be supportive. She asked me to convey this message directly and personally to President Mubarak and to inform her of his response to her on my return.

She then asked me what I thought Mubarak's reaction would be. After some traditional diplomatic procrastination to gather my thoughts, I responded that Egypt would naturally support Palestinian–Israeli peace, but probably hesitate about coming out in support of a process, which it knew nothing about. I reminded her of President Clinton's mistake in not briefing Arab leaders during the Palestinian–Israeli Camp David summit. She smiled and assured me that the administration would be transparent with its friends like the Egyptians, asserting that the objective was to conclude a peace agreement before Bush left office in 2008. She also reiterated that the basis for the negotiations were those that had helped evolve the Egyptian and Jordanian agreements with Israel, affirming that it was time to allow the Palestinians and Israelis to live in peace.

The next day I flew to Cairo where an official from the presidency met at the airport and escorted me directly to the president's offices. This was rather unconventional, given that it was late in the evening, well beyond when official business was normally done. On a second phone from his home, President Mubarak was as usual cordial and welcoming, asking about my wife and family first. Then, he specifically asked whether the message I was carrying was about the Americans intending to bomb Iran. When I clarified that it was about the Arab–Israeli peace process, I could sense Mubarak's decreasing interest; this was a broken American record that he had listened to before. Nevertheless, he had his associates arrange a meeting for me with him the next day, attended by a Prime Minister Ahmed Nazzif, the Minister for Parliamentary Affairs Mofeed Shehab, the foreign minister, and the head of intelligence.

At the beginning of the meeting, he asked me to introduce the topic and share the message I was carrying. He then asked the participants for their reactions, which were understandably overwhelmingly skeptical and suggestive of a negative response.

Mubarak then directly asked for my opinion. I responded that there was a good reason to be skeptical about another American peace process, especially one that was not yet clearly defined. Nevertheless, I told him that we could not negatively respond to anyone's efforts to pursue peace in the Middle East, unless they distorted the tenets of the peace process as internationally recognized. I added therefore that we were obliged to respond to the Americans with a well-considered but conditional "yes". I suggested this be conveyed in a letter from Mubarak to Bush, reiterating our support for Arab–Israeli peace, but registering the basic measures and steps that we thought were imperative for this process to have any potential for success. I then went on to enunciate what should be invoked in each of these areas. The foreign minister offered to have his team write a draft for the president's letter, but Mubarak responded that this should be done in consultation with the head of Egypt's intelligence who was taking an increasingly larger role in the management of the Palestinian–Israeli relations. Mubarak then instructed that the draft letter should be both reviewed and cleared by me before it was sent to him.

This was all done before my return to Washington and sent through direct communication channels from the Egyptian president's office to the White House. Having been in government already for over three decades, often entertained or frustrated by bureaucratic competition including in America, I took a copy of the message with me back to Washington. To my dismay, but not surprise, when I handed Rice a copy of the letter sent by Mubarak to Bush a few days earlier, neither had she seen it nor was she even aware of it at all. The White House had not sent her a copy of the letter. This was a reflection of inter-administration tensions and the lack of enthusiasm in some sectors of the White House, particularly from Abrams, who preferred the path of creating an interim Palestinian state rather than a full-fledged peace agreement. She thanked me for Egypt's quick response, while remarking that President Mubarak's comments were very close to those, I had initially conveyed to her.

The Annapolis Middle East Peace Conference convened on November 27, 2007, under Bush's leadership, with the aim of reviving the Palestinian–Israeli peace process. In attendance were Palestinian President Mahmoud Abbas, Israeli Prime Minister Ehud Olmert, and many others including the Arab countries and the Arab League. The 2003 Road Map for Peace proposed by the Quartet was revisited with the hope of its implementation. The conference ended with a joint statement, read out by Bush, saying that Palestine and Israel have agreed to launch bilateral negotiations. Olmert and Abou Mazen were to subsequently hold direct talks with the former showing a map of parts of Jerusalem as a Palestinian capital. Due to the sensitivity of this particular issue however, he refused to hand it over causing the Palestinians to hurriedly draw up its contours and scribble notes on napkins. Olmert's political career was, however, to quickly come to an end after being indicted on criminal charges. Consequently, nothing conclusive came of these talks or was achieved thereafter on the Palestinian–Israeli track for the remainder of Bush's tenure.[5]

THE OBAMA YEARS: WINDS OF CHANGE?

I first met Barack Hussein Obama as a Senator in the American Congress. Our discussions mostly related to the situation in Sudan and Africa. His questions impressed me because they indicated that he was thinking about the core issues rather than trying to register political positions to accommodate one or the other of his domestic constituencies. His follow-up

---

[5] After Annapolis: A Fragile Peace Process in the Middle East. (December 2005). Center for Security Studies at ETH Zurich. http://www.css.ethz.ch/content/dam/ethz/special-interest/gess/cis/center-for-securities-studies/pdfs/CSS-Analyses-25.pdf

questions also indicated that he had been attentive to what I had said. Both of these traits were to initially find expression in his handling of the Palestinian–Israeli conflict after his inauguration.

My understanding from Palestinian–American intellectuals such as Professor Rashid El Khaldi of Columbia University was that Obama had empathy for the Palestinian national aspirations well before being elected. He had recognized the double standards in denying them their rights and condoning the continuing Israeli occupation. Contrary to most new American presidents, he immediately jumped into the fray of Arab–Israeli politics in his first year in office, appointing former Senator George Mitchell, the renowned negotiator of the 1998 Irish Good Friday Agreement, as a special emissary for the Arab–Israeli conflict. He followed that by two fascinating speeches in Egypt at Cairo University in 2009, and then later at the Jerusalem International Convention Center in 2013 in Israel. In both, he showed empathy for Palestinians and Israelis, yet openly asserted that neither could fulfill their aspirations for nationhood and/or security without finding ways to accommodate the aspirations of their adversaries. Never before had an American president put the Palestinians and the Israelis on equal footing.

However, Obama missed a wonderful opportunity at the beginning of his first term by choosing incremental diplomacy over grand bold statesmanship for his Middle East efforts. After leaving government, I visited Washington in the spring of 2009 to speak at an event at Brookings Institution. Mitchell, whom I knew from years past, was there and took me aside. He told me he would focus on incremental measures that would build confidence, like reciprocally stopping settlement expansion and incitement.

I was against the expansion of Israeli settlements of course. However, I urged him to adopt a holistic comprehensive approach. The Palestinian–Israeli conflict was now down to the core issues of borders, Jerusalem, refugees, and security. In my opinion, they had to be dealt with as a package where the two parties would compromise in exchange for closure of the conflict through peace, fulfilling their aspirations for Palestinian nationhood and Israeli acceptance and security. I tried to convince him that the election of Obama, a young African American, was a larger-than-life event and that the adversarial parties would hesitate in rejecting his advice and openly opposing him during his first year in office if he called upon them to compromise in exchange for a comprehensive peace. This would not be true a year later when he would be treated like any other elected official. I stressed that these four critical issues are politically sensitive for the different parties, and they would not be able to compromise on them unless it was in exchange for complete closure of the conflict. I also very strongly cautioned Mitchell that pursuing an incremental approach was doomed to fail and would drown Obama in the minute detail of Israeli and Palestinian bickering and politics as has had many of the efforts led by Dennis Ross in the past.

Mitchell listened carefully but was clearly not convinced, emphatically reiterating that incrementalism had succeeded in the Irish negotiations, an achievement that he was legitimately proud of, but which I felt he was wrong in trying to emulate because after decades of negotiations we had already gone beyond that with regards to the Arab–Israeli conflict at that point.

After months of this incremental process, Mitchell announced the failure of his efforts in light of the Prime Minister Benjamin Netanyahu's refusal to stop Israeli settlement activity in the West Bank despite a temporary ten-month moratorium. This was the harbinger of a tense angry relationship between Netanyahu and Obama throughout the next eight years. I truly believe that initially, Obama personally wanted to move the Palestinian–Israeli conflict forward. As an ambitious politician, however, he was not about to spend political capital on something that he felt was becoming increasingly unachievable, even if he knew it was the right thing to do. In the years to follow, Obama gradually distanced himself from the Palestinian–Israeli conflict, mostly leaving it to his secretaries of state Hillary Clinton and then John Kerry. Kerry, particularly during the years from 2013 through 2016, pursued valiant but failed efforts that were often without any White House engagement whatsoever.

Between July 2013 and June 2014, when I served as foreign minister of Egypt, Kerry and I frequently met and consulted. The first topic was always what was happening in the "Arab Spring" countries. Once we went beyond that, the Palestinian–Israeli conflict was soon addressed. I was impressed by Kerry's commitment, but quickly recognized that he was making the same mistake of his predecessors by focusing mostly on the process, again with a flawed assumption that if the parties talked to each other enough, they would be able to find solutions (Fig. 4.1).

Israeli intransigence essentially deviated Kerry's goal away from concluding a detailed Palestinian–Israeli peace to achieving a framework agreement which would establish a set of principles without precisely ironing out the details. I felt strongly that the Palestinian–Israeli conflict and efforts to resolve it had gone far beyond that after the Oslo process. Any attempt to reestablish principles would in effect be at the expense of well-established ones, especially with a right-leaning Israeli government that did not believe in a sovereign Palestinian state beside Israel.

I repeatedly cautioned Kerry about limiting our ambitions under Israeli pressure and was particularly against a framework agreement, which, in many ways, would be a regression on years of work on this track. I publicly made that known at a meeting he held with Arab foreign ministers in Paris in 2014. To my astonishment, all of them including the Palestinian foreign minister went along with the idea of a framework agreement. Only a few weeks earlier, while I was passing through Paris en route to another international engagement, I had met Yitzhak Molcho, the special advisor to the Israeli prime minister. He first argued that the Palestinians were not real partners for peace. Then candidly and at length ridiculing Kerry's efforts to achieve Palestinian–Israeli peace, he asserted that the White House was no longer seriously engaged in these negotiations and that a framework agreement, which was far-fetched, was nothing but a face-saving formula that would also remain unimplemented.

READING THROUGH 50 YEARS OF HOSTILITIES AND NEGOTIATIONS

Over the past half century, Egypt has been at the center of most of the regions' battles while breaking new ground whenever possible. Gamal Abdel Nasser was a larger-than-life leader who embraced anti-colonialism and ending occupation. He was widely recognized far beyond Egypt's frontiers. However, as president, he is also politically responsible for both the Yemen debacle in the early 1960s and the 1967 Naksa with its torrential implications on Egypt's leadership and Arab interests. Anwar Sadat courageously embarked on the October 1973 War restoring confidence and stature throughout the Arab world. He wisely embraced a new direction for Egypt's foreign policy, and would insist on retrieving all of Egypt's territory. However, he signed a unilateral peace agreement with the Israelis that diluted the Arab negotiating weight and thus derailed, or at least postponed, any possibility of a comprehensive Arab–Israeli peace. Hosni Mubarak succeeded in repositioning Egypt back at the center of the Arab world. He reestablished a sense of stability and security, both in the country and beyond, without wavering in his support for the Egyptian–Israeli peace agreement, or the virtual goal of comprehensive peace.

Egypt was the first Arab country to reach a peace treaty with Israel which it did unilaterally. Without discounting the ramifications of this step on Arab negotiating weight, its national security policies remained consistent, fully supportive of Palestinian rights and a comprehensive Arab Israeli Peace. The Palestinian issue was generically part of the mindset of older Egyptians. That generation had fought four wars with Israel and achieved peace with it as well. For them, equal opportunity and national rights for the Palestinians were almost foregone conclusions and irrevocable rights. I remember Yasser Arafat once telling me in 1996 that he had confidence in Egypt because it dealt with the Palestinian national agenda as an obligation that it took on enthusiastically, but never really tried to pursue its national interest by playing Palestinians against each other.

Leaders in Syria and Jordan, each with a different paradigm, supported the Palestinian aspirations with a particular nuance intertwined with their national agenda. The Syrian leadership, the most vocal among the rejectionist front, opposed independent Palestinian decision-making, which it felt should be subordinate to their strategic plans because of the Syrian sacrifices and hosting of a large number of Palestinian refugees. The Jordanian monarchy, on the other hand, had the unique challenge of preserving the Jordanian identity with a population that was in its majority of Palestinian origin. It also felt it had special responsibilities with respect to Jerusalem. As a result, history is witness to friction and violence between the Palestinians and both the Syrians and Jordanians.

For their part, Israeli leaders to different degrees from David Ben-Gurion to Menachem Begin, Yitzhak Rabin, and Benjamin Netanyahu all pursued opportunistic, mostly expansionist, politics taking advantage of balance of power that was in their favor. They were not concerned about whether these policies were consistent with international law or not, ignoring that the State of Israel was established by the United Nations pursuant, to a formula that also included a Palestinian one, side by side.

When Rabin and Shimon Peres moved cautiously to accommodate the new Palestinian reality, this was short-lived with the assassination of the first and the political decline of the second. In essence, the right, particularly the religious right, to which present Israeli government belongs, does not believe in a two-state solution with a viable Palestinian state in the West Bank and Gaza. Their opposition to it is ideological rather than security based. At the end of the day, Israel is the party most responsible for the failure of the Arab–Israeli peace processes. Regrettably, it became less interested in the difficult choices necessary for a conclusive Palestinian–Israeli peace, as it felt more secure after its peace agreements with Egypt and Jordan.

The most aggrieved, the Palestinians, while justified in their aspirations, bear some, if a smaller, share of the responsibility for these failures. Differences between the centrists with those on the extreme right and left of the Palestinian body politic could have been a good negotiating card if the Palestinians had a functioning political system and a governing structure. In their absence, however, these factions were often at cross-purposes, even occasionally aggressively working against each other weakening the Palestinian cause. The constant in-fighting among the different Palestinian negotiators was also highly detrimental to their negotiating capacity, as their adversaries easily preyed upon them.

The United States and the Soviet Union/Russia should also be blamed for not having accorded sufficient attention to the Palestinian aspirations. Causes and conflicts in the Arab world, from within our societies as well as from our neighbors, shifted focus and priority for regional and non-regional states. A decade of a unipolar world, with America at its head, created global imbalances in favor of Israeli right, at the cost of the Palestinians. In addition, the inconclusive Palestinian–Israeli peace efforts were detrimental to the credibility of the nascent Palestinian Authority established as the kernel of future governing bodies of the state of Palestine.

A number of important lessons can be drawn from all this. If future Arab–Israeli peacemaking is to be successful, leaders need to be truly committed to peace, which will require courageous, wise decisions with respect to the process, timing, and substance. They must have a commitment to their legitimate interests; a desire for progress; and empathy for the aspirations of their adversaries, coupled with a willingness to cooperate. To reach an agreement, leaders need to develop a partnership that is based on a shared desire to achieve a win–win outcome that can withstand hostility from sections of the public on both sides. Furthermore, leaders who fail to maintain a critical mass of domestic support for their negotiating position cannot conclude peace talks. National commitment is a sine qua non for success. However, it may not suffice alone. Garnering both regional and international support for these efforts can be advantageous and even imperative.

In the negotiating process, structure and timing are also of the essence. Bold conflict resolution has its time, but successful conflict resolution is not only about grand gestures. Rigorous negotiations are equally important. Negotiating over an extended period may be necessary; it should not, however, morph into an indefinite status quo because diverse political contexts and even a new set of players with different commitments emerge over time. The Oslo process is a prime example of this. It is important to determine when to pursue incrementalism and when to go for prompt closure. Each of the numerous Arab–Israeli peace efforts, especially those involving Palestinians and Israelis, provides ample evidence confirming these conclusions.

As far-fetched as a two-state solution may appear today, I think it is still the only peacefully negotiated option that could preserve the unique national identity of both Israelis and Palestinians. The Palestinian state will have to be based on the 1967 Arab borders with Israel, with minor exchanges of territory for the sake of unifying villages and continuity between Gaza and the West Bank.

Jerusalem will have to be the capital of the two states, and cooperative arrangements must be adopted for the management of overlapping services or connectivity.

The right of return or compensation of Palestinian refugees will have to be recognized by Israel and exercised mostly, but not exclusively, by the newly established Palestinian state.

Security arrangements for both states will be needed to ensure against surprise attacks and against the use of territories as launching pads against the other.

The Israeli occupation of Arab territories occupied in 1967 should end in exchange for security and normalization with the Arab world.

Finally, non-regional interference in the Middle East peace process needs to be more balanced.

Over the past 50 years, the choice of Arabs and Israelis to go to war or even more so to opt for peace was highly influenced by the impact of, and disincentives and incentives offered by, external players. However, America's role in the peace negotiations has increasingly become overly biased, distorting the process especially on the Palestinian–Israeli track and in many respects making it increasingly untenable. Its position on Jerusalem—particularly with President Donald Trump's unilateral recognition of Jerusalem as the capital of Israel—and its passive support for a two-state solution if agreed upon are surely unacceptable. Its domestic politics lean toward Israel and in a large part against basic Palestinian rights.

It is thus time for an international coalition to become the sponsors of efforts to pursue the peaceful resolution of the Arab–Israeli conflict. This coalition would include the United States and others supportive of a two-state solution based on the Madrid peace process parameters and committed to a set timeframe. In this respect, the Secretary-General of the United

Nations must play a more prominent and proactive role. It should not be forgotten that while Egypt, Jordan, and even the Palestinians negotiated with Israel outside of the United Nations, the relevant resolutions of the organization provided the legal foundation for these negotiations, especially the Security Council resolutions 242 and 338; and many others. The United Nations is the custodian of the contemporary world order, and it should therefore not remain complacent to world events or reactive to the whims of nation-states driven by power politics rather than international legitimacy. The rules and principles governing the world order should be applied without preference or prejudice.

The dire circumstances in which peace efforts currently stand should be a clarion call for resolving this historic conflict once and for all. Nevertheless, I am anything but optimistic that this will occur in the short term because of the political balance of power in the Middle East, and many of the parties involved in the conflict have shifted in interest and conviction away from concluding an Arab–Israeli peace.

The other path, of a one-state solution, would establish one identity at the expense of the other. This is not at all conducive to a peaceful resolution through the expressions of national identity and will ultimately lead to the reemergence of violence, not only among nation-states but among the peoples themselves. This will horrifically fuel the frustrations behind violence and intolerance while perpetuating human suffering. Today, the question is no longer what a two-state solution or a comprehensive Arab–Israeli peace would look like, but rather a much more ominous question, which is whether a comprehensive Arab–Israeli peace is in fact feasible. The absence of peace and fulfillment will ultimately keep the region in continuous strife and violence even if armed conflict is sporadic.

References

Center for Security Studies. (2007, December). *After Annapolis: A Fragile Peace Process in the Middle East* (Vol. 2, No. 25). ETH Zurich. http://www.css.ethz.ch/content/dam/ethz/special-interest/gess/cis/center-for-securities-studies/pdfs/CSS-Analyses-25.pdf

Moratinos Documents. (2001). *Jewish Peace Lobby.* http://www.jewishpeacelobby.org/wp-content/uploads/2015/11/TheMoratinosDocument.pdf

Ross, D. (2005). *The Missing Peace: The Inside Story of the Fight for Middle East Peace.* New York: Ferrar, Straus and Giroux.

CHAPTER 5

Efforts to Quell Nuclear Weapons Proliferation in the Middle East

*The Treaty on the Non-Proliferation of Nuclear Weapons (NPT),
the Arms Control and Regional Security (ACRS) working group
that emanated from the Madrid peace, as well as bilateral
Egyptian–Israeli negotiations were the focus of intense
complex efforts to correct the asymmetry in nuclear weapon
non-proliferation commitments in the Middle East.*

The Middle East has probably witnessed more military conflicts, large or small, over the last half century than any other region in the world. It is therefore not surprising that regional security, arms procurement, and proliferation of new technologies especially concerning weapons of mass destruction have remained contentious between Israel, the Arab world, and Iran.

Most Arab countries are not major producers of armaments but procure weapons systems from the major international arms producers. Some of them also enter into security arrangements with different superpowers. Others like Israel, Iran, and even Turkey achieve military security by establishing a highly sophisticated military–industrial complex domestically, as well as through security arrangements with major powers like the United States and the North Atlantic Treaty Organization (NATO).

Israel, in particular, has been aggressively pursuing sophisticated weapons systems with high technology and mass destruction capacity to counter what it argued in the past was the substantial conventional numerical superiority of Egypt, Syria, and even Iraq. If that was ever true, it is not so

© The Author(s) 2020   115
N. Fahmy, *Egypt's Diplomacy in War, Peace and Transition*,
https://doi.org/10.1007/978-3-030-26388-1_5

now. In addition to its technologically advanced conventional weapons capacity, it currently has the only nuclear program in the Middle East that is not subject to the full scope safeguard system of the International Atomic Energy Agency (IAEA). Even more ominously, it is reported to have over 200 nuclear warheads. It also remains the sole Middle Eastern state non-adherent to the Treaty on the Non-Proliferation of Nuclear Weapons (NPT), nor is a member of any of the international treaties or conventions prohibiting weapons of mass destruction. Moreover, Israel today is a major exporter of weapons technology.

The peace agreement between Egypt and Israel ended any serious probability of a major outbreak of military conflict between Israel and its Arab neighbors. The Israeli military is simply far superior to the Arab armies if one discounts Egypt, which has a strong military establishment. Generations of conflict had however instilled an Israeli culture of existential insecurity, which serves as a catalyst, or excuse, for a sustained arms race that included nuclear weapons and other weapons of mass destruction.

In light of regional instability and the increasingly expansive arms race, Egypt has actively strived to ensure sustained fulfillment of its military needs. In the early 1960s, it flirted with developing a domestic military–industrial complex that included nuclear weapons. These efforts proved difficult. My father had recounted to me that in the mid-1960s the head of the Indian Atomic Energy agency had visited Egypt with instructions to develop cooperation in the nuclear field between the two countries. After visiting the Egyptian nuclear facilities and before departing, he informed him that he would report back to the Indian authorities that the nuclear infrastructure in Egypt would not sustain a serious nuclear program. Egypt had shifted to acquiring its non-nuclear military needs from international suppliers, while at the same time becoming proactive in the promotion of different global and regional nuclear non-proliferation initiatives to cap potential threats through multilateral disarmament agreements.

Over two decades later, in the late 1980s, a senior Pakistani diplomat openly told me that his country was ready to expansively cooperate with Egypt in the nuclear field. I responded that Egypt was a non-nuclear weapon member of the NPT and would respect its commitments in this respect. Our interest and paramount principle were to achieve regional security at lower levels of armament.

EGYPT AND THE TREATY ON THE NON-PROLIFERATION OF NUCLEAR WEAPONS

In 1968, the United Nations General Assembly committee for international security and disarmament considered the draft text of the Treaty on the Non-Proliferation of Nuclear Weapons (NPT). The records of the proceedings in 1965 credit the committee's chairman, Ismail Fahmy, for helping develop the basic principles that would allow for the successful conclusion of the negotiations on nuclear non-proliferation three years after. Despite this, when the treaty was open for signature, Fahmy recommended that his government sign the treaty as a gesture of good faith, but to refrain from ratifying it until Israel did so, in order to ensure parity in nuclear non-proliferation obligations and capacity. Israel refused to do so, and consequently Egypt signed without ratifying the Treaty in 1968.

In 1974, Egypt and Iran jointly submitted a resolution to the General Assembly calling for establishing the Middle East as a nuclear weapons-free zone. This proposal was to gain widespread regional and international support with the exception of Israel, which remained an obstacle toward further measures in this regard. For decades after, Egypt regularly submitted the resolution at the General Assembly's annual meetings but, as the stalemate continued, it continued to make its ratification of the NPT contingent on reciprocal measures by Israel.

This changed in 1981. The Egyptian Minister of Electricity Maher Abaza wanted to pursue nuclear power generation to accommodate growing energy needs. As expected, nuclear power plant providers and their home countries asked Egypt to ratify the NPT to facilitate the provision of this technology, citing concerns over the management of the nuclear fuel cycle.

Abaza and Boutros Boutros-Ghali, the minister of state for foreign affairs, were both supportive of the ratification. The latter canvassed the Egyptian diplomatic missions and embassies abroad with expertise in this area before making a final recommendation to the president. Nabil El-Araby, the head of the mission to the United Nations in New York, was cautiously in favor. Ahmed Osman, the head of the Embassy in Vienna who also represented Egypt at the IAEA, was also supportive but raised several considerations to be addressed along with the ratification, including what could be done with Israel's exclusiveness. The head of Egypt's Permanent Mission to the United Nations in Geneva, Omran El-Shafei, shared with Cairo Mohamed El-Baradei's opinions and mine. They were both in strong opposition to adhering to the NPT without reciprocal measures from Israel.

All of this and more was then presented to a committee convened by the two ministers, which included senior members of the Egyptian Foreign Ministry and experts in the field based in Cairo. The committee voted in support of ratification, a strange and shortsighted decision because there had been no change concerning the national security concerns that prevailed when Egypt had previously declined to ratify. Israel, in fact, was continuing its development of sophisticated weapons technology. Ironically, the only committee member who voted against this measure was the one closest to Boutros-Ghali, his Chief of Cabinet Saad El-Farargi.

Regrettably, Egypt ratified the NPT on February 26, 1981, strategically damaging its national security and losing whatever leverage it had with the international community and with Israel to pursue universal adherence to the treaty in the Middle East or as a zone free of nuclear weapons. This was puzzling domestically and globally. The Japanese ambassador to the Committee on Disarmament in Geneva even asked me immediately after the ratification to explain the logic behind the change in policy, given that Israeli policy had not changed and that the 1980 NPT Review Conference had failed to adopt a concluding document. I did my best but struggled to explain something I myself did not understand or agree with. I doubt I was very convincing.

Even more ironic was that Egypt was in fact not fully committed to pursuing a nuclear power program for peaceful purposes. Several voices were quite vocal including Salah Ibrahim, a retired Egyptian ambassador who had worked at the country's mission to the International Atomic Energy Agency. He raised a number of legitimate points about nuclear security, safety, and the long-term problems of dealing with nuclear materials. President Mubarak convened a high-level group to discuss the matter. Possibly over energized by the occasion, Ibrahim metaphorically suggested that a nuclear power station was like a nuclear bomb on the ground. The experts and technicians seized the occasion to discredit his arguments, and the proposed program received the endorsement at the pinnacle of power in the Egyptian government.

Abaza and Ghali left the meeting confident and convinced that their plan was intact and would soon gain traction on the ground now that it had Mubarak's blessing. Soon thereafter, the devastating nuclear accident in Chernobyl was to traumatize the world, and Mubarak put the proposal to start a peaceful nuclear power program in Egypt back into deep storage.

THE QUEST FOR REGIONAL NON-PROLIFERATION PARITY: THE ACRS WORKING GROUP

The pursuit of parity in the Middle East in the commitments of states to the NPT and other nuclear non-proliferation obligations such as the creation of a nuclear weapon-free zone in the region had been a consistent pillar of Egypt's foreign policy. Egypt unsuccessfully raised this issue in its negotiations of a peace treaty with Israel. In 1990, with Iraq's Saddam Hussein and Israeli Yitzhak Shamir threatening to use weapons of mass destruction against each other, Amre Moussa, Egypt's Permanent Representative to the United Nations in New York at the time, asked me to come up with a disarmament initiative to calm the situation. I suggested a proposal to create a Middle East that was free from all weapons of mass destruction, nuclear, chemical, and biological. Even this initiative was based on the pursuit of equal reciprocal measures and commitments by all states in the region. Mubarak was quick to approve the proposal, which was publicly announced in April that same year. The proposal and the principle of reciprocal commitments to arms control in the Middle East remained the essence of the Egyptian position during the subsequent Committee on Arms Control and Regional Security (ACRS), which was one of the five multilateral committees established within the Madrid Peace Process Framework.

At the second meeting of the ACRS working group in Moscow in September 1992, I presented a working paper with Egypt's vision on the topic. The senior American diplomat Dennis Ross cautioned me, before I made my presentation, that Israel was not yet in the mindset to seriously engage on these issues. I responded that Israel had been the main advocate for the need to elaborate on the post-peace relationship, and that arms control was a post-peace priority area for Egypt. We were always seriously proactive in peace building and would thus continue to present our views on arms control in the manner we see fit.

Throughout the ACRS process, the essential point of contention between the Egyptian and Israeli delegations was Israel's rejection of any serious discussion on nuclear disarmament. Even when the ACRS committee developed a draft declaration comprising of numerous items that would have allowed for a multidisciplinary, extensive, and a comprehensive peace in the region,[1] the Israelis rejected it because of its inclusion of

---

[1] ACRS Statement 1994 (see Appendix IX).

references to nuclear weapons disarmament as well as the Palestinian request to refer to self-determination.

As the months progressed, it became increasingly evident that Israel would not seriously deal with the nuclear weapons issue; therefore, the ACRS was losing its utility for Egypt. We decided not to let the other working groups in the multilateral track continue on the matters of economy, water, refugees, and environment, which were particularly important to Israel. I candidly told the Director-General of the Israeli Foreign Ministry Uri Savir that if ACRS failed, Egypt would stop the other committees as well.

AN INDEFINITE NUCLEAR IMBALANCE

Coincidentally, as the ACRS process was starting to decelerate, the date for convening 1995 NPT Extension and Review Conference, which convenes every five years, was getting closer. This placed increased pressure on Egypt not to accept the perpetuation of the nuclear imbalance, but if also provided leverage to pursue what we strongly felt was a fair national security objective.

The United States and many other countries wanted to ensure widespread support for the extension of the treaty. The more prominent options were a 25-year revolving extension or an open-ended indefinite one. Both of these options were of concern to Egypt in the absence of concrete Israeli commitments to denuclearize militarily. They would perpetuate the nuclear imbalance or at best postpone addressing it for another quarter century if the revolving extension option was adopted. We urged the United States to seize the occasion to fulfill their commitments to us to convince Israelis to ratify the treaty.

At the same time, we directly engaged the Israelis. After many rounds of bilateral discussions, I suggested[2] to the Israelis that they provide us with a commitment to join the NPT within a year after they had achieved a comprehensive peace with the Arab world. They were at first unresponsive.

Then, weeks before the NPT Review and Extension Conference, at a working lunch at the Regency Hotel in Manhattan hosted by Shimon Peres, the Israeli foreign minister; Uri Savir, the director-general of the

---

[2] Israel would commit to joining the Treaty on the Non-Proliferation of Nuclear Weapons as a non-nuclear weapon state within one year after the achievement of a comprehensive Arab–Israeli peace.

Israeli Foreign Ministry; Avi Gil, the advisor to Peres; Moussa, Egypt's foreign minister; and myself, Peres emphasized that Egypt and Israel needed to look forward in order to create a more positive environment for the new Middle East agenda. He then surprised us by agreeing to give a commitment to join the NPT one year after achieving a comprehensive Arab–Israeli peace. He added that if this was agreeable to us, Savir would visit us in Cairo within a week to finalize the agreement after they had cleared it in Israel.

Moussa leaned over toward me, asking for my opinion in Arabic. I had been regularly briefing him on the issue and he was personally closely engaged on the subject. He was therefore surprised when I gave a negative response. Perplexed, Moussa first raised other issues with Peres, before conveying his approval of the proposal. He did not, however, forget to emphasize that he expected Savir to carry with him a written letter confirming this agreement.

As we walked out, Moussa again asked me why I opposed my own proposal. He laughed when I answered that it was because Peres did not have the authority to give that approval. I added that he would not send Savir to Cairo which would cause a serious misunderstanding when these high expectations go unfulfilled, especially since we were about to report the results of this meeting to president Mubarak.

Savir never came to Cairo, nor did we get any explanation. Legitimately angry, Moussa instructed me to draft a strong message from him to Peres outlining exactly what we had agreed upon on the nuclear issue. I was happy to comply but cautioned Moussa that the Israeli political system leaked like a sieve; therefore, if we put this understanding on paper, it was bound to be leaked and create heated intra-Israeli arguments. Moussa replied, "They are not fulfilling their commitments. Please prepare the draft."

The letter Moussa sent, while legitimate, created a storm in Israel, although interestingly, the actual language that Peres had committed to on the nuclear issue was not leaked. A short while later, during the annual World Economic Forum meeting in Davos, Peres screamed at me, asking why I sent the letter. Moussa laughed loudly when I responded that the letter had been addressed from Moussa and not me because he had not fulfilled his commitments. For the rest of that extended evening, Moussa and Peres argued heatedly about disarmament issues and the Middle East as a whole, in an angry, cantankerous environment.

Our failed negotiations with the Israelis were to have implications on the ACRS process and on Egypt's positions at the NPT Extension and Review Conference. The United States was leading an intensive campaign to ensure the extension of the treaty for as long as possible and with the widest support achievable. Thomas Graham, the deputy director of Arms Control and Disarmament Agency (ACDA), repeatedly visited me and other Egyptian officials in Cairo several months before the conference to discuss this matter.

The conference was held in New York from April 17 to May 12, 1995. Although Egypt was supportive of nuclear non-proliferation and general disarmament, it could not support the indefinite extension which meant the indefinite perpetuation of regional disparities on nuclear non-proliferation obligations when it was raised in prior consultations. We had even mistakenly hesitated to support the initial proposal of a 25-year revolving extension. Although long, it would have provided its member states with leverage to negotiate in every review cycle, especially as the extension period approached its end. More importantly, it was the best option available to us because we did not have the votes to block the indefinite extension alternative if it was put to a vote.

The non-aligned countries were initially against the indefinite extension as well as hesitant to embrace the 25-year revolving extension option. South Africa at the beginning of the Mandela era was larger than life but regrettably broke ranks with the non-aligned countries agreeing to an American proposal to indefinitely extend the treaty. This was a serious blow to the African and non-aligned solidarity agreement of indefinite extension.

The support for indefinite extension gradually gained ground, albeit with some serious tactical reservations even among some developed countries. It was slowly becoming inevitable. As things progressed, the Arab countries submitted a draft resolution calling for the establishment of a nuclear-free zone in the region and Israeli adherence to the NPT in order to show global concern emphasis on the region on the occasion of the extension conference and to underline the rejection of indefinite nuclear exceptionalism. This infuriated the American delegation.

Madeleine Albright, the permanent representative of the United States of America to the United Nations, charged into one of the meetings held at the organization's headquarters castigating El-Araby who had headed our delegation. She forcefully told him that she had been informed by the American Vice President Al Gore that the instructions sent from Cairo to the delegation in New York were to withdraw the Arab draft resolution. El-Araby explained that he was not aware of such instructions. I confirmed this to him, calling on the distraught Albright to discuss the resolution if she wanted to move things forward. The Egyptian and American delegations ended up having several rounds of tense negotiations over the next few days, most of them with numerous other delegations watching us.

Those of us at the conference in New York did not know then that Gore had in fact attempted to contact the Egyptian president. Mubarak was not particularly fond of the American vice president and was always annoyed about receiving calls from anyone but his counterparts in foreign countries. He refused to take the phone call so Gore then contacted Mubarak's senior advisor Ossama El-Baz, sharing with him America's concerns. El-Baz phoned El-Araby in New York, but the latter declined to take the phone call.

With typical American heavy-handedness, President Clinton then wrote to Mubarak complaining about what we were doing in New York, asking Egypt to refrain from its insistence on a Middle East resolution and allow the extension of the NPT without a vote irrespective of what decision was to be taken on Middle Eastern issues. Robert Einhorn, a senior American diplomat, informed me of the letter and was surprised when I said he had actually made my day. I knew Mubarak was always annoyed by these kinds of complaints, and his reaction would be exactly the opposite of what the Americans were looking for. In the middle of all this, Moussa called me in New York to discuss the negotiations, mentioning in passing Clinton's letter and Gore's repeated attempts. The foreign minister had been briefing the president in detail and wanted to reaffirm, that after all this, Mubarak's instructions were to stick to the positions we had taken.

Toward the final sessions of our negotiations, Albright told us that the United States could not accept the reference to Israel in the resolution adopted by the NPT extension conference. We responded that Egypt could not submit a draft resolution on the Middle East, which it sponsored without specifically naming Israel, which had the only substantial nuclear program in the region and remained a non-member of the NPT. Albright suggested that our resolution be put to a vote, with the United States abstaining but not opposing, if the extension decision was unanimously adopted without a vote. She was shocked when I immediately responded that all resolutions and decisions would receive the same treatment, either all voted upon or all passed without a vote.

After several heated discussions and a complete deadlock, I suggested to Albright that the only way for the Middle East draft resolution not to directly name Israel was for the three depository countries—Russia, the United Kingdom, and the United States—to become the sponsors rather than the Arab States. This would clearly give the Middle East international prominence and imply a sense of seriousness on the part of the depositories even if it did not directly name Israel. At first, Albright was startled and furious at my perceived audacity. She also felt assured that Russia and Britain would not accept this proposal but was surprised later when they did. The Americans came back to us with suggested language that was acceptable after some tinkering, and all three depositories agreed to sponsor the resolution. They also agreed that all resolutions decisions would be adopted without a vote. That was fine with us, but I still wanted to see the draft text of the extension resolution before giving my complete approval.

As all of this was going on, the Sri Lankan Ambassador Jayantha Dhanapala, who was the president of the NPT Review and Extension Conference, consulted me on the language of the draft resolution extending the treaty indefinitely. An astute diplomat, he wanted to understand our parameters before asking a direct question about how we would vote. I indicated that with all of the NPT's weaknesses, for the time being, it was better than nothing. We did not, however, support indefinitely extending the treaty because this meant the perpetuation of the lack of nuclear parity between Israel and the Arabs.

I left the drafting to Dhanapala, but added that we would not oppose language that was truthful, even if we could not support the results of the decision to be taken by the conference. However, I also made it clear that we would not go along with language that implied we had supported the extension of the Treaty. Later, Dhanapala showed me a draft which said that there was "widespread support for the indefinite extension". I explained that we would not object to this because the support did exist, but that we would make a statement, after the vote, to indicate that we were not among the supporters mentioned in the resolution.

On its final day, the conference adopted three decisions that were designed to strengthen the review process for the treaty, allow for the adoption of principles and objectives for nuclear non-proliferation and disarmament, and to pass the indefinite extension of the Treaty on the Non-Proliferation of Nuclear Weapons. It also adopted a resolution on the Middle East that endorsed the creation of a zone free of nuclear weapons and other weapons of mass destruction, calling for all the NPT parties to help take practical steps toward this objective. All four were adopted without a vote. El-Araby made a statement at the closing plenary indicating that we were not among those states that were supportive of the indefinite extension.

For many countries, including us, the conference was not a major success due to the indefinite extension. However, Egypt succeeded in giving prominence to regional nuclear non-proliferation through masterful negotiations from which several lessons could be drawn.

The first is that negotiators should always understand what their interlocutors really need and leverage that to their interests. Secondly, it is important to be ambitious but careful not to overreach in negotiations, which could ultimately prove counterproductive. The non-aligned countries, including Egypt, were wrong not to initially embrace the idea of extending the NPT for 25 years when international support for it was widespread. Once its unity was broken by South Africa, the worst option—that of an indefinite extension—was bound to pass, because the major powers and their allies would carry the vote.

America for its part also overreached. It did not really need to have the extension decision adopted without a vote. By doing so, it provided Egypt with negotiation leverage and was coerced into sponsoring a Middle East resolution without a vote as well.

The third lesson is that negotiators need to be keenly attentive and have the authority to negotiate. From the very start of the conference, Egypt held a bad hand. After the failed conclusions of the non-aligned conference focusing on the subject, the indefinite extension was essentially a foregone conclusion. Noteworthy, however, is that the authority entrusted to the Egyptian delegation by its own government enabled it to promptly take decisions or draft formulas to its advantage. Thus, although starting with a weak hand, by acting quickly and decisively, the Egyptian delegation was able to have a resolution on the Middle East passed. This was to set the stage for efforts over the next decade to create a regional zone free of weapons of mass destruction. I remember a Canadian diplomat whose country's position differed from ours, nevertheless expressing his admiration for Egypt's diplomatic professionalism, as well as its courage in standing firm and on topic, challenging its main donor head on.

The fourth lesson is that on national security issues, which are strategic in nature, preserving parity in military capacity and negotiations is of paramount importance. Egypt adhered prematurely to the NPT without Israel taking reciprocal measures the former should have argued vehemently in the closing phases of the Egyptian–Israeli Peace Treaty that Israel does the same or at least offer a road map toward its adherence.

Egypt's efforts to achieve nuclear non-proliferation obligations parity were to continue. The 2000 NPT Review Conference was convened without concrete progress achieved in the implementation of the resolution adopted in 1995. Consequently, Egypt was furious and therefore successfully insisted on naming Israel in the concluding document of that Review Conference. This was directed at America as much as it was at Israel because the former had not been serious about its commitment to the compromise achieved at the 1995 NPT Conference. The United States was focused on Iraq and Iran and essentially accepted anything including the reference to Israel for the sake of a document that sufficiently reflected their concerns toward these two countries.

By 2005, at the next Review Conference, the NPT was less the focus of attention than normal. The United States and Egypt both argued openly that the NPT would not significantly suffer if the conference failed to adopt a final document, as this would be less costly than compromising on their strong positions on the issues being discussed. Egypt's focus was mostly on the Middle East. The United States opposed Egypt's positions, but also had a number of other reservations regarding nuclear disarmament and the Comprehensive Nuclear-Test-Ban Treaty. To the disappointment of most other NPT parties, the conference concluded without a final document, with Egypt and the United States reciprocally exchanging accusations about who was responsible.

At the next NPT Review Conference five years later, Egypt's proposal to undertake consultations toward the convening of a conference on the creation of a zone free of nuclear and mass destruction weapons in the Middle East was adopted. A senior Finnish Ambassador Jaakko Laajava was later chosen to lead this task. His efforts continued for about five years before breaking down on a divergence of opinion between Israel and Egypt on whether to discuss the different elements leading to the establishment of the zone at the NPT Review Conference or to first discuss creating the security environment required before serious negotiations on creating such a zone could start.

Achieving parity in the legally binding commitments of the Middle Eastern States to nuclear non-proliferation remained of paramount importance for Egypt's national security. When I assumed the position of Egypt's foreign minister, I included this issue in my speech to the United Nations General Assembly in September 2013 emphasizing that this was essential for the stability of the Middle East. To move things incrementally forward, I proposed a three-step initiative that would start with the Middle East countries and the five permanent members of the Security Council depositing official letters to the United Nations Secretary-General in support of declaring the Middle East a region free from all weapons of mass destruction. This would be followed by an appeal to the countries of the region that have not signed or ratified the international conventions on weapons of mass destruction to do so before the end of the year. The third component was an appeal for international support to convene the overdue conference to establish a Weapons of Mass Destruction Free Zone in the Middle East by the spring of 2014 at the latest. Unfortunately, not much change occurred, and the stagnation that had tainted the Middle East peace process continued through the non-proliferation process as well.

Completely frustrated by 2015, the Egyptian delegation at the NPT Review Conference essentially took the position that it was time to call a spade a spade. There was no progress on holding the conference, and it felt that Ambassador Laajava's mission should end. Egypt's anger came after long years of trying to achieve security parity through disarmament rather than an arms race. Preventing nuclear proliferation in the Middle East, in particular, has been its priority. In its pursuit of compromise between the divergent positions, it had gone further in 1990 by suggesting that measures to control all three major weapons of mass destructions be placed under one umbrella and called for the creation of a zone free of all weapons of mass destruction in the Middle East. Israel refrained from constructively reacting to any of these proposals, and the international community broke all its promises to convince it to join. For Egypt to abort its own proposal without offering or adopting an alternative was, however, not smart diplomacy and should have been carefully considered beyond anger. Counter-suggestions and proposals keeping the NPT engaged on the subject would have been more beneficial, because restarting the process will be much more difficult.

Today, Egypt remains committed to security through disarmament. It has however learned hard lessons from its mistakes which have made the fulfillment of its disarmament goals ever more difficult. After repeated unreciprocated concessions, its own positions have hardened. Since mistakenly deciding to unilaterally ratify the NPT, it has refrained from signing the Chemical Weapons Convention in 1993 despite tremendous pressures from the friendly French government. Egypt also continued to refrain from ratifying the Biological Weapons Convention, which it signed in 1975 in good faith. And, although Cairo hosted the celebratory ceremony for the African Nuclear-Weapon-Free Zone Treaty, it has refused to ratify that agreement as well. It also continues to refuse to ratify the Comprehensive Nuclear-Test-Ban Treaty, even though the essential obligations therein are already part of the NPT. All of these documents are a response to Israeli refusal to join the NPT.

In essence, the Middle East has lost one of its strongest proponents of disarmament and arms control. It is today witnessing an increasingly rapid arms race and significant concerns regarding weapons of mass destruction. Highly problematic is the continuing existence of an Israeli nuclear program beyond the IAEA safeguard system, as well as the questions raised about the Iranian nuclear program before and after America's decision to withdraw from the Joint Comprehensive Plan of Action reached in 2015 between Iran and the five permanent members of the Security Council plus Germany. This is an increasingly ominous security environment. The international community may soon seriously regret the missed opportunities it had to deal substantively with nuclear proliferation pursuant to the numerous Egyptian-led efforts in the past.

CHAPTER 6

New Engagement of Sensitive Neighbors and Long-Standing Relations

Egypt's relations with Libya and Sudan were strategic, personal, and even emotional in many respects, creating volatile ebbs, and moving away from historicism to contemporary forward-looking engagement with Africa, Asia, and Russia was imperative in the quickly changing times.

On assuming office as Foreign Minister in 2013, I established the senior position of Assistant Foreign Minister for Neighboring States in order to emphasize the priority of our relations with Libya, Sudan, as well as Palestine and Israel. Egypt's relations with Libya and Sudan have been colored by numerous considerations such as Islamism, smuggling, economic cooperation, natural resource management, and border security. With Palestine and Israel, the Arab–Israeli conflict was prominent. And with the latter, arms control issues also came into play.

APPEASING GADDAFI TO SECURE BORDERS

When I first joined the President's Office of External Communications in 1974, it had a Libya desk which was very well plugged in on the ground and was clearly determined that Egypt would never be surprised by developments there. During the October 1973 War, Libyans financed Egyptian weapons procurement and provided strategic depth including by allowing the use of its air base as a safe haven for Egyptian aircraft. Libya's Muammar

© The Author(s) 2020 129
N. Fahmy, *Egypt's Diplomacy in War, Peace and Transition,*
https://doi.org/10.1007/978-3-030-26388-1_6

Gaddafi and Egypt's Anwar Sadat did not, however, get along well, especially after Sadat started to pursue a peace process with Israel. Egypt even sent its air force for surgical strikes across the western border when Gaddafi's opposition to its policies heated up.

Relations with Libya warmed up during Hosni Mubarak's presidency and became increasingly important as an attractive venue for Egyptian searching for employment opportunities. However, the management of Egypt's relations with Libya was anything but steady or predictable. Muammar Gaddafi had slowly eliminated the revolutionary partners with whom he overthrew the Senussi monarchy becoming the singular conclusive player in Libya and Egypt's only real source of information in the country. This high-level contact is always good to have, but never enough with a neighboring state, especially one with an increasingly mercurial leader.

As Gaddafi's support for violent actions became more controversial regionally and internationally, Egypt's relations with Libya became a subject of occasional concern. In June 1993, Egypt hosted the 29th Summit Session of the Organization of African Unity. Libya was under United Nations Security Council sanctions then, but Gaddafi was expected to make an appearance. The United States Ambassador to Cairo Robert Pelletreau contacted me as the political advisor to the Egyptian foreign minister, requesting that Egypt decline to give Gaddafi clearance to fly into Cairo. I was amused by its naivety but not surprised by the request. Egypt always respected Security Council resolutions but given out mutual interests, could not realistically force Gaddafi's plane down or even reject giving him clearance if he was determined to fly into Cairo.

The Americans, who had all their observation systems watching, first seemed comforted that the Libyans had sent a presidential motorcade toward Egypt's western borders entering from the city of Salloum. When Egyptian border authorities reported this to us, it came with the caveat that they would not rule out that the motorcade was empty, which meant that Gaddafi would nevertheless fly into Cairo. This was exactly what happened.

Gaddafi arrived at the conference center in Cairo with a large number of armed guards but refused to enter the meeting hall facility without all of the armed security entourage. To allow armed security in would have been a violation of the established procedures that had been applied to all other foreign dignitaries attending the event. Mubarak, who was in the main conference room attending a session, laughed loudly when he was told of the problem outside. He walked out, greeted Gaddafi in the garden, and escorted in the smiling Libyan president with only one-armed security guard.

A few years later, I rhetorically asked President Mubarak about the policies and trappings of our relations with Libya, clearly conveying a sense of concern. Mubarak's direct answer was that Gaddafi was mercurial if not even unstable. He had, however, secured Egypt's western border from any potential threats from Islamist extremism or any other substantial criminal activity. That was more than enough for Mubarak. In an endeavor to sustain this, Egypt regularly invited Gaddafi to Cairo every couple of months. Whenever this was not possible, an Egyptian minister or the head of intelligence were sent to meet the Libyan leader. Mubarak described this process as a "policy of no surprises".

One must admit that given how long Gaddafi stayed in office, this Egyptian policy was in fact successful for a long time. However, this policy suffered a serious and fundamental flaw because it completely depended on one person. This was to have serious ramifications on Egypt's security, years later, after Gaddafi's removal.

The early months of 2011 had witnessed rising turbulence inside Libya with the increasing inability of the regime to deal with the demonstrators. As violence expanded and horrific events occurred, the Council of the Arab League's foreign ministers met to consider a resolution to be adopted by them calling for a no-fly zone to be imposed as part of a larger package to end violence against civilians.

Nabil El-Araby, Egypt's foreign minister at the time, briefed Field Marshal Hussein Tantawi, head of the Supreme Council of the Armed Forces (SCAF), which had taken charge of the country after Mubarak left office. Tantawi strongly opposed the no-fly zone, cautioning about the expected flood of refugees, extremists, and weapons across Egypt's western borders if the Libyan institutions were to completely break down. However, El-Araby explained that the Arab League ministerial committee had forcefully condemned Gaddafi's use of heavy weapons indiscriminately against civilians and that the revolution was imminent. Very soon after the adoption of the Arab League resolution, the United Nations Security Council was to adopt Resolution 1973 of March 17, 2011, which a coalition led by the North Atlantic Treaty Organization (NATO) took as a mandate for extensive aerial bombing in Libya.

About a year later, when I was still working with the American University in Cairo, I had discussions with military experts from Western countries, including France, which had played a proactive military role in the intervention. I openly criticized the NATO operations in Libya, for having gone further than originally authorized by the United Nations, without any follow-up capacity to maintain law and order thereafter. The French expert responded that it was unrealistic for the Arab countries to have assumed that a no-fly zone could be applied throughout the Libyan airspace without aggressive actions toward ground forces and anti-aircraft capacities. Other military experts openly offered that the French President Nicolas Sarkozy was determined to act against Gaddafi, even unilaterally, and had placed air force units in operational formations before the Security Council resolution was adopted. After the NATO operations ended, numerous unsubstantiated news stories circulated that Sarkozy is interested in quickly eliminating Gaddafi because of a concern that evidence was about to surface that the Libyan leader has contributed to the French president's election campaign.

Personally, I felt that Gaddafi's rule, especially toward its final years, was an unacceptable aberration for both the international community and the Arabs. He did help secure Egypt's western border, but beyond that, the situation in Libya was always a powder keg on the verge of explosion. The foreign ministers of the Arab League who had met to consider the situation in 2011 were understandably concerned by the human losses, especially with Gaddafi's excessive use of violence against peaceful civilian protesters calling for democracy in the early days of the Libyan revolution, before it turned into a civil war. Nevertheless, the ministers were wrong not to consult with their military experts as well as with different international partners. It was imperative that they first ascertain what exactly would be done to diminish civilian casualties and the destruction of Libyan institutions and ensure that there were appropriate plans for the day after the international military operations were concluded. They should have insisted on predetermined follow-up measures to ensure law, order, stability, and security in Libya. Thus, although the NATO countries bear the primary responsibility for the chaos in Libya, the meetings at the Arab League significantly share in the blame over a situation that should have been handled much more astutely.

Thus, in a short time span, Egypt found itself neighbors to a failed state, without access to real information about developments on the ground. With the accelerated state of turmoil, chaos, and insecurity following the intervention, Egypt's western border suddenly turned from a tranquil oasis to a nightmarish vast reservoir for illegitimate weapons and extremists trafficking across our borders, as Field Marshal Tantawi had cautioned. I remember an informed official telling me in 2013–2014 that the price of illegitimate weapons in Egypt had decreased because the illegal supply crossing the border from Libya was overwhelming.

Egypt's unstable and insecure western border was a recurrent topic on my foreign policy portfolio as Foreign Minister in 2013–2014. Ironically, after four decades of a one-man rule, the question now was who actually represented Libya among the many claimants. At one point at a meeting in Rome I attended, there were two delegations both claiming to represent the Libyan leadership. Egypt itself frequently received numerous Libyan officials and politicians, including Khalifa Haftar, a former Gaddafi general who had fallen out of favor with the Libyan leader and taken refuge in the United States, and Prime Minister Ali Zeidan. Each of them had competing forces on the ground who challenged the authority of the others.

Trying to develop a political platform for resolving inter-Libyan disputes was not an immediate priority for Egypt in 2013. This was understandable, given our more pressing concern about securing our western border and reducing the weapons smuggling. Egypt also had its own concerns about increasing Islamist influence from Libya, which was already an issue on our eastern and southern frontiers, in Gaza and Sudan respectively. Thus, the priority was to secure the border by supporting Haftar. Although the highest level of military command felt he could win battles, they were initially skeptical about his ability to effectively sustain control over territory in eastern Libya after winning these battles. Given the security concerns on the border, Haftar's inconclusive but dampening effect on the flow of extremists and weapons across the border was nevertheless useful and his influence continues to be so as he enhances his military capabilities.

Years later, Egyptian–Libyan border security is still a problem, although the circumstances have relatively improved. Our intelligence institutions, both military and civilian, had gradually managed to strengthen their contacts in Libya.

There remains more than one authority in Libya as well as numerous non-state parties, making political consensus still hard to establish. Thus, although preserving security on the border remains the greatest priority, Egypt's sustained foreign policy has now been expanded to support a political solution that brings the different stakeholders in the West and East together, pursuant to the efforts of Ghassane Salamé, the United Nations envoy to Libya.

Salamé had revisited the UN-brokered Libyan Political Agreement (LPA) signed in Skhirat in 2015, which provided the basis for his predecessor's scheme to bring about a Libyan reconciliation. In September 2017, he presented a revised action plan in an attempt to address the standstill in Libya, in three stages. Firstly, by amending the LPA in search of a compromise between Libya's House of Representatives and the High State Council, the two elected conflicting authorities that essentially disagree on the details of power share and the possible role of Islamists in the future of the country. Secondly, by convening a national conference under the auspices of the United Nations. The third stage would be the drafting and ratification of a constitution as a key step toward holding presidential and parliamentary elections. Salamé started working on implementing this action plan which is necessary to ensure a more stable situation in Libya, but as expected it has been a difficult task.

Stability and security in Libya serve Egypt, even if the political composition of its governing bodies is not optimum. There are concerns about the potential inclusion of Islamists in Libya's political system. Hopefully, they will not acquire conclusive influence and remain counterbalanced by secular among tribal and clan leaders who, while pious and religious, are more turf-conscious than ideological.

SUDAN AND TRANS BORDER SECURITY: SIDELINING HISTORICAL GRIEVANCES FOR MUTUAL SECURITY

I assumed my duties as Egypt's foreign minister at a time of domestic transition, with considerable concern among the Western liberal democracies about the removal of an elected president. This warranted early visits to leading Western capitals to provide a clearer contextual framing of what had happened in Egypt. I planned to do so without delay. However, I was determined to make my very first trip abroad as foreign minister to Sudan to emphasize the priority we had for relations with our neighbors and our new regional focus on the Middle East and Africa.

Egypt and Sudan have had long-standing cultural, geographical, political, and historical connections spanning centuries. Egyptians and Sudanese frequently depict themselves as natural extensions of one another. During my tenure as ambassador in Washington, my Sudanese counterpart Khidir Haroun Ahmed flippantly introduced his country to the audience of a live television cultural program in the United States as being "South of the Pyramids".

Originally, one country, Egypt's relations with Sudan were always sensitive and complex. The two peoples were generally very close with deep-rooted personal relations. On the other hand, their relations were always fodder for populist politicians flip-flopping between highlighting the distinct sovereignty of the two countries, and grand schemes of full economic and social integration. Needless to say, border security, as well as delineation issues such as Halayeb, always came into play politically.

Ideological issues, especially the emergence of Islamist trends in Sudan, were often also exacerbating forces. This was bound to be a complicating factor after the Islamists were removed from power in Egypt.

The Sudanese government then, with its Islamist ideology, had been close to the Muslim Brotherhood in Egypt and thus anxious about the removal of President Morsi in June 2013. On the other hand, they were flattered and surprised that an Egyptian Foreign Minister would choose Khartoum as his first foreign trip, a level of recognition they had long strived for because it underlined their independence and importance.

I was a strong believer that Egypt's relations with Sudan had an existential nature given our long history—extended proximity with the Nile water flowing from Ethiopia through Sudan to Egypt and up to the Mediterranean. With Ethiopia's construction of the Renaissance Dam on the Nile, the differences between Egypt, Sudan, and Ethiopia were of paramount importance to Egypt's security. There were a number of economic issues that were also the subject of considerable attention, such as illegal gold mining in Egypt by Sudanese prospectors. All of these issues remain swaying in the wind. Certain and constant however is that Egypt's direct neighbors will continue to consequently affect its foreign and domestic policies.

I sensed from my first encounter with my Sudanese counterpart Ali El-Karty that this was to be a challenging relationship. He kept suggesting that Sudan would be a bridge between Egypt, the East African countries, and Ethiopia. He was caught off guard when I countered that Egypt did not have adversarial relations with any of these countries, but that, nevertheless, given our long-standing bilateral relations and common heritage, we expected Sudan to take Egypt's side. Our subsequent meetings throughout my year as Foreign Minister were all tough but highly professional and mostly amicable, as we dealt with a long yet petty catalog of mutual grievances, none of which, in my opinion, were unresolvable with the exception of the Nile Basin issue. Karty and I were generally able to create a better environment to deal with the various security and consular issues.

The topsy-turvy nature of relations between the two countries continued. Even with mundane day-to-day issues simmering and the leadership of the two countries issuing statements about the importance of relations, larger geopolitical issues emerged. Among those of greatest concern to Egypt was Sudan providing military facilities to Turkey and its warming relations with Qatar, over and above the remaining outstanding issue of the Renaissance Dam construction project in Ethiopia.

New Roads into Africa

Egyptians are known to frequently and proudly boast that their country is Umm el-Dunya (mother of the world). In the 1950s and 1960s, they were especially proud as President Gamal Abdel Nasser's influence resonated loudly and widely throughout the world. Consistent with his populist new world view, Nasser provided material and political support to national liberation movements in African and Arab countries in their quest to end European colonialism. Then together with India's Jawaharlal Nehru, Yugoslavia's Josip Broz Tito, Indonesia's Sukarno, and Ghana's Kwame Nkrumah, he founded the Non-Aligned Movement (NAM). A movement that played a prominent role over a half century to promote and safeguard the rights and interests of the developing world outside of the North Atlantic Treaty Organization (NATO) and the Warsaw Pact alliances.

As an original founder of the Organization of African Unity and the NAM, Egypt proved time and again that its interests and influence extended well beyond its borders and across Africa. However, unfortunately, as the years passed, due to the various domestic and global developments, Egypt's foreign policy toward its African neighbors, in particular, became a less of a proactive, forward-looking approach.

The Foreign Policy of Historicism

The pioneering generations of African leaders were highly appreciative of Egypt's valuable support in their independence movements. Among many others, Nelson Mandela frequently spoke publicly and fondly about his visits to Cairo and his admiration for Nasser. However, over the years, as political independence was established, younger generations of leaders across the continent naturally became more interested in looking at the future, particularly at economic and social development.

The Egyptian presidency under Anwar Sadat was less interested in Africa. The Egyptian Foreign Ministry, however, continued believing in the regional and strategic value of the continent. The Foreign Minister Ismail Fahmy appointed young Egyptian ambassadors with exclusive experience in the African continent to key positions. They included, among others, Salah Bassiouny and Ahmed Sedqi, who represented the rising stars of the Egyptian Foreign Service. Nevertheless, toward the end of Sadat's tenure, Egypt was only paying lip service to its African relations, leveraging its historical contributions much more than engaging in concrete practical present-day or future interaction.

President Hosni Mubarak's African policy started with the active involvement of the Minister of State for Foreign Affairs Boutros Boutros-Ghali. However, it gradually fell back into diplomatic pleasantries as the Egyptian presidency separated itself from Africa, especially after the assassination attempt against Mubarak in Ethiopia in June 1995.

In 2013, the African Union (AU) froze the membership of Egypt after the elected Muslim Brotherhood president, Mohamed Morsi, was removed. This was part of the AU policies given the history of instability in African governments in the post-colonial period. As foreign minister, I quickly made a round of phone calls to a number of foreign ministers throughout Africa and the secretariat of the African Union, with the view to reactivate Egypt's AU membership, and actively put our foreign policy back on track after the transitional chaos of the previous few years. To achieve this, I laid out a plan of action and embarked on extensive visits to East, West, Central, and North Africa. On these trips, after talking about development and the future of the continent, I would then raise the issue of Egypt's return to the AU. In addition, in the talks I held with officials in East Africa, I would also firmly raise the existential issue of preserving Egypt's annual share of the Nile water.

Most of the African officials I met expressed feelings of appreciation that I was addressing the future rather than the past. I recall meeting the Ugandan President Yoweri Museveni under a Sycamore tree in the garden of his countryside home. He started the extended meeting reminiscing about his relations with past Egyptian leaders. Then he suddenly asked whether I wanted to talk about water issues and why I had not brought our minister of irrigation as has been traditionally the case. He smiled warmly when I informed him that Egypt's ministers of housing and agriculture joined me for the trip and were meeting his prime minister while I was sitting with him. This seemed to break the ice, and he interjected that Faiza Abou El-Naga, Egypt's former Minister of International Cooperation, and I were the only two Egyptian officials he met who did not start their discussions with long exposés about how much Egypt had done for Africa in the past.

Similarly, on my first trip to Senegal in 2014, the Senegalese government arranged all the appropriate meetings, including those with the speaker of parliament and head of state. The traditional fanfare for visiting dignitaries was rolled out with Egyptian flags on several main streets. However, the meetings at first seemed to be stiff and rigid, with my hosts talking respectfully but rather formally about historical relations between the two countries, before moving to the obvious questions about recent developments in Egypt.

My meeting with Speaker Moustapha Niasse warmed up considerably when he realized that I was Ismail Fahmy's son. He had been a note taker for senior Senegalese officials in the 1970s and, in this capacity, he had visited Cairo and met with my father. The meeting with the Senegalese President Macky Sall also started with a brief historical reminisce on his part before he casually asked which countries I had visited on my way from Cairo to Dakar and where else I was to stop before returning home. He was very surprised when I explained that I was coming directly from and returning to Cairo directly and that I had wanted to start with Senegal in our reengagement with West Africa. My meeting with President Sall became highly engaging and even jovial when I mentioned that the Egyptian businessman Samih Sawiris was about to initiate a new tourism investment project in this West African country.

Equally telling was how the Ugandan, Tanzanian, and Senegalese presidents ended their meetings with me by asking whether I would return to visit again, expressing the hope that this would not be a one-time visit as had been the case before with other Egyptian officials. Indeed, as foreign minister, I continued to focus on Africa throughout my term in office, personally visiting the continent more frequently than any other region.

As part of my strategy for moving forward, development and cooperation were issues of primary engagement in all of my trips to African countries. Thus, I had Egyptian investors accompany me, whenever possible, to meet with officials and their counterparts from our African neighbors to enhance the chances for cooperation. This was particularly true in Uganda, Tanzania, and Senegal where our private sector already had investments in transportation and tourism projects. I also frequently invited different colleagues in the Egyptian cabinet to come and share their expertise with their counterparts in Africa, including Engineer Ibrahim Mehlab, minister of housing at the time, and Ayman Abu Hadid, minister of agriculture.

During my meeting with Museveni, I spoke at length about the new priority Egypt was giving to Africa, banking on our long heritage of relations with the continent, but looking more so at the future in a cooperative, collective fashion. Egyptian private business, in fact, had large investments in Uganda's railway sector, and we were aiming to increase these investments.

Similarly, my meetings in Tanzania with President Jakaya Kikwete and Foreign Minister Bernard Membe were exceptionally warm, although they too appeared surprised when I mentioned Egyptian private-sector interests in their economy, first asking what products we wanted to export to them from Egypt. Their surprise was especially evident when I explained that to Egyptian investors while actually accompanying me on the visit.

The third issue of priority was Egypt's suspended membership at the AU. The organization had sent a high-level panel to Egypt in the wake of Morsi's ouster, chaired by Mali's ex-president Alpha Oumar Konaré. The AU delegation urged the Egyptian authorities to implement the road map of July 3, 2013, by promptly reestablishing the normal executive and legislative bodies to facilitate an early resumption of our participation in the AU. There was some resistance to this position from South Africa, but the tide was definitely in our favor as we implemented the 2013 road map, our national interim plan.

During my overseas trips to African countries, I could sense the predicament that most African leaders felt they were in. They all emphasized that Egypt's absence from the AU was as much a loss for the organization as it was for Egypt. They agreed that the situation was an aberration that needed to be addressed. At the same time, however, they felt bound by the organization's decision to automatically freeze the membership of any country that deposed an elected president. Numerous African leaders emphasized that they would play a more active role in lifting the suspension of Egypt's membership while urging me to expedite the implementation of the Egyptian road map, especially holding of the presidential elections.

Just before the election of El-Sisi as president, I was attending Nigeria's centennial celebration. There, Nigerian President Goodluck Jonathan received me at one o'clock in the morning in his hotel suite. The Nigerian president thanked me for coming to participate in the celebration. He also humorously thanked me for staying up until one in the morning to meet him. I decided to take full advantage of the warm and informal mood of the meeting, responding that given that Egypt was 7000 years old, we have had numerous centennial celebrations, and are always ready to share our experiences in this regard. The Nigerian president broke out in laughter and affirmed that his country would play a lead in unfreezing Egypt's AU membership as soon as the Egyptian presidential elections were over. The President of Uganda Yoweri Museveni, as well as Algerian President Abdelaziz Bouteflika, also very strongly affirmed that the aberration would be removed once the election results were announced. Bouteflika, in particular, was very forceful on the matter when it was brought up during a visit that I made to Algeria in January 2014. At the meeting, he instructed the Algerian Foreign Minister Ramtane Lamamra to ensure that a decision be taken at the relevant intergovernmental committee at the AU where Lamamra had worked and enjoyed a strong standing. Everything was put into place for Egypt's return to the organization, so I drafted the speech El-Sisi was to deliver at the AU Summit in the wake of the presidential elections in Egypt.

The committee decision was unanimously taken on June 17, 2014, two days after I left office. After Egypt's participation in the AU was restored, and as I had previously suggested to President Abdel Fattah El-Sisi, he visited Algeria on his way back to Cairo to personally express his gratitude to Bouteflika.

THE NILE: RIPARIAN NATIONAL SECURITY

Cooperation with the Nile Basin countries on water-sharing was at the top of my priorities for Africa in 2013 and 2014. It was both a national security and economic concern. Egypt's relations with East Africa were paramount, and the interim President Adly Mansour and the national security team were supportive of this readjustment of foreign policy with an increased emphasis on regional affairs.

For centuries, Egyptians had lived on only 4 percent of its land mass in the Delta and the Nile valley. There are existential reasons for this. As is frequently said, "The Nile is Egypt's most valuable gift". This majestic river is in fact the most substantial source of water for the country, providing almost 97 percent of its needs. As a result, Egypt took part in several international agreements that determined the management of rights to the shared Nile water, including the Nile Water agreements of 1929 and 1959.

Years passed, and African countries liberated themselves from European colonialists, with national demographics significantly changing as population sizes expanded, creating both an increasing need for more water and urgent demands for economic development. These changes created challenges about how to accommodate development demands with the historical water rights and the proportionately equitable use of the generous amount of water flowing through the 4000 miles of the river.

Consequently, it was becoming a contentious issue for any of the Nile Basin countries to plan the construction of dams on the river's path without the consent of the other members of the basin. Driven by economic demands, Ethiopia has, for close to 50 years, frequently considered such projects. Given that it is an upper-stream country of the Blue Nile, its plans to build dams were always the subject of concern to other lower-stream countries, including of course Egypt. Historical sensitivities and the absence of strategic cooperative thinking on all sides frequently resulted in missed opportunities for finding solutions that could have respected historical rights and met development needs.

In May 2010, Ethiopia announced its intention to build the Grand Ethiopian Renaissance Dam (GERD) on the Nile, with a water storage capacity of 74 million cubic meters, measuring 155 meters in height and almost two kilometers in length. This was highly problematic especially for Egypt, which is already suffering from water scarcity, as it gets over 80 percent of its annual water consumption from the Blue Nile. This was five times the size of the original plan that was designed a decade earlier.

As our attention toward the end of the Mubarak era had moved away from Africa. Egypt was distracted further after 2011 during its transition process. Matters deteriorated in 2012 when President Morsi held an infamous meeting on the GERD with representatives of different political trends in Egypt. Regrettably, during the meeting, some participants made bombastic and inappropriate statements regarding the Ethiopian project, with some even making appallingly racist remarks. The meeting was irresponsibly and inexplicably broadcast on live television even without prior notice to most of the participants. Its proceedings were a disgraceful episode of ranting politicians figuratively beating their chests in artificial competition to appear more patriotic using the vilest racist expressions. The overwhelming majority of the public vehemently criticized these comments as well as the presidency for broadcasting the meeting. This session was understandably found highly offensive in Ethiopia, and a number of countries in East Africa.

At the time, Foreign Minister Mohamed Kamel Amre instructed embassies across Africa to engage in a public relations campaign to contain the situation, sending personal emissaries to East African countries in particular. He also attempted to reach a trilateral agreement with the Ethiopians and the Sudanese following a series of technical and political meetings, but these were not fruitful. Ethiopia was either in no mood to trust Egypt then, or it felt it best to seize this opportunity and pursue a more aggressive and ambitious project.

Egypt's strategic water needs and the expected ramifications of the ongoing construction of the GERD was the subject of numerous national security meetings at the political and technical levels very early on after the establishment of the July 2013 government. While Egypt needed to reassess its own water policies to ensure that water was not wasted, there was no question that it would remain highly dependent on the Nile. Thus, any potential disruption to the flow and availability of significant amounts of water, even temporarily, would be tremendously damaging. In fact, even Egypt's historical right to the Nile water, which was set at 55 billion cubic meters per year in 1929, was no longer sufficient. Moreover, there were concerns over technical issues related to the design of the dam in addition to environmental concerns related to the effect of the disruption of the flow on the quality of mud and the levels of pollution. In many respects then, this was an existential issue for Egypt. It gradually became highly emotional, attracting continuous public attention and making it very sensitive political issue. Reaching an agreement with Ethiopia and Sudan on all aspects of the GERD project, whether its size and capacity, environmental implications, security considerations, or water management, thus became a pressing priority that required immediate consideration.

I often raised the GERD issue with my Sudanese counterpart Ali Karti who once attempted to calm my concerns and suggested that Sudan would try to bridge the gap between Egypt and Ethiopia. "I never expected that Sudan would choose an equidistant point between Egypt and another country", I told Karti. I then added that it was not coincidental for me as foreign minister to choose Khartoum as my first overseas trip. Karti could easily become agitated, but he had a warm heart and he immediately became apologetic. However, even then, it was obvious to me that Sudan's position would be much closer to Ethiopia with respect to the building of the GERD. Although Sudan did not frequently suffer from water shortages, it often faced problems with uncontrolled floods and extended dry spells. The GERD, built at no expense to Sudan, would resolve both of these problems. I believe that this is the primary motivation behind the Sudanese position which started years earlier and continued when Egypt had a Muslim Brotherhood president and an Islamist majority in parliament, even though this Islamic posture was shared with the ruling majority in Sudan.

The problem and its resolution were triangular. Egypt needed more water, Sudan needed more water management, and Ethiopia needed more development. All three parties could not afford to continue their water or economic development policies, which were highly inefficient and wasteful. Correcting past mistakes would not suffice. In that sense, we were faced with a win–win or lose–lose situation that could not stand on two sides alone and would only succeed through urgent but difficult detailed negotiations and collective agreement. Rhetorical threatening statements by any of the three parties toward the other or an exaggeration of the actual needs of the three countries would serve little purpose. Equally dangerous would be providing false impressions of agreements or even substantial progress when they did not exist. This would diminish the negotiating leverage of the moderates against the hardliners within all three states. Thus, it would be tiring, cumbersome, and difficult to always try to fund a triangular success, but that was the correct way to handle these negotiations.

I repeatedly made these points in my numerous discussions with my Ethiopian colleague Tedros Adhanom and with Karti. I emphatically explained to both that, unlike Ethiopia and Sudan, Egypt did not have another substantial option as a water resource. Therefore, this was a national security issue with very little room for flexibility. Simultaneously, I candidly explained that in fact, we needed more than our historical rights in the Nile water just as Ethiopia needed more development and Sudan needed more water management. Egypt was nevertheless interested in engaging in a win–win process with the readiness to provide financial resources to both Ethiopia and Sudan to achieve their goals if Egyptian interests and concerns were met. I was clear that I would not be driven by public emotions or the pressures of domestic politics, but I also left no doubt that I would personally lobby against any international support for Ethiopian and Sudanese projects on the Nile until a consensus was reached among the three countries on how to deal with the issues related to the GERD project.

This was exactly what I did due to the seriousness of the issue. I raised Egypt's position on the ongoing construction of the GERD in almost every single meeting held with influential international parties, including the World Bank, the European Union, Germany, Japan, the United Nations Security Council states, and some Arab countries, specifically asking them not to finance the construction of the dam or any projects directly or indirectly related to its construction until after the three countries reached an agreement. I did this openly and repeatedly reported to Adhanom what I had done and emphasizing that I intended to continue to do so.

This infuriated the Ethiopians. On June 9, 2014, Adhanom was received by the newly elected Egyptian President El-Sisi. The day before, El-Sisi gave an eloquent speech at his inauguration ceremony on Egypt's future, including its foreign policy, which constructively spoke about the need to cooperate with African countries, including on issues of the Nile. Following the inauguration ceremony, the Ethiopian foreign minister first congratulated El-Sisi on his election and then commended him for his approach regarding the Nile. He then pointed toward me, thanking me as well for not having been drawn into the heated public debate and the emotional rhetoric about the GERD before adding that he nevertheless wanted to complain to the president that I had succeeded in effectively withholding all foreign support for the construction of the dam throughout the previous year. Both the president and I smiled. I then admitted to having done exactly what I was accused of but added that I was willing to personally embark on a fundraising campaign for the dam, including providing some Egyptian support if there was an agreement among the three countries on all aspects of its construction. El-Sisi continued to smile and said, "You see, we are cooperative and want to work together with you." Adhanom then invited the president to visit Ethiopia and address its parliament, an invitation that El-Sisi was happy to accept with the caveat at the time that it needed the resolution of the dam issue.

Although the presidents of Egypt, Ethiopia, and Sudan later signed a declaration of intent in March 2015 in the Sudanese capital, no tangible progress was actually achieved for the following three years in the technical negotiations or most importantly regarding water management issues. Even with the best intentions behind it, the Khartoum Declaration of Principles (KDP) was superfluous and non-binding, opening the door for misinterpretations and misunderstandings as we have witnessed since then. Even more importantly, with its flowery and positive overtone, it gave the impression to the international community that significant progress had been achieved, essentially weakening Egypt's strongest negotiating position because it opened the door for international financial contributions and private investments to the dam. Thus, where very few other options actually exist, existential issues like war, peace, and natural resources should never be addressed with ambiguous language left to interpretations based on the assumption of good faith which may not stand the test of time or changing political dynamics.

ENGAGING ASIA

With its geographical location and its material resources needs, the interests and actions of prominent international players have often affected Egyptian policies. While this provided opportunities for Egypt with interested parties, it was also required ensuring diversified relations and options to safeguard against the undue influence of any foreign party. I planned to reinvigorate our relations with both the old and traditional allies but also with newer ones as part of my vision for Egypt's Foreign policy.

Traditionally, at least in terms of contemporary Egyptian foreign policy, engagements with Asia have generally focused largely on Egypt's involvement with the Non-Aligned Movement (NAM). This was particularly the case with the close rapport the Egyptian President Gamal Abdel Nasser had with the Indian Prime Minister Jawaharlal Nehru and with the Chinese Premier Zhou Enlai. There were, of course, many other Asian countries of interest to Egypt during the past six decades in or beyond the scope of NAM, either for potential economic cooperation or mutual political interests. For example, this was the case with Pakistan, Indonesia, and of course Japan.

As NAM lost its prominence toward the end of the last century, Asia's place in the Egyptian mindset, especially among its leadership, was somewhat diminished. Nonetheless, Egyptian presidents, particularly Hosni Mubarak, made it a point to annually visit a number of Asian capitals. After the revolutions of 2011 and 2013, Egypt had a clear determination to rebalance its foreign relations, including interest in Asia. As Foreign Minister, I visited China several times. I also visited Japan, South Korea, and India, among other countries in the continent. Even if Egypt had not been the theater for considerable domestic transformation during those three years, a refocused outreach to Asia made sense as we moved forward, particularly given Asia's growing global role. Added incentive for the prompt outreach to Asia was its growing economies in China, Japan, and India, in particular, and their capacity and interest to invest in the Middle East.

In December 2013, I visited Japan, South Korea, and China where I candidly and forcefully spoke about the existential threats that my country had witnessed which had necessitated the exceptional response of June 2013, with the support of the Egyptian people from all walks of life. I added that Egypt was now in the process of rebuilding the country from within and simultaneously reengaging in its foreign relations, at the highest level possible, with different international stakeholders.

In Japan, I met the Prime Minister and Foreign Minister, and a number of other high officials. Our discussions focused on the Middle East, but I also emphasized Nile water issues. I explained that the project to build the Renaissance Dam in Ethiopia was highly problematic for Egypt, insisting that international financial support for this project be withheld until an agreement was reached among Ethiopia, Sudan, and Egypt. I also asserted that Egypt would be among the first to lobby for providing financial and developmental support for Ethiopia and Sudan once there is an understanding among the three countries.

The visit to China was highly interesting to me. The different meetings, including with the Vice President Li Yuanchao, the Chairman of the National People's Congress Zhang Dejiang, and the Foreign Minister Wang Yi, had the scent of a major power coming into bloom. The Chinese wanted to know what was happening throughout the Middle East. They emphasized that a country like Egypt, with a prominent role in regional security and stability, had a particular responsibility toward conflict prevention and management. In all of the meetings, my Chinese interlocutors chose to highlight that they would neither interfere in nor accept the internationalization of Egypt's domestic affairs.

Aware of the political turbulence that Egypt has been going through for a few years, a number of Chinese companies complained about Egypt's failure to fully honor its commitments to provide infrastructural support for their investments and arranged for economic sanctions against Egypt. In fact, on arrival in Beijing, the Egyptian Embassy informed me that a substantial financial levy had been imposed. Before my departure from Beijing, the Chinese government chose to revoke the sanctions after listening to the overview of the political developments in Egypt and the Middle East. The Chinese government also unilaterally announced a ten-million-dollar unsolicited gift for Egypt. I was told this would normally be done during visits of heads of state, but that China wanted to make a special gesture on the occasion of my visit. The Egyptian Prime Minister Hazem El-Beblawi decided to allocate the money for scientific research that year. I had several other occasions to visit China for multilateral conferences, and Foreign Minister Wang Yi repeatedly made it a point to either have a bilateral lunch or meeting with me. In all cases, China was determined to help Egypt, and this was highly appreciated.

I also paid visits to South Asia. However, I planned to visit India and Pakistan on separate trips rather than couple them together as had normally been the case. Three days were spent in India in December 2013, where in meetings with a number of officials, including the Indian Minister of External Affairs Salman Khurshid, we discussed world politics, the global order, Middle Eastern and Asian developments, and our bilateral relations including, of course, economic cooperation. It was a fascinating experience, and it did not go unnoticed that I was not stopping over in Pakistan. They were also flattered when I asked to visit Nehru's memorial site, an obvious courtesy gesture that for some reason Egyptian politicians had chosen to forgo. Indian–Egyptian economic relations, including Indian investments in Egypt, continued to progress during those years in spite of the instability and some problems regarding labor laws. Regrettably, I never had the opportunity to make the intended trip to Pakistan before I left office.

Overall, I think Egypt has been for the most part quite consistent in its relations with China, Japan, and India, with an occasional recalibration from time to time. Even during his one year in office, President Mohamed Morsi visited China, Pakistan, and India. With all these countries, there has been a significant focus on economic issues, although relations with China also extended into the military and industrial domain.

As for the Koreas, it was even a more delicate balancing act. I was determined to make the most of our bilateral engagements in a mutually cooperative manner. Our relationship with North Korea had consistently progressed in the second half of the twentieth century after the 1952 Revolution. This was especially true when Egypt was closer to the Soviet Union. In addition, as the Arab–Israeli wars broke out, the North Koreans had provided highly important military hardware that supported, among other things, the Egyptian Air Force. During that period, even as South Korea's economy grew, attempts by Egyptian diplomats to open up with South Korea were rebuffed by the Egyptian leadership out of appreciation for North Korea's support. This continued beyond the rule of Nasser, even when Anwar Sadat moved westwards, and during Mubarak's tenure.

However, as Egypt's military cooperation increased and became more sophisticated with the West, particularly the Americans, the issue of Egyptian–North Korean military cooperation became a more sensitive and problematic matter. This cooperation was frequently the subject of difficult and tense arguments between Egypt and the United States. I myself had been party to some of these discussions during my tenure as Egypt's ambassador to the United States. Over time, however, Egypt established full-fledged relations with South Korea, which surpassed those with North Korea in all areas except for the military. This military relationship was later contained as the international pressure increased on Pyongyang with its declared nuclear weapons capability.

Ironically, as government relations were contained, the prominent Egyptian businessman Naguib Sawiris made a significant private investment in North Korea in the telecommunications industry in 2013. In effect, he had collaborated with the North Korean government to provide cellular telephone services. When I asked him why he would find North Korea as an attractive investment opportunity, his immediate response was that the authorities in Pyongyang had a monopoly on the telecommunications market ensuring his company 100 percent market share. It was not, however, a priority or a politically auspicious opportunity for Egypt to attempt to develop its governmental relations with North Korea in the prevailing international environment. My contacts with my North Korean counterparts were therefore generally positive but contained, albeit I was happy to see our private sector engaged as we looked forward.

The pendulum of Egyptian–South Korean relations was going in the opposite direction, with substantial room for growth in the economic field as Egypt became an attractive consumer market for South Korean goods, especially automobiles and electronics. There were also opportunities in the investment market for South Korean technology firms and construction companies. On one of my visits to Seoul as foreign minister, I also witnessed the signature of a joint venture among Egyptian, South Korean, and American petrochemical firms for a facility in Egypt, with technical and financial support from Seoul.

I was also later invited in 2015 as the keynote speaker at a South Korean Middle East conference, which they now held annually. While there, a rather amusing event occurred during an organized visit to the demilitarized zone between South and North Korea. In the sensitive holding area, we were told not to look north for more than 45 seconds. Everything went as planned until the Israeli participant introduced himself as Mr. Halawa and politely inquired whether he and his spouse could take a picture with me. I agreed but first mentioned that "Halawa" (halva) was one of the most popular Egyptian confectioneries. He knew this very well, explaining that his father was originally from Alexandria and his family had had a halawa factory on the Egyptian northern coast. As we laughed at the coincidence, our South Korean hosts became nervous in light of the activity on the North Korean side of the demarcation line that was caused by our unintentional loitering far beyond the allotted time.

Indeed, the fragile balancing of Egypt's relations with the two Koreas was not always easy to maintain. During a visit to South Korea in September 2017, the Egyptian Defense Minister Sedki Sobhy told his South Korean counterpart Song Young-moo that Egypt has "severed all military ties with North Korea". Sensitivities arose, however, just a month later when a news report surfaced about a North Korean ship passing through the Suez Canal carrying weapons allegedly purchased by Egypt, a claim that the Egyptian Foreign Ministry denied.

RUSSIA AND EGYPT, NOT A RERUN

Over and above the obvious tangible returns of our relations with the countries in Asia, I personally had a strong interest in Egypt being engaged in discussions with the leading capitals of the world, new and old. The post-World War II order was no longer relevant. We had even surpassed the unipolar world with the United States singularly dominating. I appreciated the historical experiences of the past, but wanted to look forward and break traditional practices while still maintaining ties with the old superpower allies. This was vital in our recalibrated policies.

Egyptian–Russian relations have consistently been on a roller coaster since the 1952 Revolution in Egypt. Russia and its predecessor the Soviet Union have always highly appreciated Egypt's political weight in the Middle East even when our policies differed. At the same time, in light of different experiences and especially after the fall of the Soviet Union, Russia developed a concern that Egypt only turned to it when relations with more favored allies, particularly the United States, suffered. This was not completely true though they did have justifiable reasons to draw this conclusion. In 1952, President Nasser and the Revolutionary Command Council only reached out to the Soviet Union after being rebuffed in their initial contacts with the West. After the 1967 War, when Arab armies were defeated while using Soviet weaponry, Egypt started to rebuild its military again with new Soviet Weapons. Subsequently, Sadat asked Soviet military experts to leave Egypt in 1972 just before going to war, changing the political-military paradigm in the Middle East and diminishing the credit given to the Soviet Union for the results of the war even though Arab armies were actually fighting with Eastern Bloc hardware.

After the 1973 war, Sadat's focus became increasingly Western-oriented with particular emphasis on the United States at the expense of the Soviet Union. This occurred in spite of the efforts made by his foreign minister to preserve at least a modicum of balance in relations between the two superpowers. Sadat even repeatedly insisted that 99 percent of the advantage in the Middle East peace process was in the hands of America. The more than three decades of military cooperation between Egypt and the United States thereafter further solidified Russian suspicion of a general preference in the Egyptian ruling circle toward the West.

A country like Egypt would have significant amounts of its weapon systems from both the United States and the Soviet Union, even during the Cold War. This was testimony to its strategic importance. America like the Soviet Union before it used weapons' sales as a way to expand influence in Egypt, diminishing the presence and preventing the reemergence of Russia in the Middle East. Russia was correct to assume that Egypt's sentiments in the 1980s and thereafter were definitely moving away from it toward the West. Neither Sadat nor Mubarak had any great affinity toward Russia. The Russians also had other serious concerns, particularly whether Soviet weapons technology would be made accessible to the United States through Egypt concerns that were not totally unwarranted. In spite of all this, they always left a window of opportunity through which they could address Egyptian–Russian relations, given their appreciation of the country's regional weight.

Russia considered and provided calculated support to Egypt during the Arab Awakening, and particularly the June 2013 Revolution, a further confirmation of their continued interest in developing relations. Contacts were quietly made with the Russians early on, but they took their time before publicly supporting Egypt. A number of factors, including their concern over Islamist focus, drove their position. Ultimately, they concluded that this was an opportunity to regain a better presence in the Middle East and North Africa through Egypt.

Indeed, relations with foreign powers, particularly the United States and Russia, immediately came to the fore in discussions at the highest national security level in Egypt after the political changes of 2013. There were sentiments among many segments of the public and the Egyptian security services that the West had conspired against Egypt, pushing a regime change agenda in 2011 and containing Arab nationalism or the capacities of strong Arab states even before that. Those who did not believe in overarching grand conspiracies were nevertheless concerned by American policies that seemed to target strong Arab states, especially after the debacle in Iraq. This was further exacerbated by the overzealous Western endeavors to support political Islam and especially the Muslim Brotherhood.

Consequently, very early on after June 2013, the knee-jerk reaction at the highest levels of the Egyptian intelligence and security services was to call for a dramatic shift back to Russia through some high-profile public meetings with its leadership. This was based on the assumption that Russia would be immediately responsive, creating a political deterrence for the assumed aggressive Western intervention in Egypt's domestic affairs. As an advocate of a more balanced foreign policy that included concrete public steps to openly engage Russian and Asian leaders as well as Western counterparts, I did not object to engaging the Russians. I did, however, explain that Russia was a major power, which would evaluate past practices and even more so assess the situation on the ground in Egypt before committing itself one way or the other. In all cases, I pointed out that Russia would take its time before deciding on its next step. Therefore, while initiating private contacts with the Russians was understandable, Egypt should not have high expectations that there would be a quick dividend on this effort. This was the approach that was ultimately implemented.

Reengaging leaders of the United States and Russia on Middle Eastern and world affairs was high on my priorities and I was determined to reassert that Egypt was resuming its substantive foreign policy engagement in spite of its domestic priorities. I instructed my staff to send messages to our embassies in Washington and Moscow to convey to my counterparts my wish to have bilateral meetings with each of them in their capitals, either before or after our participation in the annual United Nations General Assembly meetings in New York during the last week of September and the first week of October 2013.

Russian Foreign Minister Sergey Lavrov responded well before the American Secretary of State John Kerry, and I visited Russia in September

2013 to continue the contacts that had been started with Russia soon after June 2013. A professional diplomat, Lavrov perfectly managed the different aspects of these kinds of visits, be they the official bilateral meetings, the press conference, or the working lunch that was held on that occasion.

The Russians were in listening mode during my first visit as was evident from their body language and the questions they asked. They wanted to assess the stabilization process in Egypt and its future prospects, but they were also worried about again being engaged by us only to spite the Americans. Proactive and professionally aggressive by nature, Lavrov did not make any requests nor did he offer any promises. However, he was extremely attentive to my choice of messages in the private and media engagements. Egypt was interested in a much more energetic relationship, irrespective of our relations with others. Both in the formal meetings and in my joint press conference with Lavrov, the message was underscored. I explicitly said that my interest in Egyptian–Russian relations was not a substitute for Egyptian–American relations, which I would continue to develop, but rather in pursuit of multiple engagements that could best serve Egypt's interests. He thanked me for choosing to address this question head-on and in public. This, he found, was an indication that I understood Russian concerns and preoccupations.

After we concluded our meetings, Lavrov indicated that Vladimir Putin was out of town but that I would be meeting Nikolai Patrushev, the Secretary of the Security Council of Russia. I admit to having been a bit disappointed at first. The next day, on September 18, Patrushev who was accompanied by four senior officials received me at the Kremlin. Judging by their body language during the meeting, I gathered that at least a few of them must have spoken fluent Arabic.

Discussions were expansive and detailed, covering Egypt's domestic situation, regional trends, geopolitics, and extremism. Patrushev also welcomed our vision for foreign policy, saying his country looks forward to Egypt returning to its place as a prominent regional player. We then discussed a number of pertinent regional relationships and ongoing conflicts. The situation in Syria was, of course, one of the most pressing issues we discussed, especially because it was interconnected with our relations with other regional states.

I expressed Egypt's condemnation of the Syrian government's violence against its people but at the same time stressed that Egypt was worried if extremist factions would prevail. Patrushev said Russia shared the worry about the lack of clarity for Syria's future but added that no concrete evidence has been provided to put the blame on Bashar al-Assad's forces for carrying out anti-civilian attacks. He insisted that it was important to allow the Security Council to exercise its role and criticized the United States for what he described as its lack of clear objectives regarding its role in Syria.

Patrushev then asked about Egypt's position on how to resolve the Syrian conflict. I told him that Egypt was in the process of working out the alternatives and its most appropriate role, asserting that our priority was to protect the sanctity and territorial integrity of Syria as a nation-state. I highlighted the increasingly challenging issues ahead for the management of the situation, given that the geopolitical tensions between Saudi Arabia and Iran were extending into Syria. Turkey's increasing aggressiveness was another concerning development that needed to be followed carefully. Patrushev and I also discussed the issue of disarmament in the region as well as Egypt's concerns over the Ethiopian Renaissance Dam project and its implications on our water needs.

As the meeting was ongoing, I was impressed, not only by Patrushev's understanding of the Middle East's regional politics but also by his personal command of the details. I made it a point to be strategic in my presentation but rigorous and factual in my arguments, conveying a coherent evidence-based vision and acknowledging the challenges facing us both at home and in the region. Our discussions went well over two hours and only ended when the Egyptian ambassador to Moscow urged me to conclude in order not to miss our commercial flight back to Cairo.

Escorting me out, Patrushev said, "We were concerned about Egypt but now I am confident that you have a vision for what you want to achieve and an understanding of the challenges and opportunities ahead of you. Russia will support you." The Russians were now ready to engage. My next mission was thus to manage Egypt's expectations and have them rise gradually.

On arrival to Cairo, I submitted a report to President Adly Mansour and briefed a number of senior Egyptian officials. I emphasized that I was comfortable with the outcome of the talks and optimistic about the future of relations. However, I also emphasized that the Russian system was traditionally slow in its reactions. Shortly thereafter, I attended the Egyptian government cabinet meeting and was faced with a barrage of enthusiastic questions about what to expect from Russia. Having followed Egyptian–Russian relations since the early 1970s, I strongly felt that we had turned a corner, but I also understood that the process and the dividends would be incremental and initially slow. Noteworthy as well was that the Russian capacity to provide tangible support was much less than what was available in its previous incarnation as the Soviet Union. I, therefore, provided my colleagues in the Egyptian cabinet with a positive but conservative assessment of the visit, underlining that while this was a new beginning, Russian institutions do not act quickly, and their bureaucratic traditions could well match those of the slow Egyptian bureaucracy.

A few weeks later in September 2013, while attending the United Nations General Assembly meetings in New York, I received a notification that Russia wanted to send their ministers of foreign affairs and defense on a joint visit to meet their counterparts in Egypt. This two-plus-two formula was one that they only used with a handful of countries around the world, strongly confirming that a page had been turned in our relations. All of this occurred before Kerry even responded to my earlier message about visiting Washington.

Egyptian officials welcomed the Russian initiative to rapidly move relations forward. However, some officials, not excluding a group of those who initially supported the engagement of Russia, were worried that this meeting could provoke a negative American reaction. They argued that we should not forget that the majority of our military procurement was from Western sources, especially the United States. I reminded my colleagues that I had emphasized from the outset that trying to gain and leverage Russia versus America was an amateurish exercise that would not work. I added that now we had an opportunity to engage Russia in serious and substantive meetings on bilateral and regional affairs, an opportunity which we should make the most of.

Foreign Minister Lavrov and Defense Minister Sergey Shoygu arrived in Cairo on November 13, 2013. There were separate meetings for Lavrov with me and for Shoygu with the Deputy Prime Minister and Minister of Defense El-Sisi. President Mansour also received the four of us and then El-Sisi hosted the two delegations for lunch that was followed by a photo opportunity of the four ministers.

The political message conveyed by the Russians resonated well beyond Egypt. The public irrationally reminisced about the close relations with the Soviet Union in the past, overlooking that the widespread majority in Egypt did not previously characterize those as golden days. Our governmental institutions quickly started preparing a list of requests to be asked of the Russians, with expectations running far beyond what could realistically be fulfilled. I was happy to be credited for having opened the door to this relationship, which I believe, is mutually beneficial then and now. However, I was also worried about the reaction in some government circles in Cairo because the last thing I was looking for was another donor–recipient relationship.

As we started to reassess the present and prepare for the future of Russian–Egyptian relations, the pace of engagement and interest shown by the Russians again surprised us. On December 25, 2013, I received an invitation from Lavrov for the Egyptian Foreign and Defense ministers to visit Moscow for a second round of two-plus-two consultations. Egyptian leadership consulted on how to react, quickly agreeing that a positive response was natural and mutually beneficial, but a well-prepared visit was imperative given that expectations had already reached levels that were getting difficult to manage. The Egyptian government machinery was instructed to prepare for the forthcoming visit as quickly as possible (Figs. 6.1, 6.2, and 6.3).

On February 12, 2014, I met El-Sisi at the Almaza Air Base, northeast of Cairo, and we flew off to Moscow on a small Gulfstream official jet. Still uncomfortable flying over Turkish airspace, in light of its support for the

Fig. 6.1 Nabil Fahmy and Abdel Fattah El-Sisi

Fig. 6.2 Nabil Fahmy, Abdel Fattah El-Sisi, Sergey Lavrov and Sergey Shoygu

Muslim Brotherhood, our pilot took a long route to Moscow, avoiding flying over Turkey completely.

The Egyptian delegation had prepared itself well for the meetings, but the flight added some additional time for personal conversations between El-Sisi and myself about expectations during the visit. It was clear to me from our conversation that the military was interested in a significant new relationship with Russia. I reiterated my view that the Russians wanted this visit to succeed, adding that I expected that they would openly listen to all our areas of interest, be they military, economic, or otherwise, without ruling out a priori any particular area. I indicated, however, that I would be extremely surprised if any contractual agreements were signed during the visit, explaining that the Russian bureaucracy simply does not work that quickly.

Upon arrival in Moscow, Lavrov hosted an opulent dinner for us. The next morning, we each held our extensive and substantive separate meetings with our counterparts. The red-carpet treatment we were given clearly

Fig. 6.3   Joint press conference between Nabil Fahmy and Sergey Lavrov

reflected a desire to engage Egypt. That afternoon, before leaving our hotel to meet with President Putin in his residence, El-Sisi and I exchanged assessments of the morning deliberations and concluded that there were, as expected, many openings with considerable potential but not any concrete deliverables beyond a positive change in the Russian political attitude toward Egypt.

Our Russian counterparts joined our meeting with Putin. Putin's Advisor Yuri Ushakov, who had previously served as the Russian ambassador to Washington during my term there, was also there. After a warm welcome, Putin repeatedly conveyed a strong sense of bitterness toward the West, especially the United States, for having treated Russia in an undignified fashion. Concluding each time, that he would regain his country's dignity and proper place in the global community, but not through or for the aim of a violent confrontation with the West, which would be detrimental to both.

Putin then focused on the dangers of extremism in the Middle East, its global implications, and the threats it constituted to homeland Russia—forcefully adding that Russia could not lend a blind eye to it. He then listened to our assessment of developments in Egypt and the region, obviously receptive and clearly attentive to the concerns raised regarding extremism and the implications it had on domestic, regional, and international security.

As we ended that meeting, I was certain that Russia would gradually play a more active role in international affairs and that the Middle East would be a top priority for the expansion of its political influence and military weight, especially in view of the vacuum that existed with American policies to almost withdraw from the region. What we have seen in Ukraine and in Syria, later, were therefore no surprises to us.

Lavrov had told me before our meeting with Putin that the Russian president was attending the Olympic Games in Sochi and had traveled back to Moscow only to meet us. He and our ambassador to Russia both reiterated that this was an indication of Russia's commitment to this relationship. When we concluded our meeting with Putin, the four Russian principals escorted us out to our cars. Nevertheless, just before our departure, Putin ran into a back room and came out offering El-Sisi a Russian ice-hockey team jacket with a huge star on its right. This was a friendly gesture, but it obviously did not rest well in the West when covered in the media. However, the benefits of the gesture were more than its liabilities and therefore the photo was not of particular concern to us.

On the flight back to Cairo, I explained on my expectations of the necessary follow-up before any contractual commitments were made. We were very satisfied that the realignment of our foreign policy, as part of Egypt's national political transformation, was effectively on course. The goal of reestablishing Egypt as an active and influential regional player was shared by El-Sisi. We then quickly shifted our discussions to the tasks and challenges ahead of us in the coming months.

A significant and substantial number of arms procurement agreements between Egypt and Russia have been concluded since then. Bilateral summits between the two heads of state have been frequent with strategic infrastructure projects, like the agreed upon El-Dabaa nuclear power plant. This continued despite the tragic Russian Metrojet Flight 9268 incident on October 31, 2015, that killed all 224 people on board, mostly Russians.

From 2015 to 2017, I have had the opportunity to briefly meet Lavrov several times in Russia in conjunction with my attendance of various conferences about the Middle East. His reception was always warm and personal, but throughout these meetings, I sensed that while there was an interest in engaging, there was some disappointment at the lack of sufficient substantive Egyptian contribution in the Middle Eastern affairs. Then in 2017, while attending the annual Valdai Club Middle East Conference in Sochi, President Putin joined the last session of the event and invited ten of us to dinner. In several of his references to the Middle East, especially Syria and the Arab–Israeli conflict, he would list Egypt as among the important players. Putin himself has also made it a point to brief El-Sisi on Russia's political and later military intervention in Syria. All of this confirmed that Russia appreciated the importance of Egypt's role in the Middle East but that it now expected more efforts for Palestinian reconciliation and the deescalation zones in Syria. Russia still clearly expected Egypt to play a more influential role as a counterbalancing force against extremist groups and as a more independent player, in contrast with the Arab Gulf states, which are perceived as being genetically security-connected with the Western world and the United State of America in particular.

Notwithstanding, in comparison to the past, Egyptian–Russian relations are converging. At the same time, there remain indications of lingering concerns and suspicions on both sides, particularly with the very slow pace of negotiations and Russia's heavy-handed approach with regards to the major joint infrastructure projects in addition to the continuous delays in the resumption of direct flights between the two countries. On the Russian side, the progression in the relationship remains positive, particularly at the highest executive level. Some stakeholders in the Russian system are more reticent and cautious, particularly after the election of Donald Trump in the United States. Others even argue that Russia stands to reap bigger gains if it were to focus on Levant and the Gulf areas. In this light, Egyptian–Russian relations have significantly progressed but are still searching for a comfort zone especially after facing a setback with the air crash over the Sinai, which led to a very significant reduction in the number of Russian tourists in Egypt, and the long cancellation of some direct flights between the two countries.

CHAPTER 7

An Indispensable but Uncomfortable Relationship

Egypt and the United States, a regional and a global power, respectively, were intrinsically engaged in the pursuit of their national interests. Nevertheless, Egypt's sense of heritage and American exceptionalism were often the sources of tensions and discomforts preceding both failures and successes, especially starting in the Clinton years. Later a baptism of fire, 9/11, democracy promotion and succession and revolutions provided food for thought on Egyptian-American relations.

The relationship between the United States and Arab countries, including Egypt, is essential for the interests of both America and the Arab world. Issues like the American–Soviet competition, the American demand for oil, economic and maritime security interests, the Arab–Israeli conflict, and combatting terrorism had continued to make the Arab world important to the United States, especially since the second half of the last century. This is equally true from the Arab perspective given America's role in the pursuit of peace with Israel, combating terrorism, influence in the global economy, military weight, as well as economic and security assistance.

Arab–American relations, however, have always been volatile and have become increasingly turbulent. From June 1967 to October 1973, American relations with Egypt and Syria were probably at their worst point. For the United States, accustomed to cheap energy, the 1973 Arab oil embargo came as a shock to America and shook the post-1967 American

© The Author(s) 2020
N. Fahmy, *Egypt's Diplomacy in War, Peace and Transition*,
https://doi.org/10.1007/978-3-030-26388-1_7

apathy towards Arabs. Nevertheless, the United States continued to look at the region from a Cold War prism, with the October 1973 War bringing American and Soviet nuclear arsenals almost face-to-face in the Middle East.

Ironically, while Arab fought with Soviet, the war became the exit visa for the Soviet Union from Egypt, strengthening Egyptian–American relations and establishing this new relation as the political pivot for America in the Arab world. American objectives in the Middle East at the time were twofold: diminishing Soviet influence and safeguarding Israel's interests and security. The Egyptians for their part were keen to engage the United States, albeit still not confident of its impartiality. Economic engagement increased after the 1973 war, with Sadat opening up Egypt's economy to the international and local private sectors. A high-profile delegation of chief executive officers (CEOs) from major American multinationals like Chase Manhattan Bank, General Motors, and General Electric visited Egypt to explore business opportunities. Also, cooperation in potentially sensitive areas was pursued, with the United States agreeing to build two nuclear power plants in Egypt. At that time, Egypt did not have a peace agreement with Israel nor was it a member of the Treaty on the Non-Proliferation of Nuclear Weapons.[1]

With the conclusion of the Egyptian–Israeli Peace Agreement in 1979, the bilateral relations between Egypt and the United States entered a new stage under President Jimmy Carter. This achievement became the centerpiece of relations for years to come, opening new doors for extensive cooperation. This reached its peak a few years after 1979 with the then-generous American civilian and military aid package to Egypt.

The cooperation continued through the next decade. Relations between Egypt and the United States under Hosni Mubarak and George H. W. Bush were exceptional. The two leaders were of the same generation and had a centrist similar mindset. They personally appreciated each other and both preferred quiet diplomacy. Egypt's support for the American-led coalition to liberate Kuwait raised the relationship to yet another, new level. In appreciation, National Security Advisor Brent Scowcroft took the initiative to ensure Egypt's military debt to the United States, which amounted to USD 7 billion and was greatly appreciated and forgiven.

---

[1] This never came into fruition, however, because of a lack of focus on the Egyptian side, which was suffering from a shortages of foreign currency liquidity while having it had no immediate pressing need for the reactor, all of which led the Americans to have second thoughts about introducing this technology into Egypt, which was not yet at peace with Israel and had not in the late seventies become a member of the Treaty on the Non-Proliferation of Nuclear Weapons.

Throughout the next two and a half decades, as the foreign minister's political advisor (1991–1997), ambassador to the United States (1999–2008), and foreign minister (2013–2014), I closely observed and actively participated in the ebbs and flows of Egyptian–American relations. My main contribution was to give it a wider scope. As the century neared its end, the relationship witnessing numerous difficult challenges, including American pressure for economic reforms in Egypt, the tragic 1999 Egypt Air crash over Rhode Island, the terrorist attacks of 9/11, the invasion of Iraq, and tensions over political reform in Egypt.

EGYPT'S INDEPENDENT STREAK AND THE CLINTON YEARS

The unexpected election victory of Bill Clinton was the beginning of a slow but continuous downward trend in Egyptian–American relations. Clinton had no preconceived ideas about the Middle East. It was not a priority issue for him as a candidate. It is noteworthy that he was elected at a time when his predecessor had already started talking about a new world order at the end of the Cold War. Interestingly, one of Clinton's first achievements in foreign policy was, in fact, hosting the Palestinian–Israeli Oslo signing ceremony. Thus, a pivotal Arab country, such as Egypt, would have served the American administration well if there was a meeting of the minds. However, the Clinton team did not appreciate Egypt's role in the same fashion as the previous administration.

This was mainly due to two reasons. First, the United States was uncomfortable to find Egypt frequently taking independent positions, particularly on matters related to the Arab–Israeli peace process, especially in favor of the Palestinians. This regularly infuriated the Clinton's State Department's Middle East Peace Process team, which held a more pro-Israeli view in comparison to the previous administrations.

More importantly, however, was that the United States did not appreciate the full extent of Egypt's significance in the Middle East as a regional stabilizing power. Egypt, however, is partly to blame. Given the novelty of the Egyptian–Israeli Agreement at the time, it received strong support from the American public and politicians. Egyptian foreign policy, on the other hand, slowly and mistakenly projected itself in America, and particularly in Congress, exclusively around its pioneering role in the Arab–Israeli peace process. In doing so, it missed an opportunity to nurture appreciation in America for the country's weight throughout the Middle East. Thus, with the exception of Egypt's contribution to the liberation of

Kuwait, which was instrumental in the coalition's legitimacy by overcoming Arab concerns over the West's possible ulterior motives, American politicians, for almost a generation, only viewed Egypt's regional role through the prism of peace with Israel.

As other Arabs joined in the peace process in the early 1990s, the allure of Egyptian exclusivity slowly subsided. Moreover, with every new generation of younger American politicians or administration principals, perceptions of Egypt's significance faded further away. Consequently, its support in Congress also decreased and, over time, the pioneering Egyptian Israeli Agreement was perceived as part of history. In addition, with Egypt's increasing support to the Palestinians against American policies, the Americans were determined to put a price tag on this independent streak.

Egypt, as a leading United States partner in the Middle East, had always received advanced American weaponry before it was made available to other Arab countries. This began immediately after the 1979 peace agreement, with the United States of America giving both Egypt and Israel aid. Egypt's very significant aid package initially exceeded USD 1.3 billion in military aid and USD 850 million in economic aid.

Starting in 1996, however, there were discussions about reducing the aid package given to Egypt, as a result of the recommendation of the United States of America Envoy to the Middle East, Dennis Ross. By 1998, Israel's economy was growing substantially, and there was no rational justification for it to continue receiving economic aid at the expense of American taxpayers. Rather than face requests to cut the economic component of the aid, the Israeli Prime Minister Benjamin Netanyahu, in an astute move, succeeded in signing a memorandum of understanding with the United States of America that transferred all the American economic aid to Israel's military assistance package. Egypt assumed that its overall package would remain constant, given that Israel's overall package stayed the same; there had been a tacit maintenance of a three-to-two ratio of aid given to Israel and Egypt, respectively.

However, forces in the Congress and in the Clinton administration maintained that the Egyptian and Israeli aid packages were distinct and, therefore, opened the door for detailed consideration and micromanagement by the Congress. The American assistance to Egypt was not repackaged as Israel's. Instead, the United States administration put forth a ten-year plan to gradually reduce economic aid to Egypt by 70 percent, with no corresponding increase in the military component.

As part of the debate over the aid package, American and Egyptian officials also actively engaged on Egypt's economic reform agenda to encourage a greater role for the private sector. Officials on both sides would mention American pressures on Egypt for economic reform as being a sore point during the Clinton years, but this was not exactly true. While Egypt did complain, the truth of the matter was that reformists in the Egyptian government actually valued the American demands for economic reform. It helped them argue throughout the Egyptian bureaucracy and government that these difficult measures were necessary if we were to benefit from foreign investment, while, in fact, these policies were consistent with Egypt's own national economic reform agenda. This process was an ultimate success, at least in terms of the objectives set, with both the Egyptians and the Americans satisfied.

BAPTISM OF FIRE: EGYPT AIR FLIGHT 990

Clinton's administration was fine with what Egypt was doing domestically while being uncomfortable with its strong commitment to the Palestinians. Clinton was a charmer even with Mubarak, who was of a completely different temperament and political mindset. American officials, however, wanted to politically engage Egypt on regional issues only when it fit their purpose and only on an ad-hoc, need-to-know basis. They openly shared information or proposals. This repeatedly annoyed Mubarak, who was about to start his third decade in office upon taking up my position as ambassador to Washington in late October 1989. Clinton, on the other hand, was just about to start the last year of his second term as president.

I reached the United States on the same day that Dr. Ahmed Zewail, an Egyptian–American, was awarded the Nobel Prize for Chemistry. Congratulating him was my first official duty. From the very beginning, I planned to change the perception of Egypt in America and expand the appreciation of its importance in different regional areas. I was keenly aware of the need to engage different constituencies throughout the United States, whether officials, politicians, business communities, think tanks, or others—needless to say, to expand the areas of agreement between the two countries and, equally important, to limit the number of misunderstandings that were bound to emerge.

I started my assignment with the tragic loss of hundreds of lives. A few days after my arrival, Egypt Air Flight 990 crashed in the waters of the Atlantic Ocean near Rhode Island on October 31, 1999. This was a baptism of fire for me. Given the location of the crash, the Egyptian government agreed that the National Transportation Safety Board (NTSB) would lead the investigation and submit a formal report. Notwithstanding, a highly capable Egyptian team joined the investigation.

Search and rescue operations were undertaken in a cooperative fashion and American authorities were constructive in working with Egypt Air to help with accommodating the families of the deceased who had traveled to the United States. It was a truly painful experience of going to Rhode Island with Jim Hall, the chairman of the NTSB, to meet with the families of the victims as body parts were retrieved. A few days later, a solemn ceremony was held to commemorate the dead. Vice President Al Gore, already a presidential candidate, had asked to come and speak at the ceremony. I agreed to that proposal, considering it a compassionate gesture. On the day of the event, however, his staff phoned to inform that Gore's participation would be through a videoconference, thus transforming it into a campaign stop. I did not appreciate or approve of that scenario and withdrew the invitation for the vice president to speak.

In the search and rescue operations, the first focus of the technical teams was to find the black box that contains both the technical data and the voice recordings in the cockpit. Once found, the Under Secretary of State for Political Affairs Thomas Pickering contacted me late in the evening, requesting that I listen to the tape of the cockpit voice recording. I initially hesitated, preferring to leave the matter to the experts. However, when he explained that they wanted to make every effort to prevent any misunderstanding, I went to the NTSB offices late at night to listen to what they had.

Chairman Hall greeted me and together we listened to the tape twice. Focusing on the actual content of the tape, after overcoming the strong emotions I had when listening to the last minutes of people before their death, I had different conclusions from those originally drawn by Hall. Except for the few seconds when the pilots were losing control of the airplane, everything seemed like a casual conversation between professionals. There was the normal banter, bureaucratic criticism, flattering, and pleasantries. Then Captain Ahmed Al-Habashi told his co-pilot Gameel Al-Batouti that he would use the toilet before passengers occupied all of them after meals, and he left the cockpit. Al-Batouti took command of the plane in autopilot mode. Briefly later, with some turbulence appearing, he said "*Tawakaltu 'ala* Allah" (I rely on God), turned off the autopilot, and manually flew the plane. Shortly thereafter, the plane started to quickly lose altitude, and Al-Habashi ran back into the cockpit asking Al-Batouti what happened, before overriding him from the pilot's position and calling on him to help in regaining control of the plane. Al-Batouti first appeared to be confused and hesitant for a few seconds before starting to cooperate with Al-Habashi. The plane had been descending from 33,000 feet to 19,000 feet first in a controlled descent, before going completely out of control.

After I finished listening to the voice recording, I asked Hall for his analysis. He responded that their initial inclination was that the crash was an act of suicide. This surprised me, and I asked him to explain the reason behind that conclusion. He responded that Al-Batouti had specifically used the words *"Tawakaltu 'ala* Allah", suggesting that its religious connotation implied that someone was about to meet his God. This indicated, in his view, that Al-Batouti was about to commit suicide.

I explained that what Al-Batouti had said was, in fact, a normal habitual day-to-day expression used by Egyptians of all faiths when embarking on new tasks. Leaving home at the beginning of a day, or a student taking an exam, or a surgeon before performing an operation, would casually say "Tawakaltu 'ala Allah". It was thus not surprising that a co-pilot would use the expression while switching off autopilot, to manually fly the plane. The direct translation of the phrase "Tawakaltu 'ala Allah", "I rely on God", is, in fact, quite close to "In God We Trust", a phrase printed on the American one-dollar bill; something I mentioned to American journalist George Will during a Sunday morning television interview a few weeks after the crash. All this aside, there did not seem to be any tension in the cockpit from either pilot or co-pilot before the beginning of the events. Consequently, I urged Hall not to jump to conclusions until after the completion of the investigation with the technical and voice data properly analyzed. He assured me that that would be the case. I left the NTSB headquarters disturbed at the human loss, but naively expecting that the investigation report would be concluded without any conflict of interest. I was to be surprised later that same evening when American television networks were broadcasting that according to the NTSB sources, that the use of the Arabic phrase "Tawakaltu Ala Allah" was an indication that the accident was caused by the suicide of the co-pilot Al-Batouti.

This was only the beginning of a year full of a series of disagreements. The investigative report of the crash became a repeated source of tension between Egypt and the United States as a result of the continuous leaks from unattributed sources in the United States and, not surprisingly, strong emotional reactions from Cairo. In addition, an accident of this magnitude and dramatic nature was bound to generate numerous theories, many more false than true. One was that a delegation of over 50 military officials was on the plane. There were security reasons not to do so and, as a matter of policy, those sent for overseas training were in groups of smaller size and would not frequently overlap with each other. Another rumor emerged more recently over a decade after the crash that some officers who were later to play a prominent role in Egypt were saved by predestined fate when they delayed their departure to a later flight. I have no way to substantiate or deny this because, in the days after the accident, I was overwhelmed with many issues and did not keep track of the travel plans of our military personnel at the time. This was the responsibility of the office of the Egyptian Military Attaché in Washington, which did not provide me with information relevant to either of these two theories, and I never asked them for it.

The American and the Egyptian teams participating in the investigative report could not agree on the exact cause of the crash and, consequently, chose to provide a narrative of the event with evidence-based data. The Americans focused on the fact that the plane had made a controlled descent from 33,000 feet to 19,000 feet for no logical reason when only one pilot was in the cockpit even though at that height and in the absence of technical difficulties, it was still recoverable. The Egyptian team was convinced that two of the six actuators, which are devices that provide balance in the plane's tail, were found to be malfunctioning when retrieved, which if occurred in flight could have caused the crash. They could not, however, determine whether the malfunction occurred during the flight or as a result of the crash itself. Neither side had conclusive evidence to provide a firm conclusion and closure. The final report of the accident issued by the NTSB was a narrative that was clear and factual, but it left it open for each side to draw its own conclusions.

9/11 and the Uproar in America

Most of Egypt's political circle was enthusiastic about George W. Bush's election victory in November 2000. I understood Mubarak's antipathy towards Gore who came across as condescending, always asserting his positions and never really listening to his interlocutor's opinions. I was, however, worried about Bush's political instincts. A number of his close advisors during the election campaign, known as the "Vulcans", were hawkish neocons who strongly believed that America needed to be more assertive in pursuing its interests. Besides, Bush was a born-again Christian, and I was concerned about an aggressive ideology faith-based approach to foreign policy.

Regrettably, I proved to be correct. His first term in office was replete with arbitrary policies that throughout our concepts like the "axis of evil", "regime change", and resulted in catastrophic decisions. Some of which were not even motivated by anything but retribution for the failures or challenges faced by his father, especially for not invading Iraq and removing Saddam Hussein after Kuwait's freedom.

This desire for a regime change intensified after September 11, 2001, when terrorists attacked the World Trade Center Twin Towers in New York and the Pentagon building in Washington. The attack brought the United States to a halt and shocked it to its roots. The attacks were horrendous, inhumane acts by foreigner terrorists. Having not been attacked on the continent for over 50 years, American society was used to living in security. There was no existential threat. Its strong military-industrial complex now faced a challenging unforeseen and nontraditional threat. This was an unexpected scenario. Society's cohesion, tolerance, and domestic institutions were to be tested. This subsequently caused apprehension in the West, particularly in America, towards the Arab and Muslim world, leading to a fundamental change in their perceptions of each other.

On the morning of September 11, 2001, I entered my office to where I bewilderedly watched an attack being reported on the television screen. My immediate reaction was that this was a distasteful simulation until I sat down and realized what was actually happening. Disoriented like anyone in America at the time, I hesitated for a few minutes before recouping and attempted to fulfill my obligations to report back to Cairo on the unfolding events. I contacted the Senior Director for Middle East and North African Affairs at the White House, Bruce Riedel, but to no avail. He was only to respond 24 hours later, apologizing that while there were plans on how to secure the principals in government, the younger staff simply went out on the street, and he had felt obliged to remain with them.

President Mubarak phoned me soon after the attacks were confirmed, asking for detailed information. He was surprised but patient when I explained that the institutions of government in Washington were in disarray and not yet in a position to communicate with foreign governments. I instructed our consulates in Washington and New York to keep track of the Egyptian community in both cities and report any casualties or losses.

I told my university-going children to invite their Egyptian friends to camp out on the Egyptian ambassador's residence grounds until further clarity and a sense of security could be established.

These events first raised concerns between the two countries then brought them closer together before driving them apart again, in an unhealthy pattern of the highly important relationship. Shortly after the attack, when the American governmental offices were functioning again, Riedel called me to vehemently complain that our newly appointed Foreign Minister Ahmed Maher had issued a statement drawing a moral equivalence between Israeli attacks against the Palestinians and what had just happened in America, which was an attack against civilians in a country that was not in conflict. He was also worried that this would blur the issue in the Arab and Muslim worlds and discourage the respective regions from cooperating with America in the war against terror.

I promised to convey Riedel's sentiments in language that I felt appropriate while assuring him that that was not our foreign minister's intentions. Riedel, however, insisted that I use the language he himself used. I asked him to convey the message through the United States ambassador in Cairo. Otherwise, I would use my own language while clearly conveying the sentiments. Combative as usual, Maher first took issue with the message but then agreed to allow me to handle the situation. I later returned to Riedel, confirming that Egypt had resolutely and unconditionally condemned the attacks. Maher was also gracious enough to personally do the same later (Fig. 7.1).

This first controversy quickly dissipated when Mubarak took the initiative to declare that the war against terrorism was not a war against Islam. The White House immediately contacted me, asking that I convey Bush's personal appreciation to Mubarak, which I did. Days later, the Assistant Secretary of State for Near Eastern Affairs William Burns called in the Arab ambassadors in Washington, including myself, as did other assistant secretaries with ambassadors in their geographical domains to provide lists of what to do and not do with anyone who could be engaged in supporting terrorism. This included not allowing foreign financing, refusing safe haven, and information exchanges between security services. It was quite intrusive and thus, coldly received by other Arab ambassadors.

Burns, who clearly noticed that I appeared relaxed during all this, asked whether I had any comments. I candidly responded that Egypt had requested the same measures from everyone since the mid-1980s, expressing then the hope that all states, including the United States, would

Fig. 7.1   Nabil Fahmy and George W. Bush

cooperate in a reciprocal manner. We had asked for this cooperation after extremists who were supported by America in its attempts to bleed the Soviet Union in Afghanistan later carried out attacks in Egypt and Saudi Arabia. Yet America was not concerned then and, as always, it was only looking for its own interests with little regard for the ramifications of its policies on friendly countries. I told Burns that the United States cooperation had regrettably not been forthcoming on anti-terrorism but that Egypt nevertheless remained resolute in its conviction that combating terrorism requires international cooperation, and we would do our best to cooperate with them in a reciprocal manner.

Burns thanked me for my reactions while affirming, at the same time, that all states needed to cooperate with each other, not only with the United States. Ironically, anti-terrorism cooperation under Bush and Mubarak quickly turned sour again as America incorrectly but typically decided it had all the answers. For the United States, changing regimes in the Muslim world or exercising an overwhelming show of force were the answers. Granted, the state system in the Arab and Muslim worlds did need reform. Societies needed to be more inclusive and progressive. Most of the recent terrorists were from the Middle East. However, this was not an exclusively Middle Eastern phenomenon. The United States had played a key role in allowing it to foster. Unfortunately, rather than provide long-term solutions, American anti-terrorism policies exacerbated the situation.

POLITICAL REFORM AND GOVERNANCE: AMERICAN MEDDLING AND THE CALL FOR DEMOCRACY

In addition to the military invasion of Iraq in 2003, the regime change component of America's war against terror also affected countries that America did not directly invade. During the first term, the George W. Bush administration had come out firing on all cylinders in their regime change agenda, treating friends and foes to a heavy dose of public lecturing. Egypt, a friend, was not an easy or complacent target. The administration correctly understood that if its reform agenda in Egypt were to succeed, it would have widespread ramifications throughout the Middle East. Arab constituencies and many Arab countries continued to look towards Egypt for direction on difficult issues. Thus, the Bush administration did not miss an opportunity with every Egyptian official to raise the democracy agenda and human rights violations, except our head of intelligence and minister of defense where security cooperation had priority.

This coincided with increasingly intense public debates within Egypt itself regarding governance and political reform. In the year 2000, three key issues were the focus of domestic debate. The first was the overbearing nature of the Egyptian state institutions while being unable to efficiently provide public goods and services. These dual grievances became the focus of social movements in the industrial areas and others in the wider public sphere. Movements like Kefaya, the April 6 Youth Movement, and the March 9 Movement appealed to the middle class and academics. They became voices to be reckoned with, thus affecting the political discourse on democratic reform among youth below the age of 25, which had compromised over 50 percent of Egypt's population. In conjunction with this, the role and influence of both the military and the police elicited diverse opinions amongst the emerging political voice.

The second issue was the role of religion in our society and, particularly, the issue of political Islam. This was mostly about the political role of the

Muslim Brotherhood, which was founded in 1928 by the schoolteacher Hassan Al-Banna to promote closer societal commitments to Islamic tenets. The Brotherhood, which remains Egyptian at its core despite its international networks, was officially outlawed by Gamal Abdel Nasser before they were brought back into the political scene, albeit while remaining outlawed, by Anwar Sadat in an attempt to counter what he perceived as threats posed by leftists. During Hosni Mubarak's presidency, the Brotherhood was allowed to operate, notwithstanding some security constraints, allowing it to capture a number of seats in the Egyptian parliament. Throughout all these years, neither the Egyptian public nor the Muslim Brotherhood itself was clear as to what role this organization, which had undertaken many religious, social, economic, and philanthropic activities, could play in the political sphere.

The third issue that Egypt was debating, as Mubarak was progressing further into his third decade in office, was that of succession. This, in particular, was a long and sensitive story.

Mubarak's Succession

Given their substantial economic and political interests in the Middle East at the turn of the century; Arab, African, and international stakeholders were closely following what was taking place in Egypt. It was, however, leading Western countries, especially the United States, that were more vocal in asking direct questions and making direct public remarks in this matter. This was particularly true after the 9/11 attacks. As Mubarak aged, it was assumed that change was not only inevitable but also imminent.

The overwhelming view in Washington was that spreading democracy was the best means to secure the interests of the United States abroad. This started cautiously with President Jimmy Carter and continued with the subsequent presidents, albeit with different degrees of emphasis. Towards the end of Bill Clinton's second term and especially after the 9/11 attacks, during Bush's presidency, this posture became more assertive and aggressive.

During my nine years as ambassador in Washington, it was evident that the United States was often encouraging democratic reforms in Egypt, as well as commenting on our domestic affairs. It strongly supported the decentralization of the government authority to municipalities would make frequent demands with respect to the Christian community in Egypt and the role of the Egyptian society. As Mubarak was progressing in age,

Washington was no longer betting on him in the Middle East of the future. In fact, it was frustrated at the absence of a clear transition or a succession plan with a rational timeline. Consequently, Americans became keen followers of the Egyptian rumor mill on whether Mubarak would run for elections yet again in 2010 and who were the potential successors if he decided not to do so. Personally, I could even sense clear American preferences for particular candidates as time went on. I cannot rule out that they actually did provide support for some, but I never saw concrete evidence of direct material advocacy.

Amre Moussa

Early on in the late 1990s and early 2000, the first to be mentioned as a potential candidate to follow Mubarak as president was Amre Moussa, a former foreign minister who had been appointed Secretary-General of the Arab League in 2001. He was liked at different levels of Egyptian society but was not supported by institutions with any political weight, be that the government, including the presidency, the majority party (the National Democratic Party, or NDP), or the security services. If elections were based on public popularity alone, Moussa would have been a strong candidate had Mubarak decided not to run for reelection in 2000 or 2005. However, given the complexities of elections, which are not simply a popularity contest but an expression of the strength of a candidate's grassroots domestic network and capabilities, Moussa was bound to have a very difficult time winning.

As Egypt's ambassador in Washington, it was clear to me that the United States did not like Moussa at the time. They considered him too charismatic and nationalistic, with an independent streak that would be difficult to manage, particularly given his strong pro-Palestinian stances that quickly became equated with anti-Israeli attitudes even within Egypt.[2] This was very clear when, during Moussa's last visit to the United States as Egypt's foreign minister, an overly aggressive Condoleezza Rice, then national security advisor, antagonistically lectured Moussa about the geopolitical landscape and future of the Middle East. I was surprised by Moussa's patience and calm demeanor as he chose to avoid engaging with

---

[2] This was to the extent that a popular song by the Egyptian singer Shaaban Abdel Rahim titled "I Hate Israel" had the following lyrics: "I hate Israel, Shimon, and Sharon, and I love Amre Moussa and his judicious, wise statements."

her in what would have been a futile debate. He was clearly instead interested in future cooperation as the next Secretary-General of the Arab League. After that meeting, I took the initiative to personally inform Bruce Riedel, on Rice's staff, that I found the meeting offensive and a complete waste of time.

Omar Suleiman

The next potential candidate who emerged as a possible successor to Mubarak was General Omar Suleiman, the then director of the Egyptian General Intelligence. He had a military background with extensive experience in the intelligence services. Upon Mubarak's instructions, he had also engaged with many different international figures, especially from the United States.

Suleiman was particularly well-positioned. He had a prominent role in matters related to the war on terror and was highly involved in matters with Palestine and Israel, and thus assumed an important role in Arab–Israeli relations. His political orientation was that of a centrist with a strong pragmatist foundation. As head of intelligence, he had Mubarak's support and was respected in Egyptian political circles because of his professional record. He was not, however, particularly liked among the higher echelons of the Egyptian military, or in the Ministry of Interior, many of whom felt he was overly ambitious.

Particularly important to the United States, Suleiman believed in the importance of an Egyptian–American relationship. The Americans strongly preferred him as Mubarak's successor although they never made a public declaration or acted on this as far as I am aware. However, I could sense this from the way they asked me questions. He did not fit the bill as a democratic leader but for them, a stable, moderate centrist who could guide a complex society forward was more important to safeguard their interests than achieving democracy per se; in spite of their lecturing about the merits of democracy, they believed Suleiman was well fit to achieve this objective.

For a considerable amount of time, Suleiman remained a strong candidate to succeed Mubarak, especially as rumors increased that he was on the verge of being appointed as vice president. This position had been left vacant by Mubarak for three decades. Like Moussa, Suleiman never broached the subject of becoming president with me as Egypt's ambassador to America. Only once did he sheepishly, and with a sense of frustration, mumble that Mubarak should decide whether he would appoint him as vice president to end the rumors. Eventually, however, Suleiman's chances petered out just like Moussa's.

Gamal Mubarak

The third and most controversial potential candidate, and who drew the most attention, was President Mubarak's politically active younger son, Gamal, who had qualities that most fit the United States "democratic agenda". He had Western education and was a supporter of the private sector. Gamal became more prominent starting from 2002, as a member of the National Democratic Party (NDP), the majority party that was chaired by his father. Gradually, he acquired an increasingly prominent role as an official within the party and eventually as an advisor to Mubarak himself. He was a strong factor in changing the NDP, establishing the Policy Committee as the central decision-making body in the party structure and, to an extent, in the government. The committee included old guard as well as new young blood, most liberal thinkers, and/or private sector members. This meant challenging the state of stagnation that catered to the interests of some influential figures and groups associated with the old guard in the party. It thus created sources of friction with the traditional stakeholders in the Egyptian political system, whether in the majority party, in the government bureaucracy, or among the military and police.

At the same time, neither the quasi-reformists in this group nor the president himself intellectually embraced or publicly promoted the concept of pluralistic governance. Despite the liberal Western posture, in some quarters, Gamal was seen as representing far too little change, or the wrong kind of change, because his father, the incumbent president, had kept the office for almost three decades, allowing the state to fall into unmasked stagnation.

Gamal's basic weakness was that he represented too much change yet too little at the same time. As the president was aging, he took on a higher political profile and gained more authority. Rumors spread about what political ambitions he may have. Most Egyptians could not accept the idea of a political dynasty and public opposition grew towards this potential succession plan. Institutional stakeholders that would have lost a degree of their authority or benefits with the emerging of a new political order in Egypt also significantly grew. Meanwhile, as the centers of power focused on Gamal in the NDP, fissures occurred within the party itself, even among members who were assumed to be supporters of political reform; it was all about jockeying for positions of power.

Like the two other possible candidates, Gamal never publicly or clearly announced his political ambitions while Mubarak was still in office. For his part, the president never brought up the subject of succession in any serious discussion with me. The issue did come up a few times when he would make an angry reference to a newspaper article or a remark made by someone on the matter. But, he would always vehemently deny any suggestion that Gamal would succeed him.

The Americans, who initially disliked Moussa and were enamored by Suleiman, they did not really know where to stand on the possibility of the succession of Gamal. As ambassador, I was actively engaged with think tanks and analysts in the United States monitoring any discussion on Egypt, including American reactions to the rumors about the potential presidential candidates. Unofficial American analysts would frequently ask me about all three. American officials would only directly discuss Suleiman and Moussa as potential candidates. If I remember correctly, no official directly asked about Gamal, although they were obviously following his political progression and would have been mistaken not to.

Indeed, Gamal visited the United States in many different capacities. At first, he came as an informal member of his father's delegations. Then, as a member of large non-governmental delegations, particularly from the business community. Infrequently, he came alone on private visits in his individual capacity. Over time during all these visits, I noticed the change in his temperament and tone. Always very polite and professional, Gamal appeared more assertive in talking about events in Egypt as the years went by. He was also shifting his posture from just being a catalyst for change to that of someone who would emphasize the need for the stability and security of the regime. In one of our last meetings in Washington, I asked him about his increased focus on security and whether it reflected concern in Egypt itself. He did not respond directly but mentioned concerns about Islamist trends, especially threats from Salafi movements.[3]

During his visits, Gamal was provided with the standard courtesies that embassies offer to figures of the civil society upon their visits to Washington. He never asked for more, nor was he ever provided with uniquely

---

[3] Salafism is an ultra-orthodox political Islam trend that has its intellectual roots in Wahhabism, and it has been gaining ground in Egypt since the late 1980s.

exceptional treatment. And, he was never dealt with as an official or presented himself as such. The most formal status he assumed with was in his
capacity as a leading member of the NDP. The limelight, nevertheless, was
always a little brighter and more clearly focused on him.

American officials frequently attempted to arrange meetings with
Gamal to assess his political prospects. In May 2006, Gamal visited the
United States to renew his pilot license. As he frequently did, he flew into
Dulles Airport in Washington then took a connecting flight to his destina-
tion before taking the same route in reverse on his way back to Egypt.
Gamal would usually phone me before arriving in Washington in case
there was an urgent need to connect and similarly on his way out. On that
particular trip in May, I received a phone call from National Security
Advisor Stephen Hadley requesting to see Gamal if he was stopping in
Washington on his way back to Cairo.

As the meeting had been formally requested from me by an American
official and after acquiring President Mubarak's approval, I arranged the
meeting and went with Gamal to meet Hadley. There was nothing of any
confidential nature that was discussed in that session. Most of the questions posed were about how the NDP was evolving and the role of the
private sector in Egypt. Yet this visit caused quite a stir in Cairo, with
numerous reports circulating about confidential talks by Gamal during his
stay in Washington. These rumors were inadvertently fueled even further
by a White House press release that referred to Gamal's renewing his airplane, rather than the pilot's license. I received many phone calls from
Egyptian media enquiring why I had not issued a statement before or after
the meeting. My response then was, as always, "I do not issue statements
about meetings of private citizens." I added that it was a matter left to the
discretion of the White House or the Egyptian party concerned to issue a
statement about the meeting or not. However, I do believe that the
American evaluation of Gamal had started to enter a more serious phase,
although no direct questions regarding succession had been raised.

Two years later, in May 2008, I received a phone call from an agitated President Mubarak who launched into an inexplicable diatribe
about American amateurishness and naïveté because of their consistent
references to Gamal succeeding him as president. I carefully slowed
him down in order to inquire about the reason behind his complaint.
Clearly irritated, Mubarak referred to an invitation that had been sent
to Gamal from "the Americans", asking how this was done without any
prior notification to the Egyptian Embassy in Washington. I politely

but candidly responded that I had no idea about the invitation and suggested that he ask Gamal about it. Mubarak calmly shifted gears downward, explaining that President Bush had sent the invitation to Gamal and asked how I thought it should be handled. Upon receiving a faxed copy of the invitation from the president, I realized that it was a handwritten note from Bush on his personal stationery, inviting Gamal to visit the White House.

Within minutes, Mubarak was back again on the phone, impatiently asking for my opinion. I informed him that this was a personal invitation in both form and content. Consequently, accepting or declining it should be done by Gamal and the visit, when it happened, should be executed as a "private visit", with Gamal meetings his hosts unaccompanied by Egyptian officials from the Embassy in Washington.

Two days later, Mubarak phoned me again to inform me that Gamal would come on a "private visit". The president, however, wanted me to repeat in precise detail what this would entail, acting more in his capacity as a father and raising questions about the logistics of the visit. I explained that the only help the Egyptian Embassy could offer was to arrange for transportation to and from the airport and hotel as part of the standard gesture of courtesy that the embassy often provided to friends or acquaintances who we knew were coming into town. I then explained that diplomatic courtesies were provided at American airports only for holders of diplomatic visas. Otherwise, everyone else was treated equally and would potentially be searched by security personnel at airports.

The visit was executed as planned, without the Egyptian Embassy's participation. After concluding his meetings with President Bush, Vice President Richard B. Cheney, and possibly other American officials, Gamal phoned and asked to see me before his departure the next afternoon. I invited him to lunch the following day on a sidewalk bistro in Bethesda, Maryland. Nevertheless, I did not ask him about his meetings, and he did not dwell on them beyond simply saying that the Americans had general questions about the future of Egypt but nothing specific.

By intuition, I knew that the Americans were trying to evaluate him. A few days after the visit, all of the talk in the think tank community about Gamal's possible succession died down, at least in the well-connected institutes. To me, this was an indication that while the Americans might have an intellectual preference for a liberal civilian like Gamal, after the visit they had concluded that he would be unable to manage a country as complex as Egypt in the tumultuous environment of the Middle East.

America's investment in the Middle East was too great to put at risk for liberal values. They were probably more comfortable going with a stronger candidate who could safeguard their interests.

The Muslim Brotherhood

As the United States carefully examined the inconclusive revolving door of potential Mubarak successors, it looked at other options, including the Muslim Brotherhood. Before, the developments in Iran in the late 1970s, America had been ambivalent towards Islamists. However, immediately after the removal of America's ally, Shah Mohammad Reza Pahlavi, in February 1979, the United States became determined to never again be surprised by political forces in the Middle East, including Islamists, and took steps to learn more and have contacts with them. America also used Islamists in Afghanistan against the Soviet Union.

As the years went by, the West intensified its interactions with Islamists. Some political circles in America, especially Israeli right-wing supporters and the neocons, promoted American engagement with Islamists as a counterbalancing force to Arab nationalist as well as a way to split the Arab world's commitments to and support for the Palestinian cause. They did so on the assumption that the short-term benefits from these policies would be much greater than the long-term dangers of a faith-based coalition developing in the Middle East. They even went as far as supporting convening Palestinian elections in 2006 although they knew very well that the Islamist Hamas was more likely to win at the expense of moderates supported by the Arab world.

The shock of 9/11, which was conducted by terrorists from the Middle East, complicated the matter. However, neocon calls to counter Arab nationalism became subtler immediately after the attacks but slowly picking up later. Instead, its proponents started arguing that America should split political Islam into moderate Islamists and other more radical forces that openly rejected modernization and the West. Erdogan in Turkey and the Muslim Brotherhood were quick to seize this opportunity, projecting themselves as the modern moderate face of Islam and the best antidote to extremists attacking the West.

Consequently, during Bush's and Barack Obama's administration's, American politics gradually accepted political Islam as an inevitable component of the Middle East political landscape. With the exception of the neocons, the rest of America had, until that point, accommodated Islamists without truly embracing them. An increasing number of the Egyptian

Muslim Brotherhood members frequented the Washington think-tank circuit and organized conferences on the Middle East, many of which were held in Qatar. The United States Embassy in Cairo's relationship with the Brotherhood also changed. The embassy had, in fact, been in touch with them through intelligence operatives early on as far back as the 1980s during Mubarak's presidency, testing the waters occasionally through traditional diplomats and consistently. Once the Muslim Brotherhood candidates were accepted in the Egyptian Parliament in 2000, this status changed and they were openly invited to the United States of America Embassy. Ironically, the Egyptian government condoned the earlier contacts but complained when parliamentarians associated with the brotherhood were united at the embassy.

This new development fueled conspiracy theories amongst an increasingly sensitive Egyptian leadership given the Brotherhood in Egyptian politics.[4] American's courting of the Muslim Brotherhood was a particularly sore point for President Mubarak who became increasingly suspicious of American intentions. This was further aggravated by the Bush administration's calls for reform in Egypt and regime change elsewhere. During my final years as ambassador in Washington, high-level Egyptian officials visiting the United States frequently directly asked the American officials about their relations with the Muslim Brotherhood. When President Bush received Prime Minister Ahmed Nazif in the Oval Office in May 2005, the latter asked the American president of such connections with the Brotherhood. The Americans always adopted an evasive approach with Egyptian officials denying any engagement with the group. Nothing could be further from the truth.

Consequently, every time this issue came up during an Egyptian official's visit to America, my assessment cable afterwards would reiterate that despite American denials, the United States, in fact, had its communication channels with the Muslim Brotherhood. I would reiterate for emphasis that America had changed its approach after the Shah of Iran was

---

[4] Although the Mubarak regime allowed members of the Muslim Brotherhood to successfully run for parliament and gain over 100 of the 450 seats, the Brotherhood parliamentarians were systematically described in the media as representing "members of the outlawed organization" in perhaps a clear testimony to the cacophony of irrational contradicting policies adopted by the Egyptian government earlier this century. Then in yet another interesting but strange tactic, the government attempted to counterbalance the Muslim Brotherhood by promoting the Salafis, an even more religiously rigid but politically weaker faction of political Islam that was popular among the blue-collar sectors of Egyptian society.

overthrown and was engaging everyone. As a result, shortly after Nazif's visit in 2005, Mubarak convened a meeting amongst the high-level officials in Egypt who had visited the United States to discuss relations between the Brotherhood and America. Mubarak had been disturbed by the contradiction between the United States' announced position of non-engagement with the Brotherhood and my strong conviction that they were, in fact, doing so. He instructed Ambassador Suleiman Awwad, head of the Information Bureau of the president, to contact me urgently, to ask directly to send the president two memos. One of them was regarding the American–Muslim Brotherhood relations. When I politely asked about the urgency behind the request, Awwad informed me that the president intended to share with the Egyptian officials my assessment as well as some Egyptian intelligence information that was of concern to him.

Ultimately, and in retrospect, my overall reading of the American posture towards Egyptian leadership during Bush's administration, a decade before Mubarak was to leave office, was quite simple. The Americans, as always, were being very pragmatic. By the beginning of the century, with Mubarak at 72 years of age, America was preparing for the future. In doing so, they would deal with any candidate who could safeguard their interests, irrespective of whether he had democratic inclinations or not. This was what best explained their preference for Suleiman as a successor to Mubarak rather than either Moussa or Gamal. However, they felt that in the absence of a security establishment candidate from the military or the police, the Muslim Brotherhood enjoyed a strong mobilizing force on the ground given its long history and popular base. This was the main reason why the administrations of Clinton and Bush carefully courted the group.

The Political Reform Agenda and Human Rights

In the early years of the twenty-first century, the democracy agenda had become a prominent topic in the American engagement with Egypt. Some Republicans and Democrats were truly committed to promoting democracy worldwide, including if necessary through tough love with allies. Others used this topic as a tool to put pressure on Egyptian authorities in pursuance of the interests of their local constituencies', and even to leverage contractual business arrangements in their favor. For example, Congressman David Obey of Wisconsin was truly committed to promoting democracy and the respect for human rights, while Congressman

Frank Wolf of Virginia focused on a particular constituency, Christians in Egypt. These congressional representatives and others were particularly prominent in the appropriations process and had animated meetings with Egyptian ministers on these topics. Always in favor of Israel, Congressman Tom Lantos and Congresswoman Ileana Ros-Lehtinen used the appropriations process to try to soften Egypt's support for the Palestinians. For their part, Egyptian authorities had been rather heavy-handed in handling some cases, be that of activists or journalists, giving ammunition to their adversaries in America and bringing undue pressures on themselves. Overall, the American administration and Congress would frequently alternate roles with respect to relations with Egypt, playing good cop, bad cop, depending on the topic at hand.

As Egypt's ambassador to the United States, I listened to my fair share of American concerns with regards to human rights violations in Egypt. Not all the American references to human rights abuses were politically innocent. They occurred more frequently when they served American interests. I frequently countered American arguments when the information was questionable, incomplete, or clearly politically motivated. I did not shy away, however, from raising issues seriously with my own authorities when I felt this was warranted. The real tenuous issue then was not human rights but rather the regime change campaign, which in the case of Egypt focused on the promotion of democracy. I had repeatedly written to my own authorities about the need to promote democracy but for our own interest not because it pleased America. Indeed, constant high-profile criticism directed or orchestrated by the American administration frequently occurred throughout Bush's first four years.

In his second term, this American name-calling practice died down considerably until Ayman Nour, an Egyptian parliamentarian and runner-up against Mubarak in the 2005 elections, was arrested. Secretary of State Condoleezza Rice publicly admonished her Egyptian counterpart on Nour's incarceration at a joint press conference while he was visiting Washington in February 2006. In the summer of 2008, aware of Egyptian sensitivities, about not being recognized enough as the leader of the region. Given that Mubarak and Bush had not met since the Egyptian president's 2004 visit to the Bush ranch in Crawford, I called President Mubarak to inquire whether to encourage the American president to visit Egypt on an upcoming trip to Israel and France. Having given up on Bush, Mubarak was unresponsive, simply repeating that I should use my best judgment and take whatever decision I felt appropriate. I contacted

Hadley and suggested that Bush seriously consider visiting Egypt on the occasion of the World Economic Forum to be held in Sharm El-Sheikh in May 2008. To my surprise, a positive response came back rather swiftly. I assumed, as did others on both sides, that while it could not be a quick fix, it could at least bring relations back a step in the right direction before the upcoming presidential elections.

This was not to be the case. A few hours before President Bush's departure to Paris, I received a phone call from Elliott Abrams, who, upon Bush's instructions, read to me the president's speech to be delivered a few days later at the conference. As expected, the beginning was very flattering, focusing on Egypt's historical heritage and Mrs. Mubarak's work on the role of women. Instinctively, I asked Abrams to get directly to the part that concerned them. Not surprisingly, it was on issues of reform, with Bush falling back into the old pattern of direct name-calling, this time with specific references to Ayman Nour.

I have always supported democratic reform and respect for human rights in Egypt, but this was not the way to achieve them. Name-calling and public shaming in the presence of the Egyptian president would not be well-received. I, therefore, suggested to Abrams that Bush cancel his trip to Egypt, as this kind of speech would make relations even worse. Startled, he asked whether I wanted to get back to Cairo before making such a strong suggestion. I repeated my suggestion and responded that Bush had asked for my personal opinion and that he could have asked his ambassador to Cairo if he wanted Cairo's opinion. That was how the phone call ended.

My motive was simple. I meant to avert a troubling situation becoming even worse by having the argument at my level rather than a public presidential disagreement, which would have much greater consequences. I phoned Mubarak directly and suggested that he did not have to comment on what I was about to share. He immediately understood that there must be something ominous and silently listened, although I could sense the change in attitude from the sound of his breathing. When I finished, he simply asked, "Anything else", then hung up. A few minutes later, his Senior Information Advisor Ambassador Awwad phoned to inform me that he was instructed by Mubarak to tell me "Bravo" but did not know what this was all about.

Shortly thereafter, a worried Hadley phoned me from Air Force One, recounting what he had been told by Abrams and asking how we could move forward. I respected Hadley's professionalism and affirmed to her that it was unacceptable that the American president publicly lecture the Egyptian president. I added that this visit was supposed to be an opportunity to mend relations but that the damage had already been done. I then suggested that further contacts on details of the speech should be done with Awwad if the visit was still to go on at all.

Ultimately, the language was significantly changed, and the visit did occur. Bush and Mubarak held a bilateral meeting during which the American president affirmed that he would not have offended the Egyptian president in his own country. Strangely enough, they even agreed on a repeated visit by Mubarak to Kennebunkport, Maine, a few weeks later at the Bush family summer home. But, when Bush gave his speech at the conference, Mubarak had already left his place at the front row and walked out of the auditorium.

The point to be made here was that while the public lecturing had significantly died down mostly because Bush had been diminished by his failed policy in Iraq, it had poisoned the relationship between the two presidents, and there were elements in the administration who wanted to continue this approach. Weeks later, President Mubarak asked me to cancel the Kennebunkport visit because it conflicted with a scheduled visit to South Africa. I told the White House that the political environment between the two countries was not conducive for a successful visit and that I would not risk any further misunderstandings.

What infuriated Mubarak most was the continuous public criticism that emanated from the American administration, with repeatedly direct references to specific cases in Egypt. American officials now felt free to privately and publicly hold Egypt and its president accountable. Most of the controversial cases of individual incarceration during that era that were controversial during Bush's second term were either acquitted by Egyptian courts. This showed that the Egyptian court system was just, albeit it was also an indication that some of these incarcerations were unnecessary.

Egypt needed then, and still needs now, to expedite its political reform process to establish a pluralistic system that is commensurate with twenty-first-century norms of governance. There should be no procrastination in this regard. This cannot and should not, however, be driven by foreign countries like America or their agendas. The crippling dichotomy of choosing between no reforms at all and accepting foreign interference has proven false and problematic.

REVOLUTION AND AMERICAN REALPOLITIK

In January 2009, months after my return to Cairo from Washington, I received a phone call from Ambassador Suleiman Awwad immediately after the inauguration of President Barack Obama. Although I had been inactive in government service for months, President Mubarak asked Awwad to tell me that he had won and George W. Bush had lost, inferring that Bush had left while Mubarak had continued despite pressures from the former regarding regime change.

Indeed, in the fall of 2008, most Egyptians, including President Mubarak, felt that anyone would be better than the Bush administration for the benefit of America's relations with Egypt and the Middle East. All of Mubarak's initial high expectations about Bush, whom he and many other Arabs mistakenly felt would be an extension of his father, quickly dissipated and they chose to wait him out.

Ironically, Obama's election was a cause for celebration in many Egyptian circles. Cairo even witnessed numerous private celebrations when Obama was elected president. The exhilaration increased when he chose Cairo as the venue for his opening address to the Muslim world after some speculated that he would choose Indonesia, given that he had lived there, or Turkey, given it had promoted itself as the representative of moderate Islam. As I had said before, the visit on Egyptian public television program with the prominent political commentator, Abdel Moneim Said, Obama would discuss politics, not theology, in his speech. Therefore, he would choose Cairo University the most appropriate secular venue to address the Muslim world and the Middle East constituencies.

Obama was given a royal welcome in Cairo in June 2009. At Cairo University, he was received with numerous standing ovations even before starting his speech, which was eloquent and excellently crafted.

This was projected as a new beginning, but it did not come at the best of times. President Mubarak had gotten older but, even more so, was devastated by the death of his first grandchild. He was becoming increasingly impatient with details and less welcoming of new ideas and initiatives. About 25 years younger, President Obama came to Egypt looking for vigorous leadership but left worried about the lack of vision for the future and concerned about whether Egypt could provide sustained follow-through, as I was told by American officials afterward.

A few months later, in August 2009, President Mubarak visited Washington for the first time since his ill-fated trip to Crawford in 2004.

He did the traditional stops in Congress, the think-tank community, and, of course, the White House. The American assessment then was even more negative. Not only did they feel that the Egyptian president was distracted but they also found his delegation frequently taking calls on their mobile phones or sending messages in his presence during meetings, which they found disrespectful. They concluded that not only had the president gotten older but the position and stature of the Egyptian presidency were now being brought into question. An ominous development in a complex region for a country known for its strong centralized system.

Ironically, just as the situation in Egypt suddenly appeared like it might change towards more democratization and reforms, with the 2011 and the 2013 revolutions, America seemed more confused than ever, misreading the domestic environment in Egypt and adopting policies contrary to the demands of the majority of its people.

The timing of the Arab Awakening was surprising. Social discontent was evident and widespread throughout Egypt and numerous Arab countries. Everyone was surprised by what developed both in form and pace, including the United States. Although I had years earlier followed and cautioned our own authorities about the rising discontent, I myself did not expect the developments in Tunis to spill over that quickly in Egypt. As the January Revolution was unfolding, the Obama administration was caught off guard and did not understand what was happening on the ground. They were now suffering the consequence for years of not having respect for Arab public opinion of regularly shrugging it off. After hesitating, the United States of America decided to send Frank Wisner, one of its former and well-connected ambassadors, to Cairo as a special presidential envoy to assess the situation and pass on a few messages. He conveyed to Mubarak that he should be more inclusive, responsive to the public and prepare for a smooth transition.

As another expression of the confusion and disarray in Washington, Obama held a meeting, while Wisner was still in Cairo, with his most senior advisors of relevance to the American–Egyptian relation. All of them argued that the United States should play its cards cautiously and slowly because Mubarak had been a strong ally for decades. Additionally, they felt that quickly dropping Mubarak would raise serious concerns among other Arab allies, especially in the Gulf and had them to question whether the United States was a fair-weather friend. Susan Rice and Samantha Powers were dissenters on this decision. After some hesitation, Obama reluctantly accepted the advice to tread slowly. Then, two staffers behind him intervened, whispering to the president and causing him to reverse the decision, declaring to his surprised audience "the United States could not be on the wrong side of history". The anxious principals in the room acquiesced but ultimately believed they had convinced Obama to at least not speak publicly about the issue for now.[5]

They were to be quickly surprised, a few minutes after the meeting; however, Obama declared to the press that Mubarak had "to leave now". Secretary of State Hillary Clinton had a few days earlier been on record saying that Washington was confident in the strength of the Mubarak rule. Such unclear, inconsistent, and even contradictory messages were frankly at the very least an indication of the disarray in Washington during the early days of the revolution and could be described as nothing but an exercise of amateurish diplomacy.

In the days that followed, the United States went all out in diplomatically trying to influence events in Egypt. They contacted the Egyptian military establishment at the highest level, including the Egyptian Chief of Staff General Sami Anan, and engaged Head of General Intelligence Omar Suleiman days after he was appointed vice president. They also reached out to a wide range of civilians, including numerous old school Egyptian politicians, businessmen, civil society members, and leaders of different political trends, including Islamists and liberal leaders associated with the youth like Mohamed El-Baradei. The American administration spoke with anyone who could provide useful information.

One particularly sensitive issue was the arrest and indictment of a number of foreign and national employees of foreign non-governmental organizations (NGOs) in Egypt. Egypt had procrastinated for years about whether or not to license their operations, yet allowed them to function without official licenses. The German Konrad Adenauer Foundation had been in operation for almost three decades and had worked directly with the secretariat of the Egyptian ministerial cabinet. In my previous capacity as ambassador to the United States, I had repeatedly recommended that we either ask the American NGOs to leave or provide them with legitimate licenses and guidelines for operation. The informal modus vivendi that was reached was to conclude understandings with the different government agencies on operational procedures and consultation. These did not, however, provide the necessary transparency.

---

[5] Indeed, Wisner's message was later the subject of contradicting reports that suggested differences between Wisner's opinion and that of the administration.

With the breakdown of government supervision at the start of the 2011 revolution, many of these NGOs totally ignored the agreed consultative process and generously provided funds to numerous of these organizations leading the government to crack down and arrest many of their foreign and local employees. Under tremendous pressure, the Egyptian authorities quickly shipped the foreigners out of the country. The Egyptians working at these NGOs and who had been arrested went through a long legal process, which only recently concluded with their innocence. This is another example where everyone, the governments Egyptian and Foreign as well as the NGOs were in the wrong and had completely mishandled the situation.

Egyptian–American Relations Under the Brotherhood

After Mubarak's ouster, the American diplomatic full-court press continued even intensified, throughout the 18 months leading to the presidential elections scheduled for June 2012, with emphasis on the players they expected to be influential in the Egyptian political theater. This included a number of the candidates running for the office of the presidential, especially the two finalists, Mohamed Morsi and General Ahmed Shafik, with whom the American Ambassador in Egypt Anne Patterson was in close touch. The candidates were more than ready to engage her with a view to providing assurances that American interests would not be at risk if they were elected. Patterson, who previously served in Pakistan, was a strong believer that political Islam was the strongest political force in Egypt and thus engaged the Brotherhood most extensively. She felt they were more effective and would ultimately attain and retain power for a considerable length of time.

The election of the Brotherhood candidate Morsi as president in 2012 turned the tables on the traditional nature of American–Egyptian relations. Up to that point, businessmen were America's strongest public constituency in Egypt, with the military being the strongest supporter of the relationship within the Egyptian government. This all changed after the 2012 elections. Businesses and liberal civil society were estranged and frustrated with the American position. Reciprocally, the American ambassador in Cairo was openly disdainful of Egypt's liberal politicians, criticizing them, myself included, as being naively focused on making statements and writing opinion pieces in the printed media. The Egyptian military was clearly uncomfortable as well with the new situation. The Muslim Brotherhood, previously the black sheep in the relationship, had suddenly become an American interlocutor as a significant player in the Egyptian political spectrum before the elections and even more so once, it gained the helm of the Egyptian government.

A highly significant indication of America's interest in engagement with the Brotherhood occurred during a visit of Essam El-Haddad to Washington in December 2012. He was President Morsi's assistant for foreign affairs and international cooperation; his accompanying delegation included Khaled El-Qazzaz, an aide to Morsi. They and Egypt's Ambassador to the United States Mohamed Tawfik first met with Thomas Donilon, the United States national security advisor.

At the end of the meeting, Donilon escorted El-Haddad alone to meet Obama in the Oval Office upon the latter's invitation. Later, as they left the White House, El-Haddad very briefly conveyed to the Egyptian ambassador in Washington that Obama highlighted the importance of two points: "inclusiveness" and "helping America help them". As is tradition, the Egyptian Embassy was due to prepare a reporting cable to Cairo and the ambassador asked El-Haddad to dictate them his most important reflections. As he did this, he omitted these very two points and considerably watered down the American president's message. Interestingly, shortly thereafter, John Brennan, who was at the time the president's homeland security and counterterrorism advisor and later Central Intelligence Agency director, asked the ambassador to thank El-Haddad for their cooperation without any further detail. A similar message came through the State Department. The embassy, which had not been informed of the nature of this cooperation, interpreted this appreciation to be related to information or actions regarding assailants involved in the killing of the American ambassador and his colleagues in Benghazi a few weeks earlier.

In addition to the Brotherhood's non-transparency with other politicians within the Egyptian government and the vague American–Brotherhood cooperation mentioned, it is also noteworthy here that for three decades no Egyptian official, except the president and the prime minister, had been invited to meet the American president in the Oval Office. Since 1974, even Egypt's foreign ministers had not been invited into the Oval Office except when escorting the Egyptian president. The last foreign minister to enter the oval office unaccompanied was my father

Ismail Fahmy who was received by Richard Nixon almost four decades earlier. I mentioned the symbolism of Obama meeting El-Haddad in the Oval Office later to a senior American diplomat, who confirmed the meeting, then asserted that it had been scheduled by the White House, upon Obama's personal request, against his own recommendation.

The Egyptian government under President Morsi was equally interested in developing relations with the United States. Like others before them, they immediately chose to enter American politics by highlighting and leveraging their positive cooperation with Israel. However, they went overboard, brokering with the United States a ceasefire between Israel and Islamist Hamas, with whom the Brotherhood had strong contacts, after the breakout of hostilities in the Gaza Strip on November 14, 2012. What was unique here was not that Egypt brokered a ceasefire between the conflicting parties, but that under Morsi's rule for the first time in history; Israel was actually given an Egyptian guarantee that no missiles would be fired at Israel from Gaza. Egypt had never before provided guarantees that extended beyond Egyptian territory. This reflected how far the new Egyptian regime would go to get America's blessing and how strong relations were between the Muslim Brotherhood and Hamas.

Morsi's government also tried to attract the United States by presenting the Freedom and Justice Party, the political arm of the Brotherhood, as a symbol for moderate Islam against other more extremist Islamist elements like the Salafis or other violent Islamist forces. It was presented as an inclusive party whose symbolic deputy chairman at one point was Rafik Habib, a Christian political researcher. This was fully compatible with Anne Patterson's thinking of the inevitability of Islamism. She had once admonished me for my public criticism of the Brotherhood, asking "Aren't they better than the Salafis?" For others within the American body politic, especially those concerned about the reemergence of strong Arab state identities and its ramifications on Israel's interest such as the neocons, the Muslim Brotherhood served well as either a safe bet on a sustained winner or an additional asset to counter the potential reemergence of strong nationalist alternatives or both.

Paradoxically, throughout Morsi's year in office, continuous efforts by the United States and the Muslim Brotherhood were pursued to come closer together, while the gap between the United States and its traditional constituency of liberal Egyptians, the security establishment, and officials continued to widen.

A Revolution, Yet Again

As tensions within Egyptian society reached its peak and efforts to convince President Morsi to become more inclusive of liberals failed, the Americans started to doubt the Muslim Brotherhood's real intentions. The United States started to carefully recalibrate how closely it would publicly engage the Muslim Brotherhood (MB) or its representatives, while, at the same time, still not siding with the liberals or the security establishment. At the same time, it conveyed strong, blunt messages to the Ministry of Defense cautioning towards the elected president. The strongest supporters of the Egyptian–American relationship suddenly themselves became amongst its strongest critics. And, America's requests for meetings with its traditionally strongest Egyptian government partner, the military establishment, just before the events between June 30 and July 3, 2013, were declined.

By June 2013, however, Egyptians had opted for exceptional measures to redress the situation by pushing for Morsi's departure, irrespective of whether this was accepted or not around the world, including by America. For most Egyptians, it was an existential choice. But the American administration twisted and turned. It wanted to indicate its disapproval but carefully shied away from categorically describing events as a "coup" because this would have required more drastic measures, such as restricting its cooperation with Egypt pursuant to the United States of America Foreign Assistance Act.

Morsi was removed from office with wide popular support, and the military took charge of the country with Adly Mansour, Egypt's most senior jurist, becoming the interim president. The United States found itself in a delicate situation. Egypt was strategically important, but the administration felt compelled to argue that it could not condone the removal of an elected president. This American position was not, however, completely credible. Just two years earlier, Mubarak, an elected president, had been removed from office as well. The United States and the Western world did not complain, albeit no two situations are identical.

Gradually, as efforts to achieve domestic reconciliation between the Muslim Brotherhood and the new Egyptian authorities failed, including those by the United States. A compromise was no longer possible; the American administration had to carefully navigate a fine line between the pressures of its domestic politics and the strategic imperatives of its national security interests in the Middle East. Conflicting American domestic and foreign considerations all came into play at the same time. The United

States had to simultaneously be frank, subtle, confrontational, maneuvering, normative, and a realist. An impossible task, especially with Egyptians taking charge of their own destiny.

For their part, the Egyptian regime had growing concerns about relations with the United States. These doubts had started during the George W. Bush years, when the neocons pushed for the regime change agenda in different forms, presumably to promote and safeguard American interests. President Mubarak and many others gradually came to believe that the United States was no longer supporting his regime, looking at other options.[6] The developments of 2011 not only strengthened this belief but also helped it gain further credence with a large number of Egyptian institutions as well as the public sector.[7]

All of this was further consolidated by how the Obama administration managed the events post-Mubarak. It had infuriated the liberals, businessmen, and military because of perceived support of the Morsi presidency in spite of its rejection by an undeniably large segment of the Egyptian public, particularly the overzealous pro-Islamist posture of the American Ambassador to Cairo Anne Patterson. Now, there were rumors that her potential replacement was to be Robert S. Ford, whose career had been in troubled zones, such as post-2011 Syria, where the United States was openly attempting to influence the internal affairs of the host country.

All of this fueled a conspiracy theory, which has strong believers in Egypt to this day: that America had masterminded the 2011 Revolution as a backer of the Muslim Brotherhood. This conspiracy theory is extremely widespread, whether in Egyptian institutions or amongst officials.

[6] The Egyptian media very widely reported that the United States Secretary of State Condoleezza Rice had made specific reference to an American administration policy of constructive chaos in a speech she gave while in Egypt speaking at the American University in Cairo Ewart Hall in 2005 where she talked about the "the birth pangs" of a new Middle East. On her return to Washington, she Rice personally expressed her surprise at this, denying that the American administration had any such policy.

[7] Some analysts, especially in the Middle East, argue that the Western world and, particularly, the United States were conspirators in the 2011 events, often referring to youth being trained in Serbia or following the writings of Gene Sharp on civilian disobedience. Moreover, the American Embassy in Cairo's direct monetary support to the NGO community without coordination with the Egyptian government, contrary to past practices, and the work of American foundations like the International Republic Institute and the National Democratic Institute—both of which had been implicitly allowed by the Egyptian government to work in Cairo without being officially licensed and had thus exploited such measures—provided further impetus to such conspiracies.

Nevertheless, once emotions subsided, the overwhelming majority of Egyptian policymakers also understood that relations with America were important. The Egyptian military establishment, in spite of its criticism and complaints, would always request that the Foreign Ministry try to deftly manage the relationship and prevent an unnecessary crisis. The Egyptian intelligence services, shocked and institutionally rattled by the events of 2011, were most suspicious of American intentions.

As Egypt's foreign minister after Morsi's ouster, I argued in our internal discussions that recalibrating relations with America would take time but, in any case, these relations had to be managed differently. Egypt had to stop being reactive and was best to develop defined objectives, realistic expectations, and a clearer expression of its foreign policy, especially with major powers like the United States. Over-dependence on the United States or any other state was detrimental to our interests because it made us complacent rather than proactive and created expectations from these countries that may be inconsistent with our priorities (Fig. 7.2).

Fig. 7.2 Nabil Fahmy and the Obamas at UN General Assembly reception

Initial meetings with the American administration were professional but combative. Numerous elements in the American administration tried to delegitimize the Egyptian government after Morsi's ouster. At a meeting I had in Washington on April 29, 2014, with American Secretary of State John Kerry, the younger members of his delegations kept prodding him on to raise allegations and complaints about human rights violations in Egypt. Over time, I had to maneuver these tense meetings and work towards reorienting the focus on regional security issues, where Egyptian–American cooperation was, in fact, mutually beneficial.

With time, the American administration began to almost completely focus on moving forward with our bilateral relations, even if it was to occasionally continue to raise some Egyptian domestic issues. To preserve a balance between the different interest groups, it recalibrated its demands around, ensuring that the Egyptian roadmap would be implemented immediately with the establishment of an inclusive stable political system. It paid special attention to the Egyptian military and security establishment. After two revolutions, their weight and role in Egypt's political theater had significantly increased and, over the last two years, their relations with the United States had been tense.

In doing so, the Obama administration used its own direct channels, with the American secretary of defense Chuck Hagel frequently contacting his Egyptian counterpart Abdel Fattah El-Sisi, who was not a total stranger to the Americans. El-Sisi had attended postgraduate courses in the United States and was certainly well-connected with the Americans during his years as chief of military intelligence and minister of defense. The administration also used Jordanian and Emirati channels to create a more relaxed environment to communicate with Egypt. This became ever more important as Egyptian presidential elections got nearer and rumors spread that El-Sisi would run in the elections.

Once the two candidates for the 2014 Egyptian presidential elections were announced, realpolitik became the name of the game on both sides of the American–Egyptian relationship. However, after El-Sisi's election, which could have been a new beginning for bilateral relations, the conflicting conceptual outlooks of the two presidents did not make such progress easy.

From my work with him when we were both cabinet ministers in 2013–2014, it was obvious that El-Sisi was clearly not anti-American. While suspicious of Western maneuvering and policies throughout the Middle East, he did not appear to be amongst the American conspiracy proponents and clearly understood the importance of a well-managed relationship between the two countries. At his first Summit meeting with Obama, during the United Nations General Assembly in September 2014, the American president took the initiative to start the discussion by addressing misconceptions, including misconceptions about El-Sisi as Minister of Defense siding with the Muslim Brotherhood rather than secular liberals because he was an observant Muslim. Obama also highlighted the American administration's full support for the former Ambassador Patterson who, he felt, had been the target of severe and unjustified criticism including from within the Egyptian government institutions, which fueled public anger towards her. He concluded on a different note by affirming the American desire to move forward with Egypt as a strategic partner. El-Sisi, on his part, was determined to comprehensively explain his concerns about political Islam, its threats, particularly to Egypt's stability, security, and national identity, and did so extensively and in detail.

Both sides listened to each other, neither, however, seemed to be very comfortable with the approach of the other. The meeting was a disappointment to all. I was told that soon after that formal meeting during the General Assembly, Obama instructed his staff not to engage in unnecessary conflicts but to keep the Egyptian file completely away from the White House. He did not want to be engaged with it unless it was truly necessary. For its part, the Egyptian government became more entrenched in its belief that the Obama administration was interested in regime change and that it still supported the Brotherhood.

The two presidents never exchanged visits to the United States or Egypt after that, only encountering each other in passing or at subsequent international meetings. In fact, they probably only had three telephone conversations over the remaining two years in Obama's presidency. This was in stark contrast to the frequent, often monthly, conversations between Egyptian and American presidents in the past. The overt criticism of El-Sisi and Obama, from the respective political circles and media of the two countries, intensified even as time passed further away from the events of 2013 and Egypt concluded its interim roadmap. It became increasingly unrealistic to expect the relationship to return to constructive engagement during the remainder of Obama's tenure, so, once again, it was a waiting game.

A New and Different American President: Donald Trump

From the Egyptian perspective, the American presidential elections of 2016 had important implications for Egyptian–American relations. Donald Trump was politically unknown on the international scene, with no real track record on any foreign policy issue. He was clearly running on an anti-establishment domestic platform, which resonated well amongst some members of the Egyptian political elite. They again felt that any change in the American administration, even a risky and an unknown one, was better than four more years of the Democratic Party politics.

Trump's acerbic intolerant rants about Muslims were initially a source for embarrassment in Muslim and Arab quarters, but the establishment in the Arab world was looking for the antithesis to Obama. Trump fit that standard with flying colors. His position became more attractive, as his strong and unequivocal expressions of opposition to Iran and terrorism resonated with the Arab Gulf and with the Egyptian leadership. Hillary Clinton, the Democratic candidate Trump had defeated in the election, had been an extension of the Obama line, despite her being more of a pragmatist than Obama. The Egyptian assumptions on Clinton were further solidified after El-Sisi met the two candidates in the 2016 General Assembly. The Egyptian delegation was able to very easily agree on a joint press statement with Trump's team, which even issued a unilateral statement very strongly supportive of the Egyptian president. No statement was agreed upon with Clinton's staff who wanted to mention human rights issues in Egypt.

Many Middle Eastern leaders supported Trump's election and attempted to engage him early on. This was clearly evident when Egypt withdrew a draft resolution submitted to the United Nations Security Council against Israeli settlement activity in the occupied territories upon requests from Israeli Prime Minister Benjamin Netanyahu and President-elect Trump. Arab Gulf states were also quick to intensely lobby Trump even before the inauguration besides providing him with a regal reception on his first visit to the region, despite his previous criticism of their governments.

However, American institutions, with their separation of powers, prevent any president from continuously exercising undue power. It was, therefore, a mistake for parts of the official quarters in Cairo to assume that the president alone would determine American policy. Egypt soon learned this. After having been lauded throughout Trump's campaign, one of the first official requests they received after Trump's inauguration was, in fact, the release of Aya Hegazy, an Egyptian-American who had been arrested for the activities of an NGO she founded. When the two presidents held a meeting on the margins of the 2017 United Nations General Assembly, Trump again started by positively commending El-Sisi's efforts against terrorism before members of his delegation raised concerns regarding Egypt's relations with North Korea, its incarceration of some Egyptian-American citizens, and the draft of the new civil society law. Other policies continued including the withholding of close to USD 200 million from the assistance allocated to Egypt.

That said, the bully pulpit of the American presidency is not inconsequential; if so desired, it can set or at least correct, the tone and parameters within which the relationship is managed. Consequently, having an American president in office whose starting point was more favorable towards Egypt was understandably seen as the better option. The challenge will be how to continue to make it in the interest of the American president to do so, as well as to correctly assess the degree with which he has to re-calibrate his own positions to consider the voices in the different institutions of government and in Congress.

Not being aggressive towards each other is a good beginning, but the real question will be how Egypt and the United States can really satisfy each other. Faced with numerous challenges, the Egyptian president has concrete hard asset needs whether that is in military equipment or financial support. The military support has been resumed under Trump in response to an Egyptian transactional.

Trump, on the other hand, is transactional by desire. To provide Egypt with support, he will expect reciprocal deliverables. They will not be cash or large-scale procurement; Egypt simply does not have the resources for either. The expectation may be that Egypt provides political or military support for Trumps policies in the Middle East, such as convincing the Palestinians to be more receptive to America's proposals for Arab Israeli peace, even though they do not satisfy their national aspirations, or convincing them to accept compromises on sensitive issues like sovereignty over East Jerusalem. Another Trump desire from Egypt may be for it to provide boots on the ground to deal with threats in the Middle East given that it has the largest Arab military force, which could serve his proposal of an Arab NATO (North Atlantic Treaty Organization) to fill the vacuum that will be created as America slowly diminishes its presence in the region. Egypt may help to a degree on the Palestinian issue, but it will hesitate to extend its military forces beyond its borders and place them in harm's way.

REFLECTIONS ON EGYPTIAN–AMERICAN RELATIONS THROUGH FIVE DECADES

An objective assessment of the relations between Egypt and the United States over the last half-century will clearly conclude that it has been highly beneficial to both sides. The benefits to the United States were essentially strategic. The early 1970s saw Egypt move away from the Soviet Union and closer to the United States—cooperation with Egypt proving invaluable to the United States in defeating the Soviet Union in Afghanistan, liberating Kuwait, and combating terrorism, among other regional issues. Equally important for the United States was the pioneering role Egypt played in promoting peace between Arabs and Israel, the most prominent ally of the United States of America in the region.

Egypt also significantly gained from this relationship. Even before 1967, the emergence of the United States of America as a major global power was instrumental in confronting the trilateral British-French Israeli attack on Egypt in 1956. After the resumption of relations following the 1973 October War, America has provided over USD 50 billion in aid since the Egyptian–Israeli peace agreement. It has helped upgrade Egypt's military. But, of course, what immediately comes to mind is America's essential role in promoting Arab–Israeli peace.

Relations between the two countries have never been easy to manage. In addition, for over two decades now, they have been slowly but consistently questioned by both sides. First, the two countries made the illogical mistake of resting on their laurels and allowing their relations to be defined for too long by one issue, the Arab–Israeli conflict. Ironically, as progress was achieved in this regard from 1973 to 1995, the main tenet on which the relationship had been based gradually became less exclusive and unique, with a number of Arab countries finding a way for peace or pre-normalization with Israel.

After 1995, as the Arab–Israeli peace process itself started to slowly die down before coming to a halt, with the United States siding more and more with Israel. The relationship became costlier to defend in Egypt. The traditional stakeholders, the military and private sector, all but fell silent. The passiveness moved to criticism and a growing irritation as American administrations, one after the other, pursued a call for democratic reforms or even a regime-change agenda.

Secondly, Egyptian officials visiting Washington have chosen not to frankly and directly confront the Americans about the unacceptability of some of their requests. Most Egyptian officials choose to simply ignore or postpone addressing issues raised by the Americans if they found them disagreeable, preferring to give the Americans nuanced, unclear answers. They never really understood that with America, a misunderstanding was often more dangerous and costlier than disagreements.

Egyptian officials had also fallen into a dangerous addiction to the substantial American assistance, which further complicated diverse and false public sentiments in Egypt and America. The former assumed that the assistance was provided for Egypt being the pioneer of Arab–Israeli peace and would not entail other demands. The Americans, however, assumed that because they had been providing substantial assistance for several decades, Egypt should be at America's beck and call.

In addition, throughout most of those years, relations between the United States and the Arab world, Egypt included, were fundamentally governmental relationships with our respective societies sidelined, looking mystified, falsely enamored, or overwhelmingly suspicious of one another, without a true mutual understanding. I recall, in particular, the disdain of American officials towards any reference by Arab officials to our public opinion, which they felt was insignificant and could be ignored.

For decades, this was not only a government-to-government relationship but also essentially a relationship based on the management of only a very small number of pressing or opportune issues that served the politicians in office. It was strengthened and sustained by its indispensability for both sides but suffered severely from its containment and shortsightedness after its honeymoon period in the late 1980s.

The events of 2011–2013 and then the Egyptian presidential elections of 2014 had established a new Egyptian American paradigm that was not well-rooted. It would move forward or lurch back as forces on both sides, but especially in the United States, engaged in a tug of war. Egypt and America were both changing. They looked at each other, but for the first time in decades, not only from the perspective of Egypt's role in the Arab Israeli crisis or simply the issue of United States aid to Egypt but with a shifting unclear paradigm in play. They have not yet determined how best to deal with one another.

The Americans, on their part, are now faced with an activist Egyptian president with a determination to deliver on his commitments to his people and to try to influence events in the Middle East.

New thinking on how to best manage the Egyptian–American relationship is no longer an academic exercise or a slogan. Today, "new thinking" is imperative to serve the interests of both countries.

PART III

Egypt's Continuous Transitions

After Three Decades a Public Awakening Fueling Two Revolutions

Over his 30-year presidency, Mubarak moved from wise domestic and astute regional political repositioning through stabilization and imperative national infrastructural reconstruction but missed domestic political opportunities as the country slid from stability to stagnation to revolutions. Year 2011 generated legitimate but unfulfilled aspirations. Domestic real politic led to alienating times after the election of a Muslim Brotherhood presidential candidate and a majority in parliament inevitably by 2013 raising existential questions about identity and a reemphasis on the nation-state system.

As is the case with most politicians, especially heads of state, Egyptian presidents have often been judged, positively or negatively, by their last few years in office. Sometimes, even by a singular decision they took. This approach, particularly for Hosni Mubarak, is imprecise and, I believe, both inadequate and unfair. Historians and political analysts are partly to blame because of their penchant for focusing on highlights and isolated events. Mubarak is also responsible for this unreflective record of his tenure, given that he chose to stay in office for three consecutive decades. Given this unique longevity, it feeds the contemporary tendency to undertake piecemeal assessments centered on a singular event.

Personally, I was enamored with Gamal Abdel Nasser growing up, only realizing his faults towards the end of his presidency. I then had my first direct encounter with an Egyptian president, Anwar Sadat, and was

© The Author(s) 2020 203
N. Fahmy, *Egypt's Diplomacy in War, Peace and Transition*,
https://doi.org/10.1007/978-3-030-26388-1_8

impressed with his desire to rapidly change Egypt. Nevertheless, I found his inconsistencies and grandiose style surprising since he was most of all a grassroots politician. My closest and longest encounters were with Mubarak, both as vice president when I worked in his office and then as president during my diplomatic career. He had decided not to run for office in 2005 and managed a normal transition to a newly elected Egyptian leader. Mubarak would have probably been seen as a national hero in Egypt, even today. He had unabashedly stabilized and correctly repositioned Egypt in his first ten years in office, which should not be forgotten, then performed a reasonable job of dodging crisis in his second decade.

On a personal level, Mubarak was always considerate, courteous, and even magnanimous. I remember how nine years after I finished my post as ambassador in Washington, during which no personal contacts occurred between us, I still received a personal phone call from the former president and his wife to convey condolences after my mother passed away.

Professionally, Mubarak was always committed to national service. He instinctively understood that a country's strength is in its own environment and, therefore, prioritized stabilizing relations in the Middle East. As president, particularly during his first two decades, he would only take decisions after carefully consulting the different government officials and agencies. Indeed, he was, at first, very respectful of institutional responsibilities. Mubarak was very different from Nasser and Sadat generically, risk-averse and completely uncomfortable with grand designs and mega projects. After years of upheaval, his approach was initially best for Egypt, which was truly in need of infrastructural redesign and upgrading in both its hard assets and soft power, including human resources. Consequently, these were years where he ruled Egypt, functioning as an executive president.

These were also years when reform, both economic and political, was attempted, albeit in a restricted fashion. Egypt's population was rapidly increasing, depleting its resources while debt payments were turning into a heavy burden, creating serious liquidity shortages. Under pressures from the International Monetary Fund (IMF), Mubarak started to reform Egypt's economic policies in 1991. He also gradually brought in a number of younger cabinet ministers who were committed to economic reform particularly in 2004. Gradually, they instilled some new thinking in an archaic and resistant governmental apparatus.

Politically, one of Mubarak's first steps upon taking office had been releasing the leading opposition members arrested by Sadat and considering anti-corruption measures. Mubarak was not, however, ideologically committed to political reform; thus, he never wholeheartedly embraced its fundamental concepts of accountability or shared governance. He took these steps at the outset of his presidency out of necessity to calm a volatile domestic theater, which was a wise decision. He ultimately failed or choose not to effectively insist that these policies be instilled in his system of government and made no real attempt to promote them with the public, the majority of which did not reap quick benefits from Mubarak's considered incremental pace of economic reform. Democratic progress was, therefore, intermittent and superficial, with the inconsequential emergence of numerous political parties that lacked clear purpose or constituency, thus had no significant effect on the political landscape beyond expanding the cacophony of blowhards and attention-seekers.

Regrettably, during his last decade, Mubarak reverted strongly to his natural preference for stability, crisis management, and damage control, becoming increasingly uncomfortable with calls for change. Over time, he had also clearly become bored with governing and became less hands on. In this sense, towards the end of his term, Mubarak was essentially reigning rather than ruling, generally overseeing Egypt's functioning approach while power remained centralized with his party and close confidants. This created a situation where issues in an increasingly stagnant political system were mostly met by reactive resistance from diverse stakeholders worried about losing status and control. Less and less got done and reasonable economic growth rates had very little effect on the public at large.

This came at a moment when the large youth bulge, which benefited from accelerated IT advancements, was increasingly and anxiously calling for a more open society. Other prominent Egyptian figures, like Mohamed El-Baradei, gained a large youth following in their calls for political reforms. Starting in 2009, El-Baradei, the then director-general of the International Atomic Energy Agency, repeatedly made public remarks in a personal capacity, about the need for domestic political reforms in Egypt. This increased in 2010 upon his return to Egypt, and it culminated with the founding of the National Association for Change (NAC) and its "Declaration for Change", which comprised a set of principles to guide the desired reform, including the ending of the three-decade-long state of emergency introduced since Sadat's assassination, and the amendment of constitutional articles relating to elections. Although the Egyptian public, especially the youth, embraced him as the informal leader of the reform process, with the declaration garnering almost one million signatures from across the political spectrum within a few months, El-Baradei himself was reluctant to take any official capacity or become actively politically engaged. For his part, Mubarak was skeptical of El-Baradei's admonitions.

By then, the political environment in Egypt was in complete disarray with political forces pulling it in conflicting directions. Liberals, conservatives, strong government institutions, and religious political trends were all maneuvering to find their own way in the political process, with benign oversight on Mubarak's part. A large number of privately owned newspapers also circulated. Many of those were heavily critical. One of the forces feeding this trend was the growing space that the private sector was assuming in the Egyptian economy during the last decades of Mubarak's rule. The political landscape had gradually seen a fusion of politics and big money, with the media being considered an effective tool towards both objectives. Even the Egyptian government played a role in consolidating this trend through the recruitment of the chief executive officers (CEOs) of large private corporations to become governmental cabinet ministers. Informal arrangements among the different political parties and big business damagingly blurred the distinction between public service and personal interests.

The political party system in Egypt was only nominally expanding without the exercise of pluralistic politics, which the old guard suppressed, and in the absence of an ingrained pluralistic political culture to act as a sustained catalyst for reform. Instead, in Egypt, the exclusive one-dominant-party tradition that had been in place since the 1952 Revolution persisted. Members of government, civil society, and intelligentsia opted to join the leading party headed by the president as a shortcut to pursuing their goals.

Ultimately, Egyptian politics became a theater for inexperienced, politically well-intentioned technocrats competing with less than well-intentioned political opportunists who had louder voices and were highly experienced operationally, thus much more effective. What emerged from all this was not the aspired interaction among diverse stakeholders but rather a debasing of intellectual thought. Policies were not meant to serve the general public but personal interests. The government became more isolated from its constituency, as the different players competed in making false promises, and propaganda superseded realistic pragmatic policies.

Egypt was on a trampoline, vigorously bouncing around to increasingly higher levels beyond government control and in the absence of societal coherence or norms. The country witnessed a decade of contradictory governmental policies and tough turf battles over conflicting visions and interests. In the absence of political direction and a political forum within which consensus could be reached, it became very difficult for different government and regime stakeholders to handle the increasingly vociferous challengers.

Mubarak's measured careful management style extended not only to domestic affairs but also to foreign policy. Here, I believe he was more successful than on the domestic front. Again, the progression was much more rapid during the first decade of his presidency. Repositioning Egypt at the center of the Arab world reconnected it with its natural regional scope of influence thus reestablishing its importance globally and regionally. The continued pursuit of a comprehensive Arab Israeli peace after Israel's complete withdrawal from Egyptian territory provided credibility that it remained the main player on the regional issue of most paramount importance. Providing troops to help liberate Kuwait after the Iraqi invasion and refusing to support the American invasion of Iraq years later was evidence that he would take difficult decisions in support and in opposition of friend and foe, irrespective of their strength. Mubarak provided military facilities to friends but was reticent on long-term base arrangements, rejecting all attempts to place arbitrary constraints on Egypt's national security capacity. In essence, he took principled foreign policy decisions.

Over time, however, particularly during his last years in office, the world, and the Middle East seemed to be changing too rapidly for his measured incremental management style. The absence of a visionary foreign policy outlook towards the future, which was so prominent with Nasser and Sadat constituting one of Egypt's strengths, led regional and global players to look elsewhere. Gradually, Egypt was seen as a convener and complementary force to be reached out to as needed, rather than a regional leader to be engaged, courted, or preempted.

Nasser, Sadat, and Mubarak had their achievements that dispassionate analysts should not ignore. This is ever truer on foreign policy. Yet, none of them was a democratic leader or fulfilled the aspirations they generated in their constituencies domestically and regionally. They all preferred excessively exclusive governments and took arbitrary unilateral decisions, preventing the Egyptian political system from fully developing.

In the absence of a democratic political environment or credible political parties, youth and activists started to establish independent networks and associations for more forceful expressions of rejection. In 2004, a movement called "Kifaya", the Arabic word for "Enough", openly opposed Hosni Mubarak's continued presidency as well as the possible elevation of his son as the next president, repeatedly chanting "no reelection", "no dynasties" at meetings and demonstrations.

In 2006, workers went on strike in the industrial city of Mahalla as well as other cities demanding better treatment and benefits for workers. By spring, clashes between police and workers had become recurrent and the "April 6" movement was established embracing the same calls for political reform.

Public opinion became more aware of these efforts when the two movements joined efforts with "The National Commission for Change" to later organize repeated demonstrations in front of the Egyptian Press Syndicate, frequently confronting security forces, creating tense but generally peaceful standoffs.

On June 20, 2010, a young man, Khaled Said, died in Alexandria Police custody, with substantial evidence of torture infuriating public opinion against police brutality with tens of thousands joining the Facebook page "We are all Khaled Said".

Completely tone-deaf to public sentiment governing authorities supervised a parliamentary election in December 2010 with the most lopsided result in Egypt's history provoking even the generally politically apathetic constituencies.

Then, on December 27, 2010, Mohamed Bo Azizi burned himself alive in a public square in Tunisia in rejection of police brutality.

This desperate act had wide domestic and regional repercussions, especially after the removal of the Tunisian president and his well-established regime. It resonated loudly and clearly in Egypt, providing impetus to already peculating expressions of discontent about the police and established regime.

The events that unfolded in Egypt in early 2011 were, therefore, not surprising. I saw them as self-evident, but I did not expect them to develop or conclude at such a quick pace.

On National Police Day, January 25, 2011, a few thousand overwhelmingly secular Egyptian young men and women, demonstrated in Cairo and other large cities across the country, demanding greater civil liberties energized, in particular, by the events in Tunisia. They were quickly supported by a wide and diverse sector of the Egyptian civil society. Even more surprising, however, was the bungling, piecemeal reaction of the Egyptian authorities over the next several days. Authorities were unable to comprehend what was really happening. They inexplicitly and completely misread the magnitude of the discontent and continuously underestimating the determination of those expressing their discontent. As a result, the number of demonstrators, the level of political demands, and, for that matter, the aspirations of the people increased by the hour and with it as did the predicament and disarray of the authorities. Small demonstrations, which were initially only calling for the sacking of the minister of interior in light of recurrent violations of rights and liberties rapidly turned into a full-fledged revolutionary awakening that demanded radical constitutional reforms and eventually the president's resignation.

It is noteworthy that Islamists did not immediately join the marches. The Salafi leadership actually opposed the demonstrations on a strictly religious ground. The leaders of the Muslim Brotherhood, the most influential of the Islamists in Egypt, first hesitated and even admonished its own youth cadres who were supportive of the protests. As demonstrations gained momentum, both groups reacted opportunistically. First, the leadership of the Muslim Brotherhood announced its support for the demonstrations on January 28. The Salafi leaders then dropped their religious rhetoric and presented candidates for the subsequent legislative and presidential elections.

I happened to be living about 100 yards from Tahrir Square at that time and thus could literally see, hear, and even smell the stream of events in the square. I was also carefully following the developments because my children belonged to the generation whose voice resonated throughout the protests. As a father, I was worried. As a political analyst and practitioner, I was enthusiastically witnessing a younger generation finally express their serious interest in determining the country's future. This was a healthy development despite the generation's lack of political experience. While I wanted change, I was not a natural activist, nor did I oppose the Mubarak regime. My interest was ensuring that rational minds are committed to good governance. The country needed to do better in order to be proud again. The younger generation deserved to see their aspirations for freedom and justice fulfilled. The alternative would be a tremendous disappointment, frustration, and anger, putting the country at risk.

Two memorable episodes stand out in particular from the 18 days of the revolution. One was on January 28, the intense and infamous "Day of Rage". As I walked from my home in Garden City less than half a mile away to Qasr El-Nil Bridge, there were clashes between the protesters and the police in front of the Cairo Opera House gates at the opposite end of the bridge, where heavy security blockades had been set up. Since the first days of the protests, there had been a large security presence on the streets.

Nevertheless, against all odds, the demonstrators remained peaceful and refrained from initiating violence—although, at certain moments, scuffles occurred. Even at 100 yards away, the effects of the tear gas that the police were using against the demonstrators quickly irritated my eyes. A young man who managed to break through the police barricades ran alone towards Tahrir Square, passing directly in front of me. A few minutes later, a police officer came from the Square running in the opposite direction towards the Opera House. He looked at me and anxiously yelled, "You surround us from this side too?" That very moment, I concluded that the demonstrators had gained the upper ground and that the authorities were losing control. I realized immediately, that Egypt was at a defining moment, ending the Mubarak era. The formal announcement was only a matter of time. Later that day, the army was first deployed to the streets and issued an official declaration that it would respond to popular concerns and not open fire on demonstrating civilians.

Another turning point for me occurred on February 2. Hooligans went into Tahrir Square on horses and camels and a pitched battle broke out with demonstrators in what was called, "The battle of camels". This was broadcasted live on television. Watching this horrendous episode for 12 hours with no one intervening to stop the assault was shocking. It raised questions and anger in our communities about our very civility and humanity.

I remember asking myself at that point, "How could we as a generation claim any set of values and hand over a country like this to the younger generation?", I was overwhelmed by strong repulsive feeling as violence escalated against civilians and finally decided that I could no longer remain a passive observer.

On that same day, a group of independent public figures, who were essentially professionals and members of the business community with no partisan affiliations, came together to discuss the ongoing developments. That evening, I contacted Nabil El-Araby, a distinguished career diplomat, future foreign minister and longtime friend who was part of this group, offering to join them. I became the 12th member of this group, which was later referred to in the media as the "Wise Men Committee (WMC)".

The group quickly released its first statement calling for the president to hand over power to his vice president, while remaining in office as a titular president for the remaining six months of his fifth term in office. It also called for the dissolution of the parliament (both the People's Assembly and the Shura Council), the establishment of a transitional committee to introduce government policies and reforms, the establishment of a new government, the removal of some of the widely contested members of the National Democratic Party (NDP) leadership, as well as the end of the state of emergency.

On February 5, the group mandated El-Araby and Ahmed Kamal Abou El-Magd, a distinguished jurist and former cabinet member during Anwar Sadat's presidency, to meet the then Vice President Omar Suleiman and convey the proposal to him. According to the account later offered by both El-Araby and Abou El-Magd, Suleiman listened attentively but told them that he would not entertain a proposal for the president to hand over power. He did, however, promise to consider the ideas proposed with respect to the reforms without explaining why such measures could not be adopted immediately. El-Araby and Abou El-Magd also met Prime Minister Ahmed Shafik who had nothing different to say.

After the meetings with Suleiman and Shafik, we were very careful to continue to support the demonstrators while still looking for solutions. Our goal was to create a soft transition process for a new Egypt that would fulfill the aspirations of the demonstrators. It was evident by then that the regime was collapsing. The country needed change and greater openness. Avoiding chaos with all its potential human and material cost was the preferable path towards a new reality.

This was to be a challenging process. The demonstrators had numerous representatives with nobody in particular mandated to speak on their behalf. At any given encounter between the WMC and the demonstrators, there were at least five groups with different political and ideological beliefs claiming to represent the demonstrators. These groups included the younger generation of the Muslim Brotherhood who had supported the January 25 Revolution even when their leaders were resistant. Meeting youth from different walks of life in Tahrir was both insightful and enlightening. Some of those young men and women were affluent, while others were not economically well off. The majority were from Egyptian public universities, although a few had studied abroad. They all shared a sharp political awareness and a strong commitment to change. They acknowledged their different visions on Egypt's future but agreed that Mubarak should step down even before the suggested reforms were initiated. The young demonstrators believed the country could seriously address all the constitutional and legal issues after the president left, otherwise, they would continue protesting. One young man told me: "We have just undertaken a revolution. This is not about technicalities. It is about fundamental change, and you—the wise men group should understand this. Help us develop the way and the tools to change the system because nothing less than changing the system will satisfy us."

The WMC's incremental approach was a bit different, but the demonstrators who were uneasy with the group still respected our integrity and acknowledged our patriotism. They did not openly reject our ideas although they did not embrace our proposal when it was offered in the public statement. And, they asked us to convey our opinions to the authorities but not to negotiate on their behalf, which was fine by us. There were differing opinions amongst the youth in these very heady fluid times. No one at that point in the revolution could clearly assess how it would turn out.

Meanwhile, Suleiman was meeting with a larger group of opposition leaders from across the political spectrum that he personally chose to engage with. It did not include anyone from the youth groups we met with, or anyone from our group for that matter. Thus, there were different processes going on at the same time. Reflective of how confused the regime was at that point was that Suleiman essentially met with "political parties plus a few of the demonstrators", rather than "demonstrators plus some of the parties", at a moment when the political parties had no influence whatsoever on the demonstrations in Tahrir Square.

Day by day, the demonstrators systematically increased the pressure in different parts of Egypt. They were gaining strength from the repeated failures of the authorities. In addition, although the revolution was initiated and driven by youth and primarily supported by the middle class, the military was an equally determining factor in ensuring the outcome. Its publicly pronounced mandate was to prevent chaos and excessive bloodshed but was clearly distancing itself from the executive branch of government. In effect, it took a popular posture that became a source of strength for the demonstrators. Soon thereafter, the demonstrators started chanting, "The army and the people are one." This slogan was also quickly reiterated in the public statements issued in the name of the Supreme Council of the Armed Forces (SCAF) since the early days of the revolution. It also found its way onto stickers plastered all over the tanks and military vehicles nationwide, something that could only be done by the armed forces themselves. All this occurred without a single reference to the president or the government in the SCAF's statements.

Two weeks later, Mubarak, in an attempt to contain what had clearly become an irreversible and determined call for change, promised to commit to the reforms that had been previously proposed by the WMC, but without making any reference to the group itself. However, this offer came too late. The political tide was clearly favoring the demonstrators and their demands increased. Mubarak's new position failed to convince the masses who were ever more determined to end his rule. One day later, on February 11, 2011, Vice President Suleiman announced in a televised statement that Mubarak had decided to step down and that the SCAF would take over power for a transitional period. As Suleiman uttered these words, public celebrations broke out everywhere in Egypt.

In the final analysis, two important conclusions can be drawn from the events that rocked Egypt between January 25 and February 11. The first is that there was a huge gap in the perceptions between the president, his staff, and the realities on the ground or the commitment of the masses. Three decades in office at the pinnacle of power had blinded the regime.

Secondly, the 18 days of the revolution showed the ultimate limitations of power and was a worthy case study for a government's "don'ts" during crisis management. The revolution, especially in the first few days, saw young demonstrators lose their lives in the chaos that emerged. But, beyond the Day of Rage, it was becoming clear that nobody was prepared or able to take charge. The power of mobile phones and social media also proved stronger than that of established and substantial police services. The Ministry of Interior's security forces had already fallen in disarray before the deployment of the armed forces. The challenge during the 18 days was winning the hearts and minds of the demonstrators and the public at large. This was testimony to the great impact of the IT revolution and to the changing definition of power in the early years of the twenty-first century. Military power and law enforcement will continue to be important. However, the power of communications and networking, greatly facilitating demonstrators' ability to marshal support and organize, was becoming of extreme importance and a disruptive force in traditional security paradigms.

Watching and then participating in the intense transformation occurring in Egypt in 2011 was for me a fascinating but bittersweet and nerve-racking experience. Most Egyptians felt the same, especially those associated in the past with government institutions that had a representative role such as the Ministry of Foreign Affairs. As professional civil servants, we had all defended government choices some of which we did not necessarily agree with, of course with the exception of decisions that raised critical ethical issues. Yet, we were first and foremost Egyptians who wanted progress for our country, a paradox that poses difficult choices for many.

Interestingly, the 2011 Revolution brought Egypt back to the center of the world, with the country becoming once again a trendsetter in the Middle East with its ramifications well beyond its borders. During the 18 days, foreign embassies in Egypt and many international friends attempted to contact me by phone and email. This increased several-fold when I became active in the WMC. As a former diplomat, I completely understood their attempts to gather information as quickly as possible on this dramatic turn of events. However, for me, this was and had to remain a purely Egyptian experience. Encouraging international influence on the events was neither wise nor acceptable. Consequently, I either completely ignored the communications from my foreign friends or infrequently responded with short perfunctory messages meant to discourage further contacts until things settled.

Internationally, it was clear that the United States was lost and surprised by the ongoing developments in Egypt and the Arab world, communicating vague and contradictory messages to Cairo through former United States Ambassador to Egypt, Frank Wisner, as the Revolution was heading into its second week. These messages were later the subject of contradicting reports that suggested differences between Wisner's and the administration's opinions. This was testimony to the disarray in Washington during the early days of the Revolution in Egypt. For their part, the Egyptian youth were not focused on but appeared initially disappointed with America's slow reaction when the United States Secretary of State Hillary Clinton came out to express confidence in the strength of the Mubarak rule. When President Barack Obama remarked that he was "inspired by these kids" and called upon Mubarak to leave office, the protesters felt that they were finally being heard. Nevertheless, generally speaking, American reactions to the events in Egypt were still a lot better than European ones. Obama focused on Egypt's demonstrations and the rights and hopes of the protestors. Some of the European capitals issued statements started by reminding Egypt of the need to respect its agreements with Israel, which was not part of our domestic debate at that point in time.

In any case, the demonstrators themselves rarely dealt with foreign policy in their discussions or public statements. It did not seem to be one of their immediate top priorities. They were essentially focused on domestic issues—although the call for public accountability was also about foreign policy. As the demonstrations started to subside, the leaders of the protests said that they would respect international agreements. Similarly, when the SCAF took over, as of the evening of February 11, it quickly declared that Egypt would respect its international agreements just to calm any possible concerns among the international community.

A CHAOTIC INTERLUDE BETWEEN TWO REVOLUTIONS: THE ARMY AND THE BROTHERHOOD

After Hosni Mubarak stepped down, there was commotion, confusion, and differences of opinion. No one in Egypt expected what had just unfolded and no one had planned for the next steps. The old guard who were close to the former president saw their power usurped in less than one month, with many fleeing abroad or hiding in Egypt. Some even faced long yet futile legal processes on corruption charges. The WMC proposed a declaration of citizenship principles and constitutional provisions for national consensus, holding several meetings with many concerned figures to help develop the elements of this declaration. At the same time, Mohamed El-Baradei, who was not a member of the group, and others both the supporters and opponents of the January 25 Revolution, acted to initiate a "transitional period". These efforts remained hotly contested and somewhat vague in terms of actual implementation because diverse political opposition groups, from the far left to the far right, failed to agree on a coherent path for the future, which should not necessarily have been an impossible mission.

In addition, the revolution did not have the kind of leadership that could lead the arduous process of reform and reconstruction ahead. El-Baradei, whom the protestors had for the most part been looking up to, was not a natural politician. He had said many times that he preferred to remain a beacon for the revolution and conscience of the reform movement. Meanwhile, political opposition groups from across the spectrum also failed to present themselves as influential players in the emerging political paradigm, mainly because of their inability to compromise at that particularly crucial point in time. As for the Muslim Brotherhood and the Salafis, they had opted for a pragmatic opportunistic approach before Mubarak stepped down and continued to close with the Supreme Council of the Armed Forces (SCAF). The Islamists thus became the most adept players, but because of their rigid ideology, they did not manage to assume leadership of the revolution or develop widespread consensus among the population.

The SCAF itself also seemed overwhelmed with the process. Because of my own longstanding interest in national security and arms control, and having served as ambassador to the United States, many of the SCAF members had worked under my leadership of different Egyptian delegations or embassies. Several were and still remain personal friends. During the first few months of 2011, starting on January 25, they would regularly visit me in my apartment in Garden City to discuss the situation and ask for advice on how to move forward. Many of my suggestions were to naught but our discussions remained friendly and candid.

For the SCAF, the youth activists and El-Baradei represented fundamental and unforeseen changes that were worrisome in their ambiguity, particularly with respect to their potential consequences on the workings of the Egyptian government, which has been traditionally characterized by a strong central authority with a position of privilege for the security establishment in both its military and police components. Secular traditional politicians were seen as ineffective with a limited constituency and were, therefore, not considered serious players to accommodate. On the other hand, the SCAF believed that the Muslim Brotherhood, the Salafis, and the rest of the Islamists had influence on the street and thus chose to tactically accommodate them, particularly the Brotherhood. In pursuing the realist approach, SCAF chose to fall back on the advice of former government officials from the Mubarak era, none of whom was enthusiastic about change.

Subsequently, I became anxious at the absence of sound civilian advice for the SCAF, which had rejected suggestions of establishing a presidential troika with civilians and military to govern, albeit the SCAF created a wide-ranging but ineffective advisory board as a face-saving compromise. Then, upon the advice of Mamdouh Marei, the last minister of justice under Mubarak, the SCAF formed a small constitutional committee of legal experts, who were overwhelmingly but not exclusively Islamists, to suggest quick changes to the constitution that has been in place since 1971. In March 2011, I became increasingly pessimistic when the SCAF came out clearly in support of holding a public referendum on this committee's constitutional amendments. This step would expedite the timeline towards parliamentary elections, rather than provide giving an opportunity to draft a new Egyptian constitution first, with an inclusive post-revolution foundation, the path taken by Tunisia before us.

Concerned primarily with ensuring security and uncomfortable with the mandate to govern, the SCAF clearly preferred to quickly move into the electoral process. Friends on the SCAF did not deny these mistakes and emphasized that the military were trained in national security issues, not nation-building. They explained that when they consulted with different civilians, they received conflicting views and ultimately had to make gut choices.

SCAF, at one point, considered bringing in El-Baradei or Amre Moussa as prime minister before deciding against that. Both were viewed as difficult to manage. The first elections for the two chambers of parliament were held on December 20 and February 2012 with Islamist parties gaining 61 percent and 83 percent, respectively. SCAF, that still held the highest executive power, in the absence of a president, chose another secular civil servant Kamal El-Ganzouri, a former Prime Minister and Minister of Planning during the Mubarak rule, with a long experience in government. The new prime minister had the daunting task of also serving as a secular counterweight to the Islamists in parliament. The Muslim Brotherhood had won the largest number of Parliament seats in the first post-Revolution legislative elections. The other Islamist faction, the Salafis, had also come in second.

To achieve his objectives, the Prime Minister pulled together a team of technocrats known for their professional expertise and commitment to government service. As he was doing so, I was contacted twice, first by an intermediary and then by El-Ganzouri himself, in an effort to convince me to join the government as foreign minister. My relations with him were mutually respectful and professional in nature, but I still could not convince myself to commit to engaging in domestic politics. I declined the offer to become Egypt's foreign minister for the third time.

This was a moment when all the prominent Egyptian politicians and technocrats, from the extreme left to the Islamists on the right, including the Brotherhood, lacked practical public governance and serious political experience. All of them were eager to exercise authority and consequently pushed for minor constitutional changes as well as for early parliamentary and presidential elections. El-Baradei was the only exception amongst the leading political figures. He was in favor of a longer process that would allow first for the adoption of a new constitution commensurate with the aspirations of the 2011 Revolution and allow the political parties to gain more traction with the public.

Watching things unfold after January 2011 and recognizing the disarray of the Egyptian secular political forces, I too was in favor of the longer and more cautious process that should start with the development of an inclusive constitution to set the ground rules for governance in a new phase of Egypt before calling for elections. To this day, I strongly believe that the gravest mistake and the paramount reason for most of the problems thereafter was the failure to allow the necessary time to draft such a constitution. Holding the elections quickly not only meant we did not yet have a truly embraced constitution to place the parameters for governance, but it was also bound to result in a Muslim-Brotherhood-supported majority in the parliament.[1] This was not strictly because of the popularity they enjoyed at the time but also because of the general sense of anger towards anyone associated with the Mubarak era as well as the lack of grassroots experience of the liberals who were not associated with the former majority party. The strength and effectiveness of the Brotherhood mobilization mechanism were based on ideology, but it was also more coherent and far more efficient than any other groups after over a half-century void of true pluralistic politics.

Allowing the Brotherhood or any party to win a majority before agreeing on a constitution that established the rules of the game was an egregious affront to the revolution and its martyrs. It also consequently allowed the Muslim Brotherhood to establish a committee to write up a constitution after President Mohamed Morsi won the 2012 presidential elections. This committee was so biased that by the end of its work, every single non-Islamist member had walked out in protest. This flagrant attempt seemed determined to change the face of Egypt by including 26 different references to religion in the provisions of the constitution. It also included language that would have made the provisions of the constitution subject to the legislation by the newly elected parliament with an Islamist majority, rather than making legislation contingent on it being consistent with the provisions of the national constitution to which all walks of life relate to the normal practice around the world.

With the luxury of hindsight, one can argue that providing Islamists so much room to maneuver before learning the art of government was what brought their quick downfall. They hastily overreached, not understanding

---

[1] The Muslim Brotherhood had won the largest number of seats in the Egyptian parliament in the first post-revolution legislative elections, with the Salafis coming next in the share of seats.

that they had gained more power to implement their programs but would not be able to swiftly change Egypt's centrist cosmopolitan identity without an existential battle. Machiavellian minds postulate that the SCAF intentionally drew the Muslim Brotherhood into this trap, leading to their quick self-destruction and possibly preventing even greater bloodshed.

While calling for an early election did work in the Brotherhood's favor, I doubt that the motivation behind giving them that opportunity was enabling them to self-destruct. The rise of the Muslim Brotherhood to power presented many challenges for the SCAF. The Brotherhood was bound to target the military early on because it was the strongest institution in the country, the only one capable of resisting its authority and that is what they did. There were also no credible assurances that self-destruction would occur so quickly.

THE PRESIDENTIAL ELECTIONS

The first presidential elections held after Mubarak's ouster was, in itself, testimony to the disagreements and even chaos that permeated the political scene the year after the 2011 Revolution. Egyptian society faced choices that garnered more opposition than support.

The strongest Muslim Brotherhood candidate, Khairat El-Shater, deputy to the supreme guide of the group *(murshid)*, was disqualified from the presidential race because he would have been released from jail without concluding his necessary prohibition period before he could fully exercise his political rights.

Omar Suleiman, Mubarak's long-serving powerful head of intelligence and his only vice president, peculiarly failed to qualify after the relevant electoral committee rejected his nomination despite being an establishment person long in the security services with their penchant for detail.

Mohamed El-Baradei, the "icon of the revolution" in the eyes of many youth protest leaders and the favorite candidate of the youth, withdrew after submitting his candidature, complaining that the elections were being conducted in an unhealthy political environment.

Ultimately, out of 13 candidates who ran the course, only 5 were competitive: Abdel Moneim Aboul Fotouh, Mohamed Morsi, Amre Moussa, Hamdeen Sabahi, and Ahmed Shafik.

Aboul Fotouh was still seen by secularists as an Islamist ideologue because of his long association with the Muslim Brotherhood since his university years in the 1970s. Having already been announced as the leader of the Freedom and Justice Party, the newly established political arm of the Muslim Brotherhood, Morsi was a compromise candidate for the group, a widely noted fact that prompted critics to unkindly dub him as "the reserve candidate". Moussa, the former Foreign Minister and Secretary-general of the Arab League, was a charismatic candidate whom all others feared. But it was felt that he did not commit himself enough to change in order to attract the youth, while ironically the old guard of the Egyptian bureaucracy, the large business interests, the National Democratic Party affiliates, and the government institutions felt that he is positioning himself too close to the January 25 Revolution. A Nasserite progressive candidate, Sabahi managed to gain the support of the youth after El-Baradei decided to drop out of the presidential race. However, his candidature never really gained widespread support amongst the middle class that had emerged during the Sadat and Mubarak eras. Some analysts even suggested that he ultimately received some unannounced support from the Muslim Brotherhood to counter Aboul Fotouh. A former Air Force commander and cabinet member, Shafik had been chosen by Mubarak to head the government during the early days of the January Revolution and was removed by the SCAF in March 2011, under pressure from the youth movements. He was never a SCAF favorite because of his perceived chauvinism.

Ironically, all five candidates offered too much and too little for their opposition and their natural consistency. Egyptian society as such was still finding its way in this free-for-all, truly open elections. It was not clear then whether voters would make emotional choices or vote according to their evaluations of proposed political platforms. This made it very difficult to estimate the sustainability of public opinion trends as well as the relative efficacy of the political machinery of any of the candidates.

I myself remained resolute and consistent that I wanted a secular president. At the very beginning of the election process, before the disqualifications and withdrawals, Moussa asked whether I would join his campaign. My tentative response, which surprised him, was that I wanted my vote to have an effect and be based on an objective reading of the election prospects of the secular candidate—not on personal preferences. Therefore, I informed him, one month before the first round of votes, that I would give my support to the leading secular candidate because I wanted it to influence the result towards secularism and pluralism. I added that I would also ask the other secular candidates to withdraw in favor of the candidate who stands higher chances. I was close to both Moussa and El-Baradei and my vote would have been to one of them. That drove me to publish an article in the Egyptian Daily El-Shorouk, defending both their records, which were the target of false information campaigns.

One month before the elections, El-Baradei withdrew so I declared my support for Moussa. As promised, I also attempted to convince El-Baradei to influence the youth vote by announcing his support for Moussa. As an incentive given his interest in reform, I suggested that a declaration about constitutional change be drafted and read out by Moussa. To his credit, Moussa agreed; however, in the end, El-Baradei refused to announce his support for Moussa because he believed that the conceptual differences in their approach to government were simply too wide to overcome.

Moussa pursued a relentless substantive election campaign, traveling across the country and addressing all the issues of concern to the wider public. In many respects, he was a natural politician, always with a smile, ready to energetically press the flesh throughout the country, and ambitious enough to invest the tremendous time and effort needed to run for high office. He tried hard to address the interests of the different sectors of the Egyptian electorate. Given the capacity of both the Brotherhood and the old guard to mobilize voters, the optimistic expectation was that Moussa would run second in the first round, held on May 23 and 24, 2012, carrying him into the decisive second round in that politically heated summer. The most pessimistic estimate was that he would come in third, just missing the second round. To everyone's surprise, Moussa came in fifth, far below even the naysayer's prediction that he would barely miss out in the race for the second round. Just above him in the fourth position was Aboul Fotouh and another rank up was Sabahi. Morsi and Shafik emerged as the two front-runners.

Aboul Fotouh could not garner much liberal support because of his Islamist background although he did get some who simply wanted to reject the past. On the other hand, because he had challenged a Muslim Brotherhood candidate, he did not get the traditional Islamist vote but only those on the margins.

Sabahy, a nostalgic Nasserite candidate achieved more support than expected, but there simply wasn't enough nostalgia to win an election in an Egypt of 90 million, a majority of which are youth and, consequently, were looking forward rather than backward in history.

There were three probable reasons for the limited support that Moussa ultimately received. Moussa's team included numerous former Foreign Ministry officials who, while well-intentioned, did not have any real expertise in getting out the vote, ever so important in rural areas. They also bet too heavily on the strength of Moussa's personal communications skills at a time when the voting pattern of Egyptians had not yet been determined. Secondly, Moussa did not have any institutional support and had no serious party of his own. The NDP preferred Shafik and both the old guard and the Islamists were determined to discredit Moussa. Thirdly, he tried too hard to accommodate the numerous conflicting sectors of the Egyptian voter constituencies, consequently losing more than he gained by never being representative enough for any single one of these groups.

As we closed in on the second round of elections got closer, scheduled for June 16 and 17, 2012, the results looked increasingly unclear and uncomfortable almost for everyone. The Muslim Brotherhood supporters that originally preferred El-Shater but were left with Morsi. Meanwhile, Shafik, a gung-ho military man, was not particularly liked by the SCAF, the youth or the activists. Neither of the two was a leader during the revolution, nor were they even the preferred choices of their naturally closest constituency.

As the final count was being tabulated, a group of civil society members of diverse political associations met candidate Morsi at the Fairmont Hotel in Heliopolis, Cairo, in search of guarantees that his ideological association would not drive his government to become exclusive if he was elected. They issued a joint statement of principles that they thought would bind Morsi to their democratic secular vision. This included a commitment that the Brotherhood would appoint women and Egyptian Copts as well as a non-Islamist prime minister. This Fairmont meeting and the subsequent declaration were testimony that the Egyptian body politic, especially the liberals, had no real understanding of the Brotherhood and very little experience in electoral politics as well as multi-stakeholder governance, perhaps as a result of over six decades of nondemocratic and centralized rule. Morsi had long-standing commitments to an ideology that was not secular or inclusive. It was very improbable that he, essentially a replacement, would be willing or able to convince the Brotherhood to compromise ideologically.

On June 24, 2012, the Supreme Presidential Elections Commission announced that Morsi won the presidency by 51.73 percent, a result that some politicians and observers still question to this day. This announcement came after a curious two-day delay on the part of the committee without clear justification. The delay amongst other things generated contradicting leaks about the results and led to speculation that the United

States had contacted the SCAF in support of Morsi. I know that United States Ambassador to Egypt, Anne Patterson, had been in contact with all the candidates and that she attempted to contact the SCAF at that late stage in the election process, but I do not have firsthand information on what her message was. The election result announcement came a few days after the SCAF issued a constitutional declaration granting itself legal prerogatives, including the right to legislation and budget adoption until a new constitution was drafted and a new parliament elected.

CHAPTER 9

A Nexus of Foreign and Domestic Policy Throughout the Interim Period

The exceptional circumstances of the last few years, with the removal of a president as well as a transitional period towards the reestablishment of a traditional political system, bring into play numerous domestic and international players and considerations, underlying the importance of a more balanced foreign policy, much of which defines my tenure as a foreign minister.

ALIENATING TIMES

President-elect Mohamed Morsi was inaugurated as President of Egypt on June 30, 2012. The newly elected civilian president was now officially duty-bound to represent not only his Muslim Brotherhood constituency but also Egyptian secularists like myself who might not have voted for him and were not happy with the election results. The situation in Egypt was much more complicated than usual. While we suddenly had had true pluralistic elections, we had not developed a pluralistic political culture, where candidates won elections and thus gained the authority to pursue their programs, while citizens, whether supporters or not, continued to have equal rights and were duly represented by their elected officials. Shortly after the inauguration, I published an open letter to the new president in the privately owned and well-circulated Egyptian daily Al-Masry Al-Youm. The gist of my message was that even though I had not voted for him and was not happy with the results of the election, he was now my president,

© The Author(s) 2020
N. Fahmy, *Egypt's Diplomacy in War, Peace and Transition*,
https://doi.org/10.1007/978-3-030-26388-1_9

nonetheless. "Now", I wrote to the president, "I was his problem because he had to represent and take my interests into account as well."

This was to be a challenge for all Egyptians, but having been elected into office, the burden and responsibility fell upon on the shoulders of the Muslim Brotherhood. The year to follow was replete with political mismanagement and amateurishness on the part of the Muslim Brotherhood and Morsi's government. The bungling repeatedly gave its adversaries common cause while it was trying to establish its influence like any other elected majority would.

The Brotherhood understood that the Egyptian military, which was widely respected and supported, was the strongest institution in Egypt. But rather than tread carefully, the Brotherhood was determined to quickly tame and attain an uncontested monopoly of power. Consequently, Morsi quickly brought in the chief financial officer of the armed forces to get a clear understanding of the military budget and resources. Then, in the wake of a shocking and unprecedented terror attack that killed 16 conscripts in Ramadan, he decided to remove the Minister of Defense Hussein Tantawi and the Military Chief of Staff Sami Anan, replacing them with Abdel Fattah El-Sisi and Sedki Sobhy, respectively.

At the annual celebrations of the October War, Morsi committed one of his most serious mistakes. Traditionally, these were national celebrations with a strong military overtone. In 2012, however, Morsi's government decided to make it a reinstatement of extremist Islamists. The president rode into the parade grounds, standing in an open convertible, waving to the crowds, unaccompanied by the minister of defense. This was a misguided beginning but one that could have been accepted as a result of a lack of experience had it been the only mistake that evening.

Even more provocative, however, was the list of VIP guests at the event. Very few were present or past senior military officers. The overwhelming majority were of extremist Islamist backgrounds, including some convicted in the assassination of President Sadat at the very same celebration three decades earlier. Military leaders I later talked to were shocked by what they considered a direct affront to the armed forces, reminding them of Sadat's assassination in their midst. The surprise and displeasure were shared by the general public that took this as the beginning of an attempt to rewrite Egyptian history and legitimize violent Islamism.

A few days later, Morsi moved the confrontation to another front when he acted to remove the public prosecutor without the traditional consent of the judiciary that had already been apprehensive about his intentions.

This decision faced open resentment and considerable resistance from the judiciary even amongst some who were considered to have Brotherhood sentiments like the vice president and his brother the minister of justice. Then, in November 2012, Morsi issued a constitutional declaration that placed the position of the president above reproach and accountability, in complete violation not only of the existing constitution but also of every constitution Egypt has ever had.

At the same time that he was taking on the military and judiciary, Morsi quickly started to infuriate non-Islamist stakeholders as he ignored the commitments he had made in the Fairmont Declaration. Morsi condoned anti-Coptic agitation and egged his supporters on, condoning violent responses against the youth who were peacefully demonstrating against policies that were in contradiction with the aspirations of the 2011 Revolution.

Morsi's popularity was quickly also seriously challenged over poor state management of daily affairs. Disappointment in the newly elected president accentuated with the tragic train crash that killed close to 50 students in Upper Egypt, a reminder for many of the unchecked negligence that prevailed during Mubarak's last years of rule. The Egyptian media, which had not yet succumbed to the Muslim Brotherhood, had a field day picking on every mistake and commenting on issues candidly, bluntly, or satirically.

While protests were increasing against the November constitutional declaration, a group of liberals, die-hard activists, and old regime figures established the National Salvation Front (NSF) as an informal alliance that attempted to ensure that secular representations and voices had resonance in Egyptian politics. I was not part of the NSF, projecting my opinions instead through the local and international media as well as through a short-lived, and not particularly fruitful, membership in the Dostour Party that had been founded by El-Baradei.

As the weeks passed by, Egyptians knew that the battle for a new, more progressive Egypt was not over as more and more segments of society were alienated from the new government. I remember, in January 2013, hosting the American columnist Thomas Friedman to speak at the American University in Cairo (AUC) where I had founded the School of Global Affairs and Public Policy. As I walked him off the university campus in Tahrir Square minutes after his talk, he asked whether the president had made a mistake in taking on the military so early. I responded that Morsi had taken on everyone very early in his tenure, creating an adversary not only of the military and security institutions but also of a large number of centrists in Egyptian society as a whole.

The early questions and disappointments were not really about the Morsi-led leadership in Egypt not quickly establishing a democratic state, which we had not achieved under past presidents. This was bound to take time. The discontent that pervaded was not actually about the poor provision of goods and services, which would not have so quickly generated a call for his removal even in a hyperactive political period. No one could seriously argue that the Muslim Brotherhood ideology was foreign to Egypt, including those who opposed it like myself. It had started amongst us in the 1920s. And, it can legitimately be argued that they, like anyone else, had the right to express their views and promote their policies, provided that this does not challenge the country's identity.

My conclusion, however, was that in the agitated environment in Egypt's political scene, given the conceptual contradictions between the Islamists vision for Egypt's identity and that of all others, something was bound to burst. Morsi's political bungling, much more than bad governance, confirmed the inevitable and expedited its occurrence.

The majority of the middle class and large sectors of society were still aspiring for inclusive governance and a role in determining their future. The secretive clannish approach of the Brotherhood where the "Morshid", not the president elected in 2012, was the ultimate decision-maker was troublesome to most, even those who were ready to give it a chance. I, myself, had openly said that Morsi was my elected president, even while admitting that I had not voted for him and remained even extremely uncomfortable with the Muslim Brotherhood ideology.

President Mohamed Morsi's tactical political mistakes fed the opposition and brought it together. These steps expedited his fall and the rejection of the Brotherhood. That was not, however, the whole story or the core reason behind his demise.

However, as Morsi tried to implement his policies, it became ever more evident that the country would not be inclusive. In addition, serious concerns arose about threats to Egypt's very identity as a secular inclusive state. This had been its longstanding core niche especially since the 1919 revolution, which codified that identity in the constitution adopted a few years later, an identity that had remained unchallenged even under non-democratic presidents before Morsi.

Media in Egypt, while under pressure remained vocal and expressive frequently and vociferously criticizing both the president and the Muslim

Brotherhood. With the exception of the Muslim Brotherhood and its Islamist supporters, youth activists, liberal leaders, and secularists believed that the Brotherhood was determined to change the identity of Egypt. It was strongly felt that this was not something one could condone for three more years, pending the end of Morsi's term in office. I shared this concern and had frequently called upon the president to be inclusive but this fell on deaf ears.

Many around the world have repeated that they had had bad presidents, and Morsi was not the first nor would he be the last bad one to be elected. That is true; however, Morsi and the Muslim Brotherhood embodied all of the deficiencies and weaknesses that sparked the Arab Awakening and even took them a step further. The Muslim Brotherhood was a closed, nontransparent society operating under a strict hierarchy and absolute allegiance. In addition, Egypt had elected Morsi, but he was, in effect, a puppet of the Brotherhood's supreme leader, who was not elected by the public. Most importantly, the Brotherhood conceptualized Egypt as one part of the *Umma* or nation rather than a separate nation-state while many supporters of inclusiveness, including myself, saw the Brotherhood as part of a diverse, tolerant, and culturally rich Egypt, not the other way around.

All of this was, in effect, the antipathy of everything aspired for in the 2011 Revolution, posing fundamental questions of what Egypt, in fact, was and who would govern it. Therefore, while I would have preferred a normal transition of power, particularly after the loss of life in 2011, I also concluded that in light of all these mistakes and concerns unless there was a fundamental turnaround in Morsi's approach and that of the Brotherhood, an imminent confrontation was, in effect, bound to happen.

Sadly, nothing changed, and tensions kept intensifying. The military issued a one-week deadline for politicians to bring things together and then extended it for an additional week until the end of June. As we came closer to the June 30 confrontation, there was intensive political jockeying and some extremely unconventional attempts to bring Egypt's body politic together. A new grassroots youth movement Tamarod (Arabic for "rebellion"), which had considerable support from the business community and from within parts of the state establishment, gathered a wide number of signatures to remove Morsi and hold early presidential elections, announcing that it had collected over 22 million signatures. This was a major development but not the first popular demonstration against Morsi since his inauguration.

As efforts failed and the parties remained intransigent, Minister of Defense Abdel Fattah el-Sisi issued a public invitation to the leading politicians to gather over lunch, as his guests, at one of the army-owned facilities to brainstorm on how to reduce the political diatribes and move the country forward. Everyone initially accepted this invitation, including the president and El-Baradei. Suddenly, however, Morsi retracted his acceptance without explanation, but it was possibly out of concern that this would legitimize the armed forces as an independent political player, or it could have been due to pressures from Brotherhood leadership, or both.

Egypt was paying the price of over 60 years of non-pluralistic politics, and there were no senior political leaders of stature and experience who could garner widespread support for a middle political deal. A meeting that was at first designed to be unannounced between Amre Moussa, in his individual capacity, and Khairat El-Shater, the deputy supreme leader of the Brotherhood, also failed to deliver what could have been a last-minute exit from an escalating political crisis.

On June 23, 2013, El-Sisi again called upon the Egyptian political forces from across the spectrum to collectively find a way to move forward. He then issued an ultimatum that they had a week, which was later extended for an additional 48 hours to search for solutions after which the military would "act to safeguard the nation". With still no progress, the army visibly deployed its forces around strategic buildings.

Morsi spoke to the nation twice in a matter of three days. First, apportioning blame for the bad provision of public goods and services leaving everyone disappointed. Then, the Egyptian president's office announced that Morsi would give a second important speech on the evening of June 27. Everyone I contacted felt we were on the verge of a breakthrough that would avert confrontation. The expectation was that after huffing and puffing, Morsi would ultimately reach out to his adversaries at least symbolically, inviting them for consultations. Others, more optimistic and claiming to be better-connected, expected Morsi to call for a public referendum on whether there should be early presidential elections. Later, when I joined the government after Morsi's removal, I heard El-Sisi, still minister of defense, say that the top military brass had proposed to the president shortly before the June 30 demonstrations that he call for early presidential elections and commit to a more inclusive political approach.

That night, I impatiently waited for the Egyptian television to start the live broadcast of President Morsi's speech. As delay after delay occurred, we all assumed that the finishing touches on compromise were being put into place and that intense negotiations were ongoing. Finally, close to midnight, Morsi gave his speech. To my shock and dismay, he unabashedly blamed all of his adversaries for the country's problems. Nothing in his speech was indicative of a desire to bring the country together. He positioned himself as the single symbol of legitimacy in terms that made it inconceivable that he could during that speech, come down off that high, isolated pedestal to suggest a compromise. Being given two ultimatums to no avail, the question became not whether but when the military would act in response to secular public sentiments.

The events of the following three days were, by all accounts, nontraditional. This was not the normal way of removing an elected president, but these were exceptional circumstances. Islamists were overzealous in their political motivation albeit Supreme Council of the Armed Forces (SCAF) and most Egyptian secularists insisted first on establishing the rules of the game in a new post-2011 consensual constitution before moving to elections in which whoever won could not have exercised exclusive politics.

Like all militaries, the Egyptian military has contingency plans to intervene in unconventional circumstances to deal with foreign threats and establish order on a temporary basis if the domestic situation becomes threatening to the state's security and stability. The Egyptian military previously implemented this during the 1977 bread riots when angry protesters demonstrated against Sadat's presidential decree increasing food prices. It did so again in January 2011, with the public demonstrations against the police and the Mubarak regime. It was clearly prepared to do so again.

The military acted swiftly, gaining control of all strategic assets throughout the country and isolating President Morsi while at the same time not engaging in confrontations with the demonstrating public, except in circumstances where Brotherhood supporters aggressively confronted them.

Then, in a live televised ceremony on July 3, 2013, and in the presence of the top brass, as well as a number of prominent civilians, including El-Baradei and leaders of Al-Azhar, the Orthodox Church, Tamarod, and the Salafi Al-Nour Party, El-Sisi announced Morsi's ouster in response to the demands of the massive nationwide demonstrations. He also announced an interim roadmap, which was agreed upon by representatives of diverse political groups, including the NSF and the Salafis, and of the religious establishment, to develop a new constitution while calling for early presidential and parliamentary elections.

The Egyptian public and the country's security services, led by the armed forces, had clearly taken on the Brotherhood, as well as its representatives in government and parliament, in an exceptional, conclusive, even existential fashion. In spite of these developments, the Brotherhood was not immediately excluded. The leaders of the Freedom and Justice Party were invited to join the launch of a new political phase as well as the new government to be established. They, however, declined and insisted that Morsi was Egypt's one and only legitimate leader.

Immediately after the announcement on the evening of July 3, and Morsi's incarceration, violent protests of Muslim Brotherhood members and supporters broke out across many parts of Egypt, rendering the security situation precarious. Most significantly, thousands of his supporters started to congregate towards two major sit-ins in Rabaa Al-Adawiya, next to a mosque that carries the name of the Sufi woman saint of the eighth century in the east Cairo suburb of Nasr City, and Al-Nahda, next to Cairo University. These supporters stayed in place for over a month before security forces dispersed their camps in a violent confrontation.

As stipulated in the Egyptian constitution and upon the announcement of the July 3 roadmap, the Chief Justice of the Supreme Constitutional Court, Counselor Adly Mansour, was appointed as the interim president, mandated with negotiating the composition of a government that would return the political system, particularly the country's executive institutions, to a state of normalcy before the adoption of a new constitution and the election of a new president and parliament.

A nontraditional president whose career had been completely in the judiciary, Mansour had the political wisdom required of a statesperson facing major challenges and an unwavering commitment to supporting right over wrong and virtue over vice. Equally important was that he sought consensus in meetings of the Egyptian National Security Council (NSC), first listening to the representatives of the different government institutions before expressing himself. These were attributes ever so critical in such delicate times.

These were to be difficult times. Directly after his appointment, Mansour participated in consultations on the parameters of the new government with several political figures who were party to the roadmap announcement, most significantly the military and Mohamed El-Baradei who represented the youth. The forming of the first government after the events of June 30 was testimony to the complexity of repositioning Egypt as a cosmopolitan, centrist, politically secular country with a rich heritage and deep religious convictions. At one point, President Mansour called in El-Baradei to swear him in as the incoming prime minister before retracting the offer after he had arrived at the presidential offices. Instead, Mansour offered the position of "Vice President for Foreign Affairs". El-Baradei had a long personal experience in foreign affairs so this could have appeared natural; nevertheless, it was quite odd. Foreign policy was normally the prerogative of the head of state and El-Baradei at that point was more interested in domestic and constitutional reform. Politics, however, is frequently about compromise and this was truly strange but it seemed acceptable to all.

An immediate reflection of these contradictions was that El-Baradei first took a proactive role in helping Hazem El-Beblawi, who had been nominated as prime minister, put together the interim government. It was to be secular in nature but would open its doors to representation from Islamists, including the Muslim Brotherhood. A former finance minister but without significant party affiliation, El-Beblawi started meeting potential candidates for the ministerial positions in his cabinet but the media took advantage of the fluid and rapid developments occurring, unprofessionally floating names for the highest governmental positions at an exhausting pace.

On July 16, the first day of the Muslim holy month of Ramadan, the new cabinet was sworn in. It included inter alia El-Beblawi, Abdel Fattah El-Sisi, as first deputy prime minister and minister of defense. Two other deputy prime ministers were appointed—Hossam Eissa, as minister of higher education, and Ziad Bahaa-Eldin, as minister for international cooperation. I was nominated as minister of foreign affairs. For the most part, members of the cabinet were technocrats, generally with no strong ideological affiliations. The new prime minister announced that he had offered cabinet positions to the Brotherhood but that they had vehemently rejected his offer. Consequently, all the cabinet members were secular from both the left and the right of the economic and political landscape.

Mansour presided over the first government cabinet meeting. Challenges were underlined. Crisis management mode prevailed and the need to quickly start up Egypt once again was emphasized. This was not a war cabinet, but it was a cabinet operating in a tense volatile environment, with a historic responsibility, working under tremendous pressure with limited resources. It had to energize domestic support for stability without negating the aspirations for change, establish law and order in the face of continued violence from Brotherhood supporters and opportunists across the country, and respond to international pressures. The Western world, in particular, was generally critical that an elected president had been removed and did not give much credence to the argument that this was an exceptional response to an existential circumstance.

Another important consideration this cabinet had to deal with, like Morsi before them, was that after decades of political apathy, Egyptians from all walks of life after the 2011 Revolution were hyperventilating in the exercise of their right to free speech and in their rejection of unchecked authority. Suddenly, everyone in Egypt had an opinion. And everyone had the answers but very few had the immediate ability to exercise authority.

The process of domestic conflict resolution was spearheaded by El-Baradei with the international community initially also arguing for the Muslim Brotherhood. Violent clashes between Morsi supporters and security forces, however, broke out recurrently in different parts of the country, making reconciliation more and more difficult.

Gradually, the situation in Egypt became an existential choice between returning to the rule of Morsi and the Muslim Brotherhood and sticking to the changes announced on July 3 that had removed the Moslem Brotherhood from power. Gradually, it became clear that the mediation efforts were not making any progress. This remained the case even after it was suggested that tensions could be defused if the sit-ins would be thinned out in exchange for the authorities releasing two leading Brotherhood figures, Saad El-Katatni, the speaker of the parliament that was elected in the autumn of 2011 and Abou Elela Mady, the president of the perceived more moderate "Islamist Wasat Party".

However, with the expanding outbreak of violence, the security forces in government and a larger number of senior officials had concluded that, in the short term, no compromise was possible with the Islamists, particularly with the Brotherhood's senior leadership. Indeed, as early as July 24, 2013, during a public event attended by the interim President Mansour, El-Sisi asked the Egyptian people for a "popular mandate and order for the army and police" to fight terrorism. Two days later, there were large demonstrations supporting his call. With time, the enforcement of law and order and the dismantling of the organization of the Muslim Brotherhood and the Islamist chains of command were given priority. In the first week of August, General Mohamed Ibrahim, the Minister of Interior, convinced the cabinet to adopt a decision that would authorize the police to take necessary measures in both the El Nahda and Rabaa squares to remove the sit-ins that had blocked traffic and had disturbed the residents of the respective neighborhoods for over five weeks. I was traveling abroad that day and thus did not attend that particular meeting, but the public pressure for the government to reassert its authority was palpable.

A few days after that meeting, Prime Minister El-Beblawi and Minister of Interior Ibrahim relayed the government's decision to disperse the sit-ins to Egypt's NSC, which was chaired by the president. NSC members present in that meeting included El-Baradei, El-Sisi, myself, Minister of Interior Ibrahim, the Egyptian Army Chief of Staff Sedki Sobhi, directors of military, civilian intelligence, and presidential staff.

The records of that meeting remain legally confidential. Therefore, I will refrain from getting into specific discussions or positions taken by the different participants. Suffice to register that we listened and deliberated over the government's already adopted decision to take action to restore a sense of normalcy to both locations while emphasizing the need to keep potential casualties from all sides as minimal as possible.

Personally, I had always been skeptical and uneasy about political Islam although I had been impressed by the professionalism of some of the Brotherhood's younger members whom I met in public events. At different points in time throughout 2011–2012, I felt an Egyptian accommodation, even an uneasy one, was possible. During Morsi's one year in office, my strong doubts returned, and I concluded that unless the Brotherhood leaders made an unexpected turnaround, another violent confrontation was inevitable and very soon to break out.

El-Baradei had expressed his disapproval on the dispersal decision, as per El-Beblawi's press interview a year later.[1] El-Baradei told me after the meeting that he thought he still had time to negotiate a compromise. I did not share this assessment and felt that after the decision taken by the government, action was imminent.

In a press conference on August 7, El-Beblawi publicly announced that the government was determined to end the sit-ins. Then, Mansour issued a statement later the same day saying that diplomatic efforts to find a compromise had failed and that Egypt was not willing to receive more mediators on the matter.

A week later, on August 14, Egyptian security forces, with the Ministry of Interior at the forefront, entered the sit-ins. Government sources reported that heavy exchanges of fire occurred between the Muslim

[1] Hazem El Beblawi's speech with Al Shorouk Newspaper (2013) http://www.shorouknews.com/news/view.aspx?cdate=15082013&id=4b1fa2fe-d616-4ebf-8e9e-47fe02e40d9a&fb_comment_id=521633527902278_4397371.

Brotherhood supporters barricaded around Rabaa Al-Adawiya and Al-Nahda and the police, with significant casualties not only from the Muslim Brotherhood sympathizers but also from some law enforcement agents and a few passersby. The losses were much more so in Rabaa Al-Adawiya than in Al-Nahda. Irrespective of political affiliation or administrative function as the reason of conflict, the loss of life is highly regrettable. These were difficult, discomforting times for everyone, even for those who opposed the Muslim Brotherhood.

Subsequent to that, numerous violent demonstrations broke out in different Egyptian cities and towns. After several days of these violent exchanges, the situation slowly started to calm down with intermittent violence occurring thereafter. Whether for domestic or foreign policy purposes, it was important to establish a credible objective narrative and record of what had occurred up until then. Upon my suggestion, on December 21, 2013, the Egyptian government established a blue-ribbon legal commission led by the internationally renowned jurist Fouad Riad, to prepare a comprehensive report of the dramatic events that followed the June 30 Revolution.

With the ouster of Morsi and the suspension of the constitution that was drafted during his one year in office, Egypt was now set to draft a new constitution that was compatible with the true aspirations of reforms envisaged by the 2011 Revolution. This time, Egyptians correctly decided to draft a constitution before going to parliamentary or presidential elections, a step that, if applied earlier, would have saved us much agony—possibly even the blunders of Muslim Brotherhood that led to second revolution of June 2013.

On July 21, 2013, a ten-member committee was formed to review the suspended constitution. This committee submitted its report on August 25. By September 8, a 50-member committee was established to amend the constitution and Amre Moussa, the former presidential candidate, was elected as its chairman in the committee's opening session. Almost three months later, on December 3, Moussa delivered the draft constitution to President Mansour.

The draft constitution reflected the concerns, challenges, and prevailing societal mood. The provisions on civil liberties in this constitution responded well to the original concerns of activists behind the January 2011 Revolution and were consistent with what existed in traditional liberal Western constitutions. The provisions also stipulated that presidents could only serve two- four-year terms, in order to prevent a replay of an overstretched rule, as was the case with Mubarak. Also designed to prohibit authoritarianism were the provisions that created for Egypt an unprecedented quasi-sharing of power between the president and the prime minister, with parliamentary supervision. In addition, in view of the specific role undertaken by the minister of defense and the rest of the SCAF in championing the demands of the masses, the constitution had temporary provisions, for the following two terms of president (eight years), which specifically required the sitting president to consult with the highest military body whenever he nominated or decided to change a minister of defense.

Egyptians, at home and abroad, voted on the amended constitution. On January 18, 2014, the results were announced with the constitution approved by a considerable majority. In accordance with the constitutional declaration that the interim president had issued on July 8, 2013, to outline the stages of the transitional period, Mansour had 15 days to start the process for parliamentary elections, which was to be concluded within two months at the utmost. Once the newly elected parliament was in session, the presidential elections would then be called for.

A few days after the ratification of the new constitution, on the third anniversary of the January 25 Revolution, demonstrations and violent clashes between Muslim Brotherhood supporters, some activists, and police occurred. Twenty-nine people were killed, including three police officers. Cognizant of the need to establish a sense of normalcy, order, and authority, the following day, President Mansour issued a decision to modify his previous constitutional declaration and organize presidential elections before, not after, the parliamentary elections.

In July 2013, after some hesitation, I became part of the story of the transition process that Egypt had started going through after Mubarak was removed from office. I had joined the government after the ouster of another president, Mohamed Morsi, out of a sense of national responsibility and committed to serve for the length of the interim period of about a year, the objective of which was to restore a sense of normalcy to Egypt and its political institutions.

Ambassador Shoukry Fouad, a retired former diplomat, colleague, and close friend was the first to mention my possible nomination as foreign minister. He was aware of my dislike of domestic politics but argued that my presence provided the establishment with a centrist, non-partisan professional face, which would help garner wide domestic and international support.

A few days later, El-Baradei phoned and asked me directly if I would accept the position of Foreign Minister were it to be offered by the prime minister-designate. He did not mention Fouad but used the same argument that the country was at a historic juncture and that we were all duty-bound to serve. I told El-Baradei that in spite of my personal inclination not to take this position, if contacted by the prime minister-designate, I would meet him with an open mind. He joked that we had both rejected coming into government in the past but were now both duty-bound to share in carrying the burden. Then, he casually asked about my relations with other institutions of government, including the security services. He knew that as ambassador in Washington, I had extensive contacts with the different government institutions, including the domestic security services and the military, having led numerous Egyptian arms control delegations. My spontaneous and brief answer was that my relations had always been professional and largely amicable.

After that phone call, I spent a few hours reflecting on the idea of joining government as foreign minister, in order to have a clear and conclusive answer ready if formally asked. I was not personally attracted to such positions and did not feel I would be comfortable making the inevitable compromises required by politicians in any government around the world. I was, however, concerned about Egypt's wellbeing after living through two revolutions and seeing the country torn to its seams again. I gradually became more receptive to the suggestions that it was a national responsibility to serve.

On July 14, 2013, I was received by El-Beblawi in his office and formally invited to join the new Egyptian government as foreign minister. The prime minister-designate was naturally warm and pleasant but at first discussed very little about what kind of foreign policy was best for the country. When I asked him what he and the presidency wanted as a foreign policy, he courteously made some flattering comments about my widely acknowledged professional expertise in the area and the value-add it will bring to the cabinet.

I suggested that the prime minister-designate not to be bound by his offer to me until after listening to my comments, then concisely reiterated highlights of my reflections on foreign policy, which I had had while sitting on my living room couch after the phone call from Fouad and El Baradei. After I concluded, the prime minister-designate graciously thanked me and simply asked me to publicly announce my agreement to serve as foreign minister to the media that was waiting impatiently outside of our meeting room.

After a short statement to the media, I phoned Mohamed Amr, the Foreign Minister, a good professional who had carried the responsibility in difficult times and a close friend. I told him of the decision taken and that after swearing in a few days later, I would only enter the office of Foreign Minister if he was present, emphasizing that I wanted to thank him formally for his service. He was touched by the gesture and generously greeted me on my first day in office before we went off together for the Ramadan Iftar that same day (Figs. 9.1 and 9.2).

In effect, upon taking up the mandate of the foreign minister, I was offered no guidelines for the foreign policy from the president or prime minister, which I believed should be the normal procedure. I, therefore, developed my own one-year plan of action and announced it a few days later at a press conference for local and international media. As much as I enjoyed the freedom to do so, I was also well-aware of the fact that ministers should be given a clear mandate with a set of policies and goals

Fig. 9.1 Nabil Fahmy and President Adly Mansour

Fig. 9.2   Nabil Fahmy speaking in a press conference

to pursue when first asked to join a cabinet. Otherwise, governments would become incoherent gatherings of ambitious individuals with potentially conflicting agendas.

Inside Egypt, as per the plan, I focused on rectifying the decisions the Muslim Brotherhood took with regards to the Ministry of Foreign Affairs, whether substantive, logistical, or personnel related. I also initiated several reforms in line with the 2011 revolutionary aspirations to strengthen the workings of the ministry.

These were turbulent times with an agitated constituency, a concerned government, and a disoriented international environment. Housekeeping was essential even before seriously embarking on foreign policy endeavors.

Upon assuming the ministerial position, I had immediately received the outgoing Foreign Minister Mohamed Kamel Amre, for a discussion about foreign policy and institutional issues related to the ministry's management. I carefully listened to his reflections on how to best assess the challenges and opportunities and shared with him some ideas on how to develop our foreign policy.

I also asked Amre about substantive, logistical, or personnel issues where President Mohamed Morsi, his staff, or the Muslim Brotherhood had directly intervened. He mentioned the position taken on Syria at a highly controversial and widely criticized grandstanding conference held a few months earlier, with an incredible, if not outright, exclusive presence of ultra-orthodox Islamists that concluded with the abrupt withdrawal of the Egyptian ambassador from Damascus. Amre also mentioned the presidency's instructions to criticize the French intervention against an Islamist insurgency in Mali.

I then asked him about interference in personnel issues. President Mansour and his aides had raised concerns about the Brotherhood's "infiltration" of many ministries, with numerous Brotherhood sympathizers emerging in top government jobs at the expense of Egypt's national security interests within only one year. Consequently, questions about the possible Muslim Brotherhood influence over Egyptian Foreign Service were not uncalled for, particularly since presidents do have the ultimate authority to determine ambassadorial assignments and to confirm the most senior positions at the ministry's headquarters.

True or not, such fears were ultimately unsubstantiated when it came to the Foreign Ministry. The law governing entry to the Egyptian Foreign Service is meant to preserve it as a professional, non-political institution by confining new entry-level candidates to those passing a difficult exam and rigorous security clearance. Infrequently, more senior individuals can also enter the Foreign Ministry pursuant to a presidential decree but such appointments were rare, even exceptional, since Anwar Sadat took office.

Egypt was bound to face numerous challenges in the year ahead, and I had a large number of substantive policies to attend. Therefore, there was no time to waste on unnecessary petty amendments to personnel and administrative decisions the previous minister may have made with regards to local or foreign posts. However, if decisions were forced upon him by the former president or any of his aides out of ideological convictions, then I would immediately revoke those decisions because they curtail our ability to move forward as a professional foreign policy service with a common platform. Otherwise, I would allow myself enough time to make my own judgments on the performance of the different heads of overseas missions before considering any possible changes based strictly on professional merit.

Amre responded that only a single overseas ambassadorial posting—that to the Egyptian Embassy in the United Arab Emirates (UAE)—was decided upon the instructions of the president's office. I informed him that I would immediately withdraw that nomination and did so in my first few days in office, which had already been the subject of the expressions of discomfort from the Emirates.

Diplomacy is a highly competitive field, internationally between different countries, but also among diplomats of the same nationality. The more successful practitioners are often designated for the more high-profile posts. Consequently, the profession is never free from the inevitable downside of inter-office politics. Dealing with these issues came with the job, but given the many challenges Egypt was facing, I could not allow such petty matters to distract my attention from the more important substantive issues and goals before me.

A day or two after my discussions with my predecessor on this matter, President Mansour asked me again if I had reviewed the list of Egyptian ambassadors nominated and appointed abroad by Morsi. He suggested that I might want to revert to Amre for his reflections on the matter. From the smile on my face, President Mansour immediately concluded that I had already done so. I confirmed this, also clarifying that most of the ambassadors whose allegiances had been brought into question had actually not been nominated by Morsi but rather by the SCAF in the spring of 2012; Morsi had had no role in making any of those choices. He had simply signed their formal letters of agreement after the nominations had been accepted by the respective capitals because, by then, he had been elected president. Morsi had signed a decree appointing another cohort of professional career ambassadors, but their allegiances had ironically not been questioned by anyone.

I then assured the president that the Egyptian Foreign Ministry would work at its full capacity and that all of the already rumored allegations would be rigorously and objectively investigated. I would not take personnel decisions based on unsubstantiated innuendo, but committed to promptly withdraw any diplomat serving abroad who did not show an unwavering commitment to serving Egypt's national security.

As a distinguished jurist, he would not accept anything less than full fairness, but still, he urged me to investigate matters as they arose expeditiously, given the delicate phase that the country was going through. In the year to follow, several diplomats were accused of being Brotherhood sympathizers. In some cases, the allegations were found to be completely false, a conclusion confirmed by other relevant authorities. Other allegations were not substantiated with any concrete evidence to warrant drastic action that would carry with it a career-ending denouncement of having harmed the country's national security.

Consequently, I was resolute during my term of office in insisting that I would only make changes on the merits or demerits of professional performance. I was duty-bound to end a diplomat's service abroad if there were a legitimate national security concern or if they were not executing their job as expected of them. However, I would never prejudice a diplomat's career without concrete evidence. Those were the parameters I had in mind when later, in spring 2014, I informed President Mansour that it was time to issue the normal annual decree for ambassadorial appointments abroad. The president, however, preferred to postpone the decree until the new president was elected in June.

Of particular importance as well in those times of domestic disorientation and soul-searching was to give employees a channel to express their concerns without this creating chaos or disorder to the detriment of national interests. The Egyptian Foreign Service is responsible to publicly defend government policy in a nonpartisan fashion; therefore, challenging government policy or taking issue with domestic developments publicly, even on open social networks, was inconsistent with the role diplomats had voluntarily committed to. Some, in fact, had already started circulated their views in an informal but widely followed social network called "Lotus". I found this inappropriate in spite of my respect for free speech. I, therefore, created formal channels within the Foreign Ministry for diplomats to convey opinions on subjects beyond their direct portfolio of responsibility, to professionally criticize ongoing policies, or to creatively think about the future. I felt that diplomats are hired to unwaveringly defend and promote government policies once decided, even if they challenge them in internal discussions. If the differences were completely incompatible or there were issues of ethics, then the onus was on the diplomat to leave his position. Over time, this channel would have allowed diplomats to express views about foreign policy and the historic developments in Egypt while at the same time preserving and respecting their commitment to promote and defend government policy.

Internationally, in the action plan, the primary focus was on three areas, disseminating the accurate narrative of the domestic events in Egypt, particularly, the June 30 events and the August 14 dispersals was imperative. Restoring Egypt's stature and proactive diplomacy, both in terms of multilateral and bilateral engagements, with a particular emphasis on regional initiatives and relations, was also a priority. And, the primary principles governing our policies in the future would always be ensuring that Egypt had multiple options and that our regional role and policies had priority.

To move forward, I also felt strongly that the Foreign Ministry needed to ensure that its diplomats had the skill sets to deal with new challenges and take advantage of new opportunities. After personally and frequently facing new challenges in my own three-decade career, the need for new skills was self-evident, particularly in an increasingly interconnected global community that brings numerous issues to your doorstep at a rapid pace. These challenges had increased exponentially with nonprofessional and nontraditional stakeholders engaging in foreign affairs through empowering IT tools. Thus, I established a specialized unit on technology and several task forces on Egypt's national security and visions for the future. Needless to say, these efforts could not be successful on a sustainable basis without a process of governance reform for the country as a whole.

Like all the other ministers in the 2013 cabinet, I was starting up our operations in an increasingly volatile security situation. This was not something that the Foreign Ministry had a direct institutional responsibility for, or a role in, but we did our utmost policy wise to support the efforts that were mostly in the hands of the Ministries of Interior and Defense, along with the intelligence services. Nevertheless, the situation on the ground was bound to influence our efforts on foreign affairs because it created a challenging context for our work, with the international community carefully watching.

Vice President El-Baradei took the lead in managing or coordinating the numerous international emissaries that arrived, hoping to find a way to end the conflict between the Egyptian authorities and the Brotherhood. The Emirati and Qatari Foreign Ministers Abdullah bin Zayed Al Nahyan and Khalid bin Mohammad Al-Attiyah, respectively, United States Deputy Secretary of State William Burns, United States Senators Lindsey Graham and John McCain, European Union (EU) High Representative for Foreign Affairs and Security Policy Catherine Ashton, and Alpha Oumar Konaré, ex-president of Mali, one of the senior emissaries from the African Union, were the most prominent visitors to the Egyptian capital in the weeks that followed the political change. While these were foreign visitors, the topic of their engagement was Egypt's domestic situation and thus, their primary interlocutors in Egypt were those responsible for the transition, namely, the country's president, vice president, and, occasionally, the ministers of defense and interior.

I knew, only too well, that negotiations or reconciliation efforts never succeeded with a cacophony of negotiating focal points. And, I was not particularly comfortable with this endless stream of visitors, but given the potential ramifications of developments in Egypt throughout the Arab world, and in light of our extensive foreign relations, these visits seemed inescapable. I, therefore, left this to other Egyptian officials and did not directly engage in any conflict resolution efforts but would brief the visitors on developments as necessary. Unfortunately, this mediation process failed as violence between Morsi's supporters and the security forces intensified, culminating in the violent dispersal of the sit-ins in August 2013.

On the day of the dispersals, Vice President El-Baradei resigned, explaining that there were other peaceful ways that could have ended this societal clash and that he could no longer continue to bear the responsibility. A few years later, in January 2017, in an interview with the London-based Al Araby TV, El-Baradei elaborated further on that turn of events, explaining that he felt his efforts were futile after it became clear to him that including Islamists in the system was no longer a tenable proposition.

The local and international media had conflicting accounts on the details of the dispersals and the casualties. For their part, the Muslim Brotherhood's narrative portrayed their members in the sit-ins as pacifist protesters. They exaggerated their losses and claimed to have caused no casualties on the side of the police forces. Naturally, they tried to use this account to gain international sympathy.

As foreign minister, I decided that several steps were imperative. The first was to base my figures and opinions on addressing the public domestically and internationally on objectively substantiated information even if this meant responding at a slower pace than the cacophony of the social networks and the talk shows on satellite television. Governments, I felt, had a responsibility to be credible. That is why I had recommended the independent blue-ribbon report to be prepared by jurist Fouad Riad on the events that followed the June 30 Revolution, including ending the sit-ins at Rabaa and El-Nahda. This report clearly stipulated that it was the Muslim Brotherhood that started to shoot at a senior police officer injuring him during the dispersal of the sit-in of Rabaa Al-Adawiya. The commission did, however, also criticize the reaction of the police at different instances in these events. It remains today the most comprehensive and objective narrative and assessment of that difficult period, particularly when violence occurred.

The second goal I had, which was also of paramount importance, was preventing the internationalization of the consideration or even multilateral discussion of the situation in Egypt. During the tumultuous few months after Morsi's ouster, Egypt had many reasons to believe that even if they would not publicly use the term coup d'état, the United States and Great Britain held a strongly negative view of the summer 2013 events in Egypt. The two countries frequently initiated moves towards the internationalization of Egypt's situation by questioning the legitimacy of the government or of Egypt's delegations at international organizations and events, such as at the United Nations, the Deauville Partnership Finance Ministers' Meeting, and the annual meetings of the International Monetary Fund (IMF) and the World Bank. Yet, they refrained from formally admitting this when I asked them about their adversarial positions toward Egypt on being informed of them at different instances by credible sources, which included the IMF secretariat at its very highest level.

In the summer of 2013, the Egyptian permanent representative to the United Nations in New York informed me of efforts to convene the United Nations Security Council to discuss the situation in Egypt. When I asked Secretary of State John Kerry, he pointed to France. The French Foreign Minister Laurent Fabius, however, insisted it was the United States with British backing that was behind such efforts. Rather than waste precious time on determining who was the culprit, I immediately consulted with Russia and China to ensure that they would oppose any such measures, and gave clear, standing instructions to our embassies abroad to keep a watchful eye in order to quickly respond to such attempts.

Simultaneously, commensurate with the traditional responsibility of foreign ministers for their country's present and future international relations, I needed to shift the agenda from our domestic situation back to regional and international politics. To do so, it was imperative to first change the topic from the violent confrontations to the goal embodied in the July 3 statement of establishing a secular, civilian, democratic government. Consequently, at the beginning of every meeting with foreign dignitaries, I, myself, would start with an exposé of the situation in Egypt within the parameters I was comfortable with, before quickly and firmly moving on to international relations. The objective was to give the clear message that Egypt was well on its way back to a state of normalcy and had returned as well as an active participant in world affairs.

The annual fall meeting of the United Nations General Assembly was the most effective place to do this, given the high-profile attendance of delegates from around the world. The annual meetings were an auspicious occasion to move from a defensive reactive posture to a more proactive expansive one for Egyptian diplomacy as a strong signal that the country was resuming its activist role in regional and international politics.

President Adly Mansour had asked me, before the beginning of the annual meetings, whether he himself should attend the United Nations General Assembly; sources had informed me that some African countries might challenge the credentials of the Egyptian delegation on the grounds that its membership to the African Union had been frozen after Morsi's removal. It was also suggested by our sources in New York and elsewhere that Turkey, which was aggressively at odds with Egypt over the 2013 political changes, was instigating one of the countries in the southern part of Africa to challenge our credentials. Although this was not conclusive, we had enough reason to be concerned.

I informed President Mansour that there was bound to be some commotion if he participated in the meeting. Nevertheless, after presenting him with a thorough list of potential scenarios of what might happen, I assured him that we would come out successful at the end of any potential diplomatic battles that might occur. I had undertaken a detailed analysis of the results of a possible vote challenging Egypt's credentials and was confident that such a vote would be in our favor. Ultimately, the president decided not to personally attend the General Assembly, expressing confidence that I would successfully take on the assignment.

Upon my arrival in New York on September 21, 2013, I was briefed in detail by Egypt's permanent mission to the United Nations on the proceedings of the General Assembly. As expected, there were a few demonstrations in front of the United Nations, both against and in support of the new Egyptian regime. The permanent mission also concluded, through subtle contacts with its Turkish counterparts, that they had no instructions relating to Egypt but we remained cautious until the full delegation arrived from Ankara to confirm this. There was some grumbling about Egypt from some South African delegates but no real appetite to challenge our credentials (Figs. 9.3 and 9.4).

Sheikh Abdullah bin Zayed Al Nahyan, the foreign minister of the United Arab Emirates, was categorical that he would stand against any attempt to target Egypt. Prince Saud bin Faisal, the foreign minister of Saudi Arabia, was equally stalwart. Ramtane Lamamra, the foreign minister of Algeria, was subtler by affirming that taking on Egypt at the General Assembly would be detrimental to all Arabs. Listening to these senior officials and the generally positive even if nuanced comments from other delegates, I concluded that if there were any surprising maneuvers, we had the votes on our side as we expected. Ultimately, the relevant subcommit-

Fig. 9.3   Nabil Fahmy talking in the UN General Assembly

tee of the General Assembly accepted our credentials with those of other delegations without undue debate.

The proceedings of the General Assembly were mostly uneventful in as far as the internal situation in Egypt was concerned, with a few exceptions. During his traditional reception for heads of the delegations to the General Assembly, President Barack Obama informed me that he understood that Egyptians had been uncomfortable with Morsi, but that given the removal of an elected president from office, he was obliged to withhold or at least

Fig. 9.4 Nabil Fahmy and Ban Kee moon

postpone the delivery of some military equipment and assistance to Egypt until there was progress on the road to democracy. He added that he would announce this in his General Assembly speech the next day. I registered my strong opposition to the measures suggested as well as the venue for the announcement, adding that national security requirements were of a strategic nature and if their sustainability were not guaranteed, Egypt would resort to other sources. Obama nevertheless made the announcement in his speech after openly acknowledging the Muslim Brotherhood had governed badly and that Egypt's military intervention was supported by the majority. Minutes later, on a live American television news broadcast, I forcefully announced that Egypt would fulfill its national security needs from other sources if necessary.

The other exceptional incident was the harsh criticism of Egypt in the speech given by the President of Tunisia Mohamed Moncef Marzouki, a human rights activist who clearly sympathized with the Muslim Brotherhood. Tunisian diplomats in New York immediately urged their Egyptian counterparts to allow the incident to pass, asserting that Marzouki was simply addressing constituency rather than reflecting a new stand of Tunis on Egypt. This was not going to be possible, however, and

I decided to recall our ambassador from Tunisia in protest, after first briefing the Egyptian President Mansour, who was supportive. In a show of support for Egypt, the United Arab Emirates minister of foreign affairs rebuked the Tunisian ambassador in New York and called back his country's ambassador from Tunisia for consultations as well.

The first few months in office, I had spent a lot of time in my discussions with foreign counterparts, explaining the developments in Egypt, before gradually intentionally shifting the world's focus from the domestic situation to its international relations. Now, I used my speech to the General Assembly to emphasize that Egyptians had the right to fulfill their ambitious vision for the future, which domestically would be determined by Egyptians alone and internationally would be consistent with the United Nations Charter and the principles of good neighborly relations. The speech also projected Egypt's prominent regional status, repeatedly reiterating that our national security was interconnected with the security and concerns of its Arab and regional neighbors.

I also laid out our position on several issues of regional significance in the speech. First, I commented on the situation in Syria, condemning the use of chemical weapons there and urging all those concerned to work on a resolution for the ongoing conflict. President Obama and Secretary of State Kerry had forcefully announced that the United States would take military action against the Syrian regime to stop its war on the opposition, which was getting highly militant itself. Egypt was increasingly worried about the strategic ramifications of dismantling yet another Arab country after the debacle in Iraq and Libya. I had personal empathy for the secular Syrian opposition and felt strongly that the Syrian regime had used excessive force against its people. Emphasis was also placed on preserving the Arab nation-state order as a geopolitical priority for Egypt. Consequently, while we were supportive of a Syrian reconciliation process that could allow for better governance and more respect for human rights, we were seriously concerned about any action that could dismember Syria, which already appeared on the verge of civil war.

Secondly, I addressed the Palestinian–Israeli question, affirming that Egypt would continue supporting the right of the Palestinians to establish a sovereign state, with East Jerusalem as its capital. Lastly, I spoke about nuclear nonproliferation concerns in our region and the right to equal security for all.

All this paved the way for reestablishing and expanding Egypt's engagement in foreign affairs in subsequent meetings, where I also discussed the turmoil in the Levant, Libya, and Yemen, as well as water-resource issues, a new topic on my agenda as my interlocutors rightly pointed.

In addition to official meetings, I allocated time to the media, think tanks, and intellectual community in the West, particularly the United States. I sat for interviews with Charlie Rose and Fareed Zakaria, prominent talk show hosts for Bloomberg and CNN, respectively. I knew both from my many years as a career diplomat, but I completely understood that these were not going to be easy sessions. In fact, both Rose and Zakaria asked candid questions that were laced with criticism and skepticism. These interviews were the toughest I had had with them. However, I decided not to leave the airspace to other opinions because defense in absentia is doomed to fail.

In addition, I spoke at the prestigious think tank, the Council on Foreign Relations, upon the invitation of its president, Richard Haass, in September 2013. I knew most of the attendees in the packed meeting hall from my years as Egypt's ambassador to the United States. This was a learned, sophisticated, and engaged audience, and I made the most of the occasion, sharing my thoughts on the domestic developments in Egypt, Egyptian–American relations, and Egypt's vision for the future. A disproportionate percentage of the questions from the audience focused on El-Sisi personally and his potential future plans. However, the way I structured my presentation provoked the attention of many, who remarked after the event that they were pleased that Egypt had the calmness to look forward and plan despite its immediate, difficult day-to-day challenges.

There were, however, still some discomforting and adversarial relations with a number of countries due to their opposition to the June 30 events in Egypt. These relations were not ameliorated through our engagements in international organizations and international media but had to be addressed with a sense of urgency and meticulous handling.

Relations with the European Union (EU) were not in any sense adversarial, but they were tenuous and required continuous sensitive management throughout the interim period. As part of Western liberal democracies, EU member states were generally highly attentive to the developments in Egypt. Dealing with Europe was a multidimensional process, both at the bilateral level and within the multilateral context of the EU organizations with a sophisticated leveraging of strong points and an astute management of differences (Fig. 9.5).

Fig. 9.5 Nabil Fahmy in a meeting with the French Foreign Affairs Minister Laurent Fabius

I intensified my engagements with European countries that were, whether in agreement or disagreement with us, ready to listen, including France, Spain, Greece, the United Kingdom, Italy, and Germany. Particularly with France, Egypt had help from Saudi Arabia. Soon after the events of the summer of 2013, and upon instructions from King Abdullah bin Abdul-Aziz, the Saudi Foreign Minister Prince Saud engaged the French leadership, resolutely affirming his country's support for Egypt and its strong objection to any pressure from Europe. Faisal had contacted me before talking to the French, and I was completely comfortable with his proposed approach and felt no need to join up with my Saudi counterpart.

On the other hand, the High Representative of the European Union for Foreign Affairs and Security Policy, Catherine Ashton, made several trips to Egypt after the June Revolution. We differed on our perspectives, but she quickly realized it was futile to push too much for a deal between the new Egyptian authorities and the Brotherhood after it became obvious, during her mediation talks in Cairo, that Morsi was still insisting on resuming presidency rather than looking for a compromise as she later told me.

A number of her European countries were not comfortable with her realpolitik conclusions, especially the Nordic countries, Britain, Germany, as well as Eastern European states. Others like Greece, Malta, and Cyprus were more understanding, providing particular support to Egypt against stringent sanctions that some other European countries had suggested.

The staff of the European Commission themselves also seemed to sway from one end of the pendulum to the other. Ultimately, difficult compromises were reached among the different member states regarding the level of criticism to be addressed to Egypt in EU statements. Overall, it was clear that the EU was keen to send Egypt a message on the need to commit to the democratic path while avoiding a potential crisis in relations. The EU did not impose effective sanctions on Egypt. However, some restrictions were placed on the export of defense and law enforcement equipment. Ironically, the European Commission also slowed down the allocation of funds designed to support capacity building in countries aspiring to become more democratic, Egypt included.

This all played out dramatically in one particular meeting I had with Ashton in Brussels in April 2014. On listening to the briefings of the Egyptian delegates preparing for the meeting, it sounded like we were at a crisis point in relations. During the meeting, Ashton was professional and courteous but candid in her opening remarks, wanting to place on record that she conveyed European concerns. I did not want to waste time with a direct rebuttal of her points and said so. To the astonishment of the European and Egyptian delegations, I then announced that I would disregard my briefing notes because if relations were as bad as described in them, my delegation should have recommended that I cancel the visit. I then added that my only response was that it reflected an ill-conceived, self-defeating assumption that the EU could pressure Egypt into changing its positions on internal developments. A seasoned politician, Ashton agreed that it was a waste of time to engage in debate and that it would be much more beneficial to address how to deal with issues.

However, to emphasize my point in concrete terms, I explained that while calling for more democratic measures in Egypt, the European Commission had frozen financing for a program to enhance Egyptian capacities in ensuring best practices in respect for and the application of the rule of law. I saw faces twitching on the European side. What could be more useful in democracy promotion than the proper rule of law, I added.

Subsequently, Ashton and I mandated our delegations to have intensified deliberations to determine where collaboration was possible to help move forward in the implementation of Egypt's roadmap. This underlined that Egypt had made a commitment to establish a democratic system. It also showed that the European Commission was committed to helping develop capacities and skill sets in this regard.

Ashton and I met less than two weeks later in Cairo. Before the meeting, I was briefed that relations were taking a very positive path. I started the talks by thanking the European delegation for their work with their Egyptian counterparts, suggesting that we had now come close to reestablishing a mutually beneficial, constructive dialogue. Gradually, relations were stabilizing with the European Commission and the EU member states for the most part, although occasional tensions continued, such as during the 2014 presidential elections in Egypt.

Meanwhile, European foreign ministers and Commission officials frequently conveyed to us their astonishment at the rabid Turkish diplomatic campaign at the highest level to discredit Cairo and to urge the adoption of sanctions against Egypt. According to the accounts shared with us, Foreign Minister Ahmet Davutoğlu of Turkey's Islamist Justice and Development Party had personally spearheaded this campaign. It seemed the Brotherhood's loss of power in Egypt and the associated demonization of political Islam had burst Turkey's dreams of projecting itself as the leader of an Islamist Middle East.

An established constitutional secular country, its Islamist president, Recep Tayyip Erdoğan, seized every opportunity to privately and publicly criticize Egypt. Turkey also gave safe haven to numerous Egyptian Muslim Brotherhood leaders, including some who had court verdicts issued against them. Egypt, nevertheless, initially decided to react with measured patience in the very slim hope that strategic interest in a stable Middle East would reign. Our patience was repeatedly tested by Erdoğan's abrasiveness. Our first official response was to formally but quietly suspend joint naval exercises between the two countries. However, Erdoğan became even more vocal and vociferous.

We held internal discussions at the Egyptian Foreign Ministry on how to respond. The easiest but most provocative approach was for our public discourse to highlight both the Kurdish issue and the tragic Armenian Genocide. These were highly sensitive issues for Turkey as a whole, well beyond the Islamist ruling party or its constituency. Consequently, we took the high road out of consideration for long-term relations and chose not to focus on any of these issues. We did not want to sour our relations with the non-Islamist constituencies in Turkey. This was not necessary, and we were confident of the veracity of our policies and our ability to handle whatever Erdoğan could muster against us. As the Islamist anger became more stringent and vocal, fewer European countries were ready to be associated with the Turkish leadership, even those initially critical of the 2013 political changes in Egypt. Erdoğan, however, continued to seize every occasion to acerbically and vehemently criticize Egypt.

On November 23, during my son Ismail's wedding, in the midst of the formal religious ceremony, my office contacted me reporting another Erdoğan public statement, highly critical of Egypt. In spite of my son's unhappy glares, I immediately phoned President Mansour recommending that we withdraw our ambassador from Turkey and instruct the Turkish ambassador in Egypt to leave immediately. Mansour immediately agreed.

These steps were put into effect early the next morning, with wide-ranging public support. Egypt had been extremely patient and was justifiably angry at the Turkish actions. I, nevertheless, instructed the Egyptian protocol officials to ensure that proper professional procedures be followed during the departure of the Turkish ambassador, irrespective of our opinions about his government's policies.

Over the previous 15 years, Qatar, more than any other Arab state, was regularly in disagreement with its direct neighbors, such as Bahrain, the UAE, and Saudi Arabia, and even with countries in North Africa, particularly Egypt. The litany of complaints about its attempted intervention in internal affairs was long, but Qatar's response was simply that it has an independent foreign policy.

Qatar's position towards Egypt after the 2013 political developments was of particular consequence to our transition process. It was one of the international players that came to Egypt after President Morsi's ouster to work towards deflating the crisis that had emerged. I was informed at the time that the United States suggested that the Qataris be allowed to engage the Muslim Brotherhood directly to find a compromise and that we agreed to this with the condition that the United Arab Emirates would be present during the contacts Qatar was to hold with Brotherhood leaders.

As this mission commenced, the United Arab Emirates Foreign Minister, Sheikh Abdallah bin Zayed, asked to visit me, and I hosted him over for a private Ramadan Iftar. For his part, the Qatari Foreign Minister Al-Attiyah did not request to meet me and when our protocol officers contacted the Qatari Embassy in Cairo, they were told that their foreign minister wanted to meet the minister of defense and would determine thereafter whether he would visit the Foreign Ministry as well. I found this quite objectionable, and I told my staff to decline the request for a meeting if it were to be made by the Qatari foreign minister. Al-Attiyah later complained to Nabil El-Araby, the then Secretary-General of the Arab League, that I did not receive him. The latter was truly surprised when I explained the sequence of events, which had been misrepresented.

In all cases, the decision made by the Egyptian principals dealing with the domestic conflict resolution to allow foreign emissaries to act as a go-between amongst Egyptians was a mistake. The Qatari posture vis-à-vis Egypt post-July 2013 was overwhelmingly negative and fundamentally flawed. Not only did it offer residence to Muslim Brotherhood leaders and sympathizers, but it also encouraged their continued political activism against the regime in Egypt. It also refused to hand over those who were convicted, and the Doha-based "Al Jazeera news channels" consistently misrepresented facts in their coverage of developments in Egypt. Much of this is materially substantiated, completely discrediting repeated denials of any involvement in Egyptian affairs.

To truly understand the Qatari position, it is noteworthy to reflect on a meeting that occurred all the way back in 1995. President Hosni Mubarak had instructed Foreign Minister Amre Moussa to deliver a message to the then Emir of Qatar Khalifa bin Hamad Al Thani. As the political advisor to the foreign minister, I accompanied Moussa. After a short meeting with the Emir, he suggested we visit his son, Crown Prince Hamad, who hosted a two-and-a-half-hour lunch attended by only an aide to the crown prince, the Egyptian foreign minister, and myself.

The crown prince gave us an incredibly well-structured, conceptually coherent, and detailed overview of what he felt Qatar's challenges were and what its role should be. He openly acknowledged their inability to compete with Saudi wealth or Egyptian political and cultural power before adding that to gain some influence, they must become a regional player irrespective of the nature of events themselves, the positions they took, or the parties they sided with. He elaborated that given Qatar's small size, it could not play a traditional diplomatic role but had to have a loud voice. Finally, he metaphorically pointed towards the window, explaining that he needed to have an American airbase in Qatar, similar to the Prince Sultan Air Base in Saudi Arabia. This would serve them well to leverage his position in America, the superpower of greatest influence globally and particularly to Gulf security.

Later, when Moussa asked for my reflections, I admitted to having been impressed by the coherence of the presentations but noted that the crown prince's presentation came across more like a statement. I would expect to hear from the head of the North Atlantic Treaty Organization because I was skeptical that Qatar had the workforce or human resources to pursue such policies and implement them.

A very short time thereafter, the crown prince overthrew his father, then established Al Jazeera Media Corporation, initially bringing in former professionals from BBC Arabic programs or other Arab media. Moreover, after 9/11, Saudi Arabia became less comfortable with the presence of a large number of American forces. Qatar quickly built, at their own expense, the alternate Al Udeid Air Base, southwest of the Qatari capital. In quick succession, everything the then crown prince had said at lunch had become a reality.

It was not long before Qatar then embarked on a hyperactive regional foreign policy program to nurture its image by unabashedly becoming a host, broker, and/or sponsor on almost any discussion around regional conflict, even if it meant playing both sides. For example, America frequently complained about Al Jazeera's coverage of Afghanistan and Iraq, but it did not seriously pressure Qatar because of its willingness to host Taliban leaders and contact Islamists in several countries upon the request of Washington.

Qatar hosted numerous seminars and conferences about the new Middle East, which were often convened by prominent American think tanks and attended by high-profile American politicians. After finishing my post as ambassador to the United States, and before joining the Egyptian government in 2013, I remember attending an event in Doha about America and the Muslim world, where Secretary of State Hillary Clinton shared the opening stage with the then Qatari Prime Minister and Minister of Foreign Affairs Hamad Bin Jassim Bin Jaber Al-Thani. Tongue-in-cheek, bin Jassim started by saying that given that Qatar was not a democratic country observing freedom of speech, there was no point in discussing its domestic situation. It would be better, he continued, to address the situation of other Arab countries. The audience was astonished by his remarks and even shocked that Clinton did not bother to take issue with this very strange beginning of an event that had been promoted as part of the democratization of the Arab world. These are the kind of double standards that fuel the conspiracy theory in the Middle East.

Another very enlightening incident occurred during my year as foreign minister, which clearly contradicted the Qatari claim of non-interference in the internal affairs of other states. By then, relations between the two countries had reached a low point and Egypt's initial efforts with its Gulf Cooperation Council (GCC) allies to convince the Qataris to change course were to no avail. Then, in January 2014, as I was attending the Friends of Syria Foreign Ministers' meeting in Paris, Saudi Foreign Minister Prince Saud asked me for a private trilateral discussion with him and our Qatari counterpart Al Attiyah about Egyptian–Qatari relations. In a private dinner at his home in Paris, Prince Saud invited me to share my concerns regarding the Qatari policy, so that Al Attiyah could respond to them. I, however, asked Al Attiyah to speak first to explain what Qatar was and was not doing with respect to Egypt.

Al Attiyah jumped to the occasion and for around ten minutes energetically and unabashedly explained how it was important to have consensus among societies, to be tolerant, and to accommodate political Islam, how Qatar could not condone bloodshed, and then talked at length about different policy decisions that Egypt should pursue. After Al Attiyah finished, I remarked that everything just said was self-incriminating and that was why I had not interrupted him. Qatar had accorded itself the right to judge others, the right to interfere in their internal affairs, and even admitted to directly supporting the Brotherhood. That was more than enough of admission of unacceptable Qatari policies than anything I needed to say.

Al Attiyah was red in the face even though I refrained from adding much to what he himself had said. Refined and diplomatic, Prince Saud suggested we start reconciling by ending the reciprocal press campaign between the two countries. I rejected this request insisting that the real issue was Qatari interference in Egypt's internal affairs and was adamant that it had to stop first in order to allow for the press campaign to naturally die down.

Regrettably but not surprisingly, relations with Qatar did not get any better in the months to follow. For that to happen, it would have required diminishing their brand and regional role. Personally, I prefer taking strategic and concrete policy steps to change, in relation, aspects to other countries, rather than diplomatic actions, such as withdrawing ambassadors, which I consider to be diplomatic tools not to be removed except as a last resort. There were limits to everything, however, and as Qatari policies towards Egypt reached a truly intolerable level, I informed a number of Gulf states, particularly the UAE, Bahrain, and Saudi Arabia, that Egypt was about to withdraw its ambassador to Doha. They urged me to delay this while they worked with the Qataris for a potential solution.

Weeks later, however, the inter-Gulf contacts reached a breaking point and these three countries announced the withdrawal of their ambassadors from Qatar even before we did on March 5, 2014. Egypt had never asked any Arab ambassador to leave the country. Even in 1979, upon the Arab boycott of Egypt to protest its peace treaty with Israel, the respective Arab capitals withdrew their ambassadors from Cairo, but we did not ask them to leave. Indeed, when Egypt called back its ambassador to Qatar in 2014 to protest its interventionist policies, it did not demand a reciprocal step. Regrettably, however, relations between these four countries and Qatar continued to deteriorate. Consequently, in 2017, the ambassador of Qatar was the first Arab ambassador ever to be asked to leave Cairo.

The interim phase was initially planned to take 12 months. However, after the ratification of the new constitution, violence erupted and the interim President Adly Mansour decided on January 26, 2014, to hold presidential elections earlier to establish a sense of hierarchal normalcy in the governing system, and the whole process took several months longer.

After decades of domestic stagnation, Egyptians had feasted on two years of intense political jockeying. A campaign under the title of "Kamil Gemilak" (which could be translated as "complete your good deed or favor") had already announced on November 6, 2013, that they had collected 16 million signatures nationwide calling on Abdel Fattah El-Sisi to run for presidency. This figure rose to 26 million by February 16, 2014.

On January 27, a day after President Mansour's decision, the SCAF also issued an audio statement expressing support for El-Sisi as a candidate for president if he so decided. Given El-Sisi's role in the military and the events that Egypt had faced over the past few years, it was not surprising that the SCAF would discuss this issue. Personally, I have no directly substantiated explanation for why this statement was issued but knowing how strongly El-Sisi felt about the military and his own allegiance to it, I would not be surprised if he made the announcement of his candidature contingent on the council's approval. I do know for a fact, from him directly, that there was a candid discussion with diverse opinions among the members of SCAF before the decision was taken. Symbolism is important; however, it would have been much more appropriate for the discussion to remain within the confines of the council without a public statement to underscore that he was nominated by the people at large within the context of the full return to civilian rule. Earlier that same day, President

Mansour issued a presidential declaration promoting El-Sisi to the highest military rank of field marshal.

El-Sisi was not the first candidate to announce his intention to seek the office of president. Hamdeen Sabahi had actually already announced his intention to run for presidency on February 8. El-Sisi resigned from the army and made his announcement a month later, on March 26. He understood that he was not a traditional candidate and chose not to present an election program, which would have been the subject of detailed discussions. Instead, he successfully ran as the "hero and hope candidate". The center of Egypt's body politic had called upon the Egyptian military to intervene when it lost hope in Mohamed Morsi's presidency and grew most concerned about the Muslim Brotherhood's real plans for Egypt. El-Sisi, minister of defense at the time, had been the one to bear the responsibility of responding during the June 30 demonstrations. The public was grateful and overwhelmingly supportive of his candidature as was reflected in the results of the election.

The presidential elections were held for Egyptians abroad from May 15 to 18 and for those in Egypt from May 26 to 28, 2014. El-Sisi won receiving 23.78 million votes, an overwhelming 96.91 percent. Sabahi, the only other contender, received a modest 3.09 percent of votes. On June 8, 2014, El-Sisi was sworn in as the eighth president of Egypt, with subsequent inauguration celebrations in the presence of numerous foreign dignitaries.

Egyptians still had to complete their roadmap; the new president quickly held consultations on reconstituting the first governmental cabinet of his presidency. He asked Ibrahim Mehlib, the serving prime minister, to continue to lead that government.

A number of friends and family members had been asking me for months to withdraw from the government after an increasing number of activist youths had been incarcerated. I understood the need to robustly and forcefully deal with extremists but was myself increasingly uncomfortable with the sanctioning of numerous youth activists who, in essence, were the core of the revolution on January 25, 2011. Indeed, I had been one of three members of the Egyptian government who had previously voted against the draft demonstration law, the other two being Ziad Bahaa-Eldin and Ahmed Galal, the ministers of international cooperation and finance respectively. It was felt that the proposed law was too prohibitive and the sanctions too strict for peaceful demonstrations.

I hesitated on withdrawing from the government immediately after the presidential elections because of the commitment to fulfill the interim period if the process was still on track, but I was on the brink of changing my position and withdrawing. Just before the elections, I was impressed with El-Sisi's intervention at a cabinet meeting during a heated discussion about the detrimental effects of youth demonstrations on Egypt's security, stability, and international image. Some ministers were suggesting draconian measures against demonstrators. It seemed I was the sole remaining dissenter against the excessively harsh legal measures being suggested. Everyone then was caught by surprise when El-Sisi, who had been silent throughout the meeting, insisted on the need for compassion and accommodation towards the youth while ensuring security and stability. Immediately, I asked myself whether this was an indication of an upcoming statesman-like approach to governance.

I had remained in constant touch with El-Sisi after his election, discussing numerous pending foreign policy issues. Two days before the establishment of the new government under Mehlab, I was in conversations with President El-Sisi about several upcoming issues, including the African Union summit in Malapa, Equatorial Guinea, which would reinstate Egypt as an active member of the organization. We also agreed that he would stop in Algeria on the way back from the Summit to thank President Bouteflika for his support. Discussions dealt with a number of other forward-looking issues on the foreign policy agenda, and El-Sisi was also going out of his way to engage me in discussions about the future. He took the initiative to deny rumors that there were plans to appoint Amre Moussa as a foreign policy advisor at the presidency. I had heard these rumors but did not have any particular concern with them. The president, nevertheless, emphasized that the foreign minister's authority would not be challenged.

The composition of the new government took longer than expected and the position of the foreign minister was included in the reshuffle in its final stages. I had not been informed beforehand but was not at all disappointed with the decision. After having served faithfully, I was glad to move on.

Endless questions have been addressed to me about the reasons behind me not receiving an invitation to continue serving as foreign minister for the remaining few months until the end of the interim period. Some friends are convinced it was because of my refusal to sanction diplomats based on the security agencies' recommendations, which were without concrete evidence.

Others highlighted my independent streak and insistence on preserving the integrity of the ministry. I had always been candid about having been honored to serve despite my initial hesitation, as well as about my determination to leave at the end of the interim phase.[2] A few months earlier was absolutely fine with me, especially that had it not been for El-Sisi pronounced compassion towards youth at the cabinet meeting, I probably would have asked to be relieved of my responsibilities as foreign minister.

El-Sisi's presidency is still ongoing, now in its second term; thus, it cannot be conclusively assessed. However, at the beginning of his first term as president, he expedited Mansour's efforts to stabilize Egypt, reasserting the prominent role of government institutions, particularly the security forces and military, while working on creating an economically robust Egypt and continuing to pursue the more diversified foreign policy announced after the 2013 Revolution.

On August 30, 2015, after a long delay, partly due to issues that required approval from Egypt's top constitutional court, the Supreme Electoral Commission had announced that the first rounds of the two phases of the parliamentary elections would be held on October 17 to 19 and November 21 to 23, respectively. Political forces jockeying for advantage for seats in the elections included the Salafist Al-Nour Party and eight non-Islamist newly founded coalitions, some associated with the old guard from the Mubarak era and others more with the new centers of power. The overwhelming majority of these coalitions strongly supported the June 30 Revolution and the designation of the Muslim Brotherhood as a terrorist organization.

Parties on the coalition list of "For the Love of Egypt" received the largest number of party-based seats in the elections, with an astonishing number of 351 seats going to independents, a clear indication of the weakness of political parties. Sixty seats went to youth under the age of 35, and a particularly significant number of 87 seats went to women whose quota on the parties' nomination lists was mandated in the constitution. Ali Abd El-Aal, a member of the 50-member committee that drafted the constitution adopted in 2014, was chosen as parliament speaker in an inaugural session held on January 10, 2016.

---

[2] In the Egyptian system, it is the president's prerogative, not the prime minister's, to choose the ministers of defense, foreign affairs, interior, and justice. It is also traditionally the practice for the ministers of defense, foreign affairs, and interior to primarily, but, of course, not exclusively, report to the president.

Once this was established, Egypt's interim phase was complete, albeit with a delay of several months and a reversal in the sequence of presidential and legislative elections. This did not, in my opinion, discredit the process itself. We had two revolutions in 3 years and very little pluralistic politics in the 60 years before that. It was, therefore, quite natural that there would be a tug of war during the interim period and some delay.

The challenge thereafter was getting Egypt's political system to interact in a fashion commensurate with the aspirations of the two revolutions for efficient governance, transparency, accountability, and checks and balances. This has not been easy, and I do not personally believe that those in the position of authority have fully respected the spirit of the constitution. Nor do I believe that the Egyptian politicians and, needless to say, the general public understand that the constitution provides a comprehensive foundation upon which detailed laws should be legislated to govern public order. Nevertheless, efforts, albeit imperfect, have been made and that was incremental progress.

It was only a matter of weeks after the newly elected parliament assumed legislative authority that some of its members openly suggested amending the constitution to entrust the head of the state with more powers while simultaneously reconsidering the two-term mandate stipulated in the provisions on the regime structure. This was an affront to all those who worked for better governance in the last few years, causing serious public discontent. In 2017–2018, El-Sisi wisely dissociated himself from these initiatives. Regrettably, immediately after his election to a second term until 2022, this idea was to emerge once again.

When all is said and done, Egypt will be seen as having basically fulfilled the letter of its interim plan. That does not, however, mean that the aspirations of the two revolutions have been fulfilled. It remains today for the country to enshrine practices that are consistent with these aspirations. That will not be an easy task, but it is an imperative one.

REFERENCE

El Beblawi, H. (2013). *Speech with Al Shorouk Newspaper.* http://www.shorouknews.com/news/view.aspx?cdate=15082013&id=4b1fa2fe-d616-4ebf-8e9e-47fe02e40d9a&fb_comment_id=521633527902278_4397371

Looking Forward

CHAPTER 10

Towards a Better Middle East

Learning from a turbulent half-century in order to determine how to best move forward.

The Middle East today, with the Arab world at the center, faces a situation of tremendous flux with numerous signs of friction, conflict, instability, and human suffering—unprecedented perhaps since the post-World War II era. Anyone who has attempted political conflict resolution in the region, or truly believes in societal change, would, however, understand that even in the best of circumstances, where no serious resistance exists, all this requires a fundamental socio-political evolution that is time-consuming. No Middle East expert, or true advocate of reform in the region, would expect quick conclusive and sustainable results, which requires capacity building, changing practices, and even overhauling the political culture.

Egypt has been in an extended state of transition, and grudgingly so, since 1952, not 2011, as some analysts claim. Throughout almost seven decades, it has fought three full-fledged wars and faced serious challenges in determining a coherent socio-economic policy, while repeatedly shifting its social contract. Domestically, it has faced many serious questions, well beyond the traditional ones about economic policy. It has inconclusively deliberated on the role of religion in society, on how to reestablish a sustained culture of pluralistic politics, with an effective accountable system of governance that provides social equity, economic prosperity,

© The Author(s) 2020
N. Fahmy, *Egypt's Diplomacy in War, Peace and Transition*,
https://doi.org/10.1007/978-3-030-26388-1_10

security, and stability, as well as on how to preserve a space for the military in a civilian state commensurate with contemporary governance.

Internationally, Egypt has engaged friend and foe from all over the political stratosphere. It succeeded in liberating its territory and stood on principle, joining the liberation of Kuwait, combated terrorism but for specific reasons, some beyond its own control, failed to witness a comprehensive Arab–Israeli peace.

The travail and continuous turmoil in the Middle East have negatively affected Egypt's strongest calling card, which is its position as a pioneer and spearhead of centrism, moderation, and modernity, which the international community should invest in and depend upon.

The challenges that Egypt faced have accentuated since 2010. The Arab revolutionary awakening was, in essence, an expression of political rejection of past practice, mostly domestic, practices that did not provide social equity, prosperity, and security to the Arab people, the three fundamental and common objectives of all nations. Despite past failures, these goals remain achievable if domestic, regional, and global dynamics allow for and encourage transformation.

The reasons for the turbulence in the Arab world are numerous. The paramount generic domestic one, irrespective of the problem, discipline, or domain, is a "Resistance to Change Syndrome". Change is inevitable. In the span of time (1967–2017), encompassing events dealt in this book alone, many unforeseen opportunities and challenges emerged. The communication capacities worldwide today are just one example of changes with implications that have redefined the economic and political paradigm of the world. They have even brought into question the concepts of power and sovereignty, previously defined by material assets and formal borders.

Stability is a natural national aspiration for any government. It cannot, however, be achieved through the rejection of natural processes of incremental change. Domestic resistance to change, whether in governmental or nongovernmental positions of authority, is a source of stagnation and inefficient governance because surrounding circumstances, technologies, aspirations, and interests are in a constant state of flux. In addition, this tendency is normally coupled with those in authority resisting accountability and transparency increasing the list of unresolved problems, which fuel unfulfilled aspirations and built-up frustrations. To ensure stability, along with progress, nations must embrace incremental change in all systems that affect society.

The unique complexities we are facing, and the level of turbulence associated with these awakenings, were also exacerbated by the geopolitical competition in the region, which, in effect, not only made domestic but also foreign players consequential in our domestic problems. More frequently than not, this has been at the expense of Arab interests as a result of a "National Security Capacity Deficiency" in comparison with non-Arab members of the region.

Arab countries from the Atlantic, through North Africa to the Levant, and down to the Arab Gulf, at different points of time, have invariably made the mistake of becoming highly dependent on one or the other major superpower for their security. Even the more politically and militarily robust, like my own country Egypt, have fallen into this trap with the Soviet Union and then the United States again. On the other hand, by carefully calibrating domestic capabilities and foreign support, non-Arab states—Turkey, Israel, and Iran—have been able to preserve their national security alliances, while enhancing their own robust national security capacities at the same time. Ensuring security against existential threats by accepting the security support of a superpower or substantial regional player is justifiable. Kuwait would not have been liberated from Saddam Hussein's invasion in 1990 without the American-led international alliance. However, becoming overly dependent can lead to national security complacency, and encourage regional adversaries to become more adventurous, given that superpowers will have their own set of priorities and calculations before intervening and, more often than not, will only do so in existential circumstances.

I believe that the "Resistance to Change Syndrome' and the "National Security Capacity Deficiency" are the two most important reasons for the Arab awakenings, having occurred and caused destabilization. Resisting evolution resulted in revolutions. I would add, without any hesitation, that the Middle East will only get better when we find a remedy to this syndrome and overcome this deficiency.

Domestic transformations in the Arab world have indeed begun, albeit still with a lot of challenges. Things may get better or worse, but there will be no return to the past even if dreams of a democratic future are not immediately or easily realized. There are many indications that rampant poor governance will no longer be accepted or condoned, and one can see this in the public discourse in Arab media. In addition, even as we witness a re-centralization of authority, it is publicly promoted as a tool to better provide public goods and services, which confirm that public accountability, cannot be ignored.

Much remains to be done. To begin with, each of the Arab states must consensually develop a socio-political identity with widespread national support that is inclusive and consistent with the norms and standards of the twenty-first century. Since 1952, Egypt has essentially had a stable republican state structure. However, with every change of leadership, constituencies were pitted against each other, the marginalized and less affluent against the economically more fortunate, or supporters of private money against supporters of public ownership, or seculars against Islamists, or the youth against the old guard. These polarizing practices were, regrettably, frequently replicated throughout the Arab world.

Sound socioeconomic policies must also be adopted. Public spending in the Arab world, the traditional engine of development, has reached its limit, and the public sector can no longer absorb the number of university graduates. However, countries in the region have a large, well-educated youth population that, by global standards, has widely adopted digital and mobile technologies. This can provide a good reason for optimism as a catalyst for future growth and job creation if complemented with astute macro-socio-economic policies.

There is, however, a simultaneous need for Arab countries to become "learning societies", particularly in the Science, Technology, Engineering, and Mathematics (STEM) fields, and to create a vibrant digital service economy with a technologically capable labor force. Moreover, education systems should encourage greater openness to entrepreneurship and require students to hone their critical thinking as well as managerial skills within collaborative work arrangements. To sustain this, the digital economy will need technical infrastructure, including expanded broadband internet access and the availability of payment systems that are not just easy to use and widely available but also trustworthy. For this to occur, governments will also need to develop an approach to regulation that encourages, rather than stifles, innovation. There is a tremendous opportunity and positive potential here, but policymakers will need to work on multiple fronts to overcome economic exclusion and realize their full potential.

Economic vitality can be the engine towards prosperity, but immediate dire social challenges cannot be ignored and need to be addressed. I suggest creating an Arab social services fund that would provide matching funds to governments for the provision of basic health, housing, and educational programs. This would help shrink the size of marginalized constituencies as well as dry up significant fertile ground for extremist and terrorist recruitment.

It would also be highly beneficial for the Arab world to adopt a regional document on citizenship, highlighting the basic equality of rights and privileges for all, without discrimination on ethnic, religious, or any other basis, in order to preserve and consolidate the national identity of each of its member states.

The United Nations 2016 Arab Human Development Report reveals that Arab youth between the ages of 15 and 29 constitute nearly a third of the region's population. Another third is below the age of 15. Even though the younger generations are increasingly better educated, youth unemployment rates in the Arab World have risen to almost 30 percent, twice the global average of 16 percent. Sclerotic economies are unable to accommodate and make use of the vast amounts of human capital atrophying in the Arab World. The 2016 Arab Youth Survey reveals that there seems to be little appeal for extremist groups and their twisted interpretation of Islam among the youth. Nevertheless, many young people believe that without job opportunities and space for political expression, marginalization and frustration may increasingly be a source of tension and instability and might be an important factor in recruitment for terrorists and extremists. Youth, therefore, are an invaluable asset that should be seriously invested in because they are really the ballast of a better future. To achieve this, the fulfillment of their aspirations is a challenge that must be met.

Despite impressions to the contrary, Arab states continue to have more in common than ways in which they differ. Their historic legacy and shared cultural values should not be underestimated. A cooperative path forward is paramount if truly sustainable progress in the Arab World is to be achieved. In essence, Arab states must individually and jointly become more proactive diplomatically. The alternative, further diminution of Arab political weight, will prove disastrous to the region in this time of transition. It is imperative that the Arab states approach the changing world in wide-ranging agreement with the intention to continue building pluralistic, inclusive governments and reorienting their foreign policy away from excessive international dependency.

Traditional Pan-Arabism is neither feasible nor no longer desirable. The twenty-first-century mantra should be about constructive collaboration between independent sovereign states in the Arab world, creating a citizen identity that is responsive to national needs, taking full advantage of regional shared advantages, and consistent with modern norms. Moreover, in terms of leadership of the Arab world, it will not be about legacy but about the ability to cooperate with others in the region towards common objectives. In many ways, over the last half-century, just as the world has become multipolar, the Arab world itself has expanded to include the older and larger states of Egypt, Iraq, Syria, and Saudi Arabia. The younger smaller states of the United Arab Emirates, Bahrain, Qatar, and Oman have also shown an ability to influence regional developments, positively and negatively. Neither can act alone any longer no matter how strong or wealthy, nor independently lead the pack if a significant number of other Arab countries are not on board.

Arab countries, such as Syria and Iraq, have faced grave challenges after years of domestic injustice and foreign interference that have transformed into sectarian conflicts questioning the social coherence of once-proud civilizations. The very sustainability of the nation-state system in the Arab world, especially in the Levant, is now being questioned in favor of ethnic cultural, religious, sectarian identities that would wreak havoc on the state system, security, and stability not only in the Levant but also in the Gulf area with dangerous geopolitical implications.

Partially, as a result of these dangerous trends, the Middle East has also witnessed a geopolitical imbalance in favor of non-Arab countries in the region, especially Turkey, Iran, and Israel. Each of them poses a different unique challenge to the Arab world, from influence on insurgency, to occupation. Another important and alarming factor to take into account is the emergence of dangerous non-state actors, particularly terrorist groups such as the Islamic State in Iraq and Syria (ISIS) and the Al-Nusra Front. These groups are essentially homegrown; terrorism in the Middle East is a direct derivative of the breakdown of the social contract and the absence of effective state institutions. But these non-state actors, in different forms and with different identities, have managed to transcend borders with terrorist operations on different continents.

Then, of course, there are the regional conflicts and crises whose resolution or perpetuation will be instrumental in defining foreign policy objectives and policies in the years to come. The Arab World is rife with regional, bilateral, and domestic conflicts, from the shores of the Atlantic Ocean to the Arabian Gulf. Moroccan-Algerian tensions concerning the dispute over Western Sahara and the role of the Polisario Front remain unresolved. Libya has become a failed state, a fertile ground for extremists and terrorism, with sub-regional ramifications. Syria is a bloody battle-field, in spite of intensive diplomatic efforts sponsored by the United Nations. Iraq, while witnessing progress, is still unsettled, with terrorists able to operate across the border between Iraq and Syria. Conflict continues to consume Yemen; as with the war in Syria, the fighting there is exacerbating tensions between regional powers Saudi Arabia and Iran. The Arab-Israeli conflict, nearly seven decades old, continues to make life unbearable for the Palestinians living under occupation.

In the midst of all this turmoil, Arab diplomacy has been strangely absent. To counter support provided by non-Arab states. Some Arab countries had been providing military support for different protagonists in different conflicts, notably in Libya and Yemen, and in the war against terrorism in Syria and Iraq. Where, however, is Arab diplomacy? The diplomatic efforts are being made in every one of these cases are being led by non-Arabs or non-Arab organizations.

Arabs must look at the security paradigm in the Middle East more holistically—from within nation-state boundaries, to their immediate regional neighbors and beyond to sub-Saharan Africa and to Europe. Like the world itself, the Middle East is changing geopolitically and this needs to be addressed. The challenges ahead for a better future and regional stability are daunting, and this will require rational, proactive, and wise steps by strong and proud Arab states. Active Arab diplomacy will be a determining factor in whether the Arab awakenings are a success or a failure. This new approach will also be among the factors in determining the place Arabs will have in the future world order and in determining whether the Middle East will remain a cauldron of violence or proceed toward a more stable future.

The Arab world is amongst the largest arms buyers in the world, reaching an estimate of 11.535 billion dollars in arms purchases in 2017. However, this has not been coupled with enhanced national security capacities amongst Arab countries in terms of hardware, skills, and depth, which has diminished their influence in comparison to that of neighboring non-Arab states in non-existential crises.

Any attempt to project the future amid the prevailing volatility of today's Middle East is risky, if not foolhardy. Nevertheless, strategic planning based on well-considered assumptions is a necessity for policymakers. Domestic pressures in the Middle East will force governments to open up their systems, after initially driving them to overreact with restrictive measures in light of immediate challenges.

Given that the Middle East cannot and should not live in isolation from the global community, the path forward should be navigated by upholding international norms and practicing rational regional realpolitik in crisis management and conflict resolution. Arab and Middle Eastern states will not find stability unless they see and respect international norms, not as an imposition from foreign powers but as a response to the demand of their own people.

At the same time, sober crisis management and conflict resolution should drive the international community to preserve existing government institutions, respect the sanctity of international borders, even if shortsighted tactical gains may appear attractive and drive opportunistic policies.

No changes should be countenanced with respect to borders, irrespective of how they were originally drawn. Nor should changes involve dismantling institutions at the expense of a country's security and stability. These are roads we cannot afford to travel in the present volatility.

For the region to move forward, there must also be a reorientation of relations between Turkey and Egypt, as well as between Saudi Arabia and Iran. It is difficult to envision Middle Eastern stability with these four major players at loggerheads. Such shifts will prove challenging if not impossible in the short term. As an indication of seriousness, it would be useful to develop a series of preliminary but concrete confidence-building measures by Turkey and Iran that they would refrain from interfering in the internal affairs of their neighbors. Egypt and Saudi Arabia can reciprocate with actions acknowledging greater openness towards the legitimate interests of both countries.

Different regional organizations must be reinvigorated, such as the Arab Military Industrial Corporation, which is based in Egypt and can potentially enhance the national security capacity of different states. The Arab League, particularly in terms of its preventive diplomacy and crisis management capacities, has to redefine itself and break out of the stupor it is in.

My emphasis on reinvigorating proactive Arab diplomacy should not be mistaken for a disregard of the broader international transformations that continue to affect the Middle East. Older European states no longer reign over empires and the post-World War II bipolar security paradigms first led by the North Atlantic Treaty Organization and Warsaw Pact alliances, then by the United States and the Soviet Union, have dissipated. Both of these major powers are now moving away from prioritizing strategic "alliance" structures to short-term transactional policies with a decreased appetite for foreign military engagement as is evident in President Donald Trump's repeated reference to "America First" as the primary factor governing his international relations. It is also evident in President Vladimir Putin's policies in Syria, which, while militarily engaging, have in mind the dangers of over-extension, driving Russia to actively coordinate with Turkey, Iran, and the Syrian regime, even though these four parties do not have the same long-term goals.

This carries many implications in the Arab world as it strives to ensure its security without having a global enforcer and guarantor to rely on. Thus, it is imperative for the Arab world to diversify its relations with other states internationally rather than depend on a single superpower. They should also give increasing attention to neighboring regions, including sub-Saharan African and Mediterranean countries.

In addition, relations must be strengthened with Asian countries. China is the natural point of interest here. Its energy and raw material needs, as well as its interest in market areas, will grow exponentially. The Belt and Road Initiative and China's substantial investment capacity will raise its profile in the Arab world and make it look increasingly eastwards. The same applies with respect to India and Indonesia although to a lesser degree.

The conclusion from all this is that the Middle East will be even more complicated in the near future before it reaches its natural balance. Arab countries will pursue their foreign policies, regionally and globally, in a different context than in the past. They will preserve strong relations with the West for the near future. However, they will also strive to be less dependent on one foreign source by developing and expanding their relationships internationally. These countries will also strive to enhance their national security capacity in both diplomatic and military security terms, to independently deal with regional issues, especially as the appetite of global players to bear wider security responsibilities has diminished and regional imbalances have expanded.

Lastly, the Arab world needs to confront regional hegemonic attitudes and the illegitimate occupation of Arab lands. Solutions to current problems must respect people's aspirations for statehood and national political identity going beyond tactical or transactional approaches that provide only short-term relief. Ultimately, any policy that fails to protect national rights will not be sustainable and will perpetuate regional conflicts and thus become an obstacle to true security, stability, prosperity, and social cohesion.

Egypt should pursue a more contemporary foreign policy posture to adequately respond to the different global challenges posed by modern realities in a networked global environment, be they climate change, resource scarcity, xenophobia, or intelligence, which were not paramount when the post-World War II order was established.

To be effective and credible, this foreign policy approach should be strategic and forward-looking. Over the last decade or so, most of the developing world, as well as Egypt, has been playing catch-up on most issues. In addition, policies and positions must be announced clearly, coherently, and consistently as far as possible to avoid misunderstandings. They must be founded on a solid reservoir of earmarked resources in order to be viable and sustainable with the fundamental transformations occurring.

In the past, Egypt's political influence in the Arab world, Africa, and the developing world was unquestioned. It seemed to be a foregone conclusion or even an acquired right as a natural extension of the country's long heritage and momentous contributions of the past centuries. The overriding strategic objective for Egypt's future foreign policy will be, however, as much if not more, to provide an enabling environment for the attainment of Egypt's economic needs as to promote regional political priorities and prominence.

This is not to say that Egypt's foreign policy will uniquely pursue domestic economic goals or be driven solely by material needs. The aspirations expressed through Egypt's revolutions demand an activist foreign policy, which seeks not only to regain and strengthen but also to improve upon its historic leadership role and international standing. It is through this process of rejuvenation and assertion that Egypt can create the incentive to attract investors in economic growth and rapid social stability imperative to fulfill domestic goals and priorities.

In this context, a major and daunting challenge in which Egypt will need the help of others in the region and beyond is the fight against terrorism on its soil and nearby. This existential issue can derail any other domestic or foreign policy plans. Fighting terrorism is, of course, primarily the responsibility of the Egyptian army and security forces. However, terrorism is an international and regional phenomenon that knows no borders or frontiers and that takes full advantage of legitimate avenues of communication and resources to achieve criminal objectives. It is also a dangerous scourge that requires multidimensional security, political, and socioeconomic sustained efforts over an extended period.

However, to preserve its prominent role in the region, Egypt must, most of all, continue to be the bedrock of creative progressive intellect, which necessitates embracing new concepts of modernity and principles of governance that are responsive to the aspirations of all its people. If Egyptians want to play a central role in shaping their country's own future and that of the multiple regions their country is part of, they cannot remain complacent focusing on imminent issues of the present. They must start planning for the future now.

Personally, I believe that the winds of change in the Arab world, both domestically and regionally, were inevitable. They have created turbulent experiences that remain unsettled almost a decade later. However, they did shake governments and societies out of the state of deafening apathy that has essentially marginalized their role in determining their very own future. Therefore, while challenging and costly in the short and medium terms, the winds of change were inevitable and will be beneficial both now and more so in the future.

Very few countries in the Arab world would have survived two revolutions in three years. Egypt, in terms of the basic parameters of a strong state, human capacity, institution structures, and resiliency capacity, remains among the most stable countries in the Arab world and will continue to have a leadership role.

APPENDICES

APPENDIX I: ISRAELI DRAFT

TREATY OF PEACE
between
THE STATE OF ISRAEL
and
THE ARAB REPUBLIC OF EGYPT

Table of Contents

1. Preamble
2. Establishment of Peace
3. Recognition
4. Non-use of Force
5. Boundaries
6. Diplomatic and Consular Relations
7. Trade and Commerce
8. Cultural Relations
9. Deployment of Forces
10. Demilitarization
11. Destruction of Military Activities
12. Prevention of Terrorism

© The Author(s) 2020
N. Fahmy, *Egypt's Diplomacy in War, Peace and Transition*,
https://doi.org/10.1007/978-3-030-26388-1

13. Arms Limitation
14. Financial Claims
15. Suez Canal
16. Straits
17. Gulf of Suez and Gulf of Aqaba
18. Prohibition of Economic Warfare
19. Prohibition of Hostile Propaganda and Incitement
20. Non-interference in Domestic Affairs
21. Non-interference in External Relations
22. Hostile Organizations
23. Elimination of Prejudice in Teaching
24. Reservations to Multi-Lateral Conventions
25. Freedom of Movement
26. Aviation
27. Roads and Railways
28. Telecommunications
29. Access to Ports
30. Access to and Control of Holy Places
31. Enjoyment of Human Rights
32. Freedom of Movement
33. Right of Jews to Emigrate
34. Revocation of Hostile Resolutions
35. Promotion of Mutual Interests
36. Refugees
37. Respect for Graves and Right of Reburial
38. Nationality
39. Mutual Cooperation for Development
40. General Amnesty
41. Joint Committee
42. Conflict with Other Treaties or Domestic Law
43. Reference to Previous Agreements
44. Duration and Entry to Force
45. Settlement of Disputes
46. Registration with the United Nations
47. Languages

Israel and Egypt
With a view to ending the state of war and for the purpose of establishing permanent peace in the Area;

Desiring to prevent war, the threat of war, or the risk of war

Desiring to establish a just and lasting peace in which every State in the area can live in security

Having agreed to recognize each other's sovereignty and independence within secure and recognized boundaries

Resolved to live in friendship, co-operation, and good neighborly relations with each other for the benefit of their respective people

Desiring to remove the barriers that deny to both peoples the free exchange of information, ideas, goods, and services

Having reached agreement on the solution of all the outstanding questions between them

Have, therefore, determined to conclude the present Treaty of Peace, and have accordingly appointed the undersigned Plenipotentiaries who, after presentation of their full powers found in good and due form, have agreed on the following provisions:

(Establishment of Peace)

The state of war is hereby terminated and a just and lasting peace is established between Israel and Egypt.

(Recognition)

1. Egypt recognizes and undertakes to respect the sovereignty and political independence of Israel, and Israel recognizes and undertakes to respect the sovereignty and political independence of Egypt.
2. Neither Party shall support claims against the sovereignty or political independence of the other, if such claims are made in future by any state, group, or organization.

(Non-use of Force)

The Parties undertake to refrain from the threat or use of force directly or indirectly against each other and to settle all disputes between themselves by negotiation and peaceful means.

(Boundaries)

1. The Parties hereby establish and recognize the boundaries described in the protocol and delineated on the map attached hereto as consulting the final border between them. In the event of any discrepancy between the Protocol and the Map, the Protocol shall prevail.

2. The Parties declare that they shall respect unreservedly the territorial integrity of the other Party within these boundaries and that they have no territorial demands against each other, nor will they have such in future. They regard these boundaries as inviolable.

(Diplomatic and Consular Relations)

Diplomatic and Consular relations are hereby established between Egypt and Israel. For this purpose, it is agreed that the two parties shall proceed one month after this Treaty enters into force to exchange diplomatic representatives with the rank of Ambassador and that the question of the establishment of consulates in the territories of Egypt and Israel, respectively, shall be settled through diplomatic channels.

(Trade and Commerce)

The Parties shall negotiate and conclude a bilateral agreement on trade and commerce, for the purpose of normalizing commercial relations between then, within... years from the entry into force of this Treaty.

(Cultural Relations)

The Parties shall negotiate and conclude a Cultural Agreement within … years from the entry of force of this Treaty.

(Deployment of Forces)

Subject to the agreed security arrangements specified in this Treaty. Israel undertakes to evacuate its armed forces from all territory on the Egyptian side of the boundary established by this Treaty, in accordance with the attached timeline.

(Demilitarization)

All areas evacuated by Israel armed forces in accordance with the Articles above will remain demilitarized. In addition to that, all existing limitations as to the presence of armament and forces shall remain in effect. Details are as outlined in the attached Protocol.

1. Without derogating from the generality of the provisions of Article, the Parties agree that no part of military forces on land, at sea, or in the air shall commit, permit, tolerate, encourage, assist, or facilitate in new warlike or hostile acts of any kind in any place whatsoever, whether on its own territory or on the territory of any other state, against the military forces of the other part, or the civilians, property, institutions, territory, or airspace of the other party.

2. Each Party hereby undertakes not to enter into or remain a member of any military pact or alliance, which is directed against the other Part, or the members of which claim to be in a state of war with the other Party.

3. Neither Party shall permit the forces of any state claiming to be in a state of war with the other Party to be stationed anywhere within its territory, save with the express consent of the other Party. Neither Party shall permit the members of any group or organization whose aims are to attack directly or indirectly the other Party to be stationed under its control.

4. Each Party hereby undertakes not to incite any State to carry on belligerent acts against the other Party and not to grant aid or assistance of any kind to any State carrying on belligerent acts against the other Party.

5. Each Party shall take measures to ensure that the provisions of this Article shall be observed by its military or paramilitary forces or paramilitary forces operating from its territory.

(Prevention of Terrorism)

1. Each Party shall ensure that no act of violence against the other Party shall be committed on or originate from its territory by any organization group or individual.
2. Each Party undertakes not to grant asylum or protection to any person who has committed an act of violence against the other Party but to extradite or punish the person, as appropriate.
3. Each Party undertakes not to give any assistance or support to any individual, group, or organization planning or carrying out acts of violence against the other Part, on the territory of any other state.
4. For the purposes of this Article, acts of violence against a Party shall include acts of violence directed against (a) the territory, nationals, or population of that Party, (b) property belonging to that Party or its nationals or situated on its territory, (c) organizations, groups, or individuals in any way connected with that Party, wheresoever situated, and (d) the property of such organizations, groups, or individuals, wheresoever situated.

(Arms Limitation)

In order to eliminate the arms race, which is wasteful, and a source of tension, the Parties agree to regulate the size of their armed forces and the types of their armaments and weapon-systems. Details of such arms limitations shall be set out in a separate document to be concluded within... years after the entry into force of this Treaty.

(Financial Claims)

The Parties agree that the terms of the financial attached hereto, which is based on the principle of mutual settlement of all financial claims, constitutes a full and final settlement of all such claims, against each other, and accordingly waive all financial, economic, and property claims arising from any aspect of the Middle East dispute.

Suez Canal

Egypt declares that it regards Israel as fully entitled to all the privileges guaranteed to States under the Constantinople Convention of 1888, without any interference or discrimination, overt or covert, political or technical. Egypt shall accordingly permit and shall not interfere with free passage through the Suez Canal of ships flying the Israeli flag, under Israeli ownership, or carrying on board Israelis, or carrying Israeli cargo, or cargo destined for Israel, en route to or from Israeli ports.

Services provided to all the ships of all nations in the Canal and in the ports of access shall be provided, without any discrimination, overt or covert, political or technical, to ships flying the Israel flag, under Israeli ownership, manned by Israeli nationals, or carrying Israeli cargo or cargo destined for Israel en route to or from Israeli ports.

Tolls and charges shall be levied without discrimination, overt or covert, political or technical, from ships connected with Israel as mentioned above.

Egypt agrees not to invoke against Israel the provisions of Article X of the Constantinople Convention.

The principles enunciated above apply to the approaches to the Canal, as well as to the Canal itself.

(Straits)

The Parties recognize each other's right to unimpeded freedom of navigation and overflight through and over all straits between the area in the high seas, an exclusive economic zone, or territorial waters.

Accordingly, the Parties recognize each other's right to unimpeded freedom of navigation and overflight through and over the Straits of Tiran and Bab El Mandeb.

Each Party undertakes not to support, encourage, or assist other States in impeding freedom of navigation and overflight through and over the abovementioned Straits or other Straits.

Note: The formulation of this and next Article is drafted with reference to the latest text produced by the Third UN Conference on the Law of the Sea (A/Conf.62/W.P.10). It is therefore subject to change, depending on the ultimate outcome of the Conference.

(Gulf of Suez and Gulf of Aqaba)

(The Mediterranean Sea and the Red Sea)

1. The Parties recognize each other's right of navigation and overflight through and over the high seas, under customary and conventional international law. Such rights shall not be affected by any subsequent declaration by either Party of any part of the Mediterranean Sea or the Red Sea as an exclusive economic zone.
2. The Parties recognize each other's right to unimpeded freedom of navigation and overflight through and over the Gulf of Aqaba, the Gulf of Suez and its approaches.

(Prohibition of Economic Warfare)

Each Party undertakes to refrain from all forms of economic warfare or boycott activity aimed directly or indirectly against the other party, to prohibit any such activity from being carried out by its corporations, nationals, or within its territory, and to oppose any such activity on the part of any group or organization of which it is a member.

In particular, Egypt shall refrain from blacklisting or boycotting firms in third countries on the grounds of their religious affiliation, of the maintenance by them of economic or commercial ties with Israel, or of the maintenance of them of economic or commercial ties with other enterprises that have dealings with Israel. Egypt will consequently not require firms to declare that they do not maintain economic relations with Israel or undertake not to enter into such relations.

Egypt shall withdraw its declaration with regard to the nondiscrimination clause of the E. E. C. Treaty.

(Prohibition of Hostile Propaganda and Incitement)

Each Party shall abstain from hostile propaganda or incitement against the other Party or against organizations, groups, or individuals in any way connected with the other Party and shall take suitable measures against the dissemination of such propaganda or incitement by the media of communication operating within its jurisdiction.

(Non-Interference in Domestic Affairs)

Each Party undertakes not to interfere, directly, or indirectly, in the domestic affairs of the other Party, for any reason, whether economic, political, or ideological.

(Non-Interference in External Relations)

Each Party shall refrain from acts harmful to the other Part's diplomatic or other relations with third States or with international organizations or its relations with nationals of third States.

Egypt will support Israel's memberships in Regional Organizations.

(Hostile Organizations)

Neither Party shall accord any international or diplomatic status whatsoever to any organization whose object is the destruction or subversion of the other Party. The Parties shall oppose grant of such status to any such organization by any other state or international organization.

(Elimination of Prejudice in Teaching)

Each Party shall withdraw from its educational system all books and teaching materials that foster hatred, animosity, or intolerance towards the other Party, or its cultural or religious traditions, and shall ensure that such attitudes are not propagated in its educational system. The Parties shall introduce courses of study aimed at bringing about a positive appreciation of each other's history, values, and traditions.

(Reservations to Multilateral Conventions)

Each Party undertakes immediately to withdraw all reservations and declarations to multilateral Conventions relating to the recognition of the other Party or affecting the applicability of the Convention to the other Party, to refrain from making such reservations or declarations in the future, and to amend all internal legislative and administrative acts designed to give effect to such reservations and declarations.

(Freedom of Movement)

There shall be the maximum degree of freedom of movement between the two countries and within their respective territories, including mutual access to places of religious and historical significance, subject only to the essential requirements of public order and security.

(Aviation)

Each Party hereby declares that it regards the other as entitled to all the rights and privileges conferred by the Convention on International Civil Aviation, 1944 ("The Chicago Convention"), the International Air Services Transit Agreement, 1944, and the various regulations and annexes promulgated by the International Civil Aviation Organization subsequent to those agreements. In particular, but without derogating from the generality of the foregoing, each Party undertakes:

1. to grant to the other's registered aircraft eights of transit and overflight
2. to abrogate all Notices to Airmen (NOTAMS) and other administrative measures inconsistent with any of the aforesaid instruments or with this Treaty
3. not to invoke Article 89 of the Chicago Convention against the other
4. to permit all aircraft registered in other States Parties to the Chicago Convention to fly over and through its territory en route to and from the territory of the other Party
5. not to deny to aircraft registered in other States Parties to the Chicago Convention access to its airports on the ground that it has previously landed at any airport of the other Party

Egypt agrees to withdraw and annul forthwith the declaration contained in the letter from its Minister for Foreign Affairs, addressed to the Secretary-General of the I. C. A. O. and dated October 16, 1919, with regard to certain restrictions on the application to Israel of the Convention on International Civil Aviation.

The Parties negotiate and conclude a bilateral aviation agreement within... years from the entry into force of this Treaty.

(Enjoyment of Human Rights)

The Parties undertake to secure to all persons within their territory, without distinction as to race, sex, language, religion, or nationality, the full enjoyment of all rights and fundamental freedoms, including freedoms of expression, press, publication, religious worship, and public meeting.

(Roads and Railways)

The Parties shall ensure that roads and railways between their countries shall be reopened and maintained, and further road and train links shall be developed.

(Telecommunications)

Full and normal postal, telephone, wireless, and cable communications shall be established between the two parties, in accordance with all relevant international multilateral instruments.

(Access to Ports)

Each Party shall grant to ships flying the flag of the other Party owned by or carrying cargo of or destined for the other Party, or for its nationals, or manned by nationals of the other Party access to their ports on the same terms as those which access is granted to all other ships. No ship shall be denied access to the ports of one Party on the ground that it has previously visited any port of the other Party.

(Access to and Control over Holy Places)

Each Party shall grant to nationals of the other Party free and unimpeded access to the holy places of any religion and to all sites of cultural and historical interest situated in its territory. The Freedom of access granted by this Article may, however, be partially or temporarily restricted owing to the need for the preservation of public order.

Both Parties undertake to protect, guard, and upkeep all holy places, all sites of cultural and historical interest, and all items of cultural property situated in its territory, which are considered to be of religious or cultural value to the other Party.

(Autonomous control shall be granted to the Moslem community in Israel over all its holy places situated in the territory of Israel, in accordance with the terms of the Protocol annexed hereto. Similar autonomous control shall be granted to the other religious communities in Israel over their holy places situated in the territory of Israel.)

("Freedom of Movement")

There shall be the maximum degree of freedom of movement between the two countries and within their respective territories, including mutual access to places of religious and historical significance, subject only to the essential requirements of public order and security.

(Right of Jews to Emigrate)

Egypt shall permit all Jews resident within its territory whether or not Egyptian nationals, who wish to do so, to emigrate at any time to Israel or to any other country in accordance with their own choice, without impediment of any kind whatsoever.

(Revocation of Hostile Resolutions)

Each Party undertakes to support any draft resolution submitted to any organs of the United Nations, or any other international organization, aimed at revoking existing resolutions directed against the other Party. In particular, Egypt undertakes to support the revocation of the General Assembly Resolution No. 3379 (XXX).

Each Party further undertakes to oppose any draft resolution hostile to the other Party that may be introduced in the future.

(Promotion of Mutual Interests)

The Parties recognize that history and geography have created an objective affinity of interests between their countries and that their economic and human interests are closely related. The Parties agree to promote this natural association for their mutual benefit.

(Refugees)

Each Party shall do all that is necessary to solve the problem of the refugees situated in its territory.

(Respect for Graves and Right of Reburial)

Each Party undertakes to respect and maintain in good condition all cemeteries and graves situated in their territories in which nationals of the other Party or persons having the same ethnic or religious affiliation as any of the nationals of the other party are buried. The Parties will make arrangements for giving effect to request for the transfer for the reburial of the bodies of nationals of the other Party.

(Nationality)

(Mutual Cooperation for Development)

1. The Parties shall cooperate with each other and with universal or regional international organizations for the planning and development of the region as a whole, the raising of living standards, the eradication of disease, the prevention of pollution, the furthering of education, and the general advancement of the region. In particular, the Parties agree to enter into negotiations for the purpose of establishing joint ventures for the common exploration and exploitation of their natural resources.
2. The Parties will undertake further steps for the comprehensive development of their mutual relations. They agree that an extension of their neighborly cooperation in the economic and scientific fields, in their scientific and technological relations, and in the fields of culture, environmental protection, sport, transport, and in other sectors of their relations is in their mutual interest.

(General Amnesty)

Each Party shall grant a general amnesty to all nationals of the other Party held in its custody for criminal offenses.

Each Party undertakes to refrain from taking any measures whatsoever, including judicial proceedings, against any person, whether or not their own national, on the grounds that they have at any time shown any sympathy with or carried out any acts for the other Party. Each Party confers on the other right of diplomatic protection with regard to any such persons.

(Joint Committee)

The Parties shall set up a joint committee to supervise the implementation of the Treaty. The representative of the Parties appointed to the joint committee shall hold regular meetings for the purpose of facilitating the implementation of the provisions of this Treaty. The procedure of the Joint Committee, such as composition, frequency of meetings, competence, will be established; competence will be established in a separate Protocol.

(Conflict with Other Treaties or Domestic Law)

1. In the event of a conflict between the obligations of the Parties under the present Treaty and their obligations under any other international agreement, their obligation under the present Treaty shall prevail.
2. In the event of any conflict between the terms of this Treaty and the internal law of either Party, the Treaty shall prevail.
3. The Parties agree not to enter into any Treaty, agreement, arrangement, or understanding with any third Party, which would be incompatible with the provisions of this Treaty.
4. The Parties shall adopt all such legislative and administrative measures as may be necessary for the full implementation of this Treaty and shall not adopt in the future any legislative or administrative measures inconsistent with any of the provisions of this Treaty.

(Reference to Previous Agreements)

This Treaty supersedes all previous agreements between Israel and Egypt, including that signed by Egypt on September 22, 1975, and by Israel on October 12, 1975.

(Duration and Entry to Force)

All Maps and Protocols attached to this agreement shall be regarded as integral part thereof.

This Treaty shall remain in operation for an unlimited period.

The Present Treaty shall be ratified. It shall enter into force immediately upon the exchange of instruments and ratification.

(Settlement of Disputes)

Disputes which may arise between the two governments regarding the interpretation or application of the present Treaty or any other separate agreements concluded pursuant to the present Treaty shall be resolved by direct diplomatic negotiations.

In cases where it may have been impossible to arrive at a solution by this means, the dispute is to be submitted to arbitration at the request of either Government.

The arbitrator shall be selected by agreement between the two governments. If after two months from the date of the request of either Government to submit the dispute to arbitration, the two governments have not agreed on the choice of the arbitrator, he shall be chosen by the....

The Parties agree that the Award of the Arbitrators shall be final and binding.

(Registration with the United Nations)

The Treaty shall be communicated to the Secretary-General of the United Nations for registration in accordance with the provisions of Article 102 of the Charter of the United Nations.

(Languages)

Done at Geneva, this... Day of ....19... in duplicate in the Hebrew, Arabic, and English languages, each text being equally authentic. In case of any divergence of interpretation, the English text shall prevail.

The Alternative

(Two Possibilities)

In the event that the states bordering on Israel refuse to participate in the Geneva Peace Conference in accordance with the established framework determined by the precedent of the first session of the Conference on grounds of insistence that the organization called PLO be added to the sovereign state delegations, it is proposed:

To establish through the good offices of the United States the aforementioned three mixed commissions in keeping with the precedent determined in Rhodes in 1949.

Or: In accordance with the principle of "proximity talks", with a view to conducting in the framework of such mixed commissions the negotiations on the conclusion of the peace treaties.

TOP SECRET

7.7.77

THE FRAMEWORK FOR THE PEACEKEEPING PROCESS
BETWEEN ISRAEL AND ITS NEIGHBORS

(1) The Government of Israel will be prepared to participate, beginning October 10, 1977, in a new additional session of the Geneva Peace Conference, to be convened by the two co-chairmen on the basis of Paragraph 3 of the Security Council Resolution 338 of October 21, 1973, which states: (the Security Council) "decides that, Immediately and concurrently with the cease-fire, negotiations start between the parties Concerned under appropriate auspices aimed at establishing a just and durable peace in the Middle East".

(2) Resolution 338 includes and makes reference to Security Council Resolution 242 of November 22, 1967.

(3) Accredited delegations of sovereign states will participate in the reconvened session of the Geneva Peace Conference, namely, the representatives of Israel, Egypt, Syria, and Jordan.

(4) The participating states in the Geneva Peace Conference will present no prior conditions for their taking part in this Conference.

(5) At the public session of the recovered Geneva Peace Conference, the representatives of the parties will make opening statements.

(6) At the conclusion of the public session, three mixed commissions will be established, namely: Egyptian-Israeli; Syrian Israeli; Jordanian-Israeli.

(7) In the framework of these mixed commissions, peace treaties between the parties concerned will be negotiated and concluded.

(8) The chairmanship of each mixed commission will be fixed by the rule of rotation between an Israeli representative and a representative of the neighboring state.

(9) Having reached an agreement on the substance of the peace treaties—i.e. the termination of the state of war; the delineation of the permanent boundaries; the economic clauses, etc.—a public session of the Conference will again be convened for the purposes of signing the peace treaties.

APPENDIX II: FIRST AMERICAN DRAFT

Outline of Possible Peace Treaty Between Egypt and Israel

Preamble

The Government of the Arab Republic of Egypt and the Government of Israel:

Desirous of ending the state of war and of conducting their relations in accordance with the provisions of the United Nations Charter and the accepted norms of international law governing international relations in times of peace

Desirous also of developing between them the normal relations of states at peace with one another, and of removing the barriers between their peoples

Reaffirming that the fulfillment of Charter principles requires the establishment of a comprehensive, just, and lasting peace in the Middle East

Pursuant to the determination expressed in the Agreement between them dated September 1, 1975 (Sinai II) to reach a final and just peace settlement by means of negotiations called for by Security Council Resolution 338 of October 22, 1973

Convinced of the urgent necessity, therefore, of the establishment of peace in the Middle East in accordance with the principles and provisions of Security Council Resolution 242 of November 22, 1967:

-2-

Agree that:

Article I

This treaty and its annexes shall constitute the final peace agreement between them in accordance with the purposes and principles of the United Nations Charter and in conformity with Security Council Resolution 242 of November 22, 1967.

With the coming into force of this treaty, the conflict between them has ended and all claims or states of belligerency between Egypt and Israel will terminate, together with policies and practices deriving from them, including economic welfare or boycott activity.

The Parties undertake to respect and acknowledge each other's sovereignty and political independence, and their right to live in peace within their security and recognized boundaries.

The Parties undertake not to resort to the use of force against each other, to settle disputes by peaceful means, and to do all in their power to ensure that acts of belligerency, violence, or hostility do not originate from and are not committed from within their respective territories or by any forces subject to their control against the population, citizens, or property of the other party.

Neither Party shall support claims against the sovereignty or political independence of the other.

-3-

Article II
The permanent border between Egypt and Israel, conforming except as otherwise agreed between them to the 1949 Armistice Demarcation Line, is as shown on the annexed map (Annex 1).

Article III
Israel will commence withdrawing its forces to the permanent border in stages, beginning with the coming into force of this treaty, and synchronized with the implementation of other provisions of this treaty as provided in the annexed plan (Annex II).

Article IV
In keeping with the provisions of the preamble, the Parties accept the principle of the development between them of the relationships normal to states at peace with one another. To this end, they have drawn up the annexed protocol (Annex II), setting out the process by which they undertake to achieve such a relationship, in stages, beginning with the coming into force of this treaty, parallel to and synchronized with the implementation of other provisions of this treaty.

No later than _____ after the coming into force of this treaty, the Parties will agree to establish full diplomatic relations.

-4-

Article V
In order to provide maximum security for both parties at each stage of implementation, and for the future, once implementation is completed, security arrangements will be established that will enhance the capability of each side to protect itself against hostile military action from the other side in violation of this treaty. These measures, described in detail as to

nature and timing in Annex III, will include limited force zones in Egyptian and Israeli territory, separated by a demilitarized area patrolled by UN forces whose removal will require either the agreement of both Parties or Security Council approval. Special arrangements will be made for third-party reconnaissance and early warning facilities for both Egypt and Israel.

Article VI
In order to eliminate the arms race, which is wasteful and a source of tension, the Parties agree to regulate the size of their armed forces and the type of their armaments and weapons-systems. Details of such arm limitations shall be set out in a separate document to be concluded within _____ after the entry into force of this treaty.

Article VII
The Suez Canal will be open to the free passage of all

-5-

Israeli ships and cargoes
The principle of non-suspendable innocent passage applies to transit of the Straits of Tiran and includes the right of overflight for civilian aircraft. The association of the other littoral states of the Straits and the Gulf of Aqaba with this provision will be welcomed. An international force under UN auspices, whose removal will require either the agreement of both Parties or the UN Security Council approval, will be stationed at Sharm el-Sheikh to ensure the carrying out of this provision.

Article VIII
A Joint Commission will be established, consisting of representatives of the Parties, and operating, until the treaty is fully implemented, under UN Chairmanship, to resolve problems arising in the execution of the treaty or otherwise affecting the relations between the Parties.

Article IX
The Parties will encourage and accept guarantees for the provisions of this treaty by the United States, the Soviet Union, and the United Nations Security Council.

APPENDIX III: SECOND AMERICAN DRAFT

Outline of Possible Peace Treaty Between Egypt and Israel

Preamble

The Government of the Arab Republic of Egypt and the Government of Israel:

Desirous of ending the state of war and of conducting their relations in accordance with the provisions of the United Nations Charter and the accepted norms of international law governing international relations in times of peace

Desirous also of developing between them the normal relations of states at peace with one another and of removing the barriers between their peoples

Reaffirming that the fulfillment of Charter principles requires the establishment of a comprehensive, just, and lasting peace in the Middle East

Pursuant to the determination expressed in the Agreement between them dated September 1, 1975 (Sinai II) to reach a final and just peace settlement by means of negotiations called for by Security Council Resolution 338 of October 22, 1973

Convinced of the urgent necessity, therefore, of the establishment of peace in the Middle East in accordance with the principles and provisions of Security Council Resolution 242 of November 22, 1967:

-2-

Agree that:

Article I

This treaty and its annexes shall constitute the final peace agreement between them in accordance with the purposes and principles of the United Nations Charter and in conformity with Security Council Resolution 242 of November 22, 1967.

With the coming into force of this treaty, the conflict between them has ended and all claims or states of belligerency between Egypt and Israel will terminate, together with policies and practices deriving from them, including economic welfare or boycott activity.

The Parties undertake to respect and acknowledge each other's sovereignty and political independence, and their right to live in peace within their security and recognized boundaries.

The Parties undertake not to resort to the use of force against each other, to settle disputes by peaceful means, and to do all in their power to ensure that acts of belligerency, violence or hostility do not originate from and are not committed from within their respective territories or by any forces subject to their control against the population, citizens, or property of the other party.

Neither Party shall support claims against the sovereignty or political independence of the other.

-3-

Article II
The permanent border between Egypt and Israel, conforming except as otherwise agreed between them to the 1949 Armistice Demarcation Line, is as shown on the annexed map (Annex 1).

Article III
Israel will commence withdrawing its forces to the permanent border in stages, beginning with the coming into force of this treaty and synchronized with the implementation of other provisions of this treaty as provided in the annexed plan (Annex II).

Article IV
In keeping with the provisions of the preamble, the Parties accept the principle of the development between them of the relationships normal to states at peace with one another. To this end, they have drawn up the annexed protocol (Annex II), setting out the process by which they undertake to achieve such a relationship, in stages, beginning with the coming into force of this treaty, parallel to and synchronized with the implementation of other provisions of this treaty.

No later than _____ after the coming into force of this treaty, the Parties will agree to establish full diplomatic relations.

-4-

Article V
In order to provide maximum security for both parties at each stage of implementation, and for the future, once implementation is completed, security arrangements will be established that will enhance the capability

of each side to protect itself against hostile military action from the other side in violation of this treaty. These measures, described in detail as to nature and timing in Annex III, will include limited force zones in Egyptian and Israeli territory, separated by a demilitarized area patrolled by UN forces whose removal will require either the agreement of both Parties or Security Council approval. Special arrangements will be made for third-party reconnaissance and early warning facilities for both Egypt and Israel.

Article VI

In order to eliminate the arms race, which is wasteful and a source of tension, the Parties agree to regulate the size of their armed forces and the type of their armaments and weapons-systems. Details of such arm limitations shall be set out in a separate document to be concluded within _____ after the entry into force of this treaty.

Article VII

The Suez Canal will be open to the free passage of all

-5-

Israeli ships and cargoes

The principle of non-suspensable innocent passage applies to transit of the Straits of Tiran and includes the right of overflight for civilian aircraft. The association of the other littoral states of the Straits and the Gulf of Aqaba with this provision will be welcomed. An international force under UN auspices, whose removal will require either the agreement of both Parties or the UN Security Council approval, will be stationed at Sharm el-Sheikh to ensure the carrying out of this provision.

Article VIII

A Joint Commission will be established, consisting of representatives of the Parties and operating, until the treaty is fully implemented, under UN Chairmanship, to resolve problems arising in the execution of the treaty or otherwise affecting the relations between the Parties.

Article IX

The Parties will encourage and accept guarantees for the provisions of this treaty by the United States, the Soviet Union, and the United Nations Security Council.

Secret

APPENDIX IV: EGYPTIAN DRAFT TREATY 1977

FUNDAMENTAL REQUIREMENTS FOR FINAL, PERMANENT, AND JUST PEACE:

1. PUTTING AN END TO THE ISRAELI OCCUPATION OF ARAB TERRITORY THROUGH THE COMPLETE AND TOTAL WITHDRAWAL OF ISRAELI FORCES FROM ALL ARAB TERRITORIES OCCUPIED SINCE JUNE 1967
2. THE REALIZATION OF THE INALIENABLE NATIONAL RIGHTS OF THE ARAB PEOPLE OF PALESTINE AND THEIR RIGHT TO SELF DETERMINATION, INCLUDING THEIR RIGHT TO ESTABLISH THEIR OWN STATE
3. THE RIGHT OF EVERY STATE IN THE AREA TO LIVE IN PEACE WITHIN SECURED AND INTERNATIONALLY GUARANTEED BOUNDARIES THROUGH:
   (a) ARRANGEMENTS TO BE AGREED UPON TO PROVIDE ADEQUATE SECURITY MEASURES FOR THE INTERNATIONAL BOUNDARIES
   (b) THE NECESSARY, INTERNATIONAL POLITICAL GUARANTEES
4. COMMITMENT BY ALL STATES IN THE AREA TO CONDUCT THEIR RELATIONS IN ACCORDANCE WITH ALL THE PROVISIONS OF THE UNITED NATIONS CHARTER, IN PARTICULAR THE NON-RESORT TO THE USE OF FORCE AND TO RESOLVE DIFFERENCES BY PEACEFUL MEANS

IF THE ABOVE-MENTIONED PRINCIPLES, WHICH CLEARLY AND ADEQUATELY PROVIDE PEACE AND SECURITY FOR ALL THE PARTIES, ARE FULLY ACCEPTED AND ADHERED TO BY ALL THE PARTIES, EGYPT IS READY TO SIGN THE FOLLOWING AGREEMENT WITH ISRAEL SIMULTANEOUSLY WITH OTHER ARAB PARTIES CONCERNED.

PEACE AGREEMENT BETWEEN THE ARAB REPUBLIC OF EGYPT AND ISRAEL

REAFFIRMING THAT THE FULFILLMENT OF CHARTER PRINCIPLES REQUIRES THE ESTABLISHMENT OF A JUST AND LASTING PEACE IN THE MIDDLE EAST

RECALLING THE PURPOSES AND PRINCIPLES OF THE UNITED NATIONS CHARTER, WHICH GOVERN RELATIONS AMONG STATES

CONVINCED OF THE URGENT NECESSITY FOR THE ESTABLISHMENT OF A JUST AND DURABLE PEACE IN THE MIDDLE EAST IN ACCORDANCE WITH THE PRINCIPLES AND PROVISIONS OF SECURITY COUNCIL RESOLUTION 242

DESIROUS TO CONDUCT THEIR RELATIONS IN ACCORDANCE WITH THE PROVISIONS OF THE UNITED NATIONS CHARTER AND ACCEPTED NORMS OF INTERNATIONAL LAW GOVERNING INTERNATIONAL RELATIONS IN TIME OF PEACE

THE GOVERNMENT OF THE ARAB REPUBLIC OF EGYPT AND THE GOVERNMENT OF ISRAEL HAVE AGREED THAT:

Article 1

THIS AGREEMENT AND ITS ANNEXES SHALL CONSTITUTE FINAL PEACE AGREEMENT BETWEEN THEM IN ACCORDANCE WITH THE PURPOSES AND PRINCIPLES OF THE UNITED NATIONS CHARTER AND IN CONFORMITY WITH SECURITY COUNCIL RESOLUTION 242 OF NOVEMBER 22, 1967.

Article 2

THE ISRAELI GOVERNMENT SOLEMNLY UNDERTAKES TO:

(a) WITHDRAW ITS FORCES FROM THE EGYPTIAN TERRITORY OCCUPIED SINCE JUNE 5, 1967 TO THE INTERNATIONAL BOUNDARIES OF EGYPT.

(b) WITHDRAW ITS FORCES IN ACCORDANCE WITH AN AGREED TIMETABLE TO BE IMPLEMENTED WITHIN THREE MONTHS OF THE SIGNING OF THIS AGREEMENT. THE ARRANGEMENTS OF THE TIMETABLE ARE OUTLINED IN ANNEX.

Article 3
THE GOVERNMENT OF THE ARAB REPUBLIC OF EGYPT
SOLEMNLY UNDERTAKES TO:

(a) ENSURE THE FREEDOM OF NAVIGATION IN THE SUEZ
    CANAL   IN   ACCORDANCE   WITH   THE   1888
    CONSTANTINOPLE CONVENTION.
(b) ENSURE THE FREEDOM OF NAVIGATION IN THE
    STRAITS OF TIRAN IN ACCORDANCE WITH THE
    PRINCIPLES OF INTERNATIONAL LAW.

Article 4
THE TWO PARTIES AGREE TO:

(a) ESTABLISH DEMILITARIZED ZONES ASTRIDE AND
    ALONG THE BORDERS BETWEEN THEM, THE WIDTH
    OF WHICH SHOULD NOT EXCEED 5 K.M. ON EACH
    SIDE. THE ARRANGEMENTS FOR SUCH ZONES ARE
    OUTLINED IN ANNEX 2.
(b) ACCEPT THE STATIONING OF UNITED NATIONS
    PEACEKEEPING FORCES ON THEIR TERRITORIES
    ASTRIDE THE BORDERS.
(c) ACCEPT THE INSTALLATION OF ELECTRONIC DEVICES
    AND AN EARLY WARNING SYSTEM IN THEIR
    TERRITORIES ASTRIDE THE BORDERS.

THE DETAILS CONCERNING THE DEPLOYMENT AND
OPERATION OF THE UNITED NATIONS FORCES, THE EARLY
WARNING AND SURVEILLANCE INSTALLATIONS, AND OTHER
RELATED ARRANGEMENTS AND SIMILAR MECHANICS, AS
AGREED UPON BETWEEN THE TWO PARTIES, WILL BE IN
ACCORDANCE WITH THE PROVISIONS OF ANNEX 3.

Article 5
THE TWO PARTIES UNDERTAKE TO:

(a) RESPECT   AND   ACKNOWLEDGE   EACH   OTHER'S
    INTEGRITY AND POLITICAL INDEPENDENCE.

(b) RESPECT AND ACKNOWLEDGE EACH OTHER'S RIGHT TO LIVE IN PEACE WITHIN THEIR SECURED AND RECOGNIZED BOUNDARIES.

(c) DO ALL IN THEIR POWER TO ENSURE THAT ACTS OF BELLIGERENCY OR HOSTILITY DO NOT ORIGINATE FROM OR ARE COMMITTED FROM WITHIN THE RESPECTIVE TERRITORIES AGAINST THE POPULATION, CITIZENS, OR PROPERTY OF THE OTHER PARTY.

(d) REFRAIN FROM ANY INTERFERENCES IN EACH OTHER'S DOMESTIC AFFAIRS.

(e) NOT TO RESORT TO THE USE OF FORCE DURING THE IMPLEMENTATION OF THIS AGREEMENT.

Article 6
THE PARTIES THEREFORE DECLARE THAT THE CONFLICT BETWEEN THEM HAS ENDED AND UNDERTAKE TO TERMINATE ALL CLAIMS AND STATES OF BELLIGERENCY.

Article 7
THE GOVERNMENTS OF THE ARAB REPUBLIC OF EGYPT AND ISRAEL AGREE THAT FIVE YEARS AFTER THE FINAL IMPLEMENTATION OF THIS AGREEMENT, THEY SHALL EXAMINE WAYS AND MEANS TO PROMOTE FURTHER THE CONSOLIDATION OF PEACE BETWEEN THEM.

Article 8
THE PARTIES AGREE TO ESTABLISH A JOINT COMMISSION IN ORDER TO CONSIDER ANY PROBLEM ARISING IN THE EXECUTION OF THIS AGREEMENT. THE JOINT COMMISSION SHALL FUNCTION IN ACCORDANCE WITH THE PROCEDURES ESTABLISHED IN ANNEX 4.

Article 9
THIS AGREEMENT SHALL BE GUARANTEED BY THE UNITED STATES OF AMERICA AND THE UNION OF THE SOVIET SOCIALIST REPUBLICS. IT SHALL BE SUBMITTED TO THE APPROVAL OF THE SECURITY COUNCIL. THE PARTIES AGREED THAT OTHER STATES CAN BECOME PARTIES TO THE ABOVE-MENTIONED GUARANTEES.

FOR THE GOVERNMENT OF THE   FOR THE
GOVERNMENT
ARAB REPUBLIC OF EGYPT   OF ISRAEL

APPENDIX V: DRAFT INITIATIVE TO RECONVENE GENEVA
CONFERENCE

Strictly Confidential: Geneva Conference, 1977

  I. An international Summit Conference for Peace in the Middle East shall be convened in the Arab Sector of Jerusalem during the month of December 1977 for the purpose of achieving a just and lasting peace in the region.

    The leaders of the United States, the Union of Soviet Socialist Republics, the People's Republic of China, France, the United Kingdom, Israel, the Arab Republic of Egypt, the Syrian Arab Republic, the Hashemite Kingdom of Jordan, and Lebanon, and Mr. Yasser Arafat and the United Nations Secretary-General will take part in the conference.

  II. The Mandate of the Conference is the Establishment of a just and lasting peace based on the following terms of reference:

    a. The termination of the Israeli occupation of all Arab territories occupied since 1967.

    b. The formulation of adequate guarantees necessary to safeguard the political independence and territorial integrity of all states in the area and their right to live in peace.

    c. The realization of the legitimate rights of the Palestinian people.

    d. The termination of Belligerency and the conclusion of Peace treaties between the parties.

 III. The summit conference shall refer its decision to the president of the Security Council, so that the Security Council transmits it to the Geneva conference, which shall be convened forthwith with a view to formulate the decisions of the summit conference into peace treaties to be concluded between the parties concerned.

 IV. The Geneva Conference shall fulfill its task as soon as possible, and, at any rate, not later than June 30, 1987.

APPENDIX VI: TALKING POINTS ON THE ISSUE
OF JERUSALEM

Talking Points on the Issue of Jerusalem
Submitted July 19, 2000

Israeli Talking Points

- This concept is an attempt to address the minimum pre-requisites and of both sides without violating either red lines, first foremost:
- For Barak: no division of Jerusalem (including, no relinquishing of sovereignty at this stage).
- For Arafat: East Jerusalem as the Palestinian capital (albeit not fully sovereign at this stage) without prejudice to Palestinian Claims for sovereignty.
- Advantages to Barak:
  - A united undivided city
  - No transfer of sovereignty now
  - Recognition of the capital of Israel
  - Jewish neighborhoods in East Jerusalem incorporated and recognized
  - Expanded capital including satellite settlements
  - Preserving the religious statuesque in the holy places
  - No annexation of 200,000 Palestinians
  - Overall security authority in Israeli hands
- Advantages to Arafat
  - East Jerusalem a recognized capital
  - De facto control and full municipal authority over all Palestinian neighborhoods
  - Maintains claim for sovereignty over areas not presently included
  - Responsible for law enforcement and civic security arrangements
  - Incorporates all Palestinians as Palestinian citizens

Jerusalem Preamble

1. For centuries, the city of Jerusalem has been the focus of prayer and hope as well as a source of ongoing tension. The sides are determined

to transform the resolution of the Jerusalem issue into the corner-stone of the agreement between them and a symbol of the new era of peace and reconciliation.

2. The sides are committed to enhance the status of Jerusalem as a city of peace.
3. The sides recognize the unique status of Jerusalem as a holy city for Judaism, Christianity, and Islam and reaffirm their commitment to the freedom of worship and religious practice in the city.
4. Jerusalem shall be an open and an undivided city.
5. The undivided city shall serve as the recognized respective seat of government and capital of the two states.

Geographic Scope

6. The current municipal boundaries of the city shall be expanded to include the following areas:
   a. On the Israeli side: from Ma Ale Edumim to the French Hill and from Givat Z Eev through Givon and Har Shmuel to Ramot.
   b. On the Palestinian side: from Abu Dies through Al-Ezarieh, A-Zaim, Anata, Hizma, A-Ram, Bir Naballah, and Al Jib to Beit Iksa.
7. This entire area shall constitute the Greater Jerusalem Area (GJA).

Political Scope

8. The GJA shall compromise three types of areas:
   a. The Israeli/Jewish:
      The "Western" City, the Israeli/Jewish neighborhoods in the "Eastern" City as well as the above-mentioned expansions (6a), shall constitute the Israeli Yurushalayim, which shall be recognized by the State of Palestine as the capital of the State of Israel.
   b. Palestinian/Arab:
      The Arab "Eastern" City, as well as the above-mentioned expansion (6b), shall constitute the Palestinian Al-Quds, which shall be recognized by Israel as the capital city of the State of Palestine.
   c. The Holy Basin:
      The area including the Old City (between the Walls) as well as the adjacent areas of religious, historical, or cultural significance

(i.e. the Muslim Cemetery below the Eastern Wall, the Kidron Valley, the churches, and the Jewish Cemetery on Mount Olives, David's City, the Shiloach and Hizkiyahu, Gey Ben Hinom, and Mount Zion) shall constitute the Holy Basin and shall be subject to a special regime.

Municipal Management

9. The GJA shall be governed by four municipal authorities as follows:
   a. The Municipal of Yurushalayim:
      This municipal authority shall administer the Israeli/Jewish areas as defined above (8a). This area shall have areas in territorial contiguity and continuity of physical infrastructure, including transportation.
   b. The Municipal of Al-Quds:
      The municipal authority shall administer the Palestinian/Arab as defined above (8b). This area shall have territorial contiguity and continuity of physical infrastructure, including transportation.
   c. The Yurushalayim-Al-Quds Cooperation Authority:
      1. The two states and the two municipalities shall empower the Jerusalem Cooperation Authority (JCA) to coordinate daily activity as well as overall joint planning and municipal regulations for the GJA. The JCA shall be a parity body no majority to either side and shall have required parity subcommittees for various tasks.
         (Note: A complete draft is under preparation.)
      2. The JCA shall also oversee the implementation of "The Jerusalem Covenant" stipulating agreed-upon guidelines for the GJA.
         (Note: This document is under preparation.)
   d. The Holy Basin Joint Committee (HBJC):
      The HBJC shall be empowered by the two states and the two municipalities to manage daily in the Holy Basin. The HBJC shall be a parity body. Its main task shall be to reserve the unique character of this area. The composition, terms, and mandate of the HBJC shall be detailed in the caps. The HBJC shall establish a subcommittee for religious affairs (Joint Religious Council, JRC), which shall serve as the venue for inter-religious dialogue and for the coordination of specified religious issue.

3. The Holy Basin shall be administered according to a mutually agreed detailed agreement.

Sovereignty

10. The sides have accepted the following understandings and arrangements concerning the undivided GJA:
    a. Recognition of full sovereignty as follows:
       1. Israel:
          Full Israeli sovereignty shall apply to the "Western City", and the aforementioned Jewish areas to be incorporated in the new GJA, which are beyond the present municipal boundaries of the city (8a). This does not in any way abrogate from the Israeli claim to sovereignty over all of the current municipal area of Jerusalem.
       2. Palestine:
          Full Israeli sovereignty shall apply to the aforementioned Palestinian areas to be incorporated in the new GJA, which are beyond the present municipal boundaries of the city (8b). This does not in any way abrogate from the Palestinian claim to sovereignty over the "Eastern" sections of the current municipal area.
    b. The following arrangements shall apply to the areas not covered by section "A" above for an agreed period of time and without prejudice to the determination of the final status in this area.
       1. In the "Outer Circle" (i.e. neighborhoods such as Shoaufat, Anata, Beit Hanina, Kafr Aqab, Samiramis, Western Abu Dies, A-Shiah, Arab-Sawahara, Um Lison, Tzur Bahir, and Um Tuba). The Palestinians shall have full civilian authority. The Palestinians shall also be responsible for maintaining law and order and Israel shall have the overriding security authority. The two sides shall exercise police work in close coordination and cooperation.
       2. In the "Inner Circle" (i.e. neighborhoods such as Sheikh Jarah Wadi Joz, Bab-A-Zar, Silouan, Ras El Amud, Beit Safara, and Shsrfat). The Palestinians shall have full civilian authority, and Israel shall have full security authority. Police duties to be detailed in the cap shall be exercised by espe-

cially established joint Israeli-Palestinian unit, which shall coordinate and cooperate with the respective Israeli and Palestinian police forces.

c. The Holy Basin:
As neither side relinquishes the claim of sovereignty, yet recognizes the unique spiritual, religious, cultural, and historical importance of the Holy Basin, and wishes to promote interfaith relations and harmony among the three religions, the sides agree to establish a special regime as follows:

1. Guaranteed freedom of worship and the right to free access to all holy sites for members of all faiths and religions.
2. The prevailing religious status quo as regards to the holy sites shall be respected.
3. Legal and functional arrangements governing the Holy Basin shall be detailed in the caps. These arrangements shall determine the specific functional sphere of Israel autonomous jurisdiction and Palestinian autonomous jurisdiction, to be applied to Israeli and Palestinian citizens; joint mechanisms and regulations shall be agreed upon.
4. Sovereignty on the Temple Mount Haram-A-Sharif shall not be explicitly defined. A detailed appendix shall outline functions and jurisdictions as well as derived responsibilities. Hence, the status quo in this area shall be permanent. The administration of the area shall continue to be with the WAQF of the state of Palestine.
5. The overall responsibility for the security in the Holy Basin shall be with Israel.

In the Arab areas, "The holy Basin" joint patrols of Israeli Police and the new Special Palestinian Civic Security Force shall be carried out. Each side shall handle the illegal activities of its citizens.

Citizenship

11. All Palestinian residents of the GJA shall be citizens of Palestine, and all Israeli residents of the GJA shall be citizens of Israel. The Palestinian citizens shall no longer qualify as per residents of the state of Israel.

Appendix VII: President Clinton's Message to President Mubarak

August 9, 2000

President Clinton's message to President Mubarak, evaluating the Palestine, Israel, America Summit in Camp David

Dear Hosni:

I know Ned Walker has briefed you on the Camp David Talks. Although we didn't succeed in reaching agreement, I believe real progress was made through the efforts of both parties.

The talks broke old taboos on permanent status issues, including Jerusalem. Progress was made in narrowing many differences and pointing the way towards the outlines of an agreement.

Prime Minister Barak and Chairman Arafat moved on all issues.

As a result, I believe an agreement is possible, but we all have a historic responsibility to make this possibility a reality. I know you will continue to be my partner in this effort.

Time is not our friend in this enterprise. We must deal with the political realities for both parties. First, we must avoid September 13 becoming a point of confrontation. Second, there is a clock ticking in Israel. I believe Barack can sell a mutually beneficial agreement on peace, but I doubt this Israeli government, having exposed itself by the moves it made at Camp David, will survive if no agreement is reached soon. I fear a follow-on government will be far less forthcoming on peace. If that is the case, we will see the loss of this opportunity, with consequences in the region that will be very damaging for all of us.

As you know from Ned's briefing, we came close on most issues.

But the main sticking points were Jerusalem and specifically the Haram Al Sharif or the temple mount. This unique place is sacred to Muslims and Jews. No agreement will be possible unless BOT sides' interests and needs are addressed and both must be able to justify the outcome to their people. We cannot concede Muslim interests. But we must find a way for this sacred space to be reserved for both faiths.

Whatever the answer, I know you will support the effort to find an honorable solution. Chairman Arafat will look to you to help make tough decisions on this and other questions.

Hosni, I rely on your support as we try to end this historic conflict. I absolutely agree with you that we must stop recriminations. These are difficult issues and I believe both parties, and the region's leaders, are proceeding in good faith. The stakes could not be higher. I am convinced that either we will achieve an agreement in the next few months or we will see a slide into conflict and turmoil that could be tragic for the entire region. I remain committed to do all.

That I can to resolve this conflict, and I know you are as well.

Sincerely,

Bill

*   *   *

President Mubarak's response

Dear Bill,

Thank you for your message dated August 9th 2000 concerning the outcome of the Camp David talks, and our future efforts to achieve a just and lasting settlement of the Palestinian problem.

Your effective leadership and strong commitment to the cause of peace have helped the parties in building blocks that can move them towards reaching a final agreement. Your direct personal involvement in the negotiations has given confidence to all the parties in achieving this objective. I view your instrumental role with admiration and appreciation.

I agree with you that Camp David talks have succeeded in addressing the core issues in a direct and detailed manner, thus allowing for some progress to be made on several issues, albeit with different depths.

I wish to reiterate that Egypt stands alongside the United States as a strong partner in the quest for peace in the Middle East. Egypt has and will always be supportive of every effort aiming at transforming our shared hope into a reality, through achieving a comprehensive peace in the region. We stand ready, as always, to work with both Israelis and Palestinians to bring an end to this conflict.

Since the breakdown of the Camp David talks, I have given great deal of thought to how to help in reaching an agreement. One that builds on what was achieved in Camp David, and bridges the gaps between the parties. In this regard, I would like to share with you some of my thoughts and reflections.

First, it is clear from all that we have learned that the issue of Jerusalem and in particular that of Al-Haram Al-Sharif is one of the most sticking points hindering an agreement.

Second, it is also clear that this is not only a serious redline for President Arafat, but is also one that is of extreme sensitivity throughout the Arab and Muslim worlds.

Third, I believe that the formulas or notions of quasi or ambiguous sovereignty over Al-Haram Al-Sharif and other areas in Jerusalem will not augur well for the future. This, in turn, leads me to believe that we should address the issue of sovereignty in Jerusalem with clarity and vision for a stable future in the region.

Fourth, while focusing on ways to resolve the question of Al-Haram Al-Sharif, it is necessary to acknowledge the high sensitivity of the other core issues such as territory, refugees, security, and water.

I am of the view that the only feasible option lies in adopting what could be termed a "package within a package". A package for the issue of Jerusalem within a larger package for all the permanent status issues.

On the issue of the Holy Sites of the Old City of Jerusalem, namely Al Haram Al-Sharif and the Wailing Wall, my thoughts rest on the following lines:

- The Security Council of the United Nations would assume the ultimate authority over Al-Haram Al-Sharif and the Wailing Wall (either for a specified agreed period of time or until both parties reach a formula that would fulfill their aspirations).
- The Security Council would in-turn mandate custodial sovereignty to the government of Palestine over Al-Haram Al-Sharif, including control over access to the sites, administration, security, civic authority, ensuring the freedom of worship and free and unhindered passage, etc. The Security Council would also mandate the Government of Israel with full administration of the Wailing Wall, including control over access to the sites, administration, security, civic authority, ensuring the freedom of worship and free and unhindered passage, etc.
- Each party would pledge not to undertake, or permit acts such as digging and excavations in the respectively mandated Holy Sites, except for the requirements of repair, maintenance, and restoration of the existing site.
- No party can change the established status quo as recognized by the Security Council mandate and the terms of the agreement to be reached on this matter.

As regards other parts of the City of Jerusalem, whether its municipal boroughs or in the walled city, I envisage a settlement that builds upon what was offered at Camp David, and ensures that Jerusalem, both East and West, shall be an open city that embodies the principles of peaceful coexistence and religious tolerance, while guaranteeing the freedom of movement of all peoples. This, in my view, could only be achieved through cooperation between the parties, and by adopting joint equal arrangements to facilitate the daily operations of the whole city including in the areas of security, ensuring public order, coordinating municipal requirements of the boroughs, and so forth.

In the light of this, and as for the quarters of the Old City, my thoughts are as follows:

- The Muslim, Christian, and Armenian quarters of the Old City would be part Al-Quds and come under the full sovereignty of the State of Palestine.
- The Jewish quarter of the old city would come under the full sovereignty of the State of Israel.

Concerning the Palestinian boroughs falling within the municipal boundaries of the city of Jerusalem, they would be part of Al-Quds and would come under the sovereignty of the State of Palestine and comprise its capital while the Israeli boroughs would be part of the State of Israel and would be under its sovereignty and comprise its capital. Ensuring territorial contiguity for both sides is imperative.

Bill,

I am convinced that this package has to fall within a wider package that guarantees the settlement of all the core issues. I would like to highlight our thoughts on each of them.

On the territorial issue, I am of the strong view that this question if not dealt with appropriately, could be as explosive as the issue of Jerusalem. Some high Israeli official conveyed to us readiness to hand over 94% of the totality of the West Bank to the Palestinian side. I find it necessary that the withdrawal from the West Bank and Gaza Strip be based on the borders of June 4th, 1967. Despite the illegality of the Israeli settlements in the West Bank, and which you rightly described as an obstacle to peace, I think it is possible that the Palestinian side would agree to adopt minor rectification, in the vicinity of 3% of the West Bank, which represents the area of those settlements on or around the western border of the West Bank. The gap between the two figures are not, I believe, difficult to bridge if we work together to find an acceptable solution for this matter, based on principles such as the swap of land—which as your envoy Edward Walker relayed to us, was somewhat acceptable to both. This is of course in addition to any other idea that both parties may agree on. Furthermore, these rectifications should not in any way reflect the weight of conquest or undermine the territorial contiguity of both sides, the water rights or include Palestinian populated areas.

As regards the issue of refugees, and as you are well aware, the settlement of this matter embodies great and profound ramifications on the Palestinian People worldwide and especially in our region. Resolving this question should be based on designing a working framework to implement the principles laid out in the United Nations General Assembly Resolution 194, which include the right of return and the right of compensation. I strongly feel that resolution 194 could be implemented in a manner that will accommodate the needs and interests of both parties. I would like to emphasize that any scheme to settle the issue of refugees should give urgent attention to those residing in Lebanon.

As for security, I understand that specific arrangements were discussed, that can include a role or roles for the United Nations or multinational forces with a possible American presence. This is an important and positive substitute for any continued Israeli military presence within the boundaries of the coming Palestinian state. Other issues like limiting the armament of the Palestinian State. Other issues like limiting the armament of the Palestinian State can be addressed in a comprehensive framework of security arrangements. Moreover, the Palestinian leadership has expressed to me several times their full readiness to continue the current bilateral cooperation on security matters.

Finally, and in light of past experiences, it would be vital to create a mechanism for monitoring the faithful and timely implementation of the provisions of any agreement between the parties.

* * *

Dear Bill,

I have tailored this initiative to help you and the parties overcome the remaining challenges. I totally agree that the coming days and weeks are of historic importance, and are critical for the resolution of the Palestinian/Israeli conflict.

I have already alluded to the general idea underlying these suggestions during conversations with both Prime Minister Barak and President Arafat. Those ideas were generally discussed with your envoys (Ross- Walker) during their recent visits to the area. More detailed discussions on these suggestions are currently being undertaken with both parties.

In all frankness, I must emphasize that I do not see any other avenue that would lead us to move on the course of reaching an acceptable and reasonable solution to the issue of Jerusalem, other than seriously considering the proposal of granting the ultimate authority over Al-Haram Al-Sharif and the Western Wall; to the Security Council as explained above. I am convinced that this proposal can succeed in bridging the gap between the parties, in the context of a wider package that covers all core issues. I hope I could hear from you soon in order to accelerate the process of consultations with interested parties especially the Muslim leaders who are extremely anxious to see the problem of Jerusalem and the Holy sites equitable resolved.

At the end, I would like to express my strong commitment to work closely with you in the coming weeks to find an honorable solution to resolve this conflict once and for all.

Appendix VIII: The Moratinos Document

Taba, January 2001

Introduction

This EU non-paper has been prepared by the EU Special Representative to the Middle East Process, Ambassador Moratinos, and his team after consultations with the Israeli and Palestinian sides, present at Taba in January 2001. Although the paper has no official status, it has been acknowledged by the parties as being a relatively fair description of the outcome of the negotiations on the permanent status issues at Taba. It draws attention to the extensive work, which has been undertaken, on all permanent status issues like territory, Jerusalem, refugees, and security in order to find ways to come to joint positions. At the same time, it shows that there are serious gaps and differences between the two sides, which will have to be overcome in future negotiations. From that point of view, the paper reveals the challenging task ahead in terms of policy determina-tion and legal work, but it also shows that both sides have traveled a long way to accommodate the views of the other side and those solutions are possible.

1.   *Territory*

The two sides agreed that in accordance with the UN Security Council Resolution 242, the June 4, 1967 lines would be the basis for the borders between Israel and the state of Palestine.

1.1   West Bank

For the first time, both sides presented their own maps over the West Bank. The maps served as a basis for the discussion on territory and settlements. The Israeli side presented two maps, and the Palestinian side engaged on this basis. The Palestinian side presented some illustrative maps detailing its understanding of Israeli interests in the West Bank. The negotiations tackled the various aspects of territory, which could include some of the settlements and how the needs of each party could be accommodated. The Clinton parameters served as a loose basis for the discussion, but differences of interpretations regarding the scope and meaning of the parameters emerged. The Palestinian side stated that it had accepted the Clinton proposals but with reservations.

The Israeli side stated that the Clinton proposals provide for the annexation of settlement blocs. The Palestinian side did not agree that the parameters included blocs and did not accept proposals to annex blocs. The Palestinian side stated that blocs would cause significant harm to the Palestinian interests and rights, particularly to the Palestinians residing in areas Israel seeks to annex. The Israeli side maintained that it is entitled to contiguity between and among their settlements.

The Palestinian side stated that Palestinian needs take priority over settlements. The Israeli maps included plans for future development of Israeli settlements in the West Bank. The Palestinian side did not agree to the principle of allowing further development of settlements in the West Bank. Any growth must occur inside Israel.

The Palestinian side maintained that since Israel has needs in Palestinian territory, it is responsible for proposing the necessary border modifications. The Palestinian side reiterated that such proposals must not adversely affect the Palestinian needs and interests.

The Israeli side stated that it did not need to maintain settlements in the Jordan Valley for security purposes, and its proposed maps reflected this position.

The Israeli maps were principally based on a demographic concept of settlements blocs that would incorporate approximately 80 percent on the settlers. The Israeli side sketched a map presenting a 6 percent annexation, the outer limit of the Clinton proposal. The Palestinian illustrative map presented 3.1 percent in the context of a land swap.

Both sides accepted the principle of land swap but the proportionality of the swap remained under discussion. Both sides agreed that Israeli and Palestinian sovereign areas would have respective sovereign contiguity. The Israeli side wished to count "assets" such as Israelis "safe passage/corridor" proposal as being part of the land swap, even though the proposal would not give Palestine sovereignty over these "assets". The Israeli side adhered to a maximum 3 percent land swap as per Clinton proposal.

The Palestinian maps had a similar conceptual point of reference stressing the importance of a non-annexation of any Palestinian villages and the contiguity of the West Bank and Jerusalem. They were predicated on the principle of a land swap that would be equitable in size and value and in areas adjacent to the border with Palestine and in the same vicinity as the annexed by Israel. The Palestinian side further maintained that land not under Palestinian sovereignty such as the Israeli proposal regarding a "safe passage/corridor" as well as economic interests are not included in the calculation of the swap.

The Palestinian side maintained that the "No-Man's-Land" (Latrun area) is part of the West Bank. The Israelis did not agree.

The Israeli side requested an additional 2 percent of land under a lease arrangement to which the Palestinians responded that the subject of lease can only be discussed after the establishment of a Palestinian state and the transfer of land to Palestinian sovereignty.

1.2 Gaza Strip

Neither side presented any maps over the Gaza Strip. It was implied that the Gaza Strip will be under total Palestinian sovereignty, but details have still to be worked out. All settlements will be evacuated. The Palestinian side claimed it could be arranged in 6 months, a timetable not agreed by the Israeli side.

1.3 Safe Passage/Corridor from Gaza to the West Bank

Both sides agreed that there is going to be a safe passage from the north of Gaza (Beit Hanun) to the Hebron district and that the West Bank and the Gaza Strip must be territorially linked. The nature of the regime governing the territorial link and sovereignty over it was not agreed.

2. Jerusalem

2.1 Sovereignty

Both sides accepted in principle the Clinton suggestion of having a Palestinian sovereignty over Arab neighborhoods and an Israeli sovereignty over Jewish neighborhoods. The Palestinian side affirmed that it was ready to discuss Israeli request to have sovereignty over those Jewish settlements in East Jerusalem that were constructed after 1967 but not Jebal Abu Ghneim and Ras al-Amud. The Palestinian side rejected Israeli sovereignty over settlements in the Jerusalem Metropolitan Area, namely of Ma'ale Adumim and Givat Ze'ev.

The Palestinian side understood that Israel was ready to accept Palestinian sovereignty over the Arab neighborhoods of East Jerusalem, including part of Jerusalem's Old City. The Israeli side understood that the Palestinians were ready to accept Israeli sovereignty over the Jewish Quarter of the Old City and part of the American Quarter.

The Palestinian side understood that the Israeli side accepted to discuss Palestinian property claims in West Jerusalem.

2.2 Open City

Both sides favored the idea of an Open City. The Israeli side suggested the establishment of an open city whose geographical scope encompasses the Old City of Jerusalem plus an area defined as the Holy Basin or Historical Basin.

The Palestinian side was in favor of an open city provided that continuity and contiguity were preserved. The Palestinians rejected the Israeli proposal regarding the geographic scope of an open city and asserted that the open city is only acceptable if its geographical scope encompasses the full municipal borders of both East and West Jerusalem.

The Israeli side raised the idea of establishing a mechanism of daily coordination and different models were suggested for municipal coordination and cooperation (dealing with infrastructure, roads, electricity, sewage, waste removal, etc.). Such arrangements could be formulated in a future detailed agreement. It proposed a "soft border regime" within Jerusalem between Al-Quds and Yerushalaim that affords them "soft border" privileges. Furthermore, the Israeli side proposed a number of special arrangements for Palestinian and Israeli residents of the Open City to guarantee that the Open City arrangement neither adversely affect their daily lives nor compromise each party sovereignty over its section of the Open City.

2.3   Capital for Two States
The Israeli side accepted that the City of Jerusalem would be the capital of the two states: Yerushalaim, capital of Israel, and Al-Quds, capital of the state of Palestine. The Palestinian side expressed its only concern, namely, that East Jerusalem is the capital of the state of Palestine.

2.4   Holy/Historical Basin and the Old City
There was an attempt to develop an alternative concept that would relate to the Old City and its surroundings, and the Israeli side put forward several alternative models for discussion, for example, setting up a mechanism for close coordination and cooperation in the Old City. The idea of a special police force regime was discussed but not agreed upon.

The Israeli side expressed its interest and raised its concern regarding the area conceptualized as the Holy Basin (which includes the Jewish Cemetery on the Mount of Olives, the City of David, and Kivron Valley). The Palestinian side confirmed that it was willing to take into account Israeli interests and concerns provided that these places remain under Palestinian sovereignty. Another option for the Holy Basin, suggested informally by the Israeli side, was to create a special regime or to suggest some form of internationalization for the entire area or a joint regime with special cooperation and coordination. The Palestinian side did not agree to pursue any of these ideas, although the discussion could continue.

2.5   Holy Sites: Western Wall and the Wailing Wall
Both parties have accepted the principle of respective control over each side's respective holy sites (religious control and management). According to this principle, Israel's sovereignty over the Western Wall would be recognized although there remained a dispute regarding the delineation of the area covered by the Western Wall and especially the link to what is referred to in Clinton's ideas as the space sacred to Judaism of which it is part.

The Palestinian side acknowledged that Israel has requested to establish an affiliation to the holy parts of the Western Wall but maintained that the question of the Wailing Wall and/or Western Wall has not been resolved. It maintained the importance of distinguishing between the Western Wall and the Wailing Wall segment thereof, recognized in the Islamic faith as the Buraq Wall.

2.6   Haram al-Sharif/Temple Mount

Both sides agreed that the question of Haram al-Sharif/Temple Mount has not been resolved. However, both sides were close to accepting Clinton's ideas regarding Palestinian sovereignty over Haram al-Sharif, notwithstanding Palestinian and Israeli reservations.

Both sides noted progress on practical arrangements regarding evacuations, building, and public order in the area of the compound. An informal suggestion was raised that for an agreed period such as three years, Haram al-Sharif/Temple Mount would be under international sovereignty of the P5 plus Morocco (or other Islamic presence), whereby the Palestinians would be the "Guardian/Custodians" during this period. At the end of this period, the parties would either agree to a new solution or agree to extend the existing arrangement. In the absence of an agreement, the parties would return to implement the Clinton formulation. Neither party accepted or rejected the suggestion.

3.   Refugees

Non-papers were exchanged, which were regarded as a good basis for the talks. Both sides stated that the issue of the Palestinian refugees is central to the Israeli-Palestinian relations and that a comprehensive and just solution is essential to creating a lasting and morally scrupulous peace. Both sides agreed to adopt the principles and references which could facilitate the adoption of an agreement.

Both sides suggested, as a basis, that the parties should agree that a just settlement of the refugee problem in accordance with the UN Security Council Resolution 242 must lead to the implementation of UN General Assembly Resolution 194.

3.1   Narrative

The Israeli side put forward a suggested joint narrative for the tragedy of the Palestinian refugees. The Palestinian side discussed the proposed narrative and there was much progress, although no agreement was reached in an attempt to develop a historical narrative in the general text.

3.2 Return, Repatriation, and Relocation and Rehabilitation

Both sides engaged in a discussion of the practicalities of resolving the refugee issue. The Palestinian side reiterated that the Palestinian refugees should have the right of return to their homes in accordance with the interpretation of United Nations General Assembly Resolution (UNGAR) 194. The Israeli side expressed its understanding that the wish to return as per the wording of UNGAR 194 shall be implemented within the framework of one of the following programs:

A. Return and repatriation
  1. To Israel
  2. To Israel swapped territory
  3. To the Palestine state
B. Rehabilitation and relocation
  1. Rehabilitation in host country
  2. Relocation to third country

Preference in all these programs shall be accorded to the Palestinian refugee population in Lebanon. The Palestinian side stressed that the above shall be subject to the individual free choice of the refugees, and shall not prejudice their right to their homes in accordance with its interpretation of UNGAR 194.

The Israeli side, informally, suggested a three-track 15-year absorption program, which was discussed but not agreed upon. The first track referred to the absorption to Israel. No numbers were agreed upon, but with a non-paper referring to 25,000 in the first three years of this program (40,000 in the first five years of this program did not appear in the non-paper but was raised verbally). The second track referred to the absorption of Palestinian refugees into the Israeli territory that shall be transferred to Palestinian sovereignty, and the third track referred to the absorption of refugees in the context of family reunification scheme.

The Palestinian side did not present a number but stated that the negotiations could not start without an Israeli opening position. It maintained that Israel's acceptance of the return of refugees should not prejudice existing programs within Israel such as family reunification.

3.3   Compensation

Both sides agreed to the establishment of an International Commission and an International Fund as a mechanism for dealing with compensation in all its aspects. Both sides agreed that a "small-sum" compensation shall be paid to the refugees in the "fast-track" procedure, claims of compensation for property losses below a certain amount shall be subject to "fast-track" procedures.

There was also progress on Israeli compensation for material losses, land, and assets expropriated, including agreement on a payment from an Israeli lump sum or proper amount to be agreed upon that would feed into the International Fund. According to the Israeli side, the calculation of this payment would be based on a macro-economic survey to evaluate the assets in order to reach a fair value. The Palestinian side, however, said that this sum would be calculated on the records of the United Nations Conciliation Committee for Palestine (UNCCP), the Custodian for Absentee Property and other relevant data with a multiplier to reach a fair value.

3.4   UNRWA

Both sides agreed that United Nations Relief and Work Agency for Palestinian Refugees in Near East (UNRWA) should be phased out in accordance with an agreed timetable of five years as a targeted period. The Palestinian side added a possible adjustment of that period to make sure that this will be subject to the implementation of the other aspects of the agreement dealing with refugees and with the termination of Palestinian refugee status in the various locations.

3.5   Former Jewish Refugees

The Israeli side requested that the issue of compensation to former Jewish refugees from Arab countries be recognized while accepting that it was not a Palestinian responsibility or a bilateral issue. The Palestinian side maintained that this is not a subject for a bilateral Palestinian-Israeli agreement.

3.6   Restitution

The Palestinian side raised the issue of restitution of refugee property. The Israeli side rejected this.

3.7   End of Claims

The issue of the end of claims was discussed, and it was suggested that the implementation of the agreement shall constitute a complete and final implementation of UNGAR 194 and, therefore, ends all claims.

4. *Security*

4.1 Early Warning Stations

The Israeli side requested to have three early warning stations on Palestinian territory. The Palestinian side was prepared to accept the continued operations of early warning stations but subject to certain conditions. The exact mechanism has, therefore, to be detailed in further negotiations.

4.2 Military Capability of the State of Palestine

The Israeli side maintained that the state of Palestine would be non-militarized as per the Clinton proposals. The Palestinian side was prepared to accept a limitation on its acquisition of arms and be defined as a state with limited arms. The two sides have not yet agreed on the scope of arms limitations but have begun exploring different options. Both sides agree that this issue has not been concluded.

4.3 Air Space Control

The two sides recognized that the state of Palestine would have sovereignty over its airspace. The Israeli side agreed to accept and honor all of Palestine civil aviation rights according to international regulations but sought a unified air control system under overriding Israel control. In addition, Israel requested access to Palestinian airspace for military operations and training.

The Palestinian side was interested in exploring models for broad cooperation and coordination in the civil aviation sphere but unwilling to cede overriding control to Israel. As for Israeli military operations and training in Palestinian airspace, the Palestinian side rejected this request as inconsistent with the neutrality of the state of Palestine, saying that it cannot grant Israel these privileges while denying them to its Arab neighbors.

4.4 Timetable for Withdrawal from the West Bank and Jordan Valley

Based on the Clinton proposal, the Israeli side agreed to a withdrawal from the West Bank over a 36-month period with an additional 36 months for the Jordan Valley in conjunction with an international force, maintaining that a distinction should be made between withdrawal in the Jordan Valley and elsewhere.

The Palestinian side rejected a 36-month withdrawal process from the West Bank expressing concern that a lengthy process would exacerbate

Palestinian-Israeli tensions. The Palestinian side proposed an 18 months' withdrawal under the supervision of international forces. As to the Jordan Valley, the Palestinian side was prepared to consider the withdrawal of Israeli armed forces for an additional 10-month period. Although the Palestinian side was ready to consider the presence of international forces in the West Bank for a longer period, it refused to accept the ongoing presence of Israeli forces.

4.5   Emergency Deployment (or Emergency Locations)

The Israeli side requested to maintain and operate five emergency locations on Palestinian territory (in the Jordan Valley) with the Palestinian response allowing for a maximum of two emergency locations conditional on a time limit for the dismantling. In addition, the Palestinian side considered that these two emergency locations be run by international presence and not by the Israelis. Informally, the Israeli side expressed willingness to explore ways that a multinational presence could provide a vehicle for addressing the parties' respective concerns.

The Palestinian side declined to agree to the deployment of Israeli armed forces on Palestinian territory during emergency situations but was prepared to consider ways in which international forces might be used in that capacity, particularly within the context of regional security cooperation efforts.

4.6   Security Cooperation and Fighting Terror

Both sides were prepared to commit themselves to promoting security cooperation and fighting terror.

4.7   Borders and International Crossings

The Palestinian side was confident that Palestinian sovereignty over borders and international crossing points would be recognized in the agreement. The two sides had, however, not yet resolved this issue, including the question of monitoring and verification at Palestine's international borders (Israeli or international presence).

4.8   Electromagnetic Sphere

The Israeli side recognized that the state of Palestine would have sovereignty over the electromagnetic sphere and acknowledged that it would not seek to constrain Palestinian commercial use of the sphere but sought control over it for security purposes.

The Palestinian side sought full sovereign rights over the electromagnetic sphere but was prepared to accommodate reasonable Israeli needs within a cooperative framework in accordance with international rules and regulations.

Dispute over Ma'aleh Adumim

The importance of Israel's recognition of the June 4, 1967 border is that since 1967 (and even today), Israel's official position has been that UN Security Council Resolution 242 mandates withdrawal from "territories" conquered in the Six-Day War. The Arab position, in contrast, is that the resolution requires withdrawal from "the territories". Israel's official refusal to recognize the June 4, 1967 borders is currently an obstacle to Foreign Minister Shimon Peres in his efforts to reach an agreement with the chairman of the Palestinian Legislative Council, Ahmed Qureia (Abu Ala). There is no Palestinian confirmation of Peres' claim that the Palestinians have accepted the formulation that a final-status agreement will be based on Resolution 242.

Israel agreed to recognize the June 4, 1967 border as the basis for the border between Israel and Palestine after the Palestinians agreed in principle to discuss territorial swaps in the West Bank, as proposed by Clinton, which would enable Israel to annex parts of the West Bank adjacent to the Green Line (but not parts of Gaza). The maps presented by the Palestinians at Taba gave Israel 3.1 percent of the West Bank. That is less than the lower limit proposed in the Clinton plan (under which the Palestinians would receive 94 to 96 percent of the West Bank). Israel demanded 6 percent—the upper boundary of the Clinton plan—plus an additional 2 percent in the context of a leasing agreement. The Palestinians also rejected Israel's demand that the "no man's land" around Latrun not be considered part of the West Bank.

According to the document, Israel gave up all the Jordan Valley settlements, focusing instead on its security interests in that area. The dispute centered around the large stretch of territory between Ma'aleh Adumim and Givat Ze'ev, which contains both a fairly large Palestinian population and East Jerusalem's most important land reserves. The Palestinians retracted their earlier readiness to include these two settlements in the settlement blocs to be annexed to Israel after realizing that Israel also insisted on annexing the large tract that joins them—which would mean that Palestinian citizens would suddenly find themselves in sovereign Israeli territory. Barak instructed his chief negotiator, Gilad Sher, to tell the Palestinians that the map presented by then foreign minister Shlomo Ben-Ami, which reduced the area of the settlement bloc (including the Ma'aleh Adumim-Givat Ze'ev tract) to only 5 percent of the West Bank, had no validity.

Another dispute that remained unresolved stemmed from Israel's refusal to accept the Palestinian demand for a 1:1 ratio between the area of the West Bank annexed to Israel and the parts of Israel that would be given to the Palestinians in exchange. Israel proposed a ratio of 1:2 in its favor. In addition, the Palestinians rejected Israel's proposal that the Halutza Dunes in the Negev, the area of the "safe passage" between the West Bank and Gaza, and the part of Ashdod Port that would be set aside for Palestinian use all be considered part of the land swap. They insisted that the land they received be contiguous with either the West Bank or Gaza and that it not include any land that was merely set aside for their use, over which they would not have sovereignty. (Akiva Eldar)

How Long Is the Western Wall?

The Clinton proposal paved the way for understandings in Jerusalem, but it also created the principal dispute between the two parties.

An agreement was reached that East Jerusalem, which would be called Al-Quds, would be the capital of Palestine. Understandings were also reached regarding a division of East Jerusalem's neighborhoods such that Jewish neighborhoods would remain under Israeli sovereignty (other than Har Homa, which the first Jewish families are just moving into now, and Ras al-Amud), while Arab neighborhoods would be transferred to Palestinian sovereignty. In addition, it was agreed that parts of the Old City—the Muslim Quarter, the Christian Quarter, and part of the Armenian Quarter—would be transferred to the Palestinians.

But the Clinton proposal did not help the parties to draw mutually accepted borders between the Open City—to which both sides agreed— and the surrounding Palestinian areas, on one side, and Israeli areas, on the other. The Open City is territory that citizens of both countries can enter without passing through any checkpoints. The Palestinians wanted it to encompass all of Jerusalem, while the Israelis wanted it limited to the Old City only.

And the Clinton proposal complicated negotiations on the most sensitive issue: The Western Wall. Clinton had referred to "the holy parts" of the Wall, thereby creating an opening for the Palestinian claim that only the exposed part of the Wall (the Wailing Wall) is considered holy to the Jews, and, therefore, only this part should be left under Israeli sovereignty. Palestinians claimed the Western Wall tunnels were part of Haram al-Sharif (the Temple Mount).

Since the Taba talks ended, many meetings and seminars have taken place in an effort to close the gaps, attended by politicians and experts from both sides and from other countries as well.

Symbols of Sovereignty

Israel insisted that it retain sovereignty over the "safe passage" between Gaza and the West Bank, with the Palestinians receiving only usage rights to the land. With respect to air space, however, Israel adopted a more generous approach to the sovereignty issue. Nevertheless, it demanded rights to the use of Palestinian air space, including for air force training exercises.

The document reveals that the Palestinians expressed a willingness to accept the principle of limitations on their armaments and even took Israel's security needs into account (they agreed to three early warning stations and two "emergency locations", compared to the five "emergency locations" Israel had sought in addition to the early warning stations).

But in all matters relating to the symbols of sovereignty, the Palestinians took a harder line. They, therefore, insisted that an international force man the "emergency locations" rather than an Israeli one. And the issue of control over Palestine's international border remained unresolved for the same reason: the question of who would man the border control posts.

APPENDIX IX: STATEMENT ON ARMS CONTROL AND REGIONAL SECURITY

Statement on Arms Control and Regional Security

Preamble

The regional participants in the Arms Control and Regional Security working group, Reaffirming their respect for the Charter of the United Nations,

Bearing in mind the urgent necessity of achieving a just, lasting, and comprehensive peace settlement in the Middle East based on United

Nations Security Council Resolutions 242 and 338, and conscious of the historic breakthroughs toward such a settlement since the 1991 Madrid Middle East Peace Conference, particularly the Israeli-Palestinian Declaration of Principles and the subsequent Agreement on the Gaza and Jericho Area, and the Jordan-Israel Peace Treaty of October 26, 1994,

Agreeing that all regional parties should pursue the common purpose of achieving full and lasting relations of peace, openness, mutual confidence, security, stability, and cooperation throughout the region,

Recognizing that the multilateral working groups, including the Arms Control and Regional Security working group, should continue to complement the bilateral negotiations and help improve the climate for resolving the core issues at the heart of the Middle East peace process, and that the peace process also created the opportunity to cooperate in addressing additional issues of region-wide concern,

Embarking in this context on a process through the Arms Control and Regional Security working group to establish arms control and regional security arrangements aimed at safeguarding the region from the dangers and ominous consequences of future wars and the horrors of mass destruction, and enabling all possible resources to be devoted to the welfare of the peoples of the region, including such areas as economic and social development,

Recognizing the importance of preventing the proliferation of nuclear, chemical, and biological weapons and of preventing the excessive accumulation of conventional arms in enhancing international and regional peace and security,

Conscious that the arms control and regional security process seeks to achieve a stable balance among military capabilities in the region that takes into account quantitative and qualitative factors and also recognizes the significance of structural factors, and that provides for equal security for all,

Welcoming the special role of the United States and Russia as active cosponsors of the Middle East peace process and calling on them and other extra-regional states to provide continuing support for the objectives and arrangements of the arms control and regional security process,

Recognizing that the full realization of the objectives contained in this Statement would be facilitated by the involvement in the arms control and regional security process of all regional parties, and calling on all such parties to support the principles contained in this Statement and, in this connection, to join the arms control and regional security process at an early date,

Have adopted the following:

I. Fundamental Principles Governing Security Relations Among Regional
Participants in the Arms Control and Regional Security Working Group
In their pursuit of a just, lasting, and comprehensive peace in the Middle
East, the regional participants will be governed in their security policies by
the following fundamental principles, among others:

- The participants reaffirm their commitment to the principles of the
  Charter of the United Nations.
- Participants must refrain from the threat or use of force and from
  acts of terrorism and subversion.
- Security requires that participants fulfill in good faith obligations
  under international law.
- Security must be based on respect for and acknowledgment of sovereignty, territorial integrity, and political independence, noninterfer-
  ence in internal affairs, and reconciliation and cooperation among
  participants.
- Arms control and regional security arrangements should be aimed at
  achieving equal security for all at the lowest possible level of armaments and military forces.
- Military means, while needed to fulfill the inherent right of self-
  defense, and to discourage aggression, cannot by themselves provide security.

Enduring security requires the peaceful resolution of conflicts in the
region and the promotion of good neighborly relations and common
interests.

II. Guidelines for the Middle East Arms Control
and Regional Security Process
The regional participants recognize the following as guidelines for the
arms control and regional security process:

- The arms control and regional security process, as an integral part of
  the Middle East peace process, should create a favorable climate for
  progress in the bilateral negotiations and complement them by
  developing tangible measures in parallel with progress in the bilateral talks.

- The arms control and regional security process should strive to enhance security and general stability on a region-wide basis, even beyond the scope of the Arab-Israeli conflict, by pursuing regional security and arms control measures that reduce tension or the risk of war.
- The scope of the process must be comprehensive, covering a broad range of regional security, confidence- and security-building and arms-control measures that address all threats to security and all categories of arms and weapons systems.
- The arms control and regional security process should not, at any stage, diminish the security of any individual state or give a state a military advantage over any other.
- The basic framework of the process is to pursue a determined, step-by-step approach which sets ambitious goals and proceeds towards them in a realistic way.
- The basis for decision-making on each issue in the arms control and regional security process should be consensus by the regional participants directly concerned.
- Each regional arrangement adopted in the arms control and regional security process should be the result of direct regional negotiations and should be implemented by all those regional parties relevant to the arrangement.
- Strict compliance with arms control and disarmament measures adopted within the framework of the arms control and regional security process is essential to the integrity of that process and for building confidence among the regional participants.
- All arms control and disarmament measures adopted by regional participants within the framework of the arms control and regional security process will be effectively verifiable by the regional parties themselves and should include, where appropriate, mutual on-site inspection and other rigorous monitoring techniques and mechanisms, and such verification could be complementary with verification measures in international arrangements.

III. Statements of Intent on Objectives for the Arms Control and Regional Security Process

In the context of achieving a just, secure, comprehensive, and lasting peace and reconciliation, the regional participants agree to pursue, inter alia, the following arms control and regional security objectives:

- preventing conflicts from occurring through misunderstanding or by miscalculation by adopting confidence- and security-building measures that increase transparency and openness and reduce the risk of surprise attack and by developing regional institutional arrangements that enhance security and the process of arms control
- limiting military spending in the region so that resources can be made available to other areas such as economic and social development
- reducing stockpiles of conventional arms and preventing a conventional arms race in the region as part of an effort to provide enhanced security at lower levels of armaments and militarization, to reduce the threat of large-scale destruction posed by such weapons, and to move toward force structures that do not exceed legitimate defense requirements
- promoting cooperation among regional participants in the peaceful uses of outer space, including the pursuit of appropriate means of sharing the benefits from satellite systems, of ensuring that outer space and other environments will not be used for acts of aggression by regional participants, and of enhancing the security of regional participants, and
- (language proposed by Israel) establishing the Middle East as a mutually verifiable zone free of nuclear, chemical, biological weapons, and ballistic missiles in view of their high destructive capacity and their potential to promote instability in the region
- (language provided by the United States) establishing the Middle East as a zone free of all weapons of mass destruction, including nuclear, chemical, and biological weapons and their delivery systems—since such weapons, with their high destructive capacity and their potential to promote instability in the region, pose a grave threat to security—through a combination of regional arrangements, such as the Biological Weapons Convention (BWC), the Nuclear Weapons Non-Proliferation Treaty (NPT), and the Chemical Weapons Convention (CWC)
- (language proposed by Egypt) establishing a zone free of all weapons of mass destruction, including nuclear, chemical, and biological weapons and their delivery systems, since such weapons, with their high destructive capacity and their potential to exacerbate the arms race in the region, pose the greatest threat to its security

That all parties of the region will adhere to the NPT in the near future.

Regional participants will be guided in their conduct by the principles embodied in this Statement and will refrain from actions or activities that are inconsistent with its guidelines or principles and that preclude the attainment of its objectives.

Name Index[1]

A

Abaza, Maher, 117, 118
Abbas, Mahmoud, 72, 76, 97
Abdel Moneim Said, 186
Abdel-Shafi, Haidar, 66
Abdullah bin Zayed Al Nahyan, 244, 248
Abed Rabbo, Yasser, 95
Aboul Fotouh, Abdel Moneim, 219–221
Abou El-Magd, Ahmed Kamal, 211
Abrams, Elliott, 100, 184
Adhanom, Tedros, 143, 144
Ahmadinejad, Mahmoud, 39
Ahmed, Khidir Haroun, 134
Albright, Madeleine, 86, 122–124
Ali Abd El-Aal, 262
Ali El-Karty, 135
Aly, Kamal Hassan, 8
Amre, Mohamed Kamel, 142, 240
Anan, Sami, 188, 226
Anderson, Lisa, 15, 16, 19

El-Araby, Nabil, 7, 16, 117, 122, 123, 125, 131, 210, 211, 256
Arafat, Yasser, 61, 66, 68–70, 72–75, 79, 86–98, 102, 103, 110
Arnold, David, 15
Asfour, Hassan, 72
Ashrawi, Hanan, 66
Ashton, Catherine, 244, 252–254
al-Assad, Bashar, 153
Al-Assad, Hafez, 61, 65, 90, 91
Al Attiyah, Khalid Bin Mohammad, 244, 255, 256, 258
Awwad, Suleiman, 182, 184–186
Ayman Abu Hadid, 139
Azmi, Zakaria, 14

B

Badawi, Abdel-Hamide, 5
Baker, James, 65
Bandar Bin Sultan, 90

---

[1] Note: Page numbers followed by 'n' refer to notes.

© The Author(s) 2020
N. Fahmy, *Egypt's Diplomacy in War, Peace and Transition*,
https://doi.org/10.1007/978-3-030-26388-1

El-Baradei, Mohamed, 7, 17, 29, 30, 117, 188, 205, 206, 215–217, 219–221, 227, 230–235, 238, 244, 245
Barak, Ehud, 75, 90, 91, 93, 94
Bassiouny, Salah, 137
El-Baz, Osama, 7, 34, 72, 87, 123
El-Beblawi, Hazem, 18, 147, 233, 235, 238
Begin, Menachem, 56, 82, 111
Beilin, Yossi, 72
Ben-Gurion, David, 111
Blix, Hans, 29
Bouteflika, Abdelaziz, 140, 261
Boutros-Ghali, Boutros, 8, 10, 11, 117, 118, 137
Brennan, John, 190
Burns, William, 170, 171, 244
Bush, George H. W, 65, 95, 162
Bush, George W., 16, 29–33, 36, 96, 99–102, 104–106, 168–173, 179–186, 193

C
Carter, Jimmy, 53, 54, 56–61, 94, 162, 173
Cheney, Richard, 31, 32, 179
Christopher, Warren, 70
Clinton, Bill, 13, 73, 81, 85, 87, 90–92, 94–97, 104, 123, 163–165, 173, 182, 196, 197, 257
Clinton, Hillary, 109, 188, 196, 214, 257

D
Dahlan, Mohammed, 95
Davutoğlu, Ahmet, 44, 254
Dayan, Moshe, 57, 60
de Cuéllar, Javier, 28
Dejiang, Zhang, 146
Dhanapala, Jayantha, 124

E
Einhorn, Robert, 123
Ekéus, Rolf, 29
Enlai, Zhou, 145
Eran, Oded, 81
Erdoğan, Recep Tayyip, 180, 254, 255
Erekat, Saeb, 66, 95

F
Fabius, Laurent, 246, 247
Fahmy, Ismail, 3, 4, 8, 49–53, 56–58, 60–62, 108, 117, 137, 138, 191
Al-Farargi, Saad, 78
Fatah, Maged Abdel, 34
Fawzy, Mahmoud, 4
Feith, Douglas, 30, 31
Ford, Gerald, 4
Fouad Riad, 236, 245
Fouad, Shoukry, 237, 238
Friedman, Thomas, 97, 227

G
Gaddafi, Muammar, 129–134
Galal, Ahmed, 260
El-Gamasy, Mohamed, 48n1, 63
El-Ganzouri, Kamal, 14, 17, 217
Gil, Avi, 121
Gore, Albert, 87, 93, 122, 123, 166, 168
Graham, Lindsey, 244
Gromyko, Andrei, 4, 55

H
Haass, Richard, 251
Habibou Allele, 30
El-Haddad, Essam, 190, 191
Hadley, Steve, 100, 178, 184
Haftar, Khalifa, 133
Hagel, Chuck, 194
Hall, Jim, 166, 167

Hamad bin Jassim Bin Jaber Al-Thani, 82, 256, 257
Haroun, Medhat, 16
Hassan II, 79
Hossam Eissa, 233
Hussein Bin Talal, 68
Hussein, Saddam, 26, 28, 29, 31–34, 65, 119, 169, 269
Al-Husseini, Faisal, 66

I
Ibrahim, Mohamed, 234, 235

J
Jonathan, Goodluck, 139
Juul, Mona, 72

K
Kamel, Mohamed Ibrahim, 8, 62
El-Katatni, Saad, 234
Kay, David, 29
Kerry, John, 88, 109, 151, 154, 194, 246, 251
Khalifa Bin Hamad, 256
Khatami, Mohammad, 41
Khomeini, Ayatollah, 37
Khurshid, Salman, 147
Kikwete, Jakaya, 139
Kissinger, Henry, 4, 8n2, 48, 51, 52
Konaré, Alpha Oumar, 139, 244
Kurtzer, Daniel, 67, 78, 94

L
Lamamra, Ramtane, 140, 248
Lantos, Tom, 183
Lavrov, Sergey, 151, 152, 154–158
Levy, David, 81

Li Yuanchao, 146
Lipkin-Shahak, Amnon, 77
Lugar, Richard, 32

M
Mady, Abou Elela, 234
Maher, Ahmed, 32, 34, 170
Mandela, Nelson, 122, 136
Mansour, Adly, 140, 153, 154, 192, 232–237, 239, 241–243, 247
Marei, Mamdouh, 216
Marwan, Ashraf, 6
Marzouki, Mohamed Moncef, 249, 250
McCain, John, 244
Mehlab, Ibrahim, 139, 261
Membe, Bernard, 139
Mitchell, George, 107, 108
Mitterrand, François, 28
Molcho, Yitzhak, 109
Morsi, Mohamed, 17, 18, 39, 44, 135, 137, 139, 141, 147, 189–194, 218–223, 225–232, 234–237, 240, 242, 245, 247, 248, 253, 255, 260
Moussa, Amre, 7, 10, 12, 14, 15, 26, 65, 67–69, 72, 73, 78–80, 86, 87, 90, 96, 119, 121, 123, 174–177, 182, 217, 219–222, 230, 236, 256, 257, 261
Mubarak, Gamal, 176–180
Mubarak, Hosni, 6, 7, 9, 10, 12–17, 31–34, 38, 39, 41, 44, 61, 65, 72, 80, 82, 86, 87, 89–94, 100–102, 104–106, 110, 118, 119, 121, 123, 130, 131, 137, 141, 145, 148, 150, 162, 165, 168–171, 173–189, 192, 193, 203–207, 209–220, 227, 231, 237, 256, 262
Museveni, Yoweri, 137, 139, 140

N

El-Naga, Faiza Abou, 138
Naguib, Mohamed, 3
Nasser, Gamal Abdel, 3, 3n1, 6, 24,
    25, 37, 47, 110, 136, 145, 148,
    149, 173, 203, 204, 207
Nazif, Ahmed, 181, 182
Nehru, Jawaharlal, 136, 145, 147
Netanyahu, Benjamin, 75, 87, 108,
    109, 111, 164, 197
Niasse, Moustapha, 138
Nixon, Richard, 8n2, 48, 49, 52, 191
Nkrumah, Kwame, 136
Nour, Ayman, 183, 184

O

Obama, Barack, 106–110, 180,
    186–188, 190, 191, 193–196,
    214, 248, 251
Obey, David, 182
Olmert, Ehud, 106
Özal, Turgot, 44

P

Pahlavi, Mohammad Reza, 37, 180
Patrushev, Nikolai, 152, 153
Patterson, Anne, 189, 191, 195, 223
Pelletreau, Robert, 130
Peres, Shimon, 75, 76, 111, 120, 121
Pickering, Thomas, 28, 166
Powell, Colin, 29, 30, 34, 101, 102
Power, Samantha, 187
Primakov, Yevgeny, 28
Putin, Vladimir, 152, 157–159, 275

Q

El-Qazzaz, Khaled, 190
Qurei, Ahmed, 72

R

Rabin, Yitzhak, 53, 68, 70, 71, 73, 75,
    76, 79, 81, 86, 111
Ramzy, Ramzy Ezzeldin, 7
Riad, Mahmoud, 62
Rice, Condoleezza, 33, 34, 104,
    106, 174, 175, 183,
    187, 193n6
Rice, Susan, 187
Riedel, Bruce, 96, 169, 170, 175
Rød-Larsen, Terje, 72
Rose, Charlie, 251
Ros-Lehtinen, Ileana, 183
Ross, Dennis, 80, 86, 89, 92, 95, 108,
    119, 164
Rumsfeld, Donald, 30–32, 34

S

Sabahi, Hamdeen, 219–221, 260
Sadat, Anwar, 4–6, 8–10, 17, 25,
    37, 38, 47–53, 56–64, 82,
    110, 130, 137, 148, 150, 162,
    173, 203–205, 207, 211, 220,
    226, 231, 241
Said, Edward, 58n12, 74
Salam, Khaled, 95
Salamé, Ghassan, 133, 134
Sall, Macky, 138
Saud bin Faisal, 41, 56, 248, 252
Savir, Uri, 73, 120, 121
Sedqi, Ahmed, 137
El-Shafei, Omran, 117
Shafik, Ahmed, 189, 211, 219–222
Shamir, Yitzhak, 68, 119
El-Sharaa, Farouk, 70
Sharon, Ariel, 98, 100, 101, 104,
    174n2
El-Shater, Khairat, 219, 222, 230
Shehab, Mofeed, 87, 105
Sirry, Omar, 7

El-Sisi, Abdel Fattah, 139, 140,
    144, 154–159, 194–197,
    226, 230, 231, 233–235,
    252, 259–263
Sobhy, Sedki, 149, 226
Song Young-moo, 149
Steinberg, James, 93
Sukarno, 136
Suleiman, Omar, 103, 175–177, 182,
    186, 188, 211–213, 219

T
Tantawi, Hussein, 131, 132, 226
El-Tayyeb, Ahmed, 40
Tenet, George, 29
Tito, Josip, 136
El-Tohamy, Hassan, 60
Trump, Donald, 113, 159,
    196–198, 275

V
Vance, Cyrus, 53, 55–59
Verstandig, Toni, 80

W
Waldheim, Kurt, 4
Wang Yi, 146, 147
Weissglass, Dov, 100
Weizman, Ezer, 63
Wisner, Frank, 187, 188n5, 214
Wolf, Frank, 183
Wolfowitz, Paul, 30–32, 34

Z
Zakaria, Fareed, 251
Zarif, Javad, 39–42
Zeidan, Ali, 133
Ziad Bahaa-Eldin, 233

Subject Index[1]

A

Africa, 5, 10, 19, 45, 106, 134, 136–142, 247, 276

Ambassador, 7–9, 12–14, 29, 33, 34, 55, 62, 67, 68, 87, 89, 90, 93, 94, 96, 101, 118, 124, 126, 127, 130, 134, 137, 148, 153, 157, 158, 163, 165, 170, 173–175, 177, 181–184, 186–190, 193, 195, 204, 214, 216, 223, 237, 238, 241, 242, 250, 252, 255, 257–259

American invasion of Iraq, 24, 28, 32, 33, 36, 207

Annapolis Middle East Peace Conference, 106

Arab–Israeli conflict, 8, 11, 32, 36, 47, 48, 53, 64–66, 71, 81, 97, 107, 108, 113, 129, 159, 161, 199, 273

Arab nationalism, 24–26, 35, 48, 151, 180

Arab Peace Initiative, 97–99

Arab Spring, 109

Asia, 12, 19, 20, 145–149

B

Border security, 129, 133–136

D

Diplomacy, 4, 5, 7, 12, 14–16, 18, 32, 45, 60, 72, 78, 93, 94, 107, 127, 162, 188, 242, 243, 246, 273, 274

E

Egypt, 3, 23, 85–90, 115, 129, 204, 225, 267

Egyptian constitution, 216, 232

Egyptian revolution, 18

---

[1] Note: Page numbers followed by 'n' refer to notes.

© The Author(s) 2020

N. Fahmy, *Egypt's Diplomacy in War, Peace and Transition*, https://doi.org/10.1007/978-3-030-26388-1

F

Foreign Ministry, 4, 7, 8, 10, 16, 19, 34, 38, 40, 52, 67, 69, 73, 78, 194, 221, 241, 243, 244, 256

Foreign policy, 3–5, 9, 15, 17–20, 35, 44, 45, 50, 52, 72, 110, 119, 133, 136–140, 144, 145, 151, 152, 158, 163, 169, 194, 196, 207, 214–215, 233, 236, 238–241, 243, 255, 257, 261, 262, 271, 272, 275, 276

G

General Assembly, 42, 43, 117, 195, 196, 248–250

Geneva Conference, 52–59, 61, 65

H

Hamas, 102–106, 191

I

Iran, 9, 23, 31, 33, 35–45, 153, 180, 181, 196, 269, 272–275

Iranian Revolution, 27, 37

Iraqi invasion of Kuwait, 24, 26–28, 31, 64

M

Madrid Peace Conference, 64–76, 98, 101

Middle East, 4, 5, 12, 15, 16, 19, 49, 50, 53, 55, 56, 61, 62, 64, 65, 67, 68, 71, 72, 76–80, 82, 85–90, 96–100, 102, 104, 105, 107, 113, 114, 134, 146, 149, 150, 153, 157–159, 162–164, 169, 172–174, 179–181, 186, 192, 193n6, 193n7, 195, 198, 200, 204, 207, 214, 254, 257

Middle East North Africa Economic Summits, 76–82

Military conflict, 115, 116

Muslim Brotherhood, 17, 39, 44, 135, 137, 143, 151, 156, 173, 180–182, 190–193, 195, 209, 211, 215–222, 218n1, 225–229, 232–237, 240, 241, 245, 248, 249, 254–256, 260, 262

N

The Nile, 135, 137, 140–146

9/11 terrorist attacks, 44, 163

Non-proliferation of Nuclear Weapons (NPT), 116–118, 120n2, 124, 162, 162n1

Nuclear Weapons, 148

O

The Oslo Agreement, 74, 75, 85, 92

P

Palestine, 23, 71, 86, 99, 106, 112, 129, 175

Pan-Arabism, 24, 25, 36, 271

Peace negotiation, 64, 65, 70, 113

The Political Reform Agenda, 182–185

R

Russia, 45, 59, 65, 99, 111, 124,
149–159, 246, 275

S

Security, 9, 26, 48, 89, 115, 161, 207,
228, 268
Stability, 9, 18, 33, 110, 127, 132,
134, 146, 177, 195, 205, 231,
233, 261, 268, 272–276
Syria, 19, 23, 24, 27, 28, 38, 44, 45,
48, 50, 54, 55, 58, 61, 65, 68,
70, 71, 74, 91, 110, 115, 152,
153, 158, 159, 161, 193, 240,
251, 272, 273, 275

T

Turkey, 23, 36–45, 115, 136, 153,
156, 180, 186, 247, 254, 255,
269, 272, 274, 275

U

United States, 4, 27, 48, 115, 214, 274